Productivity

Productivity

The Art and Science of Business Management

A. Dale Timpe

Series Editor

Facts On File
New York • Oxford

This is volume seven in Facts On File's series "The Art and Science of Business Management," each volume of which provides a broad selection of articles on an important business topic of our time.

Volume one: *Motivation of Personnel*
Volume two: *The Management of Time*
Volume three: *Leadership*
Volume four: *Creativity*
Volume five: *Performance*
Volume six: *Managing People*

Productivity

Copyright © 1989 by KEND Publishing

Library of Congress Cataloging-in-Publication Data

Productivity / A. Dale Timpe, editor
        p. cm.—(The Art and science of business management ; v. 7)
        Bibliography: p.
        Includes index.
        ISBN 0-8160-1905-3
        1. Industrial productivity.   I. Timpe, A. Dale.   II. Series.
HD56.p795 1988
                                                        658.5—dc19   88-21849

British CIP data available on request
Printed in the United States of America
10 9 8 7 6 5 4 3 2 1

CONTENTS

PART III: PERSPECTIVES ON MANAGING PRODUCTIVITY

PART IV: AUTOMATION AND INNOVATION: CAUSE AND EFFECT

PART V: EVOLUTION IN THE WORK ENVIRONMENT

PREFACE

Clearly, management plays the leading role in any organization's productivity, and it is, therefore, upon management that all organizations should focus primary attention in their quest for peak productivity. Studies have shown that among qualified individuals, differences in productivity depend primarily upon attitude and motivation. Management not only directly determines its own attitude, motivation, and productivity, but is also extremely important in influencing the attitudes of the entire work force.

Management is often cited as a culprit in the current American productivity predicament. Too many layers of management and the lack of "combat" experience in the harsh realities of international competition have allowed our prior advantage to change hands. Management has been slow to respond to the deteriorating situation and unwilling to embrace change.

The entire business environment has changed and the strategies that worked during the industrial era are simply inappropriate today. For too long, American management has approached productivity issues from the perspective of prior decades, when most organizations operated on the premise that the driving competitive force in the marketplace was *quantity*. The trick to success rested on the attainment of highly efficient systems of mass production that would bring the most products into the marketplace at the lowest cost. Productivity improvement was thought to come from the physical application of more energy, better materials, faster production lines or better organization. The high quality that had characterized American goods was thought to be achieved through tighter standards and controls.

Current efforts in the quest for productivity improvement are more complex and difficult to resolve than the prior *quantity solutions*. Productivity-improvement efforts today must begin by addressing a host of interrelated issues, including technology; organizational structure; organizational culture; the changing nature of work and the worker; the need for greater production flexibility; and a shift in managerial power and authority. Another relevant factor overlaying all of these issues is the urgent need to restore and maintain the element of quality in the production process.

This compendium provides access to a broad spectrum of practical knowledge, research and theory relating to productivity. The diversity of insights, experience and theoretical concepts offers many useful and strategic solutions for encouraging, developing and managing productivity improvement. The sources represent a wide range of professional publications, including a number not readily available to most business executives. For those wanting to explore a particular aspect in more detail, the bibliography provides a valuable resource tool.

A. Dale Timpe
Series Editor

ACKNOWLEDGMENTS

The articles presented in this volume are reprinted with permission of the respective copyright holders, and all rights are reserved.

Leilani E. Allen. "Measuring Productivity in the Automated Office" from *Administrative Management* by permission of Dalton Communications, Inc., © 1986.

David R. Altany. "Faster May Soon Mean Foreign" from *Industry Week* by permission of Penton Publishing, Inc., © 1987.

B. Charles Ames. "Downsizing Your Company to Meet New Realities" from *Industry Week* by permission of Penton Publishing, Inc. © 1985.

Robert A. Becker. "All Factories Are Not the Same" from *Interfaces* by permission of The Institute of Management Sciences, © 1985.

Richard A. Bobbe, Robert H. Schaffer. "Productivity Improvement: Manage It or Buy It?" from *Business Horizons* by permission of Indiana University, School of Business, © 1983.

K. L. Brookfield. "Dimensions of Productivity Improvement" by permission from *Journal of Systems Management,* © 1983.

Ann Coil. "Job Matching Brings Out the Best in Employees" by permission from *Personnel Journal,* © 1984.

Keith Denton. "Managing 'Techies': Automation Won't Work Without People" from *Management World* by permission of the Administrative Management Society, © 1987.

Harold W. Fox. "Eliciting Latent Productivity" from *Business Horizons* by permission of Indiana University, School of Business, © 1983.

Mark Frohman, Perry Pascarell. "Creating a Purposeful Organization" from *Industry Week* by permission of Penton Publishing, Inc., © 1986.

Paul S. George. "Team Building Without Tears" by permission of *Personnel Journal,* © 1987.

Jeff Hallett. "Productivity: A State of Mind" from *Personnel Administrator* by permission of The American Society for Personnel Administration, © 1985.

Richard Pappas, Donald S. Remer. "Measuring R&D Productivity" from *Research Management* by permission of Industrial Research Institute, Inc., © 1985.

Gopal C. Pati, Robert Salitore, Sandra Brady. "What Went Wrong with Quality Circles?" by permission of *Personnel Journal,* © 1987.

Robert M. Ranftl. "Seven Keys to High Productivity" from *Research Management* by permission of Robert M. Ranftl, © 1986.

Thomas M. Rohan. "Selling Quality to the Troops" from *Industry Week* by permission of Penton Publishing, Inc., 1986.

Leonard R. Sayles. "Managerial Productivity: Who Is Fat and What Is Lean?" from *Interfaces* by permission of The Institute of Management Sciences, © 1985.

Michael Schuster. "Gain Sharing: Do It Right the First Time" from *Sloan Management Review* by permission of the Sloan Management Review Association, © 1987.

K. Dow Scott, Timothy Cotter. "The Team That Works Together Earns Together" by permission of *Personnel Journal,* © 1984.

Gregory P. Shea, Richard A. Guzzo. "Group Effectiveness: What Really Matters?" from *Sloan Management Review* by permission of the Sloan Management Review Association, © 1987.

Robert Szakonyi. "To Improve R&D Productivity, Gain the CEO's Support" from *Research Management* by permission of Industrial Research Institute, Inc., © 1985.

John Teresko. "Challenging Traditions" from *Industry Week* by permission of Penton Publishing Co., © 1987.

Lester C. Thurow. "White-Collar Overhead" from *Across The Board* by permission of The Conference Board and Lester C. Thurow, © 1986.

Timothy N. Warner. "Information Technology As a Competitive Burden" from *Sloan Management Review* by permission of the Sloan Management Review Association, © 1987.

Anthony Warren. "The Innovation Traps and How They Can Thwart Technological Leaps" from *Industry Week* by permission of Penton Publishing, Inc., © 1984.

Karl E. Weick. "Misconceptions About Managerial Productivity" from *Business Horizons* by permission of Indiana University, School of Business, © 1983.

Sheldon Weining. "Productivity Gains Still People-Dependent" from *Industry Week* by permission of Penton Publishing, Inc., © 1986.

Therese R. Welter. "Ten Ways to Mismanage Technology" from *Industry Week* by permission of Penton Publishing, Inc., © 1987.

William L. Williams, Elaine Biech, Malcolm P. Clark. "Increased Productivity Through Effective Meetings" from *Technical Communication* by permission of Society for Technical Communication, © 1987.

Wayne L. Wright. "Overcoming Barriers to Productivity" by permission of *Personnel Journal,* © 1987.

Gayle J. Yaverbaum, Oya Culpan. "Human Resource Planning" by permission of *Journal of Systems Management,* © 1986.

Part 1
THE CULTURE OF PRODUCTIVITY

1.
PRODUCTIVITY IS SHAPED BY FORCES BENEATH CORPORATE CULTURE

Michael McTague

Slow productivity growth is due to a failure of organizational morale and is a reflection on how managers and workers regard their organization. Organizations that share responsibility openly and honestly lead their industries in quality and productivity.

"Today, workers just aren't what they used to be." "The work ethic is declining." "America is in a mortal malaise." These are the ready-made explanations for inadequate productivity growth, but what are the real reasons behind this situation?

Ever since Hayes and Abernathy's article in *The Harvard Business Review* in 1980, much of the blame has unjustly centered on managers, who are now widely regarded as lacking entrepreneurial drive and technological sophistication.

Fundamentally, though, the cause is a lack of moral purpose on the part of individual executives and, ultimately, whole organizations.

Underlying any manager's actions and attitudes is a core of organizational beliefs—what the organization stands for and against.

More fundamental than organization culture—a company's common approach used for handling people, taking risks, pursuing business and competitors, developing and introducing products and so forth—these beliefs shape and determine how leadership is valued, which skills are developed and on what levels, what kinds of decisions are encouraged or discouraged, and how the organization values its managers and workers.

It is this core of moral commitments, more so than any individual manager's techniques and style, that determines the organization's character and morale.

Slow productivity growth is, in reality, a failure of organizational morale and a reflection of how managers and workers regard the organization.

PRODUCTIVITY IMPROVEMENT RELIES ON SUPPORTING BELIEFS

Efforts to improve productivity without an honest commitment to those goals—and an organizational culture and leadership to support them—will inevitably fail.

Accordingly, the difficulty many American organizations have had when attempting to improve productivity (in which quality circles and statistical process control have gone sour) stems from the reliance on techniques without beliefs.

Consider the case of the Zingo Manufacturing Company (a fictitious name). Located in Pennsylvania, Zingo makes measuring and scientific equipment.

In recent years, competition from other U.S. manufacturers, a profit slump for its major customers in the oil industry, and pressure from executives in the parent organization moved Zingo's normally conservative management to action. Four years ago, Zingo instituted a major quality circle effort. Hundreds of employees were trained in how to participate in quality circles.

For the first six months, the circles met for one hour on Friday afternoons. Then, as the idea became popular and there were demonstrated results from the effort (especially cost savings), circles began to meet during regular work hours.

Employees and engineers devoted increasing amounts of time to investigating and fixing problems. And the circles, now tightly-knit teams, were a major functional activity at the plant.

Everything seemed to be going well with Zingo's quality circles. In fact, the local newspaper had run two features on the effort and the training director received two or three calls a week from other businesses asking how they could duplicate Zingo's efforts.

Then, in early 1985 Zingo's customers sharply increased their purchases of Zingo goods. The parent company's profits began to look better than they had since 1979. And, even though Zingo's competitors were clearly present in the market, several market surveys showed that Zingo remained the industry leader, with more than 60 percent of market share and an unrivaled reputation for quality.

The training director received a call several weeks later informing him that quality circles were "no longer needed," and that although they could continue, they "should not interfere with production."

Zingo began to retreat to the conservative ways in which it had been managed (and been quite profitable) for more than 70 years. Top management felt that the difficulties of the last four years were temporary and that its reaction to those difficulties should also be temporary.

Management was happy with the results of the quality circles, but not convinced that involving employees in productivity-improvement efforts was a critical issue.

The entire effort was a product of short-term thinking. Neither an individual manager's leadership nor the existing organizational culture can make quality circles at Zingo a long-term productivity-improvement effort.

PRODUCTIVITY IMPROVEMENT REQUIRES COMPANY-WIDE SUPPORT

Some organizations, however, do achieve more. High Tech, Inc. (also fictitious) is one example. One of the most profitable companies in its size range in the U.S., High Tech is widely respected for its innovation and product quality.

Middle managers have considerable freedom to purchase or recommend the latest equipment and to develop new skills in their departments.

For the last 10 years, High Tech has offered or developed the best training programs available to enhance problem-solving and decision-making skills among managers and workers.

Individual plant and production managers have achieved significant productivity improvements and have a company-wide reputation for dedication to quality and sound people orientation.

These managers, however, are *not* in the majority. They have not been able to convince higher management to extend their approaches to other parts of the company; even their peers have characterized their efforts as "expensive" and "proletarian."

High Tech suffers from a failure of organizational morale—even though individual leaders achieve significant success and the organizational culture rewards these managers.

The improvement effort is limited because the *entire* organization lacks commitment to the principles underlying productivity improvement.

The organization is not fully committed to developing its workers' skills or encouraging them to participate in improving quality and productivity.

Although the successful "entrepreneurs" receive higher pay, promotions, and a good reputation, the long-term effect is discouragement and lack of respect for the organization.

The next productivity improvement project is likely to be greeted with indecision and fear. Many workers may develop passive-aggressive attitudes, although a few unique people will, of course, stand out in contrast to the prevailing morale of the organization.

As these two case examples illustrate, neither short-term solutions nor simply allowing individual managers the freedom to improve their effectiveness without a full commitment to productivity improvement will result in any lasting improvements.

It is critical that every organization know its basic beliefs—and this is where the personnel department or the training and development function can be a catalyst.

Assemble top managers and probe for their basic beliefs, those principles that underlie their decision making. (These beliefs *should be* shared organization-wide.)

If "remain a profit leader in the industry" drives management decision making and "develop the skills of employees to the highest level in the industry" does not, management should be aware of that.

The major advantage of this is to avoid the future frustration and division that occurs when middle managers and employees do not know or do not share top management's basic beliefs.

(It is not certain whether organizations such as Zingo Manufacturing can, or for that matter should, achieve remarkable breakthroughs in productivity and quality of work life. Zingo is, after all, a quality and market leader.)

SHARING RESPONSIBILITY IS KEY TO PRODUCTIVITY

Those organizations that have been able to install effective productivity- and quality-improvement efforts share the *responsibility* for improved results with workers and managers.

Sharing responsibility comes through a joint recognition of the need for improvement, followed by an agreement on how workers and middle managers can contribute more directly to the organization. Skills are then developed to prepare individuals to accept responsibility for improving quality and productivity.

Using the new skills and the new responsibility, workers make day-to-day decisions in an atmosphere of trust and improved self-confidence.

This concept of worker responsibility is a critical one, although it has been watered down—organizations prefer talk of "participation," which is generally regarded as a kind of industrial civil rights movement, advocated by workers as part of a long-term campaign for decision-making equality.

But worker responsibility is also a part of organizational morale. As the organization has certain basic beliefs, so do individual workers.

Several years ago, Kepner-Tregoe conducted an extensive survey to discover the cause of declining productivity and to identify how this trend could be reversed.

We concluded that approximately 85 percent of the variables affecting productivity are internal to the organization. Four-fifths of these internal variables can be changed by executive and managerial actions, while one-fifth must be effected at the workers' level.

Looking for differences between the more productive and less productive organizations, we found that the most striking difference is "the number of people who are involved and feel responsibility for solving problems."

Before designing its own quality teams, one particular organization observed other organizations using quality circles and quickly drew this conclusion: "In organizations where management sets the priorities, QC's fail."

For example, at Zingo and High Tech, top management was unwilling to share responsibility—to admit that there are problems, to train employees to solve them and to reward them for solving those problems. The result: limited gains and passive-aggressive attitudes from top to bottom.

Organizations that share responsibility openly and honestly lead their industries in quality and productivity.

In the kind of environment that does share manager-worker responsibility, leadership is a catalyst. Those individuals who have greater skill and drive, who make better decisions, who gather more information, and gain greater worker commitment achieve even more than the organization mandates.

Leaders accept greater responsibility and use their own skills to meet organizational goals. They translate organizational goals to the work level and they reward, approve, and emphasize those traits, skills, and actions that are in the organization's best interests.

The slow productivity growth of recent years, which has been partially reversed, has not come about because Americans are no longer as courageous and vigorous as we were during the pioneer days. Nor is it a reflection of great superiority of purpose on the part of managers elsewhere.

Our organizations, lulled by decades of superiority and stable consumer demand, have grown unwieldy in today's environment.

Dedication to quality and improvement of productivity cannot be left to a few individuals armed with the latest techniques. Nor is a supportive culture that permits and rewards productivity improvement adequate.

Starting at the top, organizations must develop a comprehensive framework that underlies and supports decisions on *every* level of the organization. This can only be achieved when the organization makes a total commitment, a moral choice, to achieve the best results it is capable of.

Most organizations would be better off not attempting any productivity improvement projects if their basic beliefs don't support them.

If top management does not want to share responsibility for problem solving, it has two choices: 1) not beginning any programs such as quality circles, or 2) starting to believe in sharing responsibility *before* starting the program.

If the organization is not committed to the basic beliefs required for these comprehensive change efforts—don't start them.

Michael McTague is a management and training consultant and an associate of Kepner-Tregoe, Inc., Princeton, NJ.

2.
PRODUCTIVITY: A STATE OF MIND

Jeff Hallett

Traditionally, it has been thought that improved productivity can be brought about by the physical application of more energy, better materials, faster production lines or better organization. The environment has changed, however, and the approaches that worked during the industrial era are simply inappropriate today.

The current search for "excellence" and the new emphasis on "quality" are appropriate responses to the conditions of today's emerging competitive environment. When considering the initiatives necessary to attain these objectives, we should pay close attention to our Japanese friends—once again—and avoid the mistakes of the past decade, when our attention was focused on productivity improvement.

We floundered badly during the '70s in struggling to regain the rates of productivity growth we had experienced for the five decades that began in the late '20s. We had grown so accustomed to steady improvements in our productivity that when signals that these productivity improvements might cease first appeared in the mid-'60s, they were largely ignored. When raised by some analysts of the American economy as a problem, they were dismissed as temporary aberrations that had something to do with external factors in the world economy or with normal adjustments. Five decades of extraordinary success created a bedrock faith that American productivity would soon regain its lost steam.

LOST MOMENTUM

When it became apparent in the early '70s that a problem did indeed exist, a host of federal and private initiatives were launched to try to regain our lost momentum. Productivity emerged from the realm of "givens" and became a primary objective of American management.

The result of this effort, however, didn't always produce a sudden and gratifying leap in productivity. In spite of a renewed application of the techniques and methods that had generated high levels of productivity growth

7

in prior years, there was often more frustration than success. The effort continues today.

JAPAN: A DIFFERENT PERSPECTIVE

Japan, on the other hand, charged ahead with ever-increasing gains in her productivity performance, and Americans began an ongoing stream of visits to Japan to find out what *they* were doing that *we* could learn from them. Too often, the conclusion was that they weren't doing much of anything relative to productivity performance. Many places, in fact, didn't have any formal measures of productivity. Instead, the focus was on quality, reject rates, defects, etc.

Constant inquiry of our Japanese friends regarding *how* they were able to achieve such high levels of productivity improvements, when they didn't even seem to be trying, finally produced the answer: What Americans did not understand, according to Joji Arai—Director of the Washington, DC office of the Japan Productivity Center—was that *"productivity is a state of mind!"*

This honest explanation gave our engineers and productivity experts fits—but it was the proper explanation of the difference between the Japanese approach and our own. We continued to pursue the problem from the perspective of the socioeconomic realities of prior decades. We were operating from the perspective that said the driving competitive force in the marketplace is *quantity.* The trick to success, we knew, rested on the attainment of highly efficient systems of mass production that would bring the most products into the marketplace at the lowest cost. That was productivity to us.

Productivity improvement, we thought, came from the physical application of more energy, better materials, faster production lines, or better organization; and the high quality that had characterized American goods in the past could be maintained through tighter standards and controls.

A NEW WORLD ARENA

In the meantime, however, the entire environment has changed and the approaches that worked during the industrial era are simply inappropriate today. The "ideas" of productivity, quality, and excellence are different today. What's important about each of these objectives is *intent*—the level of individual and group intent to constantly attain higher levels of performance. There is no perceived end to what can be accomplished. The assumption is that each individual and group in the process can discover things that will help achieve new levels of quality or higher levels of production.

America, as it turns out, was greatly hindered in the new, competitive world market by—surprise—quality standards. *The idea of quality standards says there is a particular level that is "good enough."* The message those standards send to the workplace and the marketplace is just that. Regardless of what any one participant in the process might be able to add that would improve the quality, the standard has been set: "good enough."

Excellence is simply a new phrase that defines the "state of mind" that must reside within a group if it is to produce goods and services of high quality and be productive in those efforts. Excellence cannot be achieved by an engineered program or project. It cannot be neatly measured and reported. Like quality, however, it *can* be seen and felt. People know excellence when they are exposed to it.

A STATE OF MIND

Finally, the state of mind that needs to be developed is in direct contrast to traditional measures of true success. Today, profit and growth can be expected to follow achievements of quality and excellence. Quality and excellence, on the other hand, cannot be expected to result from producing more products. The state of mind that should be pursued sees value in attention paid to the needs of employees and customers alike. It's one that believes that such a long-term commitment will yield higher long-term benefits than one that ignores issues of quality and excellence in a rush to exploit an apparent near-term opportunity. Today's business landscape is littered with firms that have bet the farm on short-term opportunities only to find those opportunities short-lived. Look at the personal computer and video game industries, or at financial services or airlines.

Most importantly, excellence and high-quality performance results from an organization's belief in its competence and its capabilities. It comes from respect and concern for its customers and suppliers. It is generated by a workplace that contains individuals who are both excited about and supported in their efforts to be the best. It comes from an environment where the individuals intend to be excellent, to produce the highest possible results, and to be as productive as they can.

3.
THE ART OF HIGH-TECHNOLOGY MANAGEMENT

Modesto A. Maidique
Robert H. Hayes

> For an organization to succeed, the energy and creativity of every one of its employees must be tapped. This is why many high-tech firms fight so vigorously against the usual organizational accoutrements of seniority, rank and functional
> specialization.

Over the past fifteen years, the world's perception of the competence of U.S. companies in managing technology has come full circle. In 1967, a Frenchman, J.-J. Servan-Schreiber, expressed with alarm in his book, *The American Challenge*, that U.S. technology was far ahead of the rest of the industrialized world.[1] This "technology gap," he argued, was continually widening because of the superior ability of Americans to organize and manage technological development.

Today, the situation is perceived to have changed drastically. The concern now is that the gap is reversing: the onslaught of Japanese and/or European challenges is threatening America's technological leadership.

Even such informed Americans as Dr. Simon Ramo express great concern. In his book, *America's Technology Slip*, Dr. Ramo notes the apparent inability of U.S. companies to compete technologically with their foreign counterparts.[2] Moreover, in the best-seller *The Art of Japanese Management*, the authors use as a basis of comparison two technology-based firms: Matsushita (Japanese) and ITT (American).[3] Here, the Japanese firm is depicted as a model for managers, while the management practices of the U.S. firm are sharply criticized.

Nevertheless, a number of U.S. companies appear to be fending off these foreign challenges successfully. These firms are repeatedly included on the list of "America's best-managed companies." Many of them are competitors in the R&D-intensive industries, a sector of our economy that has come under particular criticism. Ironically, some of them have even served as models of highly successful Japanese and European high-tech firms.

For example, of the forty-three companies that Peters and Waterman, Jr., judged to be "excellent" in *In Search of Excellence,* almost half were classified as "high technology," or as containing a substantial high-technology component.[4] Similarly, of the five U.S. organizations that William Ouchi described as best prepared to meet the Japanese challenge, three (IBM, Hewlett-Packard, and Kodak) were high-technology companies.[5] Indeed, high-technology corporations are among the most admired firms in America. In a *Fortune* study that ranked the corporate reputation of the 200 largest U.S. corporations, IBM and Hewlett-Packard (HP) ranked first and second, respectively.[6] And of the top ten firms, nine compete in such high-technology fields as pharmaceuticals, precision instruments, communications, office equipment, computers, jet engines, and electronics. The above studies reinforce our own findings, which have led us to conclude that U.S. high-technology firms that seek to improve their management practices to succeed against foreign competitors need not look overseas. The firms mentioned above are not unique. On the contrary, they are representative of scores of well-managed small and large U.S. technology-based firms. Moreover, the management practices they have adopted are widely applicable. Thus, perhaps the key to stimulating innovation in our country is not to adopt the managerial practices of the Europeans or the Japanese, but to adapt some of the policies of our own successful high-technology firms.

THE STUDY

Over the past two decades, we have been privileged to work with a host of small and large high-technology firms as participants, advisors, and researchers. We and our assistants interviewed formally and informally over 250 executives, including over 30 CEOs, from a wide cross-section of high-tech industries—biotechnology, semiconductors, computers, pharmaceuticals, and aerospace. About 100 of these executives were interviewed in 1983 as part of a large-scale study of product innovation in the electronics industry.[7] Our research has been guided by a fundamental question: what are the strategies, policies, practices, and decisions that result in successful management of high-technology enterprises? One of our principal findings was that no company has a monopoly on managerial excellence. Even the best-run companies make big mistakes, and many smaller, lesser-regarded companies are surprisingly sophisticated about the factors that mediate between success and failure.

It also became apparent from our interviews that the driving force behind the successes of many of these companies was strong leadership. All companies need leaders and visionaries, of course, but leadership is particularly essential when the future is blurry and when the world is changing rapidly. Although few high-tech firms can succeed for long without strong leaders, leadership itself is not the subject of this article. Rather, we accept it as given and seek to understand what strategies and management practices can *reinforce* strong leadership.

The companies we studied were of different sizes ($10 million to $30 billion in sales); their technologies were at different stages of maturity; their industry growth rates and product mixes were different; and their managers ranged widely in age. But they all had the same unifying thread; a rapid rate of change in the technological base of their products. This common thread, rapid technological change, implies novel products and functions and thus usually rapid growth. But even when growth is slow or moderate, the destruction of the old capital base by new technology results in the need for rapid redeployment of resources to cope with new product designs and new manufacturing processes. Thus, the two dominant characteristics of the high-technology organizations that we focused on were growth and change.

In part because of this split focus (growth and change), the companies we studied often appeared to display contradictory behavior over time. Despite these differences, in important respects, they were remarkably similar because they all confronted the same two-headed dilemma: how to unleash the creativity that promotes growth and change without being fragmented by it, and how to control innovation without stifling it. In dealing with this concern, they tended to adopt strikingly similar managerial approaches.

THE PARADOX: CONTINUITY AND CHAOS

When we grouped our findings into general themes of success, a significant paradox gradually emerged—which is a product of the unique challenge that high-technology firms face. Some of the behavioral patterns that these companies displayed seemed to favor promoting disorder and informality, while others would have us conclude that it was consistency, continuity, integration, and order that were the keys to success. As we grappled with this apparent paradox, we came to realize that continued success in a high-technology environment requires periodic shifts between chaos and continuity.[8] Our originally static framework, therefore, was gradually replaced by a dynamic framework within whose ebbs and flows lay the secret of success.

SIX THEMES OF SUCCESS

The six themes that we grouped our findings into were: (1) business focus; (2) adaptability; (3) organizational cohesion; (4) entrepreneurial culture; 5) sense of integrity; and (6) "hands-on" top management. No one firm exhibits excellence in every one of these categories at any one time, nor are the less successful firms totally lacking in all. Nonetheless, outstanding high-technology firms tend to score high in most of the six categories, while less successful ones usually score low in several.[9]

1. Business Focus

Even a superficial analysis of the most successful high-technology firms leads one to conclude that they are highly focused. With few exceptions, the leaders in high-technology fields, such as computers, aerospace, semiconductors, biotechnology, chemical, pharmaceuticals, electronic instruments, and duplicating machines, realize the great bulk of their sales either from a single product line or from a closely related set of product lines.[10] For example, IBM, Boeing, Intel, and Genentech confine themselves almost entirely to computer products, commercial aircraft, integrated circuits, and genetic engineering, respectively. Similarly, four-fifths of Kodak's and Xerox's sales come from photographic products and duplicating machines, respectively. In general, the smaller the company, the more highly focused it is. Tandon concentrates on disk drives; Tandem on high-reliability computers; Analog Devices on linear integrated circuits; and Culinet on software products.

Closely Related Products. This extraordinary concentration does not stop with the dominant product line. When the company grows and establishes a secondary product line, it is usually closely related to the first. Hewlett-Packard, for instance, has two product families, each of which accounts for about half of its sales. Both families—electronic instruments and data processors—are focused on the same technical, scientific, and process-control markets. IBM also makes two closely related product lines—data processors (approximately 80 percent of sales) and office equipment—both of which emphasize the business market.

Companies that took the opposite path have not fared well. Two of yesterday's technological leaders, ITT and RCA, have paid dearly for diversifying away from their strengths. Today, both firms are trying to divest many of what were once highly touted acquisitions. As David Packard, chairman of the board of Hewlett-Packard, once observed, "No company ever died from starvation, but many have died from indigestion."[11]

A communications firm that became the world's largest conglomerate, ITT began to slip in the early 1970s after an acquisition wave orchestrated by Harold Geneen. When Geneen retired in 1977, his successors attempted to redress ITT's lackluster performance through a far-reaching divestment program.[12] So far, forty companies and other assets worth over $1 billion have been sold off—and ITT watchers believe the program is just getting started. Some analysts believe that ITT will ultimately be restructured into three groups, with the communications/electronics group and engineered products (home of ITT semiconductors) forming the core of a "new" ITT.

RCA experienced a similar fate to ITT. When RCA's architect and longtime chairman, General David Sarnoff, retired in 1966, RCA was internationally respected for its pioneering work in television, electronic components, communications, and radar. But by 1980, the three CEOs who followed Sarnoff had turned a technological leader into a conglomerate with flat sales, declining earnings, and a $2.9 billion debt. This disappointing performance led RCA's new CEO, Thornton F. Bradshaw, to decide to return RCA to its high-technology origins.[13] Bradshaw's strategy is to now concentrate on RCA's traditional strengths—communications and entertainment—by divesting its other businesses.

Focused R&D. Another policy that strengthens the focus of leading high-technology firms is concentrating R&D on one or two areas. Such a strategy enables these businesses to dominate the research, particularly the more risky, leading-edge explorations. By spending a higher proportion of their sales dollars on R&D than their competitors do, or through their sheer size (as in the case of IBM, Kodak, and Xerox), such companies maintain their technological leadership. It is not unusual for a leading firm's R&D investment to be one and a half to two times the industry's average as a percent of sales (8-15 percent) and several times more than any individual competitor on an absolute basis.[14]

Moreover, their commitment to R&D is both enduring and consistent. It is maintained through slack periods and recessions because it is believed to be in the best, long-term interest of the stockholders. As the CEO of Analog Devices, a leading linear integrated circuit manufacturer, explained in a quarterly report, which noted that profits had declined 30 percent, "We are sharply constraining the growth of fixed expenses, but we do not feel it is in the best interest of shareholders to cut back further on product development . . . in order to relieve short-term pressure on earnings."[15] Similarly, when sales, as a result of a recession, flattened and profit margins plummeted at Intel, its management invested a record-breaking $130 million in R&D and another $150 million in plant and equipment.[16]

Consistent Priorities. Still another way that a company demonstrates a strong business focus is through a set of priorities and a pattern of behavior that is continually reinforced by top management: for example, planned manufacturing improvement at Texas Instruments (TI); customer service at IBM; the concept of the entrepreneurial product champion at 3M; and the new products at HP. Belief in the competitive effectiveness of their chosen theme runs deep in each of these companies.

A business focus that is maintained over extended periods of time has fundamental consequences. By concentrating on what it does well, a company develops an intimate knowledge of its markets, competitors, technologies, employees, and of the future needs and opportunities of its customers.[17] The Stanford Innovation Project completed a three-year study of 224 U.S. high-technology products (half of which were successes, half of which were failures) and concluded that a continuous, in-depth, informal interaction with leading customers throughout the product-development process was the principal factor behind successful new products. In short, this coupling is the cornerstone of effective high-technology progress. Such an interaction is greatly facilitated by the long-standing and close customer relationships that are fostered by concentrating on closely related product-market choices.[18] "Customer needs," explains Tom Jones, chairman of Northrop Corporation, "must be understood *way ahead of time*" (authors' emphasis).[19]

2. Adaptability

Successful firms balance a well-defined business focus with the willingness, and the will, to undertake major and rapid change when necessary. Concentration, in short, does not mean stagnation. Immobility is the most dangerous behavioral pattern a high-technology firm can develop; technology can change rapidly, and with it the markets and customers served. Therefore, a high-technology firm must be able to track and exploit the rapid shifts and twists in market boundaries as they are redefined by new technological, market, and competitive developments.

The cost of strategic stagnation can be great, as General Radio (GR) found out. Once the proud leader of the electronic instruments business, GR almost single-handedly created many sectors of the market. Its engineering excellence and its progressive human-relations policies were models for the industry. But when its founder, Melville Eastham, retired in 1950, GR's strategy ossified. In the next two decades, the company failed to take advantage of two major opportunities for growth that were closely related to the company's strengths: microwave instruments and minicomputers. Meanwhile, its traditional product line withered away. Now all that remains of GR's once dominant instruments line, which is less than 10 percent of sales, is a small assembly area where a handful of technicians assemble batches of the old instruments.

It wasn't until William Thurston, in the wake of mounting losses, assumed the presidency at the end of 1972 that GR began to refocus its engineering creativity and couple it to its new marketing strategies.[20] Using the failure of the old policies as his mandate, Thurston deemphasized the aging product lines, focused GR's attention on automated test equipment, balanced its traditional engineering excellence with an increased sensitivity to market needs, and gave the firm a new name—GenRad. Since then, GenRad has resumed rapid growth and has won a leadership position in the automated test equipment market.

The GenRad story is a classic example of a firm making a strategic change because it perceived that its existing strategy was not working. But even successful high-technology firms sometimes feel the need to be rejuvenated periodically to avoid technological stagnation. In the mid-1960s, for example, IBM appeared to have little reason for major change. The company had a near monopoly in the computer mainframe industry. Its two principal products—the 1401 at the low end of the market and the 7090 at the high end—accounted for over two-thirds of its industry's sales. Yet, in one move the company obsoleted both product lines (as well as others) and redefined the rules of competition for decades to come by simultaneously introducing six compatible models of the "System 360," based on proprietary hybrid integrated circuits.[21]

During the same period, GM, whose dominance of the U.S. auto industry approached IBM's dominance of the computer mainframe industry, stoutly resisted such a rejuvenation. Instead, it became more and more centralized and inflexible. Yet, GM was also once a high-technology company. In its early days when Alfred P. Sloan ran the company, engines were viewed as high-technology products. One day, Charles F. Kettering told Sloan he believed the high efficiency of the diesel engine could be engineered into a compact power plant. Sloan's response was: "Very well—we are now in the diesel engine business. You tell us how the engine should run, and I will . . . capitalize the program."[22] Two years later, Kettering achieved a major breakthrough in diesel technology. This paved the way for a revolution in the railroad industry and led to GM's preeminence in the diesel locomotive markets.

Organizational Flexibility. To undertake such wrenching shifts in direction requires both agility and daring. Organizational agility seems to be associated with organizational flexibility—frequent realignments of people and responsibilities as the firm attempts to maintain its balance on shifting competitive sands. The daring and the willingness to take "you bet your company" kind of risks is a product of both the inner confidence of its members and a powerful top management—one that either has effective shareholder control or the full support of its board.

3. Organizational Cohesion

The key to success for a high-tech firm is not simply periodic renewal. There must also be cooperation in the translation of new ideas into new products and processes. As Ken Fisher, the architect of Prime Computer's extraordinary growth, puts it, "If you have the driving function, the most important success factor is the ability to integrate. It's also the most difficult part of the task."[23]

To succeed, the energy and creativity of the whole organization must be tapped. Anything that restricts the flow of ideas, or undermines the trust, respect, and sense of a commonality of purpose among individuals is a potential danger. This is why high-tech firms fight so vigorously against the usual organizational accoutrements of seniority, rank, and functional specialization charts: often they don't exist.

Younger people in a rapidly evolving technological field are often as good—and sometimes even better—a source of new ideas than are older ones. In some high-tech firms, in fact, the notion of a "halflife of knowledge" is used; that is, the amount of time that has to elapse before half of what one knows is obsolete. In semiconductor engineering, for example, it is estimated that the halflife of a newly minted Ph.D. is about seven years. Therefore, any practice that relegates younger engineers to secondary, nonpartnership roles is considered counterproductive.

Similarly, product design, marketing, and manufacturing personnel must collaborate in a common cause rather than compete with one another, as happens in many organizations. Any policies that appear to elevate one of these functions above the others—either in prestige or in rewards—can poison the atmosphere for collaboration and cooperation.

A source of division, and one that distracts the attention of people from the needs of the firm to their own aggrandizement, are the executive "perks" that are found in many mature organizations: pretentious job titles, separate dining rooms and restrooms for executives, larger and more luxurious offices (often separated in some way from the rest of the organization), and even separate or reserved places in the company parking lot all tend to establish "distance" between manager and doers and substitute artificial goals for the crucial real ones of creating successful new products and customers. The appearance of an executive dining room, in fact, is one of the clearest danger signals.

Good Communication. One way to combat the development of such distance is by making top executives more visible and accessible. IBM, for instance, has an open-door policy that encourages managers to talk to department heads and vice presidents. According to senior IBM executives, it was not unusual for a project manager to drop in and talk to Frank Cary (IBM's chairman) or John Opel (IBM's president) until Cary's retirement. Likewise, an office with transparent walls and no doors, such as that of John Young, CEO at HP, encourages communication. In fact, open-style offices are common in many high-tech firms.

A regular feature of 3M's management process is the monthly Technical Forum where technical staff members from the firm exchange views on their respective projects. This emphasis on communication is not restricted to internal operations. Such a firm supports and often sponsors industry-wide technical conferences, sabbaticals for staff members, and cooperative projects with technical universities.

Technical Forums serve to compensate partially for the loss of visibility that technologists usually experience when an organization becomes more complex and when production, marketing, and finance staffs swell. So does the concept of the dual-career ladder that is used in most of these firms; that is, a job hierarchy through which technical personnel can attain the status, compensation, and recognition that is accorded to a division general manager or a corporate vice-president. By using this strategy, companies try to retain the spirit of the early days of the industry when scientists played a dominant role, often even serving as members of the board of directors.[24]

Again, a strategic business focus contributes to organizational cohesion. Managers of firms that have a strong theme/culture and that concentrate on closely related markets and technologies generally display a sophisticated understanding of their businesses. Someone who understands where the firm is going and why is more likely to be willing to subordinate the interest of his or her own unit or function in the interest of promoting the common goal.

Job Rotation. A policy of conscious job rotation also facilitates this sense of communality. In the small firm, everyone is involved in everyone else's job: specialization tends to creep in as size increases and boundary lines between functions appear. If left unchecked, these boundaries can become rigid and impermeable. Rotating managers in temporary assignments across these boundaries helps keep the line fluid and informal, however. When a new process is developed at TI, for example, the process developers are sent to the production unit where the process will be implemented. They are allowed to return to their usual posts only after that unit's operations manager is convinced that the process is working properly.

Integration of Roles. Other ways that high-tech companies try to prevent organizational, and particularly hierarchical, barriers from rising is through multidisciplinary project teams, "special venture groups," and matrixlike organizational structures. Such structures, which require functional specialists and product/market managers to interact in a variety of relatively short-term problem-solving assignments, both inject a certain ambiguity into organizational relationships and require each individual to play a variety of organizational roles.

For example, AT&T uses a combination of organizational and physical mechanisms to promote integration. The Advance Development sections of Bell Labs are physically located on the sites of the Western Electric plants. This location creates an organizational bond between Development and Bell's basic research and an equally important spatial bond between Development and the manufacturing engineering groups at the plant. In this way, communication is encouraged among Development and the other two groups.[25]

Long-term Employment. Long-term employment and intensive training are also important integrative mechanisms. Managers and technologists are more likely to develop satisfactory working relationships if they know they will be harnessed to each other for a good part of their working lives. Moreover, their loyalty and commitment to the firm is increased if they know the firm is continuously investing in upgrading their capabilities.

At Tandem, technologists regularly train administrators on the performance and function of the firm's products and, in turn, administrators train the technologists on personnel policies and financial operations.[26] Such a firm also tends to select college graduates who have excellent academic records, which suggest self-discipline and stability, and then encourages them to stay with the firm for most if not all, of their careers.

4. Entrepreneurial Culture

While continuously striving to pull the organization together, successful high-tech firms also display fierce activism in promoting internal agents of change. Indeed, it has long been recognized that one of the most important characteristics of a successful high-technology firm is an entrepreneurial culture.[27]

Indeed, the ease with which small entrepreneurial firms innovate has always inspired a mixture of puzzlement and jealousy in larger firms. When new ventures and small firms fail, they usually do so because of capital shortages and managerial errors.[28] Nonetheless, time and again they develop remarkably innovative products, processes, and services with a speed and efficiency that baffle the managers of large companies. The success of the Apple II, which created a new industry, and Genentech's genetically engineered insulin are of this genre. The explanation for a small entrepreneurial firm's innovativeness is straightforward, yet it is difficult for a large firm to replicate its spirit.

Entrepreneurial Characteristics. First, the small firm is typically blessed with excellent communication. Its technical people are in continuous contact (and oftentimes in cramped quarters). They have lunch together, and they call each other outside of working hours. Thus, they come to understand and appreciate the difficulties and challenges facing one another. Sometimes they will change jobs or double up to break a critical bottleneck; often the same person plays multiple roles. This overlapping of responsibilities results in a second blessing: a dissolving of the classic organizational barriers that are major impediments to the innovating process. Third, key decisions can be made immediately by the people who first recognize a problem, not late by top management or by someone who barely understands the issue. Fourth, the concentration of power in the leader/entrepreneurs makes it possible to deploy the firm's resources very rapidly. Lastly, the small firm has access to multiple funding channels, from the family dentist to a formal public offering. In contrast, the manager of an R&D project in a large firm has effectively only one source, the "corporate bank."

Small Division. In order to recreate the entrepreneurial climate of the small firm, successful large high-technology firms often employ a variety of organizational devices and personnel policies. First, they divide and subdivide. Hewlett-Packard, for example, is subdivided into fifty divisions; the company has a policy of splitting divisions soon after they exceed 1,000 employees. Texas Instruments is subdivided into over thirty divisions and 250 "tactical action programs." Until recently, 3M's business was split into forty divisions. Although these divisions sometimes reach $100 million or more in sales, by Fortune 500 standards they are still relatively small companies.

Variety of Funding Channels. Second, such high-tech firms employ a variety of funding channels to encourage risk taking. At Texas Instruments managers have three distinct options in funding a new R&D project. If their proposal is rejected by the centralized Strategic Planning (OST) Systems because it is not expected to yield acceptable economic gains, they can seek a "Wild Hare Grant." The Wild Hare program was instituted by Patrick Haggerty, while he was TI's chairman, to insure that good ideas with long-term potential were not systematically turned down. Alternatively, if the project is outside the mainstream of the OST System, managers or engineers can contact one of dozens of individuals who hold "IDEA" grant purse strings and who can authorize up to $25,000 for prototype development. It was an IDEA grant that resulted in TI's highly successful "Speak and Spell" learning aid.

3M managers also have three choices: they can request funds from (1) their own division, (2) corporate R&D, or (3) the new ventures division.[29] This willingness to allow a variety of funding channels has an important consequence: it encourages the pursuit of alternative technological approaches, particularly during the early stages of a technology's development, when no one can be sure of the best course to follow.

IBM, for instance, has found that rebellion can be good business. Arthur K. Watson, the founder's son and a longtime senior manager, once described the way the disk memory, a core element of modern computers, was developed:

> [It was] not the logical outcome of a decision made by IBM management; [because of budget difficulties] it was developed in one of our laboratories as a bootleg project. A handful of men . . . broke the rules. They risked their jobs to work on a project they believed in.[30]

At Northrop the head of aircraft design usually has at any one time several projects in progress without the awareness of top management. A lot can happen before the decision reaches even a couple of levels below the chairman. "We like it that way," explains Northrop chairman Tom Jones.[31]

Tolerance of Failure. Moreover, the successful high-technology firms tend to be very tolerant of technological failure. "At HP," Bob Hungate, general manager of the Medical Supplies Division, explains, "it's understood that when you try something new you will sometimes fail."[32] Similarly, at 3M, those who fail to turn their pet projects into a commercial success almost always get another chance. Richard Frankel, the president of the Kevex Corporation, a $20 million instrument manufacturer, puts it this way, "You need to encourage people to make mistakes. You have to let them fly in spite of aerodynamic limitations."[33]

Opportunity to Pursue Outside Projects. Finally, these firms provide ample time to pursue speculative projects. Typically, as much as 20 percent of a productive scientist's or engineer's time is "unprogrammed," during which he or she is free to pursue interests that may not lie in the mainstream of the firm. IBM Technical Fellows are given up to five years to work on projects of their own choosing, from high speed memories to astronomy.

5. Sense of Integrity

While committed to individualism and entrepreneurship, at the same time successful high-tech firms tend to exhibit a commitment to long-term relationships. The firms view themselves as part of an enduring community that includes employees, stockholders, customers, suppliers, and local communities: their objective is to maintain stable associations with all of these interest groups.

Although these firms have clearcut business objectives, such as growth, profits, and market share, they consider them subordinate to higher order ethical values. Honesty, fairness, and openness—that is, integrity—are not to be sacrificed for short-term gain. Such companies don't knowingly promise what they can't deliver to customers, stockholders, or employees. They don't misrepresent company plans and performance. They tend to be tough but forthright competitors. As Herb Dwight—president of Spectra-Physics, one of the world's leading laser manufacturers—says, "The managers that succeed here go *out of their way* to be ethical."[34] And Alexander d'Arbeloff, cofounder and president of Teradyne, states bluntly, "Integrity comes first. If you don't have that, nothing else matters."[35]

These policies may seem utopian, even puritanical, but in a high-tech firm they also make good business sense. Technological change can be dazzlingly rapid; therefore, uncertainty is high, risks are difficult to assess, and market opportunities and profits are hard to predict. It is almost impossible to get a complex product into production, for example, without solid trust between functions, between workers and managers, and between managers and stockholders (who must be willing to see the company through the possible dips in sales growth and earning that often accompany major technological shifts). Without integrity the risks multiply and the probability of failure (in an already difficult enterprise) rises unacceptably. In such a context, Ray Stata, cofounder of the Massachusetts High Technology Council, states categorically, "You need an environment of mutual trust."[36]

This commitment to ethical values must start at the top, otherwise it is ineffective. Most of the CEOs we interviewed consider it to be a cardinal dimension of their role. As Bernie Gordon, president of Analogic explains, "The things that make leaders are their philosophy, ethics, and psychology."[37] Nowhere is this dimension more important than in dealing with the company's employees. Paul Rizzo, IBM's vice chairman, puts it this way, "At IBM we have a fundamental respect for the individual . . . people must be free to disagree and to be heard. Then, even if they lose, you can still marshall them behind you."[38]

Self-understanding. This sense of integrity manifests in a second, not unrelated, way—self-understanding. The pride, almost arrogance, of these firms in their ability to compete in their chosen fields is tempered by a surprising acknowledgment of their limitations. One has only to read Hewlett-Packard's corporate objectives or interview one of its top managers to sense this extraordinary blend of strength and humility. Successful high-tech companies are able to reconcile their "dream" with what they can realistically achieve. This is one of the reasons why they are extremely reticent to diversify into unknown territories.

6. "Hands-on" Top Management

Notwithstanding their deep sense of respect and trust for individuals, CEOs of successful high-technology firms are usually actively involved in the innovation process to such an extent that they are sometimes accused of meddling. Tom McAvoy, Corning's president, sifts through hundreds of project proposals each year trying to identify those that can have a "significant strategic impact on the company"—the potential to restructure the company's business. Not surprisingly, most of these projects deal with new technologies. For one or two of the most salient ones, he adopts the role of "field general": he frequently visits the line operations, receives direct updates from those working on the project, and assures himself that the required resources are being provided.[39]

Such direct involvement of the top executive at Corning sounds more characteristic of vibrant entrepreneurial firms, such as Tandon, Activision, and Seagate, but Corning is far from unique. Similar patterns can be identified in many larger high-technology firms. Milt Greenberg, president of GCA, a $180 million semiconductor process equipment manufacturer, stated: "Sometimes you just have to short-curcuit the organization to achieve major change."[40] Tom Watson, Jr. (IBM Chairman) and Vince Learson (IBM President) were doing just that when they met with programmers and designers and other executives in Watson's ski cabin in Vermont to finalize software design concepts for the System 360—at a point in time when IBM was already a $4 billion firm."[41]

Good high-tech managers not only understand how organizations, and in particular engineers, work, they understand the fundamentals of their technology and can interact directly with their people about it. This does not imply that it is necessary for the senior managers of such firms to be technologists (although they usually are in the early stages of growth): neither Watson nor Learson were technical people. What appears to be more important is the ability to ask lots of questions, even "dumb" questions, and dogged patience in order to understand in-depth such core questions as: (1) how the technology works; (2) its limits, as well as its potential (together with the limits and potential of competitors' technologies); (3) what these various technologies require in terms of technical and economic resources; (4) the direction and speed of change; and (5) the available technological options, their costs, probability of failure, and potential benefits if they prove successful.

This depth of understanding is difficult enough to achieve for one set of related technologies and markets; it is virtually impossible for one person to master many different sets. This is another reason why business focus appears to be so important in high-tech firms. It matters little if one or more perceptive scientists or technologists foresees the impact of new technologies on the firm's markets, if its top management doesn't internalize these risks and make the major changes in organization and resource allocation that are usually necessitated by a technological transition.

THE PARADOX OF HIGH-TECHNOLOGY MANAGEMENT

The six themes around which we arranged our findings can be organized into two, apparently paradoxical, groupings: business focus, organizational cohesion, and a sense of integrity fall into one group; adaptability, entrepreneurial culture, and hands-on management fall into the other group. On the one hand, business focus, organizational cohesion, and integrity imply stability and conservatism. On the other hand, adaptability, entrepreneurial culture, and hands-on top management are synonymous with rapid, sometimes precipitous, change. The fundamental tension is between order and disorder. Half of the success factors pull in one direction; the other half tug the other way.

This paradox has frustrated many academicians who seek to identify rational processes and stable cause-effect relationships in high-tech firms and managers. Such relationships are not easily observable unless a certain constancy exists. But in most high-tech firms, the only constant is continual change. As one insightful student of the innovation process phrased it, "Advance technology requires the collaboration of diverse professions and organizations, often with ambiguous or highly interdependent jurisdictions. In such situations, many of our highly touted rational management techniques break down."[42] One researcher, however, proposed a new model of the firm that attempts to rationalize the conflict between stability and change by splitting the strategic process into two loops, one that extends the past, the other that periodically attempts to break with it.[43]

Established organizations are, by their very nature, innovation resisting. By defining jobs and responsibilities and arranging them in serial reporting relationships, organizations encourage the performance of a restricted set of tasks in a programmed, predictable way. Not only do formal organizations resist innovation, they often act in ways that stamp it out. Overcoming such behavior—which is analogous to the way the human body mobilizes antibodies to attack foreign cells—is, therefore, a core job of high-tech management.

The Paradoxical Challenge. High-tech firms deal with this challenge in different ways. Texas Instruments, long renowned for the complex, interdependent matrix structure it used in managing dozens of product-customer centers (PCCs), consolidated groups of PCCs and made them into more autonomous units. "The manager of a PCC controls the resources and operations for his entire family . . . in the simplest terms, the PCC manager is to be an entrepreneur," explained Fred Bucy, TI's president.[44]

Meanwhile, a different trend is evident at 3M, where entrepreneurs have been given a free rein for decades. A recent major reorganization was designed to arrest snowballing diversity by concentrating its sprawling structure of autonomous divisions into four market groups. "We were becoming too fragmented," explained Vincent Ruane, vice-president of 3M's electronic division.[45]

Similarly, HP recently reorganized into five groups, each with its own strategic responsibilities. Although this simply changes some of its reporting relationships, it does give HP, for the first time, a means for integrating products and market development across generally autonomous units.[46]

These reorganizations do not mean that organizational integration is dead at Texas Instruments, or that 3M's and HP's entrepreneurial cultures are being dismantled. They signify first that these firms recognize that both (organizational integration and entrepreneurial cultures) are important, and second, that periodic change is required for environmental adaptability. These three firms are demonstrating remarkable adaptability by reorganizing from a position of relative strength—not, as is far more common, in response to financial difficulties. As Lewis Lehr, 3M's president, explained, "We can change now because we're not in trouble."[47]

Such reversals are essentially antibureaucratic, in the same spirit as Mao's admonition to "let a hundred flowers blossom and a hundred schools of thought contend."[48] At IBM, in 1963, Tom Watson, Jr., temporarily abolished the corporate management committee in an attempt to push decisions downward and thus facilitate the changes necessary for IBM's great leap forward to the System 360.[49] Disorder, slack, and ambiguity are necessary for innovation, since they provide the porosity that facilitates entrepreneurial behavior—just as do geographically separated, relatively autonomous organizational subunits.

But the corporate management committee is alive and well at IBM today. As it should be. The process of innovation, once begun, is both self-perpetuating and potentially self-destructive: although the top managers of high-tech firms must sometimes espouse organizational disorder, for the most part they must preserve order.

Winnowing Old Products. Not all new product ideas can be pursued. As Charles Ames, former president of Reliance Electric, states, "An enthusiastic inventor is a menace to practical businessmen."[50] Older products, upon which the current success of the firm was built, at some point have to be abandoned: just as the long-term success of the firm requires the planting and nurturing of new products, it also requires the conscious, even ruthless, pruning of other products so that the resources they consume can be used elsewhere.

This attitude demands hard-nosed managers who are continually managing the functional and divisional interfaces of their firms. They cannot be swayed by nostalgia, or by the fear of disappointing the many committed people who are involved in the development and production of discontinued products. They must also overcome the natural resistance of their subordinates, and even their peers, who often have a vested interest in the products that brought them early personal success in the organization.

Yet, firms also need a certain amount of continuity because major change often emerges from the accretion of a number of smaller, less visible improvements. Studies of petroleum refining, rayon, and rail transportation, for example, show that half or more of the productivity gains ultimately achieved within these technologies were the result of the accumulation of minor improvements.[51] Indeed, most engineers, managers, technologists, and manufacturing and marketing specialists work on what Thomas Kuhn might have called "normal innovation,"[52] the little steps that improve or extend existing product lines and processes.

Managing Ambivalently. The successful high-technology firm, then, must be managed ambivalently. A steady commitment to order and organization will produce one color Model T Fords. Continuous revolution will bar incremental productivity gains. Many companies have found that alternating periods of relaxation and control appear to meet this dual need. Surprisingly, such ambiguity does not necessarily lead to frustration and discontent.[53] In fact, interspersing periods of tensions, action, and excitement with periods of reflection, evaluation, and revitalization is the same sort of irregular rhythm that characterizes many favorite pastimes—including sailing, which has been described as "long periods of total boredom punctuated with moments of stark terror."

Knowing when and where to change from one stance to the other, and having the power to make the shift, is the core of the art of high-technology management. James E. Webb, administrator of the National Aeronautics and Space Administration during the successful Apollo ("man on the moon") program, recalled that "we were required to fly our administrative machine in a turbulent environment, and . . . a certain level of *organizational instability was essential if NASA was not to lose control*" (authors' emphasis).[54]

In summary, the central dilemma of the high-technology firm is that it must succeed in managing two conflicting trends: continuity and rapid change. There are two ways to resolve this dilemma. One is an old idea: managing different parts of the firm differently—some business units for innovation, others for efficiency.

A second way—a way which we believe is more powerful and pervasive—is to manage differently at different times in the evolutionary cycle of the firm. The successful high-technology firm *alternates* periods of consolidation and continuity with sharp reorientations that can lead to dramatic changes in the firm's strategies, structure, controls, and distribution of power, followed by a period of consolidation.[55] Thomas Jefferson knew this secret when he wrote 200 years ago, "A little revolution now and then is a good thing."[56]

REFERENCES

1. See J.-J. Servan-Schreiber, *The American Challenge* (New York: Atheneum Publishers, 1968).

2. See S. Ramo, *America's Technology Slip* (New York: John Wiley & Sons, 1980).

3. See R. Pascale and A. Athos, *The Art of Japanese Management* (New York: Simon & Schuster, 1981).

4. See T. J. Peters and R. H. Waterman, Jr. *In Search of Excellence* (New York: Harper & Row, 1982).

5. See W. Ouchi, *Theory Z: How American Management Can Meet the Japanese Challenge* (New York: John Wiley & Sons, 1980).

6. See C. E. Makin, "Ranking Corporate Reputations," *Fortune*, 10 January 1983, pp. 33-44.

7. M. A. Maidique and B. J. Zirger, "Stanford Innovation Project: A Study of Successful and Unsuccessful Product Innovation in High-Technology Firms," *IEEE Transactions on Engineering Management*, ; M. A. Maidique, "The Stanford Innovation Project: A Comparative Study of Success and Failure in High-Technology Product Innovation," *Management of*

Technological Innovation Conference Proceedings (Worcester Polytechnic Institute, 1983).

8. See E. Romanelli and M. Tushman, "Executive Leadership and Organizational Outcomes: An Evolutionary Perspective," *Management of Technological Innovation Conference Proceedings* (Worcester Polytechnic Institute, 1983).

9. One of the authors in this article has employed this framework as a diagnostic tool in audits of high-technology firms. The firm is evaluated along these six dimensions on a 0-10 scale by members of corporate and divisional management, working individually. The results are then used as inputs for conducting a strategic review of the firm.

10. See R. Vancil and P. C. Browne, "General Electric Consumer Products and Services Sector" (Boston, MA: Harvard Business School Case Services 2-179-0707).

11. Personal communication with David Packard, Stanford University, March 4, 1982.

12. See G. Golvin, "The Re-Geneeing of ITT," *Fortune*, 11 January 1982, pp. 34-39.

13. See "RCA: Still Another Master," *Business Week*, 17 August 1981, pp. 80-86.

14. See "R&D Scoreboard," *Business Week*, 6 July 1981, pp. 60-75.

15. See R. Stata, *Analog Devices Quarterly Report*, 1st Quarter, 1981.

16. See "Why They Are Jumping Ship at Intel," *Business Week*, 14 February 1983, p. 107; M. Chase, "Problem-Plagued Intel Bets on New Products, IBM's Financial Help," *Wall Street Journal*, 4 February 1983.

17. These SAPPHO findings are generally consistent with the results of the Stanford Innovation Project, a major comparative study of U.S. high-technology innovation. See M. A. Maidique, "The Stanford Innovation Project: A Comparative Study of Success and Failure in High Technology Product Innovation." *Management of Technology Conference Proceedings* (Worcester Polytechnic Institute, 1983).

18. See: Maidique and Zirger; Several other authors have reached similar conclusions. See, for example, Peters and Waterman (1982).

19. Personal communication with Tom Jones, chairman of the board, Northrop Corporation, May 1982.

20. See W. R. Thurston, "The Revitalization of GenRad," *Sloan Management Review*, Summer 1981, pp. 53-57.

21. See T. Wise, "IBM's 5 Billion Dollar Gamble," *Fortune*, September 1966; "A Rocky Road to the Marketplace," *Fortune*, October, 1966.

22. See A. P. Sloan, *My Years with General Motors* (New York: Anchor Books, 1972), p. 401.

23. Personal communication with Ken Fisher, 1980. Mr. Fisher was president and CEO of Prime Computer from 1975 to 1981.

24. At Genentech, Cetus, Biogen and Collaborative Research, four of the

leading biotechnology firms, a top scientist is also a member of the board of directors.

25. See, for example, J. A. Morton, *Organizing for Innovation* (New York: McGraw-Hill, 1971).

26. Jimmy Treybig, president of Tandem Computer, Stanford Executive Institute Presentation, August 1982.

27. See D. A. Schon, *Technology and Change* (New York: Dell Publishing, 1967); Peters and Waterman (1982).

28. See S. Myers and E. F. Sweezy, "Why Innovations Fail," *Technology Review*, March-April 1978, pp.40-46.

29. See *Texas Instruments* (A), 9-476-122, Harvard Business School case; *Texas Instruments Shows U.S. Business How to Survive in the 1980's*, 3-579-092, Harvard Business School case; *Texas Instruments "Speak and Spell Product,"* 9-679-089, revised 7/79, Harvard Business School case.

30. Arthur K. Watson, Address to the Eighth International Congress of Accountants, New York City, September 24, 1962, as quoted by D. A. Shon, "Champions for Radical New Inventions," *Harvard Business Review*, March-April 1963, p. 85.

31. Personal communication with Tom Jones, chairman of the board, Northrop Corporation, May 1982.

32. Personal communication with Bob Hungate, general manager, Medical Supplies Division, Hewlett-Packard, 1980.

33. Personal communication with Richard Frankel, president, Kevex Corporation, April 1983.

34. Personal communication with Herb Dwight, president and CEO, Spectra-Physics, 1982.

35. Personal communication with Alexander d'Arbeloff, cofounder and president of Teradyne, 1983.

36. Personal communication with Ray Stata, president and CEO, Analog Devices, 1980.

37. Personal communication with Bernie Gordon, president and CEO, Analogic, 1982.

38. Personal communication with Paul Rizzo, 1980.

39. Personal communication with Tom McAvoy, president of Corning Glass, 1979.

40. Personal communication with Milt Greenberg, president of GCA, 1980.

41. See Wise (September 1966).

42. See L. R. Sayles and M. K. Chandler, *Managing Large Systems: Organizations for the Future* (New York: Harper & Row, 1971).

43. See R. A. Burgelman, "A Model of the Interaction of Strategic Behavior, Corporate Context and the Concept of Corporate Strategy," *Academy of Management Review* (1983): 61-70.

44. See S. Zipper, "TI Unscrambling Matrix Management to Cope with Gridlock in Major Profit Centers," *Electronic News*, 26 April 1982, p.1.

45. See M. Barnfather, "Can 3M Find Happiness in the 1980's? *Forbes,* 11 March 1982, pp. 113-116.

46. See R. Hill, "Does a 'Hands Off' Company Now Need a 'Hands On' Style?" *International Management,* July 1983, p. 35.

47. See Barnfather (March 11, 1982).

48. *Quotations from Chairman Mao Tse Tung,* ed. S. R. Schram (Bantam Books, 1967) p. 174.

49. See: D. G. Marquis, "Ways of Organizing Projects," *Innovation,* August 1969, pp. 26-33; T. Levitt, *Marketing for Business Growth,* (New York: McGraw-Hill, 1974), in particular, ch. 7.

50. Charles Ames, former CEO of Reliance Electric, as Quoted in "Exxon's $600-million Mistake," *Fortune,* 19 October 1981.

51. See, for example, W. J. Abernathy and J. M. Utterback, "Patterns of Industrial Innovation," *Technology Review,* June-July 1978, pp. 40-47.

52. See T. Kuhn, *The Structure of Scientific Revolutions,* 2d ed. (Chicago, IL: University of Chicago Press, 1967).

53. After reviewing an early draft of this article, Ray Stata wrote, "The articulation of dynamic balance, of ying and yang . . . served as a reminder to me that there isn't one way forever, but a constant adaptation to the needs and circumstances of the moment." Ray Stata, president, Analog Devices, letter of 29 November 1982.

54. Quoted in "Some Contributions of James E. Webb to the Theory and Practice of Management," a presentation by Elmer B. Staats before the annual meeting of the Academy of Management on 11 August 1978.

55. See Romanelli and Tushman (1983).

56. See J. Bartlett's *Familiar Quotations,* 14th ed. (Boston, MA: Little, Brown), p. 471B.

Modesto A. Maidique is associate professor of engineering management at Stanford University. Robert H. Hayes is professor of business administration at the Graduate School of Business Administration at Harvard University.

4.
ELICITING LATENT PRODUCTIVITY

Harold W. Fox

Who says the Japanese have the only answers to productivity gains? This profile of an Indiana "miniconglomerate" outlines methods for using excellent employee relations to boost productivity in uncommon but very effective ways.

Two decades after Bill and Gayle Cook sacrificed $1,500 and one room of their Bloomington, Indiana, apartment for their new business, the sales of Cook Group Incorporated were well over $90 million. Internally generated funds financed this spectacular growth. Sales and profits soared, as did employee morale and income, after president William A. Cook, the cofounder, discarded some traditional principles of management in favor of a home-grown employee participation and productivity-sharing system for motivating companywide achievement. (See Credos and Practices). "We foster a family atmosphere at the workplace," declares Cook. "In my opinion, many other businesses—from a mom-and-pop operation as we were until the mid-sixties, to a corporation the size of General Motors—could put our philosophy to profitable use."

Cook adds two provisos: 1) The company must generate a rising stream of profitable orders, enabling employees to keep increasing their output and earnings in a secure environment. Nobody fears that improved productivity could jeopardize employment. 2) The establishments or branches must be structured to employ fewer than 400 people, enabling participants of all ranks to keep identifying themselves with the organization. Friendliness, not formality, should mark labor-management relations. (See Cook's Philosophy of Industrial Relations.)

MANAGEMENT-LABOR INTERDEPENDENCE

This philosophy evolved after years of exploration and experimentation at Cook Incorporated, the flagship company of the Cook Group. The company specializes in medical instruments for probing and correcting abnormalities in blood vessels and the heart. Unobstrusive, this closely held enterprise is

29

The Cook System—Credos and Practices

1. Small work units with minimum number of employees.
2. Fewer excused absences. Focus on attendance.
3. Top management interacts frequently with employees at all levels.
4. Management believes that unionization has no place at Cook Incorporated.
5. Although the company is privately owned, it reveals shipping and sales data monthly to all employees.
6. Middle managers promote output in a harmonious atmosphere.
7. Middle managers must be fully knowledgeable about company policies.
8. Despite curbs on their authority, middle managers are held responsible for results.
9. Personnel advisor, backed by top management, intervenes in disputes between a manager and a subordinate to guard overall company interests.
10. Incompetent managers are removed promptly from their positions.
11. Some employees alternate between operative and supervisory status.
12. Versatility of employees is encouraged.
13. The company trains employees at all levels.
14. Guidance to employees explains what to do, but attempts not to prescribe how.
15. Peer pressure for high output at required quality.
16. Reliance on the responsibility and initiative of work units.
17. Management compliments groups only, not individuals.
18. Personnel policies apply to everybody.
19. Enforcement is impartial and strict.
20. Employees may bypass their supervisor to air grievances.
21. One incentive plan for all full-time employees.
22. The incentive plan treats all employees as a single group.
23. Opportunities for higher earnings.
24. Incentive bonus is paid monthly.
25. Employees can try to remedy their deficiencies between evaluation time and decision on merit raises.
26. The company appreciates employees as participants in the conduct of the business.
27. Concise manual of personnel policies.
28. Insistence on perfect quality.
29. Employees want to increase output.
30. Production and marketing are integrated.
31. Joint problem solving by operative and quality-control technician.
32. Secure employment for a small work force.
33. Sincere, rational appreciation of employees.
34. Incentive pool derives from companywide improvement.

35. Nearly all new hires are unskilled persons, recent high school and college graduates.

---

nestled in a suburban area of modestly priced homes and light industry. Densely planted pine trees enhance the local scenery and conceal the factory. Workers depend on this plant for employment.

Employees must exercise painstaking care in manual crafting of catheters (long, thin tubes) and other medical products, one unit at a time. Product perfection is imperative to protect the health of patients. Speed, although secondary, is an important commercial consideration. The tasks are intrinsically repetitive. Altogether, considerable training and acculturation are necessary to qualify new recruits, mainly female high school graduates, for this work.

A policy against overstaffing exacerbates this dependence on a small work force with special qualifications. Lateness, nonattendance, and turnover cause the company severe problems. Unexpected absences reduce output, which is difficult to recoup. Thus each employee is highly valued, for both humanitarian and commercial reasons.

CHAOTIC CONDITIONS

But this recognition of the workers as critical participants in the company's operations was a long time in coming. After overflowing operations were moved from the founder's apartment to larger business facilities, the type of apathy at the workplace common in many companies plagued this one. Prior to 1976, while top management was developing new products, production systems, and loyal customers, supervision of employees had been delegated to a hierarchy of administrators. Political infighting, antagonisms between and within the ranks, and squabbles about policy interpretations diverted attention from work. Output per worker rarely increased with experience. Shipments lagged behind orders by several months. Some goods had to to be recalled as defective.

To improve production, top management supported executive efforts in classical fashion. Clear lines of authority extended from top to bottom. Explicit rules governed everyday conduct. Specific problems were patched up, bringing transitory relief from the turmoil. Soon, however, the deteriorating trend resumed.

Operatives were indifferent. Symbolizing their frustration, employees kept demanding more pay for less work. Absenteeism and quit rates kept rising. Productivity continued to decrease. Exhortations to the personnel and special privileges or concessions were to no avail. Neither were threats, penalties, suspensions without pay, or even selected dismissals.

Middle managers despaired. At their request, top management tightened labor policies further and granted middle managers additional authority to enforce them. But mid-level managers abused their authority. Their prerogative unchecked, they were dictatorial and overbearing. As Lord Acton observed 100 years ago, "Power tends to corrupt and absolute power corrupts absolutely." Employees viewed managerial decisions as arbitrary or capricious. Rumors and innuendos about favoritism, procedural changes, and various intrigues created jealousies, worries, and tensions. Insecurity permeated all levels.

Trying frantically to meet the rising demand for its products, management had twice, over two-year periods, doubled the size of the work force. Of course, this rapid influx exacerbated the reorganizational problems. Eventually the disordered situation dampened sales.

Bill Cook was relatively inactive in his company for a two-year period in the mid-seventies, as he recuperated from open-heart surgery. Nevertheless, he blames himself for the chaotic conditions in his shop. "We had lost personal contact." When he set about to rectify this omission, his employees told him bluntly, "You don't know what's going on here."

Indeed, he did not. For example, at the outset it was not clear whether the operatives of the middle managers were at fault. But Cook's investigation concluded that conventional policies and bureaucratic administration were preventing employees from functioning effectively. Standard procedures stifled creativity. Individual norms and rewards discouraged cooperation. Autocratic supervision intimidated subordinates.

Radical changes were a necessity.

TOWARD A FRAMEWORK FOR PRODUCTIVITY

Instinctively, Cook based his reform effort on gaining the trust of the employees. He encouraged them to pose questions, all of which he answered candidly. Together, they identified problems and groped for practicable solutions. Of course, the transition to a new relationship was not smooth.

In his quest to fasten the worker's allegiance solely to Cook Incorporated, the president found himself contending with union overtures to his employees. He conveyed his intense opposition. "Our company policy states clearly that unions have no place at Cook Incorporated." Convinced of Cook's sincerity, or perhaps fearing the company might relocate from Bloomington, the workers rejected the union's membership drive.

One of Cook's first acts was to terminate a major executive and several supervisors to whom personnel administration had been entrusted. The emerging approach curtailed the power of the successor supervisors, yet held them responsible for results. Eventually, fifteen senior and middle managers who could not adjust to this unorthodox concept departed (some of them transferred to other work at the company). Meanwhile, from discussions between

William A. Cook's Philosophy of Industrial Relations

A productive and congenial work environment that yields high income to all participants derives from direct dealings between management and labor who recognize their mutual dependence, demonstrate mutual respect, and pursue the mutual goal of corporate prosperity.

1. Interdependence of management and labor
   a. Management and subordinates must cooperate in furtherance of company profit. Management is responsible for providing a steady stream of work and employees for filling customers' orders with care and speed. Everyone's interests must be protected with vigilance and vigor.
   b. In a labor-intensive business that requires excellent craftsmanship, as Cook Incorporated does, workers are a critical resource. This resource must be developed and maintained.
   c. Training of employees heightens manager-worker inter-dependence. The trained worker has specialized skills that render him or her more valuable to the business, yet confine this extra commercial worth to the present place of employment.
2. Working conditions for productivity
   a. Work units should be subdivided into establishments employing fewer than 400 people. These people must be eager workers, fully committed to their jobs, obviating the costs of hiring and training extra employees or supernumeraries as fill-ins for absentees. In effect, if regular employees are not producing, the company has no way of making up the lost output.
   b. In such a small workplace, managers and employees should have genuine concern for each other. Compensation should promote teamwork, not conflict. Each human being should have unlimited and monetary reward.
   c. These psychic and financial conditions preclude a role for labor unions.

management and workers, a framework for productivity emerged, based on harmonious working conditions and universal financial incentives.

PERSONNEL ADVISOR PROMOTES HARMONY

Under the new policy, employees may bypass the chain of command whenever complaints are not settled satisfactorily. To facilitate the implementation of this option, Cook Incorporated instituted the position of personnel advisor, who reports directly to top management.

The personnel advisor compensates for the power of supervisory management and audits the latter's performance. She promotes higher productivity as the goal that employees of all ranks share. She also helps resolve disputes between a manager and a subordinate.

Employees are free to air grievances or personal problems at any time, and specify whether or not the personnel advisor should relay the contents of a talk to the complainer's supervisor or higher management. Either way, this ombudsman tries to soothe the aggrieved person and solve the problem. Frequently, however, she is more of a counselor than an advisor. Her services as a sympathetic confidante are in wide demand.

An office clerk, promoted to this new position, inspired universal credibility. Management believed that she was eminently suited to be the first personnel advisor. But power tends to corrupt. Management now suspects that, after a while, she succumbed to the temptation of exploiting her position as a springboard for greater power. "She was feared."

Her successor, Jackie Wikle, is deemed ideal for this work at the present stage, when personnel methods are stable and enjoy general acceptance. She had earlier demonstrated her versatility by progressing from the factory floor to the office and thence to customer service. This hands-on experience taught her to understand problems and recommend solutions. "She uses judgment," observes Cook. A young, cheerful person, Mrs. Wikle says that she loves her job. "It's challenging." Employees contact her day and night.

WORKING CONDITIONS FOR PRODUCTIVITY

Another new function was created in 1977, when erstwhile secretary Phyllis McCullough, a customer service manager, was appointed executive assistant to the president in charge of employee communications. "A title without power," quips Cook. But she did restore calm. Now as a vice president, Mrs. McCullough has since assumed responsibility for all corporate communications and operations with the exception of sales and R&D. As part of her continuing personnel work, she is in charge of the productivity program.

She inaugurated a series of weekly meetings (lasting one to one and a half hours on company time) at which attendance by all leaders, supervisors, and managers is mandatory. These get-togethers feature, on a first-name basis, uninhibited discussions of problems, suggestions, and other matters of concern to the work force. Debates help mold and clarify the philosophy of channeling individual interests to corporate welfare.

McCullough carefully explained the personnel policies to the middle managers. At the same time she reassured them that this explicit demarcation of their scope and a pledge of management support replaced the former climate of uncertainty and retroactive criticism.

Nowadays, middle managers nurture achievement with a focus on the entire operation, not on their prerogatives or individual predilections. Despite curbs on their authority, confident managers with good communications skills succeed in this setting, according to Cook. "We want autonomy [for managers], but not at the sacrifice of checks and balances." Of course, eager workers do not need detailed supervision and pressure as apathetic employees do. The productive climate frees managers for more constructive tasks such as training, operations improvement, and scheduling.

The company gives qualified employees much discretion on how to do their jobs. "Managers, supervisors, leaders, and production people must determine what an adequate capacity is," states Cook. In the plant, each person has an individual workstation within which he or she has near-total freedom. Private radios with ear phones entertain their owners without disturbing coworkers. Pinups, family photographs, pet phrases, and drawings adorn the partitions. Management does not interfere when some people stop for a short conversation. The subject could be an idea to speed up production or it could be a personal matter. The workers judge.

Rules apply only where absolutely unavoidable. For example, safety regulations (shatterproof eyeglasses, protective hairnets) are strictly enforced. So are adherence to product specifications and compliance with edicts of the Food and Drug Administration. A typical penalty is temporary forfeiture of incentive pay. Termination is reserved for the most flagrant, repetitive violations. "Once workers are trained, we really hate to lose them," explains McCullough. "We work with them a long, long time, trying to salvage them."

Any problem that disciplinary actions cannot solve is adjudicated by an employment review board. Sessions require attendance of at least two corporate officers, the employee's department manager, the personnel advisor, and five other members. In practice, however, formal sanctions are rare. Peer pressure for performance makes them unnecessary.

In fact, at times middle managers shield assemblers and inspectors from overly zealous shipping clerks. The managers reiterate that the company needs perfect workmanship and complete orders. They encourage production workers and quality-control technicians to cooperate in a joint quest for improvements. Collective creativity is espoused, not solo speed-ups.

Accordingly, superior performance does not draw individual compliments; management addresses all kudos to the team. This group orientation is reinforced by the company's compensation policy.

FINANCIAL INCENTIVES FOR PRODUCTIVITY

The company's key motivator is high total income, contingent on group productivity. Over the years, Cook Incorporated has welded a work force of compatible, career-minded people of high capacity and initiative who respond favorably to incentives. Remuneration has three levels; base pay, supplementary benefits, and productivity sharing.

Initial wages and salaries are below the median of the competitive range.

This relatively low starting level discourages persons who seek a job for just a brief period. Rewards are ample for those who stay a long time—exactly the type of worker that Cook Incorporated wants to hire.

Most entrants are unskilled. Training and experience at the firm develop their ability to contribute. Wages vary according to such things as skill requirement, length of employment, and adjustments for shift differentials.

A generous benefits package supplements this base pay. Besides the usual extras, the employer defrays the full premiums for employees' health, dental, and life insurance. A bonus rewards perfect attendance, and capricious absences are penalized. Special allowances cover absences for jury duty, death in the family, and personal days. The company also has profit-sharing and savings plans.

Further, an incentive program at Cook Incorporated and many of its affiliate companies rewards all permanent full-time employees at a uniform percentage premium of their basic wage or salary. Payment is prompt. Although the company promises distribution of this bonus fifteen days after the month in which it was earned, disbursement usually occurs within five days. "Monthly payment is a 'nifty' idea," notes Cook. It is a feature adapted from the Scanlon plan.

Cook's provision for determining the total pool and allocating it to individual employees is simple. Illustrative calculations appear in Table 1. The total employee dividend is 5 percent of monthly sales (shipments) if they meet an established goal plus 8 percent of excess sales over the goal. The resulting total, divided by the total payroll, yields the incentive percentage on base compensation. In recent years this override has averaged more than 35 percent of base pay.

Table 1
Illustrative Bonus Computations

Example	Last Month's Shipments	Pool Basis	Amount of Pool	Computation of Incentive	Bonus per $100 Base Pay
1	$ 900,000		none		none
2	$1,000,000	5% of $1,000,000	$50,000	$\dfrac{\$\ 50,000}{\$250,000}$	$20.00
3	$1,400,000	5% of $1,000,000 8% of $ 400,000	$82,000	$\dfrac{\$\ 82,000}{\$250,000}$	$32.80
4	$1,600,000	5% of $1,000,000 8% of $ 600,000	$98,000	$\dfrac{\$\ 98,000}{\$250,000}$	$39.20

General assumptions: Established shipping goal is $1,000,000 per month. Current total payroll is $250,000.

Why total dollar shipments? A sales base is unambiguous. Any other figure might trigger arguments or suspicions over accounting methodology. Shipments correlate quite closely with production—the activity that the majority of employees can influence most directly. And, although the company is private, it does not object to disseminating its sales figures monthly, informing all personnel about its current performance. Altogether, the base of sales instead of profit or some other criterion has many advantages.

The bonus percentage formula meets two criteria. One is, the higher the value of shipments, the larger the amount distributed among the employees. "We have no cap," avers William Cook. Two, a rising incentive amount does not depress the company's profit percentage on the higher sales.

Yet fixed costs (for base pay) are relatively low. And the company saves extra training costs and other high overhead, such as extra administration and space, that a larger work force would create. Moreover, improvements are real. The company does not reward a department's savings that merely transfer costs to another section. Finally, the goal is updated every three months. It has been rising fast.

Promotion from within offers another opportunity for higher pay. Cook Incorporated encourages employee versatility. As noted, Cook Group keeps individual workplaces small. Smaller yet is the team to which a worker belongs. In these little sections, people know each other and understand the company's operations—key qualifications for advancement.

Most middle mangers started as operatives. "We have not brought in many outsiders at the management level," notes Phyllis McCullough. "Our biggest success has been the development of people internally." An additional opportunity for managers with super-achievement records and potential is a top position and equity participation in a satellite company. The original firm has sprouted into Cook Group Incorporated, a mini-conglomerate of sixteen semiautonomous corporations. Several are headed by former employees of the parent company. Many have adopted the same employee policies.

RESPONSIVE PERSONNEL

After the personnel had overcome their initial misgivings, enthusiasm for the productivity-sharing plan gathered momentum. People settled down to work. Unexcused absences became negligible. "The incentive program blew the lid off production," exults McCullough. Acceptable output zoomed. In the first four years, sales of Cook Incorporated approximately tripled. Price increases averaged 7 percent annually. Employment increased a total of 5 percent over the entire period. The implied increase in real output per worker is 150 percent, or more than 20 percent annually. Customers' orders are shipped promptly.

McCullough credits the spectacular escalation in productivity to employees, not labor-saving machinery. Over the years, the company installed additonal equipment, mainly to improve product quality. A computerized bank of telephones has rendered customer service more efficient.

Operatives who had previously restrained their coworkers now prod them to turn out more units. Ideas for shortcuts, structural improvements, and other savings pour forth. They are unstintingly passed on to others.

In one department, for example, a new employee with six weeks of training outproduced the two top recordholders. Thereupon the former champions vowed to show up the neophyte. Soon, production doubled, causing disruptions everywhere. Quality control asked for more technicians, but management challenged it to find ways of monitoring the increased volume without increase in staff. It did. The company, however, had to restructure various related operations and buy additional packaging machinery.

The record-breaking employee is still with the company. "This incident is quite typical, observes Cook. "Some employee discovers a better way; he or she tells others and they revolutionize production."

The personnel office is swamped with applications for employment. Even though it purges its list annually, during a normal (nonrecession) year it has a backlog of 1,000 applicants for some 400 jobs with virtually no turnover.

Through careful hiring followed by probation, the company selects individuals who, apparently, are eager to learn and work hard for high income. Each is paired with a trainer, who is an experienced production worker or supervisor. Instruction is on-the-job, not in a classroom. The marketing and office departments have similar procedures.

Individual evaluations precede semiannual wage decisions. Lagging producers get adequate time and training to improve before their raise is set. But not everybody reacts to the financial incentives the same way, and attitudes change over a person's lifetime.

SOME LIMITATIONS

"The incentive plan does cause some problems," acknowledges McCullough. Management must be vigilant lest some workers sacrifice quality for speed. Impatience can focus on the one whom a team perceives as the "weakest link." Thus, insistence on higher output can be harmful here, just as employee-enforced restrictions are in other firms. The personnel advisor helps middle management quell incipient disputes.

Occasionally, discord arises between a sick person who wants to return to work and her physician who asks Cook Incorporated to extend her leave. Personal health is, of course, uppermost, but the company is not sympathetic toward a doctor's unwarranted self-protection or overindulgence.

As the years pass, many people's primary goal turns from financial to social, observes vice-president McCullough. At first, the main motivator is the incentive system. Moreover, entrants can look forward to higher pay bases as their tenure lengthens. After eight to ten years of employment, ambition and productivity flatten. By that time, their base pay has risen substantially over the entry level. Most people are more satisfied financially, and doing a consistent, good job becomes its own reward. Their interests emphasize group membership, job security, and the prestige of affiliation with a successful organization known to be selective and to make products of high, social value. "Yet they still want a merit raise," observes McCullough. And, of course, as a person becomes older, the expectation of a pension takes on increasing importance.

Since all employees share in the incentive pool in proportion to their base pay, mature workers receive higher total compensation than the more productive youngsters. Management considers this paradox justified. Longevity deepens and diversifies experience. "I can fill in on any job in the place," an old-timer announced proudly. Experienced operatives teach the newcomers. They preserve a stable culture even though operations are dynamic.

This system gives management much flexibility. Operations are revamped often to accommodate changes in demand, product, technology, procedures, or personnel assignment. Yet the income of the employees is secure. For example, a supervisor whose performance has peaked may return to production at no cut in pay. Her position becomes available to a more imaginative worker. This has happened more than once. It is not unusual for a production worker to have a higher wage than his or her supervisor. Flexibility in work assignments helps the company keep the work force small. It substitutes for alternating hires and layoffs that typify personnel practices at some other companies.

MAINTAINING THE MOMENTUM

William Cook is almost fanatical in his dedication to the productivity system. He has given talks on the subject and is eager to share his experiences with others. "Adoption of this type of program takes willingness to experiment and to overcome resistance. One must be prepared mentally to admit failure and change." Interestingly, a recent survey by the U.S. General Accounting Office found that fewer than 1,000 companies throughout the United States run a productivity-sharing system program. Some 52 percent of a sample of companies researched by this government agency were unionized.

Management takes care to nurture the enthusiasm for its program and forestall any abatement. From time to time management injects small surprises and innovations into employee relations, keeping the program fresh. New employee activities replace events with flagging interest and heighten worker involvement in the firm.

Recently the company began giving each worker a carton of cookies to take home at Thanksgiving. An employee's birthday continues as a paid vacation benefit, but the company just added to this celebration by giving a personalized box of candies. A recent issue of the company's house organ reported on an awards banquet, Halloween party, and news from other Cook companies. It also featured items that employees submitted through stringers in their midst.

Close quarters and constant interaction obviate a need for morale surveys, management believes. From high school vocational teachers and from others who have worked in the plant for a few weeks or months come glowing reports about employee attitudes. More formally, the company monitors quarterly the percentages by which goals are attained or surpassed. Most significant, of course, are the happy faces, the general spirit of satisfaction, and the continual increases in output that are evident daily.

Drawing on his two decades in business management, William A. Cook summarizes his philosophy: "The individual must learn to think of himself or herself as a part of a group. The highest form of individuality is being able to remain productive as a team member without sacrificing creativity. Our company will survive if we continue to find those individuals who can identify new products and create new management methods. Our top-level managers must continue to train new managers and instill in them the desire to excel within a group. Also we must continue to manage by reaction to a problem or goal—not to a specific long-range plan."

Harold W. Fox is a professor of marketing at Ball State University, Muncie, Indiana.

5.

TO IMPROVE R&D PRODUCTIVITY, GAIN THE CEO'S SUPPORT

Robert Szakonyi

The CEO is the key player in improving R&D productivity. A nontechnical CEO can provide the support needed only if he is given handles with which to manage the interaction between R&D and other departments.

In most companies improving R&D productivity is the R&D director's job. However, this job is not quite as simple as it might seem because it is the chief executive officer, *not* the R&D director, who is the key player in improving R&D productivity. The R&D director can do his job, therefore, only if he realizes that his first responsibility is not determining priorities among new technologies or recruiting excellent researchers, but *gaining the CEO's support for R&D*.

Literally, improving R&D productivity means that the R&D organization increases its output. Almost everyone, however, agrees that measurements of R&D output in technical or financial terms are not very valid. Consequently, another view of what improving R&D productivity involves is needed.

Interest in improving R&D has stemmed originally from concern that a company's R&D organization has not been contributing its share. Operationally, this concern has been expressed in terms of two questions: Is the R&D organization doing the right R&D? Is the R&D being used?

R&D directors, of course, worry about these two questions—all of the time. Most R&D directors also know that the best way to get these questions answered in the affirmative is through improving the management of the interfaces between the R&D organization and the rest of the company (i.e., manufacturing, marketing, finance, etc.).

This is where the CEO's support for R&D comes in. The R&D director cannot manage these interfaces, because the R&D organization makes up only part of the interfaces. Usually it is only the CEO who can manage the interfaces. It is the CEO, not the R&D director, who can only try to persuade executives in other functions to work more closely with the R&D organization, which sometimes is like pushing a string.

In order to gain the CEO's support, the R&D director must consider 1) the background of the CEO, 2) the CEO's job, and 3) how the CEO handles his job in relation to R&D.

1. Most CEOs do not have a scientific or engineering background. Some CEOs may have worked in technical operations for a while, but few of them have had much experience with technology. Companies, on the whole, are run by people from manufacturing, marketing, finance, etc.
2. The CEO's job consists of seemingly contradictory elements. It is extremely abstract, but very operational. Managing 50,000 to 100,000 people in a very large corporation, for example, forces the CEO to be far removed from producing or selling products. At the same time, although he deals in abstractions, the CEO's job is to make hard-nosed business decisions about tough operational problems.
3. In theory, most CEOs probably would like to support R&D. The background of any CEO, however, will greatly influence whether he will support R&D in more than theory. A CEO with a technical background usually will, for he is on the same wavelength as the R&D organization. Such a CEO understands the operational problems of making technical advances aimed at increasing business.

On the other hand, a CEO without a technical background usually will support R&D as an abstract idea, but will deal with the R&D organization in terms of the only operational tool that he has—the crude tool of the budget. When dissatisfied with R&D productivity, a nontechnical CEO frequently thinks that his only resource is to cut the R&D budget.

Those R&D directors whose CEO has a technical background escape having their dealings with him solely around the narrow issue of budgets. For the preponderance of R&D directors, however, widening the area of mutual concern that they have with their CEO is one of their major problems.

The two approaches that R&D directors usually have taken in trying to solve this problem often have not worked.

First, documenting all that the R&D organization has contributed frequently does not work. Because of the exploratory nature of R&D, many R&D projects do not succeed. In addition, placing a value on fruitful R&D is difficult. In such a situation, the overall value of the R&D is a matter of judgment. If the CEO is not on the same wavelength as the R&D organization, he will probably not be satisfied with any documentation.

Second, demonstrating how the development of a new technology will lead to business payoffs often does not work by itself. The commercial prospect of a new product rests on a combination of its market potential and the technical leverage that the new product will have. Because the technical developments leading to this new product are uncertain—and, in turn, its leverage can only be estimated—one cannot get a good fix on its market potential. Consequently, what may look like a good business argument to the R&D director may not appeal to the CEO, especially since he probably does not understand the technology that is at the core of the new product.

R&D directors, therefore, need to take another approach to widening the area of mutual concern between their CEO and themselves. Rather than simply emphasizing technical or business payoffs, they need to emphasize *sound management.*

When a nontechnical CEO evaluates the expenditure of resources and the risks involved, he looks not only at the probability of technical or commercial success, but also at the credibility of the estimates. The CEO wants to make sure that the entire operation will be managed well. Consequently, an argument by the R&D director that is based on technical and business payoffs probably will only satisfy the CEO if executives in manufacturing, marketing, finance, etc. concur in their estimates.

Furthermore, although a concurrence of estimates by various executives may satisfy the CEO on a particular issue, something more is needed to gain the CEO's support for R&D in general. Before the CEO gives this type of support, he wants to see two things: 1) A demonstration that the R&D organization is working effectively with other functions; and 2) some handles for the CEO so that he can manage the interfaces between the R&D organization and other functions.

Given that the CEO probably is not managing these interfaces and that therefore the R&D organization is not working as effectively with other functions as it should, the R&D director will have to propose management changes to gain the CEO's support. Neither the CEO nor executives in other functions will accept any management changes, however, unless they first see business payoffs that will stem from these management changes.

Consequently, the R&D director should/must move on two fronts more or less simultaneously, though leading on the business front. The approach involves five steps.

1. *Develop ideas on how technical developments will lead to business payoffs.* The R&D director needs to show why any technical developments will provide the basis for a better business strategy than, say, acquisitions or diversification into financial services. Essentially, the R&D director has to develop sound business strategy that happens to rest on technology.
2. *Gain support from executives in other functions for these ideas.* The R&D director needs to build a coalition of supporters throughout the company. Ideas on how technical developments will lead to business payoffs provide the basis for building such a coalition. Moreover, by testing the waters with other executives through discussing these ideas, the R&D director will also be starting to lay the foundation for improving this coordination.
3. *Develop better procedures on both sides for coordinating the R&D organization with other functions.* The R&D director and executives in other functions need to evaluate—and then make improvements in—eight areas pertain-

ing to the relationship between the R&D organization and other functions: generating research ideas; selecting and evaluating R&D; transferring R&D; organizational structure; lines of communication; mix of skills; linking technological and business planning; and linking R&D to manufacturing.

4. *Establish handles for the CEO so that he can manage the interfaces between the R&D organization and other functions.* These handles should not be designed to make a nontechnical CEO a glorified R&D director. This is not the CEO's job. The CEO needs information that enables him to evaluate the many business and management risks that one sees from his perspective. Consequently, if a nontechnical CEO is ever going to be induced to rely on more than budgetary controls, he must help design his own handles. The CEO will not spend time designing these handles, however, unless he first sees significant business payoffs stemming from improving this coordination.

5. *Implement a step-by-step plan aimed at reaching these business and management goals.* Neither the business payoffs nor the improved coordination will be achieved overnight. Consequently, not only must phases in these efforts build on their predecessors, but the business phases and the phases in management changes must reinforce each other. Business payoffs pull improved coordination; improved coordination underlies business success.

In conclusion, the CEO is the key player in improving R&D productivity. A nontechnical CEO can play this role only if he is given handles with which to manage the interfaces between the R&D organization and other functions. It is the R&D director's responsibility to provide the CEO with these handles. Once the R&D director does this, he can gain the CEO's support and then do his job of improving R&D productivity.

Robert Szakonyi is a project director at the School of Engineering and Applied Science, George Washington University.

6.

HOW TO RECOGNIZE—
AND AVOID—
ORGANIZATIONAL DECLINE

Peter Lorange
Robert T. Nelson

Although there is a high probability of corporate decline following a
period of success, managers can learn to recognize early signs of deterioration.

Corporate performance almost always declines following a period of success.
The denial of this likely reality can make it difficult, if not impossible, for upper
management to recognize signs of decline. Corporations are sometimes
criticized for being "bloated, risk-averse, inefficient, and unimaginative" and
for not spending enough on research and development.[1] Commenting on this,
a leading economist noted that, "Big business has an aging process that can
weaken it."[2] While, to a considerable extent, we agree, we also believe preventive actions to anticipate and counteract decline are possible.

We will examine some of the *underlying* organizational characteristics that
contribute to declining performance and describe approaches that promise a
significantly higher probability of sustaining success. These approaches will
address behaviors that contribute to performance decline and also shed light on
some underlying causes of declining momentum.

There is a considerable body of recent literature on the broad subject of
corporate culture. This paper is not a review or a summary of this subject.[3] It is,
rather, a specific look at how internal organizational factors may precipitate
decline. Our discussion refers to large, established corporations rather than
smaller unique organizational and performance concerns.[4]

Our study of threats to organizational performance is based on both U.S. and
European corporate industrial experiences. Observations are based on two
workshops with executives from a variety of corporations, plus in-depth experience and work with six companies, drawn from the electronics, building

materials, metals, chemicals, energy, and machinery industries. In most cases, the companies are multinational and multidivisional.

This paper will examine the following issues: * observations of organizational decline,

- reasons for organizational decline,
- early warning signals,
- intervention alternatives, and
- underlying beliefs that safeguard against decline.

While our emphasis is on internal factors contributing to performance decline, we do not dismiss the importance of other classical strategy issues. Delineation of a competitive strategy *is* key; the industry structure *will* have an impact; technological breakthroughs and innovations *can* disrupt one's path to success; and economic and political factors *do* affect performance. We only suggest that examining how organizations cope with degeneration provides a useful complement to these critical theoretical outlooks.

OBSERVATIONS OF ORGANIZATIONAL DECLINE

Although the art of strategic management seems to have become more highly developed than ever before, a wide range of corporations' performance has declined. Conventional measures such as total sales, profitability, market share, and loss of technological leadership all indicate this deterioration. Many corporate leaders blame these setbacks on largely uncontrollable elements in the external environment such as currency fluctuations, interest rates, and low-cost foreign competition. While these explanations have some validity, they only partially explain decline. There are usually early indicators of trouble that alert managers should recognize and address at an appropriate time. Instead, problems are not recognized. Eventually managers take desperate, precipitous steps to correct long-standing problems. Such problems, which tend to be relatively easy to correct if addressed early, are often pointed out by industry observers or by some executives within the corporation itself. Refusal or inability to see problems early can lead to escalating negative effects that, over time, can set organizational decline in motion.

Well-known examples include the U.S. automobile industry, which once had a dominant position in the world automobile market. Gradually it began to produce autos of a quality well below standard; the manufacturers were slow to respond to the market's demand for smaller cars, and the industry paid wages well above the U.S. average for comparable industries. These three factors created an unstable U.S. automobile industry.[5] The U.S. steel industry, too, used increasingly obsolete processes and paid its workers wages well above the national average. Loss of competitiveness is well documented.[6]

Significantly, both of those industries also seemed to experience a deterioration of performance-oriented management climate. The change in climate may have prevented management from acting when the necessity for doing so should have been obvious.

CAUSES OF ORGANIZATIONAL DECLINE

It seems that success itself often appears to blur perceptions of the market and the competitive environment, thereby setting organizational decline in motion. Paradoxically, *competitive success itself* may trigger organizational decline by encouraging complacency. Companies often gain an extraordinary competitive advantage through technical innovation in a growth niche.[7] DuPont, for example, had long been dominant in the field of artificial fibers. In such cases, with very heavy demand, no in-kind competition, and high profitability, normal competition disappears. Expansion becomes the only strategy and marketing becomes the recording of orders. Success validates the strategy of the moment; as long as success lasts, the organizational characteristics that evolve are also validated.

We propose five specific factors that play a major role in organizational decline. Taken together they help to suggest how to avoid a slowdown in organization momentum.

Decline, Entrapment, Self-Deception. Indicators of decline, often obvious to the objective observers, are discounted by responsible top managers, usually because of some commitment to an outdated view of the business's basic nature.[8]

In a large multinational corporation that we observed (a world leader in parts of the metals business) management became used to high and low cycles as the norm. Over time, however, the business matured. The upturns became fewer and weaker, while the downturns lasted longer. Top management was so committed to its belief that downturns were insignificant that it failed to note the new pattern. The brief occasional upturns, with their accompanying temporary upturns in financial results, seemed to confirm their now out-of-date strategic picture. This kind of almost willful blindness on the part of top management may be much more common than is generally known.

Hierarchy Orientation. A business's growth phase is typically characterized by a strong orientation toward the primary market and competitive goals. This focus is often replaced by a "hierarchy" orientation once success has been achieved. (By *hierarchy orientation*, we mean the use of decision criteria based primarily on the perceived desires and politics of the organization hierarchy, rather than on basic business demands.) New employees may no longer absorb the sense of urgency that gripped the founders.[9]

A large multinational electronics corporation we observed had experienced extraordinary growth and financial success. Then so-called "coordination" problems became evident: in a given market, for instance, several divisions had independent manufacturing, distribution, and sales activities. R&D was carried out without adhering to common, over-all standards. Market research in various divisions had led to competition for the same customers. In response to these developments, top management instituted massive coordination staffs to centralize marketing and R&D. New vice presidencies were created. The results: a massive increase in hierarchical orientation and organizational complexity—but no one any longer had "uncluttered" business responsibility.

Cultural Rigidity. With economic success, a change in emphasis from innovation to tightened administration tends to create an increasingly rigid culture. The new culture inhibits the rapid changes often necessary to respond to a rapidly changing business environment.[10] In the electronics firm just described, for instance, elaborate coordinating requirements were instituted. These included formal, numbers-oriented strategic planning documents, a detailed budgetary control process, and manpower reporting routines. Producing these documents took up enormous amounts of time and none of the documentation came out on a timely, as-needed basis.[11]

Desire for Acceptance; Conformity. If top management is perceived to be averse to change or to criticism, then potentially independent voices within the organization will not be heard. A strong desire for acceptance and a hierarchical orientation leads managers not to "rock the boat" unless rocking is explicitly encouraged.[12] In the metals company, for instance, several maverick executives frustrated their superiors and led others to imitate them by "breaking the norms." Their lack of success and ultimate departure led to an even stronger emphasis on the prevailing manufacturing-process, engineering-oriented focus. Similarly, in the electronics firm, it was considered in poor taste to raise problem issues in large meetings because that might come across as criticism of a colleague.

Too Much Consensus and Compromise. When multidivision companies try to develop synergy opportunities in R&D, manufacturing, and distribution, the organization tends to become more complex. New staff groups often emerge. The results can be a gradual increase in the amount of time key managers spend on planning meetings, as well as increased focus on reaching consensus. Such activities often produce compromises that are timed poorly and that do not "belong" to any specific management group. The need to achieve consensus causes bickering and waters down managerial responsibility.[13]

In a large multinational machinery corporation, there was considerable tension between the global strategy managers and the country managers. No effort was made to assess which of these groups should be given the stronger hand. Instead, top management introduced extensive planning coordination processes structured around "global strategy teams" and "country strategy teams." The outcome was disappointing. Compromises were abundant, important problems were left unresolved, and the final plans reflected no sense of urgency or resolve.

Taken together, these five factors gradually separate managerial employees from basic, immediate business goals. Also, the momentum generated by success may mean that individual employees feel no sense of urgency—no sense that daily performance has a significant effect on business performance. However, sustaining dynamism often requires high levels of energy and effort, and the difficulty of sustaining such a light energy level may ultimately lead to decline in effective performance.

EARLY WARNING SIGNALS

Certain organizational characteristics can serve as early indicators of performance decline. Even though they are sometimes difficult to measure objectively, it is obviously important to evaluate these indicators. A considerable time lag may occur between the first "weak signals" and the ultimate decline in measurable business performance. Usually, the negative characteristics become more deeply entrenched as time passes; the correction of deeply entrenched problems is often painful and disruptive.[14]

The dilemma is that weak signals are much harder for managers to see, understand, and take seriously. They are not perceived as sufficiently dramatic to demand immediate attention. For this reason, we recommend that organizations systematically monitor weak signal factors, then "amplify" them through institutionalized analysis so as to be prepared to launch appropriate, timely responses.[15] Nine characteristics in particular can give useful early warnings—and, if not monitored, can contribute to the business's decline.

Excess Personnel. A swollen staff and an excess of managerial levels can magnify the problems described above. Effective communication, difficult under the best of conditions, is virtually impossible when information flows through too many levels. Managerial levels and personnel are often added to provide quick solutions for control and coordination problems. Compensation systems and title structures may further encourage expanding the hierarchy. Such trends are rarely challenged during a company's success phase. As the organization grows, small "kingdoms" develop; each has its own agenda and the stage is set for turf battles. The electronics, metals, and manufacturing firms described above had all added significantly to their head-count. Interestingly, however, the number of lower-level jobs had gone down in each case—but the number of managerial-level jobs had increased dramatically. All three organizational structures had become much more complex and headquarters size had grown substantially.

Tolerance of Incompetence. Many large corporations have great difficulty coping with managerial incompetence. The uncoupling of managerial personnel from immediate, basic business goals—which typically happens following a highly successful phase—can create an environment where inability to perform is masked. In addition, cleaning out incompetent managers is a hot potato that upper-level managers often do not want to touch. For instance, fast-track managers, who are the future leaders of the organization, typically find it unrewarding to address competence problems as they pass through various corporate assignments. They chose instead to focus on areas that will provide them with "positive visibility" and so enhance their image.

In one energy-related company we observed, there was an amazing consensus within management ranks that certain key executives had reached their "level of incompetence," yet it was unheard of to change job assignments ahead of schedule. The executives in question had supposedly "earned the right" to be treated with understanding because of their past service. Mediocrity and incompetence gradually became so entrenched that a massive shakeup was inevitable.

Cumbersome Administrative Procedures. When examining performance decline, one encounters numerous examples of excessive paperwork, slow approval systems, endless alternative evaluations, and inappropriate committee decisions. These inefficiencies tend to build up over a long period of time. Increasingly, they become a part of various internal agendas in a bloated organization. In the machinery manufacturing company, for example, capital appropriations procedures had become extremely rigid over the years. Considerable delays led, in several instances, to serious strategic-timing problems. An outsider could quickly see that the vice president in charge of capital budgeting clearly enjoyed the power he had as "interrogator" of the line.

Disproportionate Staff Power. Staff groups, originally designed to supplement the line with specialized knowledge, or to facilitate coordination, grow over time. As a hierarchical orientation develops, various staff groups (legal, finance, public affairs) increase their influence to the point where the operating groups lose their client status; staff groups begin to co-manage the company. An increasing ratio of staff to line is often a good early indicator of excessive growth in staff's relative power. The energy company we studied had a large, centralized strategic planning staff. The planners considered the line unsophisticated, conventional, and too ready to criticize. The line saw the planners as too theoretical, arrogant, and irritating. Needless to say, as this expensive staff grew in size—and grew away from its support role—its real contribution diminished.

Replacement of Substance with Form. Managers can easily become too absorbed by form and insufficiently concerned with substance. Many strategic planning processes, for example, produce thick binders full of numbers that do not improve management's understanding of environmental trends. Urgent business challenges do not receive the attention they deserve.

In a building materials company we studied, the formal planning process featured an elaborate planning review schedule that put heavy demands on top management's time and booked up their calendars months in advance. Little came of these formal, rehearsed meetings. Yet line managers who urgently needed ad hoc strategic reconsiderations could rarely reach top management to discuss such unexpected events.

Scarcity of Clear Goals and Decision Benchmarks. In a growth phase, the whole organization tends to understand what the key competitive challenges are.

When the business moves into success and maturity phases, though, large segments lose their day-to-day focus on the basic business. The benchmarks for decisions may become less defined. In fact, when a decision must be made, managers often spend more time sorting out the criteria for the decision than making the decision itself. This lack of common vision can contribute significantly to the dissipation of available managerial energy.

A company from one of our workshops reported an example in which a business manager decided against a geographical expansion based on a clear business analysis. He was then overruled by upper management, which used ill-defined criteria to make their decision—corporate image, market presence, personal bias. After heavy losses the decision was reversed, but the business manager and others were left uncertain about decision criteria.

Fear of Embarrassment and Conflict. One of the more interesting outcomes we have noted is that when a company goes through its success phase, a shift occurs in the outlook of many managers. Where they were once no-nonsense and business oriented, they become increasingly concerned with avoiding embarrassment and side-stepping conflict. Many high-level executives think they have more to lose from making mistakes and rocking the boat than they have to gain from pursuing potentially controversial, issue-oriented positive accomplishments.

In the energy company, major funding had gone into a new business development for several years. This project was spearheaded by the CEO; the manager in charge was given a free hand to spend what was needed. The losses became staggering and several senior-level committees were established to analyze the project strategy. No one identified any problems. While the managers involved were not untruthful, they failed to report their concerns about the *timing* of the new product. Because they did not want to embarrass anyone, least of all the CEO, they preferred to sweep this issue under the rug—even though they had serious misgivings.

Loss of Effective Communication. Business success requires that accurate information flow vertically and horizontally throughout an organization. When an organization is in decline, healthy communication becomes extremely difficult.

One typical example we encountered was the case of a division vice president who routinely combed his staff for good news to report to management committee meetings. He wanted to provide good, not bad, news. Since in fact serious problems existed, he created a false, and very dangerous, sense of euphoria.

Outdated Organizational Structure. An organizational structure often reflects a corporation's past rather then its present or future. Outdated organizational constraints can inhibit the interactions necessary to succeed in the future. To overcome difficulties imposed by rigid structures, many companies have created task forces, planning teams, and so on. For these structures to be successful, the organizational climate must encourage a manager to develop a more broad sense of responsibility than his or her formal job entails. Unfortunately, in degenerating organizations this broad vision often seems unworkable. Managers prefer to be cubbyholed, not to consider the broader issues.

In the electronics firm, for example, a number of ad hoc task forces were in place. Senior managers tried to avoid these assignments, even though they readily proclaimed their importance. Instead, they placed their third-string management on the task forces, then pulled them off for "more pressing" operational duties. De facto, a rigid structure prevailed.

Clearly, it will be difficult to measure many of these danger signals. Nevertheless, they are useful and qualitative early indicators of a potential threat to future economic performance. If management is willing to periodically examine these issues, signals may cause managers to "unfreeze" their thinking and confront, evaluate, and take action as needed. Where direct measurements are possible (such as line to staff ratios or number of managerial levels), these can and should be compared with current and potential competitors. Where number measurements are not possible, an anonymous organizational survey can produce valuable insights.

INTERVENTION ALTERNATIVES

When an organization is facing decline, it is more or less a given that it needs to change strategic direction. The often frustrating reality, however, is that the various conditions we have described can make change difficult.

The following four-step thinking model, if included in the strategic planning process, can help a company to maintain strategic vitality. It is based on the classical model for executing organizational change, which consists of "unfreeze," "change," and "refreeze" modes.[16] Table 1 gives an overview of this model.

We will review each of the steps in this process in some detail.

Unfreezing: Establishing the Likelihood of Decline. Senior management must recognize the high probability of decline. Strategic planning efforts should include a process that monitors early performance indicators, as outlined in the previous section. The members of the organization should be challenged to identify indications of performance decline as they arise, and to suggest pragmatic solutions for counteracting these dysfunctions. Different businesses within an enterprise may develop unique problems, so area leaders must be attuned to specific relevant signals that will affect price, quality, service, or design.[17]

The degree to which an organization is "unfrozen" is determined by the extent of the decline and the depth of the "corrupting effects" as shown by the early indicators. Determining how far to "unfreeze" is an important decision.

In the electronics firm, for instance, executives focus particularly on potential problems concerning strategic momentum. Several times every year the top group of managers has a frank and thorough discussion of each business

Table 1
A Management/Intervention Change Process
for Counteracting Organizational Degeneration

UNFREEZE

- Recognize Potential Problems
- Sensitize Organization
- Establish Early Indicator-Review System for Each Business

CHANGE

- Assess Effect of Organizational Problems on Strategic Business Plans

REFREEZE

- Establish Effective Overall Communication to Overcome Organizational Problems and Address Business Strategy
- Continue to Evaluate Validity of Early Indicators

---

division. From these eclectic meetings emerges a renewed sensitivity to keeping up the momentum in each business.

Reconcile Degeneration Signals with Strategy. As a second step in the planning process, management should examine the extent to which organizational danger signals might affect the implementation of strategic business plans. Doing this will clarify the consequences of taking no ameliorative action. Most executives do not readily make changes that bring their previous judgements into question.[18] Thus, upper management may need to institute formal internal review taskforces or hire an outside consultant to ensure that proper attention is given to characteristics that could impede strategy implementation. In the building-materials firm, each strategic implementation program is reviewed regularly with the goal of identifying potential "derailing" factors that could threaten programs within the firm. A list of potential problem areas, not dissimilar to the one we identified earlier, is examined. Outside experts are brought in regularly to assess reasons for setbacks in critical areas.

Top-Down Bottom-Up Dialogue. A two-way conversation might at this stage realistically help to recreate vitality and improve the probability of developing and implementing a successful plan. Even this phase is difficult. Unilateral top-down dictates will not work. Bottom-up demands are similarly ineffective. Even if all sides appear to want change, open communication is still difficult. Often more effective communication, including descriptions of problems and recommendations for improvements can threaten an individual's power base.

This real or perceived diminishment is not welcomed by those it affects. To keep the change process open, upper management must continuously express its resolve to solve the problem. If particular managers are impediments to change, they should be removed. The dilemma, however, is that top management itself can be the problem. In these extremely difficult circumstances, we still emphasize the point that bottom-up pressure is the only way to effect change.

In the metals firm, a vibrant top-down bottom-up dialogue is based on an assessment of what issues will be particularly meaningful for businesses in different situations. New, emerging divisions reason together about strategic direction; line management gets access to top management to discuss initiatives and objectives. For a more established business, the discussion typically shifts toward improving competitive performance based on cost containment, delivery promptness, securing quality levels, and so forth. Line management thus gets access to the top to discuss these issues. Ad hoc teams of managers participate in the various discussions based on their ability to contribute to the issues at hand. A more issue-oriented, competence-driven interaction seems to result.

Follow-up Monitoring. The early warning indicators should be continually reviewed, and the effort to shelter strategy implementation from degenerative forces must continue. Otherwise, the process becomes a one-shot attempt to attract attention from key management levels.

Ideally, if the early indicators are monitored closely and the organization is operating well overall, the changes resulting from intervention will be gradual—the organization should be capable of revolutionary changes, however, should the conditions warrant.

SAFEGUARDING AGAINST DECLINE

If management merely settles for a "mechanical" interpretation of these steps, not much progress will be made. It is not enough merely to be aware of—and address—the symptoms of organizational decline. It is also necessary to introduce and reinforce institutional beliefs about how to counteract organizational degeneration.

In our opinion, the single biggest challenge is sensitizing top management to the fact that decline is almost unavoidable unless deliberate steps are taken to prevent it. Then a series of guidelines can be proposed:

- Organize the company into definable ventures that have explicit goals. The clarity and immediacy of the goals provide decision benchmarks that are understood by executives.
- For each business, single out and concentrate on the toughest competitors and the most difficult customers.

- Define each job so that it is closely tied to a venture and has a "daily effect" on the success or failure of the venture.
- Promote individual diversity in order to challenge the hardening of outdated organizational concepts. Make room for experimentation and look for managers who are winners.
- Strengthen the participative, interactive, and integrative sides of strategic management process. Emphasize more effective information flow.

In principle, these managerial goals are simple, obvious, and familiar. In practice, however, they are by no means easy to achieve. The seriousness with which they are considered will affect how well strategic progress is sustained.

In summary, we have reached the following conclusions. Organizational performance almost always slacks off following a period of economic success. Organizational complacency sets in if it is not zealously avoided. While it is difficult for the top management team to recognize gradual performance decline, several steps can be taken to increase the capability of coping with degeneration. These include instituting a set of measures to assess common early warning signals. They also include building into the strategic planning a set of formal considerations regarding potential problems. Finally, appropriate managerial beliefs can provide a context for fighting organization degeneration.

Maintaining a desirable management climate requires a high and continuous energy input. A proactive approach can improve the probability of business success. A laissez-faire approach, on the other hand, is likely to result in an organization's demise.

REFERENCES

1. Speech by R. G. Darman, deputy secretary of the treasury, before Japan Society's conference, "Tax Reform in Japan and the United States: A Stimulus to New Economic Vitality?" (New York, 7 November 1986).
2. J. K. Galbraith, quoted from *The New York Times*, 11 November 1986, p. D4.
3. For recent reviews, see R. H. Kilmann, M. J. Saxton, R. Serpa, and associates, *Gaining Control of the Corporate Culture* (San Francisco: Jossey-Bass, 1985); and E. H. Schein, *Organizational Culture and Leadership* (San Francisco: Jossey-Bass, 1985).
4. For a case study of change processes in a large, successful corporation, see A. M. Pettigrew, "Examining Change in the Long-Term Context of Culture and Politics," in *Organizational Strategy and Change*, ed. M. J. Pennings (San Francisco: Jossey-Bass, 1985). For a fascinating analysis of how inner management factors and style differences between Ford and Sloan seemed to count considerably in explaining GM's success and

Ford's demise in the 1920s, together with an epilogue on GM's decline in the 1980s, see A. J. Kuhn, *GM Passes Ford, 1918-1938* (University Park: Pennsylvania State University, 1986). For a general discussion of decline in U. S. industry, see, for instance, B. Bluestone and B. Harrison, *The Deindustrialization of America* (New York: Basic Books, 1982).

5. See for instance, R. Phillips, A. Way, et al., *Auto Industries of Europe, U.S., and Japan* (Cambridge, MA: Ballinger, 1982); and B. Yates, *The Decline and Fall of the American Automobile Industry* (New York: Empire Books, 1983).

6. See for instance, P. Tiffany, *The Roots of Decline* (New York: Oxford University Press, 1987).

7. See A. D. Chandler, *Strategy and Structure* (Cambridge: MIT Press, 1962).

8. J. Brockner, J. Z. Rubin, and E. Lang, "Face-Saving and Entrapment," *Journal of Experimental Social Psychology*, 17 (1981): 68-79.

9. M. Crozier and E. Friedberg, *Actors and Systems* (Chicago: University of Chicago Press, 1980).

10. B. M. Staw, L. E. Sandelands, and J. E. Dutton, "Threat-Rigidity Effects in Organizational Behavior," *Administrative Science Quarterly* 26 (1981): 501-524.

11. S. Rosen and A. Tesser, "On Reluctance to Communicate Undesirable Information: The MUM Effect," *Sociometry*, 33 (1970): 253-263.

12. See J. Irving, "Group Think," *Psychology Today*, November 1971.

13. See T. C. Cummins, "Designing Effective Work Groups, in *Handbook of Organizational Design*, P. Nystrom and W. H. Starbuck, eds. (New York: Oxford University Press, 1981).

14. P. Lorange, M. S. Scott Morton, and S. Ghoshal, *Strategic Control* (St. Paul, MN: West Publishing, 1986).

15. P. Lorange, "Strengthening Organizational Capacity to Execute Strategic Change," in M. J. Pennings (1985). (Reference 4.)

16. D. Kolb and A. L. Frohman, "An Organization Development Approach to Consulting," *Sloan Management Review*, Fall 1970, pp. 51-66.

17. T. Gilmore and L. Hirschhorn, "Management Challenges Under Conditions of Retrenchment," *Human Resource Management Journal*, 22 (1983); 341-358.

18. P. Block, *The Empowered Manager* (San Francisco: Jossey-Bass, 1987).

Peter Lorange is professor of management at The Wharton School, University of Pennsylvania, and director of Wharton's Center for International Management Studies. Robert T. Nelson is a general management consultant based in Huntington, NY.

7.
HUMAN RESOURCE PLANNING

Gayle J. Yaverbaum
Oya Culpan

For years, organizations have recognized the importance of worker satisfaction. In today's rapidly changing work environment, managers must take care to consider human-resource problems when integrating technology into the organizational structure.

Office and factory automation are progressing rapidly. Computers are replacing typewriters and filing cabinets; a paperless office is becoming a reality. What was once written material is being forwarded over communication lines, and we are talking to computers. Even a paperless federal bureaucracy appears possible with the Office of Management and Budget investigating ways for government agencies to set up computerized systems to collect, analyze, and disseminate information.[1]

More and more people are working at home using telecommunications. In the workplace itself, robots are providing the means to automate factories. Some predict the factory worker of the future will be an operator at a computer terminal rather than an assembly-line worker. The Japanese postulate factories with glass-enclosed, air-conditioned workstations, with the lines between office and factory becoming less distinct.[2]

For example, people utilizing telecommunications to perform work away from the office are reporting feelings of loneliness and isolation. Talking on the phone or through a computer is not enough personal contact for some people; they need face-to-face interaction. Fear of stepping off the corporate ladder and becoming less promotable under isolated work environments is especially prevalent among telecommuters.[3]

Erasing the lines between office and factory in the future will lead to automation of office tasks and centralization of many functions that were previously decentralized, and make management of systems a corporate priority. People already fear that they will be displaced by new technologies, or be unable to perform satisfactorily. Job insecurity creates resistance to change.

Craig Brod defines "technostress" as the inability to cope with changes caused by computer technology in a healthy manner.[4] "Cyberphobia" is another term applied to fear of computers.[5] Much of this fear is associated with lack of "hands on" experience by the first-time user; people are afraid of making a mistake, appearing foolish, or losing control. Managers themselves often experience these fears as they are forced to interact with computers in order to effectively carry out their jobs. The fears exist at every organizational level.

Stress of any sort has a multitude of consequences that will eventually have an effect upon an organization. Schermerhorn provides a list of new behaviors that result from stress.[6] They include absenteeism, errors in judgment, carelessness, mistakes, poor humor, negative attitude, resistance to change, tardiness and poor interpersonal relations. Cox includes many of the same effects plus high accident and turnover rates, poor organizational climate and general job dissatisfaction.[7] Therefore, it is critical that organizations understand the possible negative effects stress in technological environments can have and take measures that will counteract them.

PERSONAL FULFILLMENT MODEL

Organizations have for years recognized the importance of worker satisfaction. In the enigmatic and rapidly changing computer environment, individuals develop different levels of need and different levels of expectations regarding the organizations in which they are involved.

The Model of Personal Fulfillment introduced in Figure 1 establishes the interrelationship between the individual and the organization and demonstrates that a variety of activities affect worker satisfaction. It is assumed that higher levels of satisfaction result in greater productivity for each individual, and, therefore, higher levels of productivity for an organization.

The Personal Fulfillment model also includes external activities. These occur outside of the organizational environment and include family interrelationships, sports, volunteer work, hobbies and personal entertainment. Although most organizations do not yet realize the importance of these activities to employee job satisfaction, interesting results from studies of those who do have given support to the value of such activity.

A typical reaction to change is the diminishing of self-esteem, precipitated by uncertainty. The resulting stress is felt throughout an organization. Figure 2 proposes a Wheel of Action, a plan to counteract the negative aspects of rapid technological change. It implies a relationship to the Model of Personal Fulfillment by presenting specific actions to promote the personal satisfaction.

WHEEL OF ACTION

The Wheel of Action is divided into four sections—individual characteristics, task, external activities and organizational support.

Individual Characteristics. Individual characteristics can only be indirectly adjusted, although an organization can provide new experiences for an

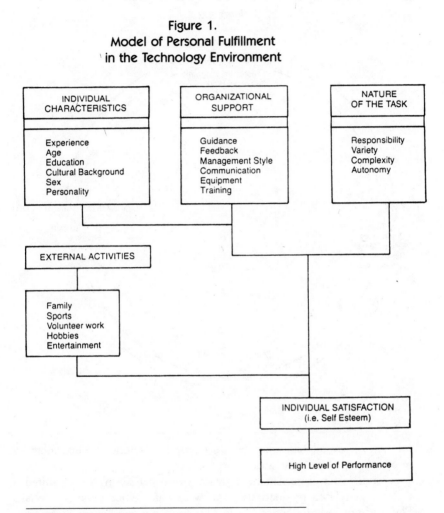

Figure 1.
Model of Personal Fulfillment
in the Technology Environment

employee and offer educational programs to ease fears. A number of companies are turning to personality assessments as an aid to recruiting in order to select the employees who are the most likely to fit into a particular environment. Hiring persons who adapt easily to change will benefit an organization that is involved in rapid technological growth.

The Task. Stress can be a consequence of jobs that are either too complex or too routinized. It is management's responsibility to eliminate stress-producing factors in the design of tasks. This will facilitate better relationships between employees and management, and between individuals and their jobs.

Some tasks can become too routinized as computers take over complex chores, and changes in the nature of these tasks may be necessary to enrich the jobs which have been affected. It is essential to vary the task or expand it; the

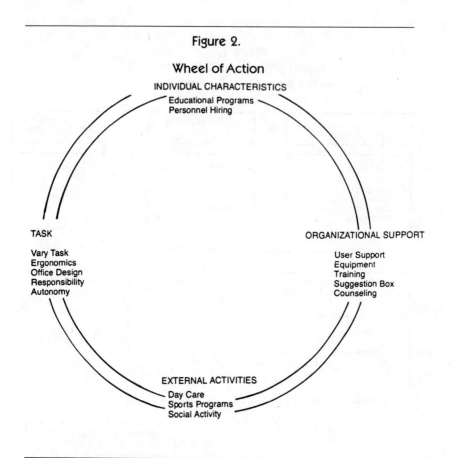

Figure 2.

Wheel of Action

INDIVIDUAL CHARACTERISTICS
Educational Programs
Personnel Hiring

TASK

Vary Task
Ergonomics
Office Design
Responsibility
Autonomy

ORGANIZATIONAL SUPPORT

User Support
Equipment
Training
Suggestion Box
Counseling

EXTERNAL ACTIVITIES

Day Care
Sports Programs
Social Activity

rotation of several tasks may be an appropriate solution. Also, increased responsibility often stimulates a bored worker.

Ergonomic furniture can help create a physical setting better suited to technology-related productivity than were older office desks and chairs. Placement of desks for better personal interaction is another simple means to achieve higher employee satisfaction.

Tasks that become more complicated also can lead to feelings of frustration. Education and user support are primary vehicles for stress reduction in such situations. Too many organizations are spending enormous amounts of money on equipment and software, and little or nothing on training. User support centers need to be established on an ongoing basis. A simple misunderstanding of working in a manual can be a major cause of tension.

External Activities. Organizations are beginning to comprehend the significance of support for activities external to the daily operation. These are important both to employee mental health and to the overall personality of a worker. For example, as more and more women enter the work force, some organizations have taken over the job of child care by establishing day-care centers. The worker, relieved of anxieties about children, finds greater job satisfaction, and the result is increased productivity.

Loneliness, leading to low self-esteem and low productivity, can be prevented by planned socialization. A sports league may provide the support necessary to eliminate these feelings. Organizations that address these external influences will benefit by increased employee motivation.

Organizational Support. Aforementioned factors such as user support centers, ergonomic furniture, and training are sources of organizational support. In addition, organizations that provide counseling staffs will benefit by an escalation in employee morale. Personal contact by top management, regular feedback mechanisms, and public recognition of accomplishments are all ways of demonstrating management support. Conversely, suggestion boxes are a means by which an organization can receive feedback from employees.

SUMMARY

Inadequate concern with human resource planning has created problems in integrating technology into the organizational structure. Management is confronted with the ongoing task of employee motivation and job redesign in a new setting. This calls for new strategies to promote a better balance between the individual's goals and the organization's goals. The Model of Personal Fulfillment is the foundation for specific actions which can improve worker personal fulfillment and job satisfaction. Each organization must look at its own environment to decide which strategies will be of most benefit.

REFERENCES

1. "Pressing for a Paperless Government," *Business Week,* March 25, 1985, p. 29.
2. Messina, Andrew, "Automated Factory, Automated Office," *Office Automated Computerworld,* June 13, 1984, Vol. 18, No. 24A, pp. 71-75.
3. Larson, Erik, "Working at Home; Is It Freedom Or a Life of Flabby Loneliness," *Wall Street Journal,* February 13, 1985, p. 33.
4. Brod, Craig, *Technostress: The Human Cost of the Computer Revolution,* Addison-Wesley Publishing Company, Reading, MA, 1984, p. 16.
5. DeMaagd, Gerald R., "Management Information Systems," *Management Accounting,* October, 1983, Vol. LXV, No. 4, pp. 10, 71.
6. Schermerhorn, John R., *Management for Productivity,* John Wiley, New York, New York, 1984, p. 708.
7. Cox, T., *Stress,* University Park Press, Baltimore, Maryland, 1978.

Gayle J. Yaverbaum is an assistant professor in the Department of Computer and Information Science at Temple University, Philadelphia, PA. Oya Culpan is an assistant professor of management at Pennsylvania State University, Middleton, PA.

8.
CREATING THE PURPOSEFUL ORGANIZATION

Mark Frohman
Perry Pascarella

> The purposeful organization has neither the high-risk orientation of the start-up organization nor the low-risk orientation of the typical mature company. Through moderate risk taking and change making, it constantly introduces tactical corrections in course as it drives into the future.

In mature companies, top management often scrambles to loosen things up when it faces strong pressure for change. In young organizations, management fears that it will inevitably be infected with the bureaucratic lethargy that comes with age.

Organizations typically move through three stages—start-up, growth, and maturity. Prolonged maturity generally seems to lead to rigidity and, sometimes, rigor mortis.

Many executives seem to think that what they need is a little more of Stage 1, if not a complete return to the simplicity and freshness of it. But a return to entrepreneurialism is neither sufficient nor even necessary to lead a mature company onward.

"Onward" is a key word. Rather than seeing the mature organization as the end of the line, management should consider that a fourth stage is possible. Let's call it the *purposeful organization*.

Many of the prescriptions for remedying a mature organization's ills attempt to replicate earlier stages of organizational development. Unfortunately, most organizations are ill-equipped to go backward. The direction for the future is *the future*—going beyond the third stage to a fourth one with a set of practices and procedures that builds on the firm's history and success while adapting to the competitive environment. Management should look at the present organization as evolving from earlier stages and as a platform for the next stage.

TRADITIONAL GROWTH STAGES

An emerging company is launched by an entrepreneur who does almost everything, including designing the product, financing the business, finding customers, and delivering the goods. The risk level is quite high. The organizational structure is flat. As the firm grows and people are added, roles and responsibilities remain loosely defined. Planning and control are handled by the entrepreneur while operating functions may be assigned to others. Overall, the style is one of individualism, informal relationships, and close attention to marketplace success.

The organization next evolves into the *growth stage* as the entrepreneur adds people, equipment, and facilities beyond what he can handle with loose management and control methods. Hierarchy and division of labor become more pronounced. Personal relationships give way to job definitions and formal reporting systems. Management, looking to gain control of the mushrooming organization, starts to rely on more formal procedures. To become more efficient, it initiates standards and mechanisms. The earlier close contact between the owner and customers diminishes and is replaced by the introduction of marketing and sales functions. Risk is no longer as great because the organization has a stronger business base.

In the *mature stage,* growth has given rise to the need for complex budgeting and planning systems and substantial increases in staff to handle administrative and reporting requirements. With the slowdown in growth and the large investment in resources, management exhibits a low propensity for risk taking. Management strives for stability and focuses on improving the planning and control processes.

The stability-and-control orientation of Stage 3 is an adaptive response to a history of growth in a fairly predictable political, legal, and technological environment—and a marketplace characterized by familiar and non-volatile competitive and economic pressures.

But that environment has changed dramatically in recent years, rendering many Stage 3 organizations far too rigid to meet the onrush of change or to manage leaps in innovation, even when management calls for them. Transition to a fourth stage would represent a purposeful evolution as the organization adapts to external and internal forces.

TYPICAL RESPONSES

The usual responses to the changes buffeting organizations today fall into four categories: cost control, introducing new technologies, adopting new management methods, and attempting to return to entrepreneurialism. Unfortunately, these responses may not sufficiently address the new conditions. Furthermore, they may damage the existing organization if they are blindly inserted. They may be incompatible with some of the existing operations or create conflict between the "old" and the "new."

COST CUTTING

Many executives try to cut out the "fat" when their Stage 3 organizations start to sputter. Inventories, travel expenses, equipment purchases, and maintenance are common candidates for the budget knife. However, these one-time-only savings often do little to help the organization become better poised to compete.

NEW TECHNOLOGY

Introduction of new technology into manufacturing processes or products may require new skills, procedures, and relationships. The organization, having been accustomed to standardization and incremental change, may be ill-prepared to handle new products or processes. Also, management's motivation for moving into new technology is sometimes a negative one—trading off technology costs for people costs. In short, it is mere cost reduction, rather than a means of opening doors to innovation, and expanded markets.

NEW STRATEGY

A third response, with a more positive orientation, is to initiate new methods of management by developing a corporate mission statement, engaging in strategic planning, or nurturing employee involvement. Each of these measures can serve a useful role, but they are often applied as "Band-Aids" and may not meet the adaptive needs of the organization.

Offering a statement of strategic significance is rarely sufficient to leverage a Stage 3 organization onto a new growth track. A new statement serves little purpose in the absence of a fully conceived management program that takes into account internal and external conditions.

ENTREPRENEURIALISM

The desire for innovation may produce still another response: the notion that the organization needs employees who take risks, push new ideas, and buck the establishment. A great deal of popular literature advocates the introduction of entrepreneurs (or "intrapreneurs") into mature organizations. But Stage 3 organizations operate with orderly, sequential procedures that do not encourage or support creativity. Managers who advocate injections of entrepreneurialism here and there are trying to drive their organization with one foot on the brakes and the other on the gas pedal.

CONFLICTS

Research indicates that entrepreneurs have a need for achievement, a need to be masters of their own destiny. They do not like structure or control by others.

Entrepreneurs clash in a number of ways with those things that make a Stage 3 organization work. They:

- Seek to be autonomous and self-controlling—to do something different; mature organizations have reporting systems and controls geared to minimizing deviation.
- Have a high tolerance for uncertainty; mature organizations try to reduce uncertainty and ambiguity for efficient processing of information and decisions.
- Tend to be independent and unstructured; Stage 3 organizations breed interdependence and team-oriented work through structures and rewards.
- See their success primarily as a function of their own personal energy and efforts; Stage 3 managers see their effectiveness as a result of their ability to work with, and influence, others.

In a mature organization an entrepreneur is, by definition, an exception. Conflict between the entrepreneur and the conventions of the organization are inevitable, and rob both of opportunities to perform the functions for which they were intended. Even when top management deliberately injects an entrepreneur—or "intrapreneur"—into the organization and is willing to tolerate exceptional behavior, the entrepreneur clashes with peers and others in the organization who see him as an added burden in meeting their objectives and as someone receiving unfair rewards.

An entrepreneur is like a foreign object introduced into a body. The body's immune system will try to reject it in order to defend the existing functions. The challenge facing most companies will be met, not by the introduction of a foreign object, but by reconditioning the "body" to meet changed conditions.

STAGE FOUR

Rising interest in such things as worker involvement, strategic management, mission statements, and entrepreneurialism reveals the need of many organizations to move on to a fourth stage.

Perhaps no company today would fully fit the description "purposeful organization." Yet, numerous chief executives are searching for a definition of their company's purpose or mission and trying to isolate those values that represent both a destination and a means of getting there. They are near Stage 4 without realizing it.

Full transformation to Stage 4 will require the top manager's decision and commitment to move on to this stage because it is relevant to him or her as an individual. The move forward is both an individual and an organizational transformation. Corporate purpose has to be built on personal purpose to give it validity and energy. Without a link to someone's personal purpose, a mission or purpose statement is merely propaganda.

There is no set formula for an organizational purpose. It must be a statement that gives direction and engenders commitment. It must balance a number of seemingly paradoxical factors. The time horizon should be short- and long-term; the strategy should realize the need to optimize ongoing operational aspects of the organization while, at the same time, leaving room for anomalies, new ideas, and the unplanned. A Statement of Purpose conveys the important quantitative and qualitative dimensions of the organization. It expresses what the organization wants to accomplish, how it is to be measured, and the values it intends to use as a foundation for its policies, systems, and decisions.

A complete Statement of Purpose reflects the belief that, at some time, every organization needs new ideas and every idea need organization. It will explain the necessity—that is, purposefulness—of apparently incompatible goals such as improving manufacturing controls and providing freedom and resources to develop new products. For example:

A large manufacturing company states: *"We're in the electronic instruments business—to meet the needs of our customers in research and design throughout the world. We want to be a rapidly growing company that is the industry leader in shareholders' equity and return on sales. We want to provide opportunity and satisfaction for our people based upon their individual creativity and performance. We want to be the best at what we do and will strive to be the technological leader in those areas in which we choose to concentrate. We want to be famous for our level of quality and service."*

FOCUS

In a Stage 4 organization the major focus of top management is communication of—and adherence to—the Purpose. The Purpose is a written statement generated after much thought and discussion of internal competencies. The Purpose expresses the values or core beliefs of the organization, setting the direction for what the organization strives to accomplish and how it intends to go about it.

Top management's job is to enroll employees in the Purpose so that they can turn their efforts to achieving it. The challenge to top management of a purposeful organization is to develop an organization-wide set of processes and systems that communicate, drive, support, and reward action consistent with the Purpose. Top management's role is to champion the implementation of these processes and systems. Experience has shown that a new-product idea requires a champion to nurture its development. So does a Purpose.

PLANNING

Purpose drives the planning process which companies at any stage must have if they are to allocate their attention, energies, and resources effectively.

Like all good planning processes, the purposeful organization's planning does not begin with the present and outline a course of intended action. Nor does it try to superimpose meaning on present or intended actions. It is a system to translate the Purpose into action and, therefore, backs down to the present through long- and short-term objectives. It builds on the basis of "what counts," rather than insisting: "This is the way we do it around here."

In its concern for relationships, the purposeful organization integrates its actions with those of its suppliers and customers. It thereby provides opportunities for synergism as people come to know one another's present capabilities more thoroughly and anticipate future capabilities together.

STYLE

Style is a personal expression of leadership that cannot change like a suit of clothes. While it is important, style is not what leaders in purposeful organizations focus on.

A popular story in management circles describes the "boiled frog phenomenon." A frog is not sensitive to change in water temperature if the temperature is raised slowly. Consequently, it will boil to death. Unlike the frog, managers are aware of the rising "temperature" around them. They do perceive the need for change. What is missing is another pot to jump into.

Most prescriptions suggest changes that leave the manager in the same pot of water and simply give him different "swimming" strokes to use—write a mission statement, walk around the plant, and so on. Top management must examine the "pot"—or organizational purpose—first. New strokes or style will follow.

Although the typical entrepreneur is not team-oriented, his need for people to pitch in produces involvement. Purpose is the overriding force, not the style of the founder. Leaders aspiring to Stage 4 can take a lesson from Stage 1. People are energized when they have a sense of purpose and can see how they can contribute and make a difference.

In a start-up organization, the founder believes in himself. In a purposeful organization, the leaders must believe in others; whatever the style, there must be trust. The organization is coping with a complex environment, conflicting market and technological pressures, demands for short-term results and long-term viability. Because they need the help of others to deal with uncertainty and ambiguity, managers must develop trust by being open and sharing information.

STRUCTURE

In a purposeful organization the structure is designed to support the goals assigned to each unit. The question to be asked is: "What structure will best enable us to carry out our purpose?" Too often, the question is reversed—"What functions should we perform that fit our current structure and organization?" In either case the existing strengths, capabilities, and competencies are major considerations. Yet, in a tough, turbulent environment an organization must first serve the Purpose or—like the oversized dinosaur—it will become nonadaptive and extinct.

There are inherent incompatibilities in an organization where management tries to mix optimization of both existing operations and cultivation of new ideas. Peter Drucker and many others suggest the separation of product- and business-development units from existing operations. This separation should reduce opportunities for conflict and confusion.

Furthermore, decentralization has many advantages that fit the nature of a purposeful organization. People want to work in a place where they feel part of something special—something they can identify with. Certainly, largeness mitigates against that. However, decentralization and small units do not guarantee that people will be turned on. People need to know what is expected, and have high standards, adequate resources, and trust. With these forces in place, small units are beneficial. Then the most powerful control system is in place—intrinsic control exercised by responsible people who trust one another in their pursuit of Purpose.

In Stage 4 the challenge is to manage organization boundaries. The objective and interests of different parts of the organization must be integrated to advance the total organization. In a Stage 4 organization the need to accommodate differences in structure, staffing, time horizons, and the like are recognized and addressed. Integration is accomplished through the planning process, which articulates the need for the different units and their value and contribution to the organization.

CONTROLS AND REWARDS

The Stage 4 organization lets its people know what counts—and it counts on their sense of responsibility. The often-elaborate systems for controlling people and reporting on their performance tend to be superfluous—or even detrimental to effectiveness. As an organization moves from Stage 3 to Stage 4, these systems would be eliminated or altered to support responsible responses to the sense of purpose.

All kinds of control—budgets, performance evaluation, plans, policies and procedures, short- and long-term objectives—are designed to create stability and predictability in a Stage 3 organization. But a Stage 4 organization's "control" comes from individuals' sense of responsibility.

Organizations can further influence behavior through their reward systems—official and unofficial. Financial compensation, recognition, promotions, new responsibilities, special assignments, access to more resources, and educational opportunities favor certain kinds of behavior over others. In the purposeful organization, rewards are carefully monitored to promote taking moderate risk, team effort and individual effort, meeting both short- and long-term goals, maintaining and improving the old business, developing the new business, and involvement in the corporate Purpose.

FOSTERING INNOVATION

"Skunkworks"—or outside-of-the-mainstream groups—have often been used successfully to bring innovation to large organizations. But the Stage 4 organization strives to make innovation occur within the organization itself.

Many management theorists contend that innovation occurs when people are encouraged to take risks without fear of being punished—and with the promise of tremendous reward for success.

Research suggests, however, that achievers are driven more by the *likelihood* of success itself than the *consequences* of failure or success. David McClelland, well-known researcher on the subject of achievement, has studied the motivation profile of entrepreneurs and discovered that these people are not high risk takers; they are comfortable when they assess the probability of success to be moderate—neither a "sure thing" nor an "impossible dream."

Innovative, entrepreneurial people seek a challenging environment where attainment is truly possible. People who are achievement-oriented are not going to be motivated if failure is likely, even though accepted. In fact, they may leave the organization to find an environment where they can get the support needed to increase the chance for success with a new idea.

Companies interested in accelerating their rate of innovation often try to establish climates that appeal to gamblers, not achievers. Gamblers respond to the promise of payoffs; achievers to the provision of resources that improve their perception of the probability of success. Achievers do not want to bet the company.

The purposeful organization, then, has neither the high-risk orientation of the start-up organization nor the low-risk orientation of the typical Stage 3 company. Through moderate risk taking and change making, it constantly makes tactical corrections in course as it drives toward its Purpose.

Mark Frohman is head of Organizational Resources, a Chagrin Falls, Ohio-based consulting firm that specializes in corporate strategy and organizational design. Perry Pascarella is editor-in-chief of Industry Week *magazine.*

Part II
PRODUCTIVITY IMPROVEMENT: MANAGE IT OR BUY IT?

9.

PRODUCTIVITY IMPROVEMENT: MANAGE IT OR BUY IT?

Richard A. Bobbe
Robert H. Schaffer

In today's business world, expanded productivity can no longer be purchased through investments in technology and pay incentives. High performance is the product of sophisticated managerial actions that assure the full exploitation of resources and investments over long periods of time.

The decade of the eighties will see unprecedented attention given to productivity improvement. The reasons transcend the usual concerns of individual businesses for growth and profitability. The Joint Economic Committee of the U.S. Congress in its 1979 mid-year analysis of economic prospects stated that the average American is likely to see his standard of living dramatically reduced in the 1980s unless productivity growth is accelerated. It described productivity growth, or greater output per man-hour, as the "economic linchpin of the 1980s."

Historically, productivity gains have been produced by major investments in new technology, mechanization and automation, as well as by motivational and pay incentives to spur individual efforts. These approaches have produced tremendous gains and have helped to propel the U.S. into world leadership. But these approaches—even expanded—are no longer enough to produce the kinds of results needed to meet the unprecedented productivity challenges of the eighties.

For example, the president of a $700 million manufacturer of consumer products has said: "Tax incentives for capital investment may be useful to very large corporations, but except for relatively minor investments, we and the vast majority of companies simply must learn to increase productivity from what we already have in place. We haven't even seen the big productivity gains we expect from the investments we've made in recent years."

A corporate human resources vice president says: "Frankly, I'm skeptical of incentive plans based on sharing gains in productivity or value added with production employees. I've seen too many plans go down the tubes after high expectations and lots of initial fanfare."

Executive vice president of a multi-billion dollar international corporation: "We have all kinds of fancy computer systems, yet our inventories are eating us alive! I told my guys over and over again we must cut inventories. But nothing happens. What must I do—make heads roll?"

Many top managers who have adopted the best in modern management technology are frustrated and dissatisfied with the lack of results. Many of these managers miss a fundamental point: all of the individual management actions, investments, programs and improvements will not, in themselves, yield much productivity improvement. High performance is the product of the highest order of managerial actions that assure the full exploitation of resources and investments. Productivity improvement is influenced, above all, by sophisticated managerial action and commitment over long periods of time. By managing productivity, the organization gains greater return from its current investments and expenses. It is also able to assess more clearly the *additional* investments or systems that may be needed. And it will know how to get the most out of these additional investments. Without managing productivity, management may invest, but will not get an adequate return on its investment.

We here outline some of the critical dimensions of that aspect of the management job that we refer to as *management of productivity and performance improvement*. Put another way, we describe what top management must do to get greater output from available resources, in contrast to the investments it can make to get more resources. As such, we focus on the highest return area, getting more from what management is already paying for. We describe a three-part strategy for accomplishing these results.

Creating the high-performance culture: Make performance improvement a routine aspect of everyday management.

Providing the leadership for performance improvement: Put in place the management disciplines and mechanisms essential to productivity and performance improvement.

Getting started with short-term improvement projects: Design these as building blocks for sustained performance improvement.

Taken together, these three provide a framework for launching and sustaining a total process for managing the improvement job.

CREATING THE HIGH-PERFORMANCE CULTURE

In many organizations managers who are asked to improve their performance respond with, "What's wrong? Aren't we doing a good job? We're meeting the budget, aren't we?" These comments reflect an all too prevalent view: "We must be doing all right since nobody told us we aren't." Generally, such organizations are stimulated to improve only by an external threat—erosion of market share, rapidly escalating material costs, technological changes, new government regulations, a supplier's problem, a customer's need.

The alternative is to generate a set of expectations, an organizational culture, geared to achieve continual improvement. In such a culture, performance improvement is not a fluctuating activity, turned on when the need arises and turned off when the pressure is off. It is a central, continuing, and ubiquitous character of the company management. The elements of creating that environment are outlined below. These include the establishment of expectations, the focus on exploiting resources, the integration of improvement with every aspect of management, the selection of critical focal points for concentrated performance-improvement effort, and the blending of management development and management achievement.

CREATE EXPECTATION OF CONSTANT IMPROVEMENT

The foundation for constant improvement is a managerial climate in which continuous performance improvement is expected, no matter how good current performance may be. Where this climate exists, managers, even those who have done outstandingly well, never feel "we have arrived." Instead, the planning and execution of significant improvements are key dimensions of each manager's job. These occupy a significant share of time and attention, in contrast with managing the routine and repetitive aspects of the organization's work. Job descriptions and performance reviews focus on results, not activities. Goals and objectives push far beyond what normal efforts and momentum will produce.

DEVELOP EXPECTATION OF FULL EXPLOITATION

Managers in our culture have been indoctrinated with the idea that increased output or productivity must be purchased with additional investment. When managers think about improvement, they see programs and systems, investment for mechanization, automation, computerization, R&D, incentives, reorganization, training, additional staff, and so on. These are all things that money can buy to improve the system. If quizzed, most managers would assert that they are producing about as much as can be produced from the resources available to them, considering the constraints they face.

In fact, most managers are not making the most of what is available to them, and there's plenty that can be done to get greater returns. The questions that are far too infrequently asked are these: What can we do to get far greater returns from the human and physical resources we're already paying for? How can we do a better job of managing improvement? It is these questions that management must ask itself in order to cause its organization to look to itself for sustained performance and productivity improvement.

For example, a high-technology specialty steel mill, having made a large investment in a new melt shop, was meeting its production goals but was far over its cost goals. In response to top management's demands to get costs in line without reducing production, operation managers cited bottlenecks, which, they said, required additional investments in service facilities, such as tracks for movement of molds. When it was made clear by top management that additional investment would not be made, the bottlenecks were overcome through more thoughtful planning and collaboration among the departments concerned.

Managers must be much more insistent in exhausting all possibilities for extracting greater results from available resources before searching for additional ones. Not only does this yield maximum return on current investments, it also helps to assure clearer assessments of needs for additional resources. Under those conditions, when additional investments are made, the know-how and motivation to exploit them fully will have been developed to a significantly greater extent.

INTEGRATE IMPROVEMENT WITH REGULAR PROCESSES

In organizations in which aggressive pursuit of improvements is not a regular activity, crises often trigger urgent campaigns for cost or performance improvement. Task groups are organized, reorganizations occur, studies and analyses are performed. Often these campaigns produce results. But if they are produced without changing the way the organization manages and conducts its activities, they are short-lived once the crisis is over. Expectations are reduced and people begin to slip back into previous work habits, staffing patterns, and lower levels of performance and productivity.

To be more productive and long-lasting, the management of improvement should use existing organizational mechanisms, management systems, and controls to the greatest extent possible. To the extent that the ongoing budgeting, goal setting, planning, operations review, performance review, salary administration, and other management processes do not lend themselves effectively to this purpose, they should be improved, rather than adding special new mechanisms to the old.

The annual goal-setting and budgeting process can serve as major vehicles for formulating performance improvement demands for organizing tangible improvement efforts that go well beyond the budget numbers. These processes may need strengthening or better integration to assure that challenging, yet achievable, goals are set, and that short-term sub-goals are properly identified, communicated, and regularly reviewed for process and appropriateness.

Performance reviews and salary administration can then, in turn, be modified to provide further reinforcement. For example: A business unit of a large chemical company redesigned its annual goals-setting process. The aim was to produce results in excess of what they believed could be achieved by their normal management processes and by the expected momentum of their business. A series of interfunctional work-planning sessions was conducted, beginning with the development of mutually agreed-upon work assignments and work plans for developing their proposed business and functional goals for the new year. At the final three-day session they reached agreement on their business goals; each function identified one or two important goals that it committed itself to achieve, which would be the subject of intensive planning, work, and reviews throughout the year; and they developed action plans for accomplishing two- or three-month "stepping stone" sub-goals.

FOCUS ON A FEW CRITICAL ISSUES

Another characteristic of the high performance culture is that at all times the organization is devoting concentrated attention to achieving substantial improvements in a few focused target areas. This is in contrast to company-wide or plant-wide programs that often are perceived as threatening to many people and which involve many variables—thus high risks of failure.

Top management must usually be involved in identifying, selecting, and defining these few issues. These demands must then be translated into well-planned and coordinated work programs throughout the organization.

The increasing use of such disciplined management methods to achieve targeted improvements assures both the endurance of the improvements after top management shifts its concentration, and enhancement of managerial capabilities to expand the improvement methodologies to other important targets.

The specialty steel mill referred to above began by focusing on two areas in the melt shop—to reduce turnaround time for ladles needing repair, and to accelerate moving of molds. Through improved planning, setting of targets and tracking progress, and methods of involving hourly workers, output increased almost 50 percent in eight months with the same people and the same equipment. They then moved to the finishing operations and, using the same methodologies, increased on-time deliveries by 15 percent.

A computer systems company began an organized attack on working capital reduction by designating a few managers from different functions to serve as a task group with an initial assignment of reducing inventories by 10 percent within three months and by an additional 20 percent by year-end. Following accomplishment of the first 10 percent reduction, they were to develop procedural and operational changes for effective ongoing inventory management. After successfully reaching the three-month target, the effort was expanded in stages over the next few months to include order entry, billing, and production control, with other areas to follow, step by step.

INTEGRATE PERFORMANCE IMPROVEMENT AND MANAGEMENT DEVELOPMENT

Continuing and expanding productivity and performance improvement requires constant strengthening of the company's managerial and organizational capabilities. The two must be mutually reinforcing, for the quest for productivity improvement cannot be successfully sustained without the requisite managerial methodology, capability, and collaboration.

Rather than mounting special managerial development programs—communications, team building, participative management, behavioral workshops, MBO, and so forth—the performance improvement process itself can be designed to increase the organization's most important managerial and organizational skills and abilities. It has been demonstrated time and again that the most lasting, the most meaningful, and the most personally rewarding development of managers occurs when new methods and concepts are applied immediately in the successful achievement of an important and challenging goal. The improvement process provides excellent opportunities for building in such developmental experiences.

For example, a manufacturer of industrial products was completing a large new plant that would double the output of a major product. In order to double production and sales rapidly, it was imperative that all functions—production, engineering, personnel, customer service, sales, and marketing—integrate their activities with utmost precision and maintain a new level of effective collaboration. A series of workshops was conducted in which interfunctional groups of 15 to 20 managers and other key people were helped to use some new managerial disciplines to identify and define their few most urgent goals related to the expansion challenge. They created managerial work plans and assignments for subordinates and task groups to carry these out, and designed a monitoring process to track progress, reveal problems, and work out appropriate and timely resolutions.

Thus, to make significant and lasting improvement in its productivity, an organization must strive constantly for high levels of excellence. This is as true for any enterprise as it is for a championship baseball team, for a marathon runner, or for a champion tennis player.

Such striving, and such accomplishment, cannot be produced in a one-time or sporadic effort. It must become an ongoing aspect of everyday management, as the five key elements that have been described are at work making the company a "high performance culture."

It is one thing to understand the importance of these five elements to performance and productivity improvement. It is another to provide the leadership, the disciplines, and the mechanisms for actually achieving results.

PROVIDING LEADERSHIP FOR
PERFORMANCE IMPROVEMENT

The previous section outlines some key concepts for creating the culture, the attitudes, and the approaches for generating and sustaining substantially higher performance of the organization. It is the responsibility of top management to translate these concepts into concrete and well-integrated actions on a continuing basis, ultimately with all levels and functions of the organization involved.

There are five essential contributions to top management in providing the leadership methods and disciplines for launching and sustaining organized improvement.

1. Establish specific demands and expectations.
2. Assign responsibility for managing the effort.
3. Assign responsibility for results.
4. Use disciplined management work plans.
5. Make help available to managers for accomplishing results.

Many managers who look at this listing will say, "But we already do this!" And indeed they very well may—to some degree or other. The key point is this: These five elements must be woven carefully together so that they are mutually supportive strands in a total improvement fabric. And they must be applied effectively and consistently, and be ongoing over time. The leader whose initial reaction is, "There's nothing new here," may find it useful to check his or her organization's behavior and personal behavior against what is stated below to see if any of these ingredients are missing, and if these are as integrated as they might be in the organization.

ESTABLISH DEMANDS AND EXPECTATIONS

Significant performance improvement does not take place in the absence of clear-cut, well-focused performance-improvement requirements that make each manager at every level accountable for accomplishing specific results. A process must be created through which top management can sharpen its own sophistication in deciding and in communicating appropriate levels of expectations.

Management should approach this as an evolutionary and developmental process. Gaining commitment to and understanding of the goals, first among themselves and then with subordinate managers, takes time, discussion, resolution of ambivalences, and the determination to move ahead despite resistances that may arise from subordinates.[1] Successful achievement of initial goals through better methods of goal definition, management work planning, and control help top managers to gain increasing skill and sophistication for setting more ambitious and longer-range goals. As the process continues, these capabilities gradually expand.

A good vehicle for beginning the improvement process is the goal-setting conference, a retreat of three to five days or longer for the top management group. This can be the forum for a well-planned, thoughtful exploration of the concepts outlined in the section on creating the high performance culture, which should underlie the improvement effort. In that context, the key strategic issues and goals of the organization are considered, and near-term stepping-stone goals set. Initial demands, expectations, and assignments can also be developed.

ASSIGN RESPONSIBILITY FOR MANAGING

The goal-setting conference can also be used to assign responsibility to an existing "operating committee" or other small group of key functional managers for launching and managing the improvement effort. This "performance improvement committee" can initiate and coordinate the first few productivity improvement projects in response to the goals set at the goal-setting conference. They can see that the projects are mutually reinforcing, and can review progress, provide assistance as the projects proceed, and be sure that appropriate communications are maintained to keep all people informed who should be. They also provide that continuing sense of urgency, constancy, and determination that is a critical element of successful leadership.

As successes are gained from initial projects, the committee also sees that key learnings about performance improvement are identified and disseminated. And they organize an expanding and coordinated series of improvement projects on a continuing basis.

A control system must be developed that reveals how well people are performing in accordance with their commitments and plans. The right kind of control system helps the people concerned carry out their tasks and helps top management avoid surprises. This means that work must be measured, reports of progress against the work plans generated, and reviews of progress conducted regularly.

Inasmuch as performance and productivity improvement is to be never-ending, this control system becomes a regular part of the ongoing managerial process.

ASSIGN LINE RESPONSIBILITY

One of the first jobs of the performance-improvement committee is to think through the questions of which individuals, functions, or task groups should be assigned the responsibility for accomplishing which specific improvement results. Normally there are people whose line responsibilities coincide or inter-sect with the improvement areas concerned, with staff people in a support role where appropriate. Designated members of the committee can then create written assignments, and review and adjust these with the assignees.

Why in writing? Most managers pride themselves on being busy with many tasks and responsibilities. How often have you experienced the phenomenon of the "forgotten" assignment? How often have you had a subordinate report back to you weeks later on an assignment, only to discover that his understand-ing of what was to be done was quite different from yours? Both understanding and commitment are essential for the assignments to be undertaken successful-ly. Putting the assignment in writing is crucially important. This becomes a key tool in the process.

USE DISCIPLINED WORK PLANS

Key managers and task groups must go beyond agreement with the goals established and assignments accepted. Level by level they must develop specific functional and interfunctional goals and management work plans that spell out when and *how* they will move from current levels of performance to the required levels.

Work plans should be quite specific, particularly for those actions to be taken in the near term. This requires more than a time line on a scheduling chart. It requires not only the "what" and the "when," but the critical substeps, who is to be responsible for each, and how completion of each step is to be measured. It should be tested against such crucial questions as these:

1   Does the work plan include steps to gain commitment of those who must contribute to, or who can influence, its accomplishment?
2   What are the areas or steps which entail the greatest challenge or con-cern?
3   Which entail significant human relationship challenges? What can you do to increase your sense of confidence?
4   What is the probability of success? Is this good enough to warrant proceeding? Does this suggest that alternative strategies should be con-sidered?
5   Will assignments to people be a factor in accomplishing the project? If so, is this reflected in the work plan?
6   Have you built a reporting process into the work plan?
7   With whom should you review or discuss your work plan?

Without very specific goals and work plans, managers can fall into the trap of passing these targets on to their subordinates, with each level "accepting" the targets, but not knowing whether progress really will be achieved. Work plans from subordinates provide tangible evidence that they will accomplish the goals. Better to discover at the start that adequate thought has not been given to how to achieve a goal than to wait until later on to discover that progress will not be forthcoming.

MAKE HELP AVAILABLE TO MANAGERS

If the demands are sufficiently tough, subordinate managers will soon reach the limits of their own capacities. They should have access to staff and/or consulting support in learning how to break through to new levels of performance in innovative ways.

For example, they may need assistance on such things as achieving inter-functional collaboration, brainstorming, and other creative ways of identifying and gaining agreement on opportunities for improvement; defining these opportunities as discrete, measurable, near-term goals; creating project sub-assignments, and gaining commitment of their subordinates and/or task groups to these assignments; organizing task groups and making them effective; applying work-planning disciplines; rationalizing time demands for both special and ongoing responsibilities; managing coordinating and review processes; and increasing the effectiveness of meetings.

All of these disciplines and methods, however, should be introduced as needed in the context of working toward achievement of the improvement goals, rather than as isolated training packages. They will have maximum meaning this way, and will be more likely to be successfully applied. Many managers have had little or no experience in these methodologies. To ensure success, and as an integral part of the process of strengthening their managerial capabilities, staff or outside consulting assistance may be called upon.

Taken together, these are the five elements that management must apply to meet the challenge of providing leadership for productivity and performance improvement. As the process advances, the details can be strengthened or adjusted. They should all develop together, since the overall effort will be limited by the weakest of the elements. When coupled with a culture and climate in which high performance is the expected norm, these mechanisms for providing leadership drive the organization toward ever-increasing productivity.

A LOW-RISK WAY TO GET STARTED

Thus far we have offered some principles and outlined the essential management disciplines for generating constant performance improvement. It can take some time for all of these elements to operate effectively. Moreover, this goal will not be reached unless people gain enthusiasm, which comes from a sense of reward and success along the way, as well as from continual top management reinforcement of the efforts. So let us consider how to move into results-producing action based upon these principles and disciplines.

It is not necessary to start with a massive company-wide program. In fact, such an approach can actually divert energy from performance improvement, stimulate unnecessary anxieties and political maneuvers, and encourage focusing on the mechanics and the record keeping. It is preferable to start with a series of discrete, measurable performance improvement projects. Such projects become the bricks and mortar of the sustaining improvement process, and generate the essential enthusiasm and energy to sustain progress.

To get started, begin by selecting an area where improvement is needed, and where there is a real sense of urgency. This might be a product that has become uncompetitive because of high cost, a plant with a quality problem, or a sales region not meeting its quotas. Secondly, and this is the tricky part, instead of attacking the whole goal, carve off a first-step sub-goal that can be accomplished in a relatively short time with available resources. This is important because you want to produce some momentum and success, not more delays, more studies, and more frustration. For example:

A large bank with many branches selected a few branches for the first step. In each of these one critical goal was selected, such as increasing deposits within a six-week period, reducing errors, or improving customer service.

A national sales organization with high aspirations selected one sales branch. In that one branch two strategies were selected to increase sales within a matter of weeks.

A plastics manufacturer, during a period of suddenly increased opportunity, was unable to respond because of plant quality problems. Quality improvement began by a controlled program of testing improvement ideas on the line.

These initial modest-success undertakings are called "breakthrough projects," because they not only achieve improved performance, but also develop some new managerial skill and confidence. They generate the momentum for expanding the improvement process.

The best way to assure the success of these projects is to involve the people who will have to make them succeed. This not only provides practical ideas for improvement, but also stimulates readiness and the desire to collaborate in making the improvement projects successful. The ground rules should specify defining the goals so that no significant addition in resources or people will be required. Also, if the project is one which will take many months, the first sub-project should be defined for a matter of weeks.

The project would be carried out in a fairly rigorous and sophisticated fashion, beginning to use all of the performance improvement disciplines outlined in the section on providing leadership for performance improvement above: clear-cut demands and expectations, responsibility for overseeing the projects, clear-cut accountability for results on the project, the requirement for work plans to help ensure that the projects will be accomplished, and consultative or staff assistance for the managers responsible.

Thus, all of these broad principles, instead of being introduced into the organization through grand pronouncements, new policy decrees, training, or missionary work, are built into the accomplishment of the specific breakthrough projects. In effect, each of these breakthrough projects becomes a microcosm of the overall disciplined improvement process.

On a broader level, as projects are begun in more and more places in the company, as projects are expanded, and as they are related across the boundary lines of functions and divisions, the overall management processes discussed originally can begin to come into play. People learn that they can get more done with current resources, that they are expected to produce improvement as part of the regular management process rather than as some separate staff-driven project, and that the breakthrough projects themselves blend management development with management achievement.

Further, this process generates important personal rewards to participating managers as they experience increasing success in contributing to strengthening the performance results of the organization.

Thus specific short-term (increasing in length as the effort expands) performance improvement projects are the basic vehicle. They are used for developing the leadership tools for performance improvement and for developing the ingredients of the high-performance culture. This three-part strategy begins with rewards and reinforcements and increasingly provides them as the organization expands its capacity for performance and productivity improvement.

REFERENCE

1. For in-depth discussion of management demand making, see Robert H. Schaffer, "Demand Better Results—and Get Them," *Harvard Business Review*, November-December 1974: 91-98.

Richard A. Bobbe and Robert H. Schaffer are principals of the management consulting firm of Robert H. Schaffer & Associates located in Stamford, Connecticut.

10.
SEVEN KEYS TO HIGH PRODUCTIVITY

Robert M. Ranftl

A review of the Hughes productivity study shows that skilled, responsible management is one of the most important factors in achieving high productivity in technology-based organizations.

Since 1973, Hughes Aircraft Company—a high-technology electronics organization of some 77,000 employees—has been conducting an extensive study on means of optimizing productivity in technology-based organizations.

The study reveals that the basic factors common to high productivity totally complement the factors common to high creativity and innovation; i.e., the organizational chemistry required to optimize productivity is synonymous with that required to optimize creativity and innovation. (It should be emphasized that creativity and innovation are by no means the exclusive province of the R&D sector; to assure high organizational productivity, creativity and innovation should permeate every discipline and every job within an organization.)

After reviewing the many hundreds of study findings and the insights of the thousands of managers throughout the country who have participated in the author's seminars on productivity, the following factors were selected as constituting seven keys to achieving high productivity and creativity.

1. Skilled, Responsible Management. Clearly, management is the chief factor with respect to any organization's productivity, and, as such, is the factor upon which all organizations should focus primary attention in their quest for achieving peak productivity.

The critical tie between an organization's management and productivity is evident in the basic definition of productivity itself. Basically, productivity is the ratio of valuable output to input; i.e., the efficiency and effectiveness with which available resources—personnel, machines, materials, capital, facilities, energy, and time—are utilized to achieve a valuable output.

Virtually anyone could manage if resources were unlimited. However, as we are all well aware, this is seldom, if ever, the case, and, therefore, the challenge of creative management is to get the job done optimally with the available resources. And, looking forward in time, there will very likely be fewer rather than a greater abundance of resources at management's disposal, thus creating an even greater challenge.

Inherently, all resources are bipolar; i.e., they can be fully engaged and productivity utilized, or, just as readily, they can be underutilized, permitted to lie fallow, or counterproductively abused. The final outcome, or "bottom line," of an organization's endeavors depends primarily upon the effectiveness with which management deploys the available resources. First and foremost, the responsibility of management is, and always has been, the deployment or "stewardship" of available resources, thus making management the key link in the entire productivity chain.

Further confirmation of management's critical tie to productivity is evident when one considers personal productivity. The Hughes study showed that personal productivity does not correlate significantly with such factors as IQ, excellence of education, schools attended, curricula pursued, grades achieved, or courses taken since graduation. These factors are extremely important as indicators of a person's qualifications, aptitude, and potential to perform; i.e., they represent one's credentials. Therefore, such factors are of great significance when hiring someone. However, study participants consistently pointed out that among qualified individuals, differences in productivity primarily depend upon two factors, namely, attitude and motivation—first and foremost, the attitude and motivation of management, and that, in turn, reflected downward and coupled with the attitude and motivation of the work force.

To achieve high productivity, it is particularly important that every member of management be highly motivated, positive, and totally committed. Correspondingly, the same posture is necessary relative to the entire work force. But, it must be remembered that the psychological work environment is a critical factor in this regard, and it is management that establishes the psychological work environment. (See Figure 1.)

It is management that gives the challenging assignments or lack thereof; it is management that establishes the equity (fairness) within the organization or lack thereof; it is management that exhibits the genuine interest, encouragement, and appreciation or lack thereof; the equitable incentives and rewards or lack thereof; and so on. As can be readily seen, management not only directly determines its own attitudes, motivation, and productivity, but through its managerial style is extremely catalytic in influencing the attitude and motivation—and, therefore, the productivity—of the entire work force.

Still further confirmation that management is the key driving factor relative to an organization's productivity is evident in another study finding, which showed that the overall productivity of an organization depends heavily upon its management personnel and the top five percent of the staff, i.e., people who deal largely in the realm of creative and innovative ideas, judgment, major decisions, and actions. Participants did not diminish the importance of high productivity on the part of everyone else in the work force, but the point they clearly made is that it is the managerial personnel and the top five percent of the staff who set the pace for productive operations, i.e., it is their ideas, judgment, direction, example, etc. that set the pace for organizational productivity down the line.

Figure 1.
Primary Elements of an Effective
Psychological Work Environment

- Skilled and effective management and leadership with outstanding people in key positions.
- Clearly identified organizational objectives and performance goals.
- Simple organization structure featuring clear lines of direction.
- High standards of operation, stressing personal, organizational, managerial, and product excellence.
- Effective communication and technology exchange.
- A high degree of personal job freedom.
- Minimal constraints, procedures, and red tape.
- A stimulating, open, creative climate where people can be themselves.
- A prevailing sense of equity in all operations.
- An absence of fear, politics, and gamesmanship, and avoidance of any connotations of "insiders" and "outsiders."
- The absence of a caste system: i.e., the differentiation between first-class and second-class roles.
- Equitable, parallel promotion ladders.
- A climate conductive to career planning, wherein job security is directly tied to contribution.
- Equitable system of incentive and rewards.
- A prevailing positive "can do" attitude coupled with the spirit of "thinking improvement into everything."

Study findings clearly show that skilled, responsible management and superior productivity are inseparable. We are entering a far more demanding era requiring greater professionalism in management. Tomorrow's manager, in addition to being technically qualified in his or her field, must be a respected people-oriented leader skilled in the latest techniques of behavioral science and sound business practice.

2. Outstanding Leadership. Of all factors, managerial leadership has, by far, the greatest leverage on productivity. Ultimately, the destiny of any organization hinges on the quality of its leadership.

True leaders bring out the best in people and organizations. This is largely because leaders elicit strong positive emotional reactions, and people tend to fulfill their needs and grow under effective leadership. Such leaders have an uncanny knack for cutting through complexity, providing practical solutions to difficult problems, successfully communicating these solutions to others, and instilling enthusiasm and a "can-do" attitude.

However, while leadership is readily recognizable, it is difficult to define. No two leadership styles are the same—each style is, and should remain, unique to each individual. Furthermore, a good leader in one situation may not be a good leader in a different situation. Also, the type of leader needed depends specifically on the group to be lead. Yet, even the same group may require a different kind of leadership at different times in its evolution.

During the Hughes study, senior executives, managers, scientists, engineers, educators, and consultants were asked what indicators they use most frequently to identify highly productive employees, managers, and leaders. In addition, the literature search revealed a number of such observations. While the inputs from all these sources were expressed in a variety of ways, they focused on a few basic characteristics. The profiles of "A Productive Employee," "A Productive Manager," and "An Outstanding Leader" are shown in Figures 2, 3 and 4 respectively, with typical observations listed under each. These three profiles should be viewed as three concentric circles, with the "Profile of a Productive Employee" at the center and the "Profile of an Outstanding Leader" forming the outermost circle. Thus, an outstanding leader encompasses the cumulative characteristics of all three profiles.

Most managers have some leadership ability, but unfortunately very few are outstanding leaders. It is important, therefore, that management be catalytic in enhancing the leadership potential already present within the organization by (1) selecting for advancement to key managerial positions those who show leadership promise, and (2) providing the appropriate climate, opportunity, challenge, encouragement, incentive and reward for those selected individuals to further develop their leadership skills and grow.

3. Organizational and Operational Simplicity. Organization structures should be kept simple, flexible, and adaptive to change, always striving for the minimum number of levels consistent with effective operation. This affords clearer lines of direction, provides for less fragmented responsibilities, and is conducive to the taking of greater initiative by everyone in the organization. Also, it augments communication and technology exchange, and enhances decision making throughout the organization.

Correspondingly, work elimination and simplification techniques should be applied to all operations, and simplicity should be stressed in the products, themselves. Products should represent the simplest construction capable of achieving design objectives.

All operational constraints should be reduced to those absolutely necessary. Regulations, procedures, and red tape should be minimized, providing employees the maximum degree of job freedom. Of particular importance, authority should be delegated as far down the organization as reasonably possible.

4. Effective Staffing. Much attention should be devoted to selecting the right people to begin with—stressing quality not quantity. Adding more people does not necessarily equate to increased productivity. And, before hiring new people, one should ensure that the present people are performing to capacity.

Figure 2.
Profile of a Productive Employee

Many study participants felt that while no two individuals are alike, an envelope might be developed to include common characteristics of particularly productive employees. Key characteristics contained within this envelope are listed below.

Is well qualified for the job. Job qualification was considered basic to R&D productivity. Without the proper job qualifications, high productivity was considered out of the question. Typical observations:

- Is intelligent and learns quickly.
- Is professionally/technically competent—keeps abreast of his/her field.
- Is creative and innovative—exhibits ingenuity and versatility.
- Knows the job thoroughly.
- Works "smart"—uses common sense—organizes work efficiently—uses time effectively—doesn't get bogged down. Is consistently concerned with design performance, quality, reliability, maintainability, safety, producibility, productivity, cost, and schedules.
- Looks for improvement, but knows when to stop perfecting.
- Is considered valuable by supervision.
- Has a record of successful achievement.
- Continuously develops self.

Is highly motivated. Motivation was termed a critical factor—a "turned on" employee is well on the road the high productivity. Typical observations:

- Is self-motivated—takes initiative—is a self-starter and self-driver—has a strong sense of commitment.
- Is persevering—productively works on an assignment until it is properly completed—gets the job done in spite of obstacles.
- Has a strong will to work—keeps busy.
- Works effectively with little or no supervision.
- Sees things to be done and takes appropriate action.
- Likes challenge—likes to have abilities tested—enjoys solving problems.
- Has a questioning mind—demonstrates a high degree of intellectual curiosity.
- Displays constructive discontent—"thinks" improvement into everything.
- Is goal/achievement/results-oriented.
- Has a strong sense of urgency and timing.
- Has a high energy level and directs that energy effectively.
- Gets satisfaction from a job well done.
- Believes in a fair day's work for a fair day's pay.
- Contributes beyond what is expected.

Has a positive job orientation. A person's attitude toward work assignments greatly affects his/her performance. A positive attitude was cited as a major factor in employee productivity. Typical observations:

- Enjoys the job and is proud of it—looks to it as the primary source of need satisfaction.
- Sets high standards.
- Has good work habits.
- Becomes engrossed in the work.
- Is accurate, reliable, and consistent.
- Respects management and its objectives.
- Has good rapport with management.
- Takes direction well—readily accepts challenges and new assignments.
- Is flexible and adaptive to change.

Is mature. Maturity is a personal attribute rated important by study participants. A mature employee displays consistent performance and requires minimal supervision. Typical observations:

- Has high integrity—is genuine, honest, sincere.
- Has a strong sense of responsibility.
- Knows his/her personal strengths and weaknesses.
- Is self-reliant, self-disciplined, and self-confident.
- Has deserved self-respect.
- Lives in the "real" world—deals effectively with the environment.
- Is emotionally stable and secure.
- Performs effectively under pressure.
- Learns from experience.
- Has healthy ambition—wants to grow professionally.

Interfaces effectively. The ability to establish positive interpersonal relationships is an asset that does much to enhance productivity. Typical observations:

- Exhibits social intelligence.
- Is personable—is accepted by and interfaces effectively with superiors and colleagues.
- Communicates effectively—is clear and concise—is open to suggestions—is a good listener.
- Works productively in team efforts—is cooperative—shares ideas—helps colleagues.
- Exhibits a positive attitude and displays enthusiasm.

Figure 3.
Profile of a Productive Manager

The characteristics used to identify productive employees are also applicable to managers. However, since management plays such a key role in organizational productivity, the study also sought special *additional* indicators, which identify productive managers. These indicators are listed below, with typical observations included under each.

Is competent at staffing. Typical observations:

- Has high recruiting standards.
- Is skilled at recognizing talent.
- Attracts and holds capable, productive people.
- Is not afraid to hire top people—does not feel personally threatened by them.
- Maintains an optimal balance of the talents and capabilities needed to achieve the objectives of the organization.
- Continually introduces "new blood" into the organization.

Directs the organization's efforts effectively. Typical observations:

- Responds to the organization's current and long-range needs.
- Applies sound, practical technical and administrative judgment.
- Exhibits conceptual skills—keeps everything in proper perspective.
- Integrates and synchronizes the application of available resources.
- Is results-oriented.
- Supplies goals and keeps work properly focused.
- Delegates effectively—clearly defines assignments, responsibilities, and commensurate authority—tries not to second-guess subordinates.
- Is competent in dealing with people—is candid and straightforward —skillfully influences others to work effectively.
- Always keeps things under control—continually monitors performance, e.g., technical progress, schedules, and costs.
- Knows when to stop work on a project.
- Continually assesses productivity and strives to improve it.
- Manages effectively in good times and bad.
- Consistently sets a good example.
- Is willing to be held accountable for stewardship.

Is competent at handling complexities and problems, and in dealing with new concepts. Typical observations:

- Has a good understanding of the work and problems involved.

- Does the job with full consideration for all associated limitations and trade-offs—keeps realities in perspective—adapts strategies accordingly.
- Recognizes good ideas and accurately senses their intrinsic value.
- Skillfully identifies potential new technologies and product lines.
- Is not easily misled—sees things in their true light—readily detects inconsistencies, inaccuracies, and inefficiencies.
- Is skilled at improvising—effectively identifies and removes roadblocks and bottlenecks.
- Effectively develops and applies preventive and corrective measures—considers contingencies and is prepared.
- Pinpoints problems quickly—digs into problems, distills them down to their simplest terms, asks pertinent questions, gets critical information, considers all alternatives, makes necessary assumptions and trade-offs, and arrives at effective decisions.
- Is willing to take calculated risks.
- Handles emergencies decisively—is not prone to "crisis management."

Is a skillful communicator. Productivity in the R&D environment depends heavily on effective interfaces between individuals and groups whose areas of specialization often have a minimum of common ground. The manager frequently must provide that common ground. Typical observations:

- Interfaces with superiors, peers, and subordinates.
- Keeps superiors, peers, and subordinates properly informed.
- Maintains an effective flow of two-way communication.
- Is readily accessible—maintains an open-door policy.
- Encourages effective exchange of information.
- Is skillful at oral and written communication—conveys ideas clearly, concisely, and persuasively—makes effective presentations.
- Conducts meetings skillfully—sets proper tone and pace—maintains focus, draws out and clarifies relevant points, and channels discussion effectively toward productive conclusions and actions.

Supports and guides subordinates in their work and encourages their full participation. Typical observations:

- Knows subordinates, their capabilities, and their aspirations.
- Respects subordinates and their individual differences—is sensitive to their feelings—earns respect.
- Makes everyone involved a party to the action—involves employees in decisions that affect them—makes all members feel they are important to the team effort.
- Provides effective assignments and background information necessary for performance of those assignments.
- Holds subordinates responsible for performance—requires thorough and timely completion of assignments.

- Provides effective feedback—appraises performance skillfully.
- Helps subordinates in their personal development and career pursuits.
- Serves an ego-building role with respect to subordinates—supplies necessary motivational reinforcement.
- Gives appropriate credit—rewards fairly—praises publicly (criticizes privately).
- Is receptive to employee's concerns, ideas, and suggestions—is empathic and a good listener.
- Gets involved when subordinates have problems—helps them and backs them up—promptly corrects employee grievances.
- Serves as a buffer to protect subordinates from many of the daily administrative and operational frustrations.

Figure 4.
Profile of an Outstanding Leader

Although many managers have distinct leadership abilities in certain aspects of their jobs, very few qualify as outstanding leaders. The few who do are unusually competent, dynamic, confident individuals who somehow "have it all together." Study participants identify the following as distinctive qualities of an outstanding leader:

Sets a particularly positive example as a person. The outstanding leader exhibits characteristics that stamp him/her as a "person of note." Typical observation:

- Is unusually competent.
- Has quality and quickness of mind.
- Is particularly creative, innovative, and nontraditional—a unique individualist.
- Is highly self-motivated, self-confident, and self-directing.
- Has extremely high integrity, values, and standards—stands above organizational politics and gamesmanship.
- Has unusually high motives—is dedicated—has a firm sense of purpose and commitment—is never self-serving.
- Has a strong positive orientation.
- Displays total self-command.
- Has a high level of deserved self-respect and self-esteem.
- Accepts the role of leader with appropriate humility—enjoys the role and is clearly accepted as a leader.
- Is willing to work harder than other members of the team.
- Has particularly high vitality, stamina, an reserve energy.
- Is continually searching/learning/developing/expanding/evolving.
- Is a "winner."

Takes a dynamic approach to activities. The outstanding leader approaches tasks with verve and enthusiasm, is always oriented toward improvement. Typical observations:

- Is action-oriented—has a compelling drive to accomplish and achieve.
- Is quick to size up the merit of people, ideas and opportunities.
- Uses a persuasive personality rather than force of power to get things done.
- Is tenacious—perseveres in the face of obstacles—always sees things through to successful completion.
- Is always willing to "stand up and be counted"—makes necessary decisions and does what has to be done, even though such action may be unpopular and results in adverse criticism.
- Continually seeks new and better ways.
- Is a visionary—is unusually skilled at predicting future technological and operational needs and applications.
- Always sees new challenges and new fields to conquer.

Brings out the best in people. Typical observations:

- Is strongly people-oriented.
- Exhibits great respect for human dignity.
- Is particularly skilled in motivational processes and in dealing with people.
- Has well-defined, meaningful goals and successfully inspires associates to help achieve them.
- Has confidence in people and effectively communicates that confidence.
- Brings about dynamic synergism within groups.
- Is stimulating and catalytic—instills enthusiasm—maintains an exciting organizational climate—communicates a "can-do" attitude in all actions.
- Helps subordinates achieve their full potential.

Demonstrates great skill in directing day-to-day operations. Typical observations:

- Conceptually integrates all facets of the operation.
- Has a strong sense of timing and limits—accurately senses "when" and "how much" in each situation.
- Has an uncanny knack for cutting through complexity—effectively sorts out irrelevancies and identifies the real driving factors—provides practical solutions to difficult problems and successfully communicates these solutions to others.
- Senses what might go wrong and develops contingency plans.
- Maintains control of all situations, performing with relative ease during times of stress.
- Displays an "elegant" simplicity in all actions.

Standards for managers and key personnel must be particularly high. If these positions are filled by competent people, other competent people will be drawn to the organization. If however, second-rate people are selected for key roles, they usually attract third or fourth-rate people to positions below them.

"New blood" should continually be introduced into the organization. New, talented, people, regardless of their age, act as a stimulus to the organization and often lead directly to some of the most valuable innovations.

Low producers should be weeded out early—often, employees who are low producers at 15 years could have been just as readily identified in the first six months or first year of employment. However, before terminating a low producer, one should strive to identify the reasons for poor performance. Frequently only a change in assignment or supervision is necessary to remedy the situation.

Delay, when feasible, replacing personnel lost through normal attrition, e.g., retirement and voluntary termination, allowing the responsibilities and workload of the remaining individuals to increase until an optimal level is reached. In this manner retirement and attrition frequently open the way for effective job enrichment.

5. *Challenging Assignments.* Assignments are key to the creative and productive processes. Each individual has a particular sphere of highly creative and productive activity. But the right person must be matched to the right problem. (See Figure 5.)

The work, itself, should be motivating. This is particularly key to the creative/innovative process. The optimal combination of work and environment creates a resonance within a person; work becomes play. On the other hand, if one's job does not provide fulfillment, a person will frequently divert his or her attention and energies to personal and outside pursuits.

Special attention should be given to a new employee's first assignment since it introduces the employee to responsibilities, people, and paths of communication that can significantly influence his or her long-term effectiveness and ultimate position in the organization.

By definition, one should never give an assignment to a person who just has the required skill; give it to the person who wants to and loves to do it: and, never give an assignment which, under other circumstances, you wouldn't be willing to accept yourself.

6. *Objective Planning and Control.* Ineffective planning causes major drains on productivity, e.g., people not knowing what is expected, tasks proceeding out of phase with each other, peripheral activities, over or underperforming, and start-stop operations.

Conversely, effective planning improves operational productivity, e.g., helps ensure the best possible use of resources, integrates all aspects of a program into an efficient, synchronized effort, minimizes false starts and the pursuance of counterproductive efforts, provides for future risks and contingencies, and precludes continual crisis management.

Figure 5.
Twenty Effective Job Assignment Practices Identified
by Study Participants as Enhancing Productivity

- Provide assignments that lead, through successful completion, to a feeling of accomplishment and a sense of contributing/belonging.
- Ensure assignments are pertinent to the organization's overall objectives and have management's active interest and support.
- Assign work in keeping with individual capabilities and interests—avoid misemployment—don't get employees "in over their heads."
- Ensure assignments make effective use of employee's existing skills and talents while, at the same time, affording them an opportunity to develop new skills and grow.
- Keep assignments in scope—avoid too many simultaneous tasks.
- Keep assignments from being overspecialized—jobs should not be divided too finely.
- Ensure assignments are clearly defined and involve specific responsibility: avoid open-ended assignments whenever possible.
- Focus on end results (technical performance, cost, schedules, etc.), giving the employee as much freedom and opportunity for work-planning and decision-making as possible.
- Make schedules tight but realistic; permit adequate time to do the job effectively.
- Use the most capable people for the most critical jobs. (This does not mean continually using the same tried-and-proven employees; capable but untried people must be given a chance—this is the only way junior employees can develop.)
- Provide particularly creative people with highly challenging job assignments, minimizing boring, repetitive and trivial tasks.
- Minimize the amount of nonengineering work done by engineers.
- Strive for equity of workload among employees; don't overload good people just because they "always come through."
- Consider special assignments for key people in addition to their primary responsibilities; e.g., identify them as consultants in specialized areas in addition to their normal work.
- Change or expand employee assignments periodically; don't destroy capable people by trapping them in "indispensable" functions that lead nowhere.
- Minimize loans of employees to other organizations—this is usually an unsatisfactory arrangement for the employee.
- Establish work teams of people who are particularly productive when working together. (Selection of personnel whose backgrounds differ widely often enhances cross-fertilization of idea and has a synergistic effect.)

- Maintain an adequate backlog of work. The productivity of people waiting for new assignments is usually relatively low and existing projects tend to overrun if there are no new assignments is sight.
- Provide job security consistent with the employee's job performance.

In like manner, it is important that effective control systems be established that measure progress against plans, detect deviations, pin-point responsibility, indicate corrective action, and assure that out-of-tolerance performance is improved.

Controls should always be applied judiciously, ensuring they are valid, simple, objective, timely, and cost-effective, and they should be reviewed regularly for effectiveness. Also, one must be keenly aware of the cost of control, itself—always keeping control systems within scope, and continually monitoring the "watcher"-to-"doer" ratio.

In the final analysis, we must strive to achieve the most valued of all forms of control, "self-control": that brought about through the daily actions of dedicated, skilled management and subordinates who hold themselves responsible and accountable for their personal performance.

7. *Specialized Managerial Training.* Since management is clearly the chief factor with respect to any organization's productivity, it is particularly important that organizations strive to develop a commitment to productivity improvement throughout their managerial team, and provide the members of that team with useful tools for implementing effective productivity improvement efforts thoughout the organization. A highly effective vehicle in achieving this objective, as experienced by Hughes, is specialized managerial training.

The initial productivity training thrust at Hughes was a long-term series of voluntary, after-hours productivity courses for line and staff managers. Four basic courses were provided, comprising 25 class-hours each. The four courses focused on personal productivity, managerial productivity, organizational productivity and combating counterproductivity.

After teaching more than 1,000 hours of such classes the author recognized that a more streamlined approach would be necessary in order to reach all the management of a company comprising 77,000 employees. Furthermore, although the classes were always fully subscribed, it was evident that those manager already predisposed to productivity improvement were more likely to volunteer than those most needing the training. A transition was, therefore, made to a long-term series of mandatory, off-site seminars on personal, managerial, organizational, and operational productivity for all levels and sectors of line and staff management. The content of these one-day seminars is a distillation of the 100 class-hours of material originally contained in the four basic productivity courses.

The seminars are not intended to constitute a "cookbook" approach to productivity improvement, nor is there any attempt to cast participants into a common mold. Quite to the contrary, at the start of each seminar, managers are advised to develop and maintain their own personal style of management, and particularly their own unique style of managerial leadership, adding and substracting to that style only as they, themselves, see fit. Therefore, the seminars do not present a productivity gospel; rather, they provide a sharing of insights and a shopping list of ideas and productivity tools. the intention is to inspire participants to subsequently take productive action when returning to their respective work areas.

Productivity improvement cannot be dictated or legislated from the top. Those at the head of organizations can be highly productive themselves, set an outstanding example, and be catalytic in enhancing productivity down the line. However, peak organizational productivity will only be achieved when each manager stimulates productivity improvement within his or her respective organizational sector, with all subordinates performing productively in their incumbent positions.

The author has conducted more than 100 seminars in this Hughes series, involving more than 3,000 members of management. Each seminar is composed of four modules of approximately equal length.

The first module deals with the anatomy of productivity; i.e., what is it, why is it important, what are the key factors that impact it, how it can be evaluated, and, on an overall systems basis, how it can be improved. The second seminar module focuses on managerial and organizational productivity. A number of counterproductive factors common within many organizations are identified and analyzed, with focus entirely on effective managerial techniques of precluding or effectively combating such counterproductivity. Particular emphasis is placed on managerial leadership.

The third module focuses on personal productivity. A number of counterproductive factors commonly experienced in one's personal life are identified, with the emphasis on effective means of precluding or combating such counterproductivity. It is the author's firm conviction that each individual should continually grow in the direction of becoming a more creative and self-fulfilled person. Therefore, within this third module, significant time is devoted to exploring potential means of enhancing one's personal motivation, creativity, and sense of self-fulfillment.

The fourth module comprises a workshop on identifying effective means of improving the productivity of the particular organizations involved. Major sources of internal counterproductivity are identified along with suggested means of combating such counterproductivity.

One might assume that most organizations' lists of major counterproductive factors would be very long; however, the opposite tends to be the norm. Nevertheless, those lists, although relatively short, are extremely important when it comes to improving productivity.

Each organization has its own unique profile of counterproductive factors. However, the subject of counterproductivity has been widely probed during the course of the Hughes productivity study since its inception in 1973, and a resulting list of typical counterproductive factors within industry is given in Figure 6.

The approach to productivity improvement must be totally professional, avoiding all gamesmanship, fads, and buzz words. A well-qualified, highly

---

Figure 6.
Twenty-five Factors Identified by Study Participants as Most Likely to Cause Serious Counterproductivity Within R&D Organizations.

- Ineffective planning, direction, and control.
- Overinflated organization structures.
- Overstaffing.
- Insufficient management attention to productivity, and to the identification and elimination of counterproductive factors within the organization.
- Poor internal communication.
- Inadequate technology exchange.
- Insufficient or ineffective investment in independent research and development (IR&D) efforts.
- Poor psychological work environment.
- Lack of people-orientation in management—insufficient attention to employee motivation.
- Misemployment.
- Ineffective structuring of assignments.
- Lack of effective performance appraisal and feedback.
- Insufficient attention to low producers.
- Technological obsolescence.
- Ineffective rewards systems that inadequately correlate individual productivity and compensation.
- Lack of equitable parallel managerial and technical promotion ladders.
- Lack of equity in operations.
- Ineffective customer interface.
- Ineffective engineering/production interface.
- Ineffective subcontractor/supplier interface and control.
- Operational overcomplexity—constrictive procedures and red tape.
- Excessive organizational politics and gamesmanship.
- Excessive provincialism.
- Ineffective management development.
- Inadequate investment in, and lack of proper maintenance of, capital facilities.

---

motivated and dedicated management team that optimally deploys the organization's resources—particularly the human resources—is the ultimate foundation upon which to productively and creatively build.

The productivity seminars are making a valuable contribution in this regard. To inspire others, one must first be inspired. In like manner, to inspire the work force to higher levels of productivity, the management team, themselves, must first be inspired. The seminars are intended to spark that inspiration, permitting dedicated commitment and productive action to follow.

Participants' reactions to the seminars has been particularly favorable. On the anonymous evaluations conducted upon seminar completion, participants have given the seminar an overall evaluation that averages between 5 and 6 on a scale of 1 to 6. Of particular significance, 97 percent of the thousands of managers who have participated in the productivity seminars to date, within Hughes and many other companies, have suggested that other members of their organization's management participate in subsequent seminars. Thus a domino effect is being achieved, which is important when striving to make productivity improvement an integral part of the daily way of life throughout an entire organization.

Robert M. Ranftl is president of Ranftl Enterprises, a consulting firm totally dedicated to helping organizations achieve their full potential. He is the author of an award-winning book, R&D Productivity.

11.
DIMENSIONS OF PRODUCTIVITY IMPROVEMENT

K. L. Brookfield

Improving organizational productivity is a much wider challenge than improving employee productivity: it requires policies and programs designed to improve the "organizational 3Rs"—the results-resources ratio.

We hear a lot these days about the need to improve productivity in organizations. It has become widely recognized among managers and in the media that a significant increase over the low North American national rates of the past decade is essential for economic competitiveness, improvement in living standards and social health.

As commonly defined, productivity is the relationship between goods and services produced and the resource inputs used, usually expressed as a ratio of a measure of output(s) to a measure of inputs(s). A total productivity ratio takes into account all outputs and inputs, but to date very few organizations have established such a measure. The complexities of valuing or indexing numbers of different outputs and inputs and maintaining valid statistics between organizations over time have caused the general use of partial productivity measures.

The commonest partial measure is output per labor hour. A consequence of using labor input as the sole denominator in the ratio is the tendency to create the inference that it is the personal productivity of the work force that is being measured. This is unfortunate and the Bureau of Labor Statistics of the US Department of Labor has found it necessary to warn the readers of its productivity bulletins that measures based on labor inputs reflect the joint effect of a number of interrelated influences, such as changes in technology; capital investment per worker; level of output; utilization of capacity; layout and flow of material; managerial skill; and skills and effort of the work force.[1]

A New York Stock Exchange survey of US private sector corporations estimates that a total of 13 million workers are taking part in human resource programs to improve productivity. A minority of corporations have such programs, most of which are less than five years old. In reply to the question about the reasons for the programs, the most striking response, and perhaps the one most fundamental significance, is the acknowledgment of a change in management philosophy.[2]

However, it was found that the most common programs are directly aimed at better individual performance and include formal training, employee appraisal and feedback, and employee goal setting.

Clearly, this represents a partial focus on productivity improvement, even within the human resources area, and though its importance cannot be denied—particularly in organizations where human resource costs are the major cost component—it reinforces the idea that productivity means personal productivity.

ACTIONS TO IMPROVE PRODUCTIVITY

Actions to improve productivity in organizations may in fact be of many kinds, as the following examples illustrate:

- Reduction in the range of products made, with savings throughout the manufacture and supply chain
- Introduction of a management decision-support system
- Opening a central warehouse having automatic storage and retrieval to replace several smaller obsolescent facilities
- Re-establishment and upgrading of a quality control program
- Installation of ergonomically designed workstations to allow better working comfort and efficiency
- Work flow smoothing to avoid hiring more staff to cover activity peaks
- Provision of computing facilities in user areas
- "Working smarter" by individual employees
- Adoption of a management training program
- Designing a new office tower to be energy-efficient

These changes are all aimed at improving the "organizational 3Rs"—the Results-Resources Ratio. The list could of course be extended enormously: every aspect of an organization's operation can be questioned with a view to improvement. Often there are many possible changes to system features, with new ones arriving frequently in technological areas, such as computing. Which changes are adopted will depend upon contingency factors like understanding of the change; decision processes; availability of implementation resources, including finance, management time and skill; and acceptability to individuals and groups.

A systems view would suggest that proposed changes be evaluated for their possible interactions with existing or impending practices and other proposed changes. Some changes may conflict with each other and cause an overall loss in productivity. Some may complement each other and yield synergistic benefits.

ACTION MODES

The organizational action modes that originate such innovations can be of a number of kinds. Starting within working groups and moving outwards we see for example:

1. Initiatives by individual managers to improve performance and reduce unit costs in their areas of responsibility. For many years it has been asserted in the literature that this is a fundamental part of the management task. In practice its common neglect in favor of system-maintenance activities has led to the highlighting of system improvements goals in such programs as MBO and ZBB
2. Adoption of employee suggestions, perhaps submitted through a formal suggestions plan with rewards for ideas adopted
3. Discussions in management-employee groups teams/committees resulting in changes
4. Investigations and recommendations for action by teams or task forces of managers
5. Initiatives by functional groups such as research and development, information systems, industrial engineering, or human resources development, which are exercising their role of importing new knowledge, technology, systems and practices into the organization
6. Planned change projects and programs, such as new technology projects, a corporate performance-improvement program, and organization development and job redesign programs
7. Decisions by top management: to restructure the organization or to cease providing a product or service, for example
8. Use of proposals by outside specialists such as suppliers and consultants
9. Adoption of recommendations arising from external reviews by auditors, management consultants or regulatory bodies
10. Mandatory change imposed on the organization by an external authority—an agency of government for example

In larger organizations in recent years, changes will have originated in all these modes and combinations of them. Those modes that have been incorporated into basic organization functioning operate continuously (e.g., modes 1 and 5) or periodically (e.g., modes 4 and 9). Senior management's responsibility is to ensure the best use of whatever modes are available to them; when necessary, existing modes must be returned and new ones introduced for single or repeated use.

Assessment of opportunities for improving innovation performance and modes must depend upon an analysis of possible actions, their characteristics and implications in relation to the features of the organizational setting. What follows suggests the nature of the variables to be considered.

INNOVATION VARIABLES

A literature survey distilled the variables bearing upon innovation under project characteristics, communications, organizations, and personal factors.[3] The variables identified are indicated in more detail:

A. Project Characteristics

1. Advantage—awareness of relative benefits
2. Conformity—compatibility with established values, procedures, facilities
3. Comprehensibility—ease of understanding and implementing; teachability
4. Capability—fiscal, manpower and physical resources
5. Demonstrability/Revocability—observable gains/trialability; reversibility
6. Championship—advocacy by influential persons or sources

B. Communications Variables

1. Mode, e.g. person-to-person
2. Involvement of users

C. Organization Variables

1. Goals—environment pressures; goals clarity
2. Structure—power distribution, flexibility, occupational specialization, size
3. Communication and Decision Making—communications content, form and direction—support from superiors and colleagues—decision mode; individual or participative
4. Leadership and Staff—personality and role of leaders—tenure; vested interests—staff morale and cohesiveness—staff professionalism

D. Personal Variables

1. Ages
2. Economic and social status
3. Access to knowledge
4. Sense of security

These variables apply generally to innovations or knowledge transfers in organizations, and hence also to the subject of actions aimed at productivity improvement. They can provide the basis of a situational assessment that will suggest the possible success of a given change project or program and where alterations could be made in it and its context in order to improve its chances.

MAJOR VARIABLES OF PRODUCTIVITY IMPROVEMENT ACTIONS

Independently of the preceding analysis, the writer has distilled from the literature and from experience the following list of variables applying specifically to productivity improvement efforts. This again may be used as a basis for the assessment of existing or proposed projects or programs.

1. Management philosophy and style of managing
2. Management levels involved and nature of involvement
3. Organization areas involved
4. Subject or system scope—some or all of, for example, output quality, management processes, production processes, job redesign
5. Organizational mode—normal line-functional; steering committee and task groups; external consultants
6. Initiative—manager acts on intra-unit basis/manager expected to call on specialists as required/external review
7. Techniques used—for project planning, data collection and analysis, creativity, evaluation of ideas
8. Awareness in the organization of the need to act; degree of inertia
9. Human resource factors:

   - availability of manager/specialists time and energy
   - extent of manager/specialist skills
   - influence of key people involved
   - employee/union involvement; industrial relations implications and constraints
   - use of consultants
   - training needs: orientation; skills
   - "ownership"—Whose show is it?
   - motivation and commitment: credibility of project; rewards for involvement

10. Relationship to existing or proposed management systems and practices, such as MBO and quality circles, and to previous productivity related programs and persisting attitudes toward them
11. Uniformity or flexibility of application across the organization
12. Timing and urgency:

- moment in time in relation to recent and impending changes, internally and externally
- duration—short or long-term
- phasing of action

13. Improvement objectives—specific targets or open-ended
14. Communications:

   - vocabulary used: jargon of business performance/system/industrial engineering/human resources development
   - feedback to participants
   - publicity about policies, actions, and results

15. Degree of planning of projects, programs, and changes versus ad hoc or evolutionary action
16. Benefits vs. cost estimation and methods of evaluating program success, including productivity measures and trends

PROGRAM ANALYSIS AND PROFILING

A list of variables like this may be developed into a frameworks for a systematic analysis and profiling of productivity programs by:

a. Defining the variables in greater detail.
b. Regrouping or adding/deleting variables to improve the usefulness of the characterization in a given situation.
c. Setting a spectrum of possible alternatives against each variable to allow profiles of existing or proposed programs to be drawn. A complicating factor is that a program may in different parts of phases be characterized by several points on a spectrum, because, for example, of combinations of subject areas or organization modes. This can be obviated to some extent by defining variables so that numerical or high-medium-low scales may be attached. For example, see the spectra of increasing user responsibility for DP activities in reference 4.

Even if a systematic analysis is not done, a list of variables provides a good starting point for a management discussion of key factors and alternatives in the design and operation of productivity programs. Whether done formally or not, "spectrum thinking" about options and implications along multiple dimensions is increasingly important in management systems work.

Further than this, there is the vital need to see the interactions between the features and to synthesize effective action patterns for particular organization settings. Also, evaluation of options calls for considerable judgment and knowledge of productivity improvement techniques, management systems, and organizational behavior. Program features often have both positive and negative implications of significance. An emphasis on using performance measures, for example, has obvious logic in the context of management planning and control; negative outcomes may, however, lie in the attitudinal field if the application of measurement conflicts with the values of those measured or results in the focusing of efforts on producing the right numbers, to the detriment of ultimate organizational goals. Over the years many methods and programs for productivity improvement have been tried, with widely varying degrees of success. The following analysis of experience suggests the basis of a successful approach for the future:

> Much evidence in the form of past work-life/productivity improvement programs exists to suggest that to achieve both sustained quality of work life and productivity gains, behavioral science or human factors, plus learning and motivational considerations, need to be blended with production engineering principles and economic requirements of work organizations. Enduring gains are most likely to come from a systems approach, in which all important considerations or variables receive simultaneous attention.[5]

SUMMARY

Improving organizational productivity is a much wider challenge than improving employee productivity and requires policies and programs aimed at all significant inputs, processes, and outputs, with the purpose of raising the overall organizational results-resources ratio. Actions to improve productivity may take a range of modes, from local manager initiative, to combined efforts of internal groups, to action by agents external to the organization. The outcomes of change efforts are decided by the operation of a number of key variables of the programs and the settings. The design of programs and their assessment against the variables calls for "spectrum thinking" to expose the possible alternatives and implications for each variable, and systems design skills generally. A situational analysis will assist the development of productivity improvement programs that are likely to succeed in particular organizational settings.

REFERENCES

1. Quoted in National Research Council, *Measurement and Interpretation of Productivity* (National Academy of Sciences, 1979), p. 20.
2. Quoted in *Industrial Engineering* (February 1983), p. 11.
3. Human Interaction Research Institute. *Putting Knowledge to Use* (National Institute of Mental Health, 1976), pp. 10-29.
4. Buchanan, J. R. and Linowes, R. G. "Making distributed data processing work," *Harvard Business Review*. (Sept.-Oct. 1980), pp. 146-147.

5. Employers' Council of British Columbia, *Changing Times in the Workplace* (1980), pp. 45-46.

Kenneth L. Brookfield is a professional engineer and teacher of management subjects in the continuing education programs for graduate engineers at the University of British Columbia. He is also an independent systems consultant and trainer.

12.
FASTER MAY SOON MEAN FOREIGN

David R. Altany

The United States is currently in the process of losing its status as the world's premier producer. According to an expert from the American Productivity Center, the U.S. must repair the long-standing adversarial relationship between labor and management if it wants to improve its productivity.

When it comes to productivity, the U.S. has long been king of the hill. Despite long-standing concern in the U.S. about slow productivity growth, American workers still produce more product per hour than workers in any other country in the world.

In 1986 the cumulative yearly value of products and services produced by each American worker was $37,600, followed by Canadians ($35,700), Netherlanders ($32,400), and the French ($31,700).

Unfortunately, the hill of productive efficiency we stand atop is fast eroding underfoot. Countries now trailing the U.S. in productivity have become trailblazers. Conversely, the massive size and management structure that enables the U.S. to gain dominance in the industrial world have in recent years slowed productivity innovations to a crawl.

Ten years of repeated warnings that slow productivity growth could lead to forfeiture of America's productive preeminence are now inching toward realization. C. Jackson Grayson, founder and chairman of the American Productivity Center, projects that by the year 2000, the U.S. won't even place among the world's five most productive countries.

INDICATORS

Signs of America's sinking status as the world's premier producer are apparent in the latest manufacturing-technology-assessment report conducted by the U.S. Department of Defense. Its findings:

- The ratio of white-collar to blue-collar workers for Japanese manufacturing is 4:1. In the U.S. the ratio is 8:1.
- Japanese manufacturers maintain inventory levels to two months' use on average. U.S. producers hold up to nine months inventory.

- The average time between an order and the shipment of the product is five to six months in the U.S. Japan requires only one to two months.
- Though Japan's manufacturing base is smaller than America's, it employs four times as many robots (40,000 versus 10,000).
- The average age of plants and equipment in Japan is ten years. In the U.S. the average age is 17 years. Capital spending in Japan makes up 17 percent of its gross national product, compared with 10.2 percent in the U.S.

CAUSES

Mr. Grayson contends that management and labor alike are responsible for our slow productivity growth. Business is quick to condemn the government for policy actions that impair productive efforts. And the public looks to policymakers first to improve competitiveness.

But the lawmakers are limited in their ability to influence productivity and competitiveness. Only business managers set strategy and allocate funds, and only labor makes the machinery run.

"If the U.S. wants to improve its productivity, it should act to repair the long-standing adversarial relationship between labor and management," Mr. Grayson says.

Most of the management abuses that occurred early in this century have been eliminated as a result of unionization. But workers still lack a sense of commitment and concern from top managers distanced by several management layers and an elitist culture that excludes nuts-and-bolts communication.

On the labor side, union's role as a guardian of workers has also veered astray. Union efforts to limit workers' responsibilities to specific job descriptions, and more important, their role in promoting opposition to management, have done great harm to U.S. competitiveness. The threat of labor strikes induce managements to hold large inventories.

ACTIONS

Mr. Grayson suggests a number of changes—both organizational and attitudinal—that businesses can take to improve performance. Some of his suggestions include:

- Rework accounting systems.
- Implement gain-sharing.
- Involve employees in company plans.
- Make jobs more secure.
- Flatten management structure.
- Improve management/employee communications.

Much of the success of U.S. businesses' attempts to improve productivity will rely on long-term investments. As technology assumes a greater role in U.S. industries, the educational requirements for workers will increase with it.

It was assumed in the U.S. that computers and advanced technology would reduce the skills required for routine clerical jobs in industries such as banking and insurance. But research conducted by the Center on Education & Employment concludes that computer technology has helped make once-simple jobs more complex, many of them requiring high-skill levels.

13.

INFORMATION TECHNOLOGY AS A COMPETITIVE BURDEN

Timothy N. Warner

Information technology is seen by many companies as a new competitive weapon. This paper will argue, however, that it can be a competitive burden unless a company's existing production system has already been restructured for maximum efficiency using conventional means.

A major electronics manufacturerer established an automated warehouse for incoming components. Robots glide up and down the high-rise bays, selecting bins of components under computer control; the bins are passed to a conveyor system; they move around on a path determined by bar code scanners that identify each bin and route it to a stock picker. The stock picker removes items for dispatch to the factory floor as instructed by a computer workstation. An automated guided vehicle rolls off to the factory along a track painted on the floor.

At a cost of many millions of dollars, the system epitomizes the technology of the "factory of the future." But it is now idle. The firm now delivers the bulk of its supplies directly to the factory floor, bypassing the automated warehouse.

Perhaps the managers of this firm thought that information technology was a competitive weapon; perhaps they thought that advanced manufacturing technologies incorporating microelectronics were the key to manufacturing cost reduction. At least, finally, they recognized an organizational design alternative to the use of information technology. Had they not done so, information technology would have continued to be, for them as for many others, a competitive burden.

The purpose of this paper is to review the role of information technology in manufacturing enterprise and to point to alternative strategies for achieving the results that information technology promises. It will also argue that the proper role of information technology in a production system cannot be correctly assessed until the system had been restructured for maximum efficiency using conventional means.

INFORMATION TECHNOLOGY IN MANUFACTURING

When we consider the use of information technology in manufacturing, we find three main components. The first is the use on the shop floor of devices containing some level of intelligence—robots, numerically controlled machines, flexible manufacturing systems, automated guided vehicles, and the like—and falling under the rubric of *flexible automation, or advanced manufacturing technologies*. The second is the use of computer-aided design techniques, and the third is the use of computerized manufacturing information and control systems. Together these components are capable of becoming computer-integrated manufacturing systems (CIM). Businesses most affected by them tend to be from the aerospace, automotive, electrical equipment, electronics, machinery, and metal-fabricating industries. Many observers see these technologies as truly strategic in impact. For example, rapidly shifting consumer tastes and increased global competition necessitate short product design cycles and responsive manufacturing facilities; economies of scope replace economies of scale. Indeed, some observers see in these information-technology-based approaches the solution to the problem of North American competitiveness.[1]

INFORMATION TECHNOLOGY AND ORGANIZATIONAL DESIGN

Information systems, whether they incorporate "information technology" or not, serve a coordination function in the firm, allowing it to cope with complexity and uncertainty. Jay Galbraith's work provides a framework for understanding how this occurs.[2] He starts with the issue of how to organize for a task that grows in complexity and uncertainty, and considers the problems of coordination. As soon as the task becomes so large that several persons are engaged in it, they face a management problem. This can be resolved in a variety of ways. For example, a hierarchy of authority is more or less essential, as are agreed-upon rules, programs, and procedures. If the task to be performed is known and standardized, little more needs to be done. But uncertainty in the task creates problems because, to resolve the issues created by uncertainty, more and more information passes up the channels of authority, ultimately overloading them. Galbraith suggests a number of generic strategies for dealing with this problem, which he divides into two broad categories.

Reduce the need for information processing:

• Give organizational units more discretionary authority so that the need for upper-management intervention is diminished. Doing this is associated with redesign of tasks into larger, firewalled modules that are carried out by craft or skilled workers.

- Manage the environment to reduce the amount of uncertainty.
- Create slack resources, often in the form of inventory or order backlogs.

Increase information-processing capacity:

- Increase vertical-channel capacity in the hierarchy.
- Increase the amount of lateral coordination, not involving higher levels of management.

These strategies are not so much mutually exclusive as they are complementary. The important thing to realize is that sometimes one can meet an apparent information-processing problem not by throwing computer power at it, but by removing the conditions that caused the need for information processing in the first place. The example with which I opened this paper demonstrates this possibility well. The control of raw-materials inventory and of its movement within the factory are such complicated jobs that advanced computer systems, and computerized devices, are needed to cope with them in an efficient manner—that is, in an analysis comparing manual and automated systems, the automated system would appear more efficient. A better alternative (ignored if one focuses on the use of information technology) might be to remove the conditions that cause inventory to be held.

The Japanese have taught us to regard inventory as "waste." Galbraith's analysis shows us that, if inventory is waste, then information-processing capacity that serves the same function as inventory is also waste.

Information-processing capacity is used to cope with uncertainty and complexity, but much of the uncertainty and complexity faced by a firm is created by the firm itself because, for example, the product is too complex, contains components from too many suppliers, and is produced by systems of high variability. Let us examine four cases where dealing directly with these conditions replaces attempting to compute one's way around them.

DESIGN FOR MANUFACTURABILITY

Complex products are reflected in complex production systems. It is instructive to analyze examples where sophisticated companies have taken a hard look at their production systems, intending to raise the level of manufacturing efficiency, perhaps to become the industry's low-cost producer. Generally there are three elements in their strategies: product design, automation, and manufacturing control systems. While it is hard to disentangle the relative benefits of each, a strong case can be made that much of the gain in efficiency comes from a process of change that may well have been precipitated by the adoption of automation but is otherwise unrelated to it.

Consider the example of Northern Telecom, a major multinational corporation in the telecommunications industry that was faced with the challenge of low-cost telephones produced in Pacific Rim countries. The company's response was to redesign the telephone and reduce its labor content through automation. The redesign is especially interesting because it succeeded in reducing the parts count from 325 to 156.[3] The original labor content was twenty-three minutes per handset. A crude computation shows that if labor content were proportional to parts count, then manual assembly of the revised product would take eleven minutes. Actual labor content, after automation, was nine minutes. It is clear where the major leverage was achieved.

A similar analysis could be conducted with another well-documented automation success—the IBM Proprinter.[4] Redesign for manufacturability reduced the parts count by 60 percent (the printer has 60 parts, compared to 150 in a competitor's product), and the product was simplified for robotic assembly. A similar emphasis on product design at Ford Motor Company reduced the number of pieces in a car-body side panel from 15 to 2. What these examples tell us is that product redesign has tremendous leverage to reduce complexity and its concomitant variability. The important thing is to manage what we might call the internal environment; automation is secondary.

GROUP TECHNOLOGY

A second example, from the secondary manufacturing sector, is the job shop—a production system in which jumbled flow dominates. Scheduling problems in job shops are severe. The result is that the typical machined part spends 95 percent of its total time on the factory floor waiting, and only 5 percent on a machine, being cut. A machine tool might spend only a small fraction of its time cutting metal, the bulk of its day being taken up waiting for work to be set up. The consequent waste of resources has motivated considerable research into job-shop scheduling, and the development of shop-floor data acquisition systems to aid in managing the flow of work through the shop. With a few exceptions the North American solution has been to throw computer power at the problem.[5]

Information processing is not the only, or necessarily the best, solution. People who didn't have the luxury of computers established the concept of "group technology," which in essence is the classification of parts produced by the job shop in terms of similar fabrication sequence, shape, and size.[6] Suppose we can, via such a classification scheme, allocate 80 percent of the shop's volume to families of like parts. Then we can process each family through a manufacturing cell whose machines are placed in the correct sequence and are tailored for the family. The job shop starts to look like a flow shop; scheduling problems are reduced; the prospect for dramatic reductions in work-in-process inventory is enhanced. (As it happens, information technology can play a key role in the application of group technology concepts, and is perhaps essential to that process, but at least when this is the case we know that the technology is being applied reasonably.) In Galbraith's terms, we have redesigned the task into self-contained modules, as opposed to finding the information-processing capacity to schedule the more complex task.

MANUFACTURING CELLS

Jelinek and Goldhar have pointed out that the new technologies of flexible automation—particularly the use of numerically controlled machine tools, robots, and flexible manufacturing systems—give rise to new production system possibilities based on short production runs and rapid switching (at near-zero cost) from one product to another.[7] These provide economies of scope, contrasted with economies of scale. The essential component here is the programmable device, say the NC machine or industrial robot, that can switch immediately from performing one kind of task to another under program control. Once switching costs are zero, then small lot sizes become feasible, indeed optimal. Combining the concepts of rapid changeover through programmability, and group technology, one arrives at the flexible manufacturing cell—the first step toward CIM.[8] It may consist of an integrated multifunctional NC machining center, or a circle of NC tools with automatic tool-changing and raw-material loading and unloading, perhaps with automated guided vehicles moving the pieces from one machine to the next. Its purpose is to produce, in small lot sizes, the components in a particular family.

It is incorrect to think that only programmable multifunctional machines are capable of instant zero-cost switching. The Japanese have shown us that conventional technology can be used in the same way.[9] The trick is to reduce setup times to very small amounts through ingenious engineering and the application of what is, in retrospect, common sense. The "multifunctional" machine can be created from an assemblage of low-cost conventional machines in a manufacturing cell. Hence a concept—economies of scope—that appeared to depend on the advent of high technology on the factory floor is applicable in a much more modest manufacturing environment.[10]

In its simplest form a manufacturing cell is a line (or U-configuration, or circle) of simple machine tools, say, for the production of a family of parts. In order to produce a part, a worker starts with the raw material piece and walks in down the line, performing each operation sequentially, until he or she reaches the end. Note, lot size equals one, and setups must be one-touch, not involving other workers. To speed up the line one simply adds another worker; each takes roughly half the work of the cell. One can keep adding workers until the physical ability of the cell to accommodate them is exhausted.

The conventional manufacturing cell achieves flexibility with slack machine resources (which can be cheap, because the machines are simple) and multifunction workers. (Galbraith suggests that a function of "craft" workers is to reduce the costs of coordination.) The cell is a low-fixed-cost increment to a firm's manufacturing capacity, a feature not shared by the information-technology-intensive flexible manufacturing cell, which achieves flexibility through machine-based intelligence.

There is a further consideration—the flexibility of the fully automated "flexible manufacturing cell" is deceptive, because of the extend to which inflexible materials-handling equipment is integral to its operation. This factor limits the number of different items that can in fact be processed by the cell, rather undermining the notion of flexibility.[11]

JUST-IN-TIME SYSTEMS

Another complementary approach to uncertainty and complexity arises out of the problem of management control in repetitive discrete manufacturing (of cars, airplanes, computers, or lawnmowers, for example). In this situation, an information-technology approach (material requirements planning) contrasts strongly with a non-information-technology approach (continuous flow manufacturing).

The manufacturing of such goods is information intensive. It is said, for example, that the engineering documentation for a Boeing 747 weighs more than the plane itself. The manufacturing process involves many separate suppliers, spread across the globe, whose activities must be coordinated. The production system for these goods is an industry, not a single enterprise. The sheer volume of transactions required to manage such a production system makes it a natural target for information technology.

Material requirements planning (MRP) is an approach to the management of fabrication and assembly of products of this type. The key concept is that the demand for low-level components derives from the production of an end product whose production level is planned. Traditionally a component of, say, a lawnmower (a particular blade, perhaps) is manufactured in an economic lot size, stored in a warehouse, and used as needed until a reorder point is reached, at which point another batch is fabricated. The inventory of blades constitutes slack in the sense that it exists because nobody bothered to figure out exactly when the blades would be needed based on the production schedule for end-items, or perhaps because the number of end-items required could not be accurately forecasted or determined.

Clearly, if we know the precise production schedule of all the lawnmowers into which this particular blade goes, then we can establish, by back scheduling, when to produce or order the blades, so that inventory never builds up much in excess of requirements. MRP, then, substitutes information processing for slack in the way that Galbraith envisions. But MRP systems are notoriously difficult to implement and consume substantial resources in the form of computing power and indirect manufacturing labor.[12] Further, although they deal with the slack created by the earlier inability to back schedule production, they trap and institutionalize other slack that is generally more significant. In order to back schedule you have to estimate lead times for production. As mentioned earlier, 95 percent of the manufacturing lead time in a job shop is wasted, and building this exorbitant lead time into a computer system merely institutionalizes waste. In addition, the buffering function of inventory—allowing for variations in lead time or quantity delivered—is generally handled by artificially inflating the lead time or the quantity produced, which again casts inefficient organizational processes in stone. A final point is that the occurrence of stockouts on the shop floor can be ascribed to "the computer" rather than to some individual who could take corrective action. The system does not contain the levers that would motivate the work force to more efficient behavior; standing apart from the system on the shop floor, the MRP system introduces a fatal bifurcation of responsibility for overall performance.

Contrast this with what has been called Just-in-Time (JIT) or Stockless Production, or Continuous Flow Manufacturing.[13] Suppose for a moment that production of all components could be accomplished instantly. Then back scheduling from the number of different lawnmowers required to the number of blades required in a given period is simplified. But even this is unnecessary. If there is almost no work-in-process inventory (WIP), then replacement of the components required for a particular lawnmower must occur soon after its production. All we need is a signaling system that lets the blade production worker know when to produce. This is accomplished through the well-known *kanban* system. No computers are necessary to accomplish job-order release and dispatching, since these happen because of the pull system in place.

But there is a radical change in the organization of production. Setup times must be very low; lot sizes are correspondingly small—otherwise a machine would be occupied running large lots at the time it is required to produce a component "on demand." The flow of work might be reorganized so that travel times between successive workstations are minimized, and so that visual signaling methods (*kanban* squares, colored golf balls, etc.) can be used. There can be absolutely no defective parts passed along the system, because there is little WIP to absorb the discrepancies between planned and actual production.

Because there is so little WIP, it can all be located on the factory floor. No elaborate materials-handling or inventory control systems are required. The benefits are legion, well-documented, and persuasive to the increasing number of U.S. manufacturers adopting these techniques.

In Galbraith's terms, the firm adopting JIT seems to be doing the impossible—lowering the information-processing requirement *and* removing slack from the system. This is not a complete picture, because the JIT firm plans slack resources in the form of machinery running more slowly, people working less than complete shifts, heavy maintenance, and idle equipment. In addition, the JIT firm eventually manages the uncertainty in its external environment by negotiating supply and delivery schedules to which all parties firmly adhere.[14]

We see here the competitive use of information systems, to be sure, but the use is not necessarily based on high technology. We also see whole industries being transformed by the impact of JIT methods, and corporations such as Hewlett-Packard and IBM relying on the cost and quality benefits of JIT to achieve a competitive edge.[15] One authority at IBM, which has reportedly invested $22 billion in manufacturing in the last five years, comments, "Of all the aspects of IBM's investment in manufacturing . . . the least expensive—Continuous Flow Manufacturing—is the most significant."[16]

I do not intend to give the impression that JIT systems are universally applicable in place of MRP systems. A balanced view might be that each has its place, or that some blend of the two is appropriate.[17] Certain conditions (long lead times for production, uncertain reject rates, fluctuating demand, high setup costs) favor MRP systems.[18] The tragedy is that an information-technology approach treats these conditions as immutable, whereas in many cases they are not. Rather than reducing waste, an information-technology approach adds to it by burdening an already inefficient system with the cost of computation.

CONCLUSIONS

Just as piles of work-in-process inventory can signal inefficient production, so also can the elaborate information system, or the machine tool with more axes than it needs, or the automatic storage and retrieval system. The paradox here is that some of the finest examples of manufacturing efficiency incorporate the most advanced computer control systems and factory automation. For example, comparing North American to Japanese manufacturers, we find in North America a lower rate of adoption of NC machines and robots, the building blocks of flexible automation. The reason is that for the well-organized production system the benefits of automation are clear. The Japanese, having paid more attention to basics than the North Americans, are in a better position to evaluate new technologies *and* have production systems into which devices such as robots and NC machines more readily fit.

The analysis presented above suggests that the twin strategies of product design and production system design around conventional technologies can achieve the lion's share of the benefits associated with moving from an unexamined, poorly organized production system to a world-class manufacturing facility. The issue is one of timing—a firm should forego information-technology-based approaches to solving production problems until it has exhausted conventional approaches, and then move forward into flexible automation. At that point it can examine the benefits of flexible automation relative to the best alternative practice.

Information technology is seen as a new competitive weapon; "strategic systems" take their place alongside decision support systems and traditional data processing; and the "chief information officer" commands a seat at the table where strategic decisions are made.[19,20] Indeed, in the five years or so since early work on information technology as a competitive weapon appeared, the topic has achieved the status of cliche. Cliche or not, many firms look to information technology as a key weapon in their strategic arsenal.

When one considers what kinds of competitive advantage firms hope to achieve using information technology, one finds a depressingly high proportion of firms hoping to reduce competition through raising switching costs, reducing the amount of information available to the customer, and so forth—that is, using information technology to secure a local monopoly.[21] Depressing, because innovations in the service sector, or in the distribution, marketing, or purchasing functions of manufacturing enterprises, do little to counter the concern that North American enterprises are becoming "hollow corporations."[22] Meanwhile, a naive faith in technological silver bullets diverts manufacturers from the hard work of rebuilding North America's industrial base, and tempts them into alarming, high-risk forays toward the factory of the future. A recent report describes the experience of Deere and Company:

> The giant farm equipment manufacturer broke fresh ground a decade ago with factory automation that was then regarded as the model for all others to emulate. FMS technology worth $1.5 billion was designed to provide a choice of 5,000 process changes on ten basic tractor models.

As Deere had to weather a depressed farm equipment market and then a strike, it became apparent that the company had invested too much in its state-of-the-art FMS without regard to the process being automated . . .

> Billion-dollar losses were followed by rationalization of the production process, and today automated manufacturing at Deere is a much more organized, simplified affair. John Lardner, a company vice-president, said: "The FMS was a retrofit to a production design problem that shouldn't have existed in the first place."[23]

Manufacturing competitiveness is the only enduring base for a viable modern economy. Information technology will play a key role in transforming manufacturing. But not now, not for most firms. For them it is the hard road of conventional process improvement and production system organization that will lead to manufacturing competitiveness.

REFERENCES

1. R. I. Benjamin, J. F. Rockart, M. S. Scott Morton, and J. Wyman, "Information Technology: A Strategic Opportunity," *Sloan Management Review*, Spring 1984, pp. 3-10; R. M. Cyert, "The Plight of Manufacturing: What Can Be Done?" *Issues in Science and Technology* 1 (1985): 87-100.
2. J. R. Galbraith, *Organization Design* (Reading, MA: Addison-Wesley, 1977).

3. R. McClean, "Quality and Productivity at Northern Telecom," in *Proceedings of the Fourth Annual Operations Management Association Meeting*, 1985, pp. 1-9.

4. "Less Is More in Automation," *IBM Engineering/Scientific Innovation*, Fall 1986, pp. 4-5.

5. W. K. Holstein and W. L. Berry, "Work Flow Structure: An Analysis for Planning and Control," *Management Science* 16 (February 1970): B324-B336.

6. N. L. Hyer and U. Wemmerlov, "Group Technology and Productivity," *Harvard Business Review*, July-August 1984, pp. 140-149.

7. M. Jelinek and J. D. Goldhar, "The Strategic Implications of the Factory of the Future," *Sloan Management Review*, Summer 1984, pp. 29-37.

8. P. Huang and B. Houck, "Cellular Manufacturing: An Overview and Bibliography," *Production and Inventory Management*, Fourth Quarter 1985, pp. 83-92.

9. S. Shingo, *A Revolution in Manufacturing: The SMED System* (Stamford, CT: Productivity Press, 1985).

10. U. Wemmerlov and N. L. Hyer, "Research Issues in Cellular Manufacturing," *International Journal of Production Research* 25 (March 1987): 413-431.

11. R. Jaikumar, "Postindustrial Manufacturing," *Harvard Business Review*, November-December 1986, pp. 69-76.

12. J. C. Anderson, R. G. Schroeder, S. E. Tupy, and E. M. White, "Material Requirements Planning Systems: The State of the Art," *Production and Inventory Management*, Fourth Quarter 1982, pp. 51-66.

13. R. W. Hall, *Zero Inventories* (Homewood, IL: Dow Jones-Irwin, 1983); R. Schonberger, "Applications of Single-Card and Dual-Card Kanban," *Interfaces*, August 1983, pp. 56-67; "Integrated Manufacturing: Nothing Succeeds Like Successful Implementation," *Production Engineering*, May 1987, pp. IM4-IM32.

14. S. Chapman and M. Schimke, "Towards a Theoretical Understanding of Just-In-Time Manufacturing," *Operations Management Review*, Summer 1986, pp. 32-36.

15. R. C. Walleigh, "What's Your Excuse for Not Using JIT?" *Harvard Business Review*, March-April 1986, pp. 38-54.

16. "What Did IBM Buy for $22 Billion?" *Computerworld*, 15 June 1987, pp. 69-83.

17. Schonberger (August 1983).

18. L. J. Krajewski, B. E. King, L. P. Ritzman, and D. S. Wong, "Kanban, MRP, and Shaping the Manufacturing Environment," *Management Science*, 33 (January 1987): 39-57.

19. M. E. Porter and V. E. Millar, "How Information Gives You Competitive Advantage," *Harvard Business Review*, July-August 1985, pp. 149-160.

20.   "Management's Newest Star: Meet the Chief Information Officer," *Business Week*, 13 October 1986, pp. 160-172.

21.   G. L. Parsons, "Information Technology: A New Competitive Weapon," *Sloan Management Review*, Fall 1983, pp 3-14; B. Ives and G. P. Learmonth, "The Information System As a Competitive Weapon," *Communications of the ACM*, December 1984, pp. 1193-1201; J. Y. Bakos and M. E. Treacy, "Information Technology and Corporate Strategy: A Research Perspective," *MIS Quarterly*, June 1986, pp. 107-119.

22.   "The Hollow Corporation," *Business Week*, 3 March 1986, pp. 56-78.

23.   T. Davis, "Manufacturers Revise Their Strategy on Factory Automation," *Globe and Mail*, 4 July 1987, p. B7.

Timothy N. Warner is assistant professor of management science in the faculty of administrative studies, York University, Toronto.

14.
BEYOND THE NUMBERS: WHAT PRICE AUTOMATION?

Daniel J. Meyer

Traditional economic-justification methods are often inadequate when it comes to evaluating new automation technologies, but this article argues that decisions to invest in these new technologies can be reasonably justified.

Manufacturing managers know that they have to automate, that in the long run it's inevitable. On the other hand, they'd like to have the assurance that the company won't go broke before the automation begins to pay off.

Unfortunately, traditional economic-justification methods are often inadequate when it comes to evaluating new automation technologies. The inadequacies stem from three sources.

First, we don't have a good enough handle on the cost accounting of our current operations. Let's face it: ultimately, justification implies a comparison with one's present mode of operation. In effect, someone always says: "Show me, in dollars and cents, why we should change anything at all."

The problem is that we haven't developed the tools to measure and assess all the "intangibles" commonly lumped into the burden rate of manufacturing cost—the "catchall" element of total cost excluding materials and direct labor.

Take quality, for example. We may know the cost of scrap and rework, but can we measure the costs that deviations in quality have on downstream operations such as assembly? Can we place a dollar value on lost business due to questionable quality?

If we can't measure the cost of quality in our present operations, how can we evaluate the worth of a technology that promises, say, a 15 percent or 25 percent quality improvement?

Another example is flexibility. Many managers are looking to new automation to give them greater flexibility—flexibility to produce a wider variety of products with shorter lead-times, better response times to changes in the marketplace, and so on.

Just as we have never developed the tools to measure the complete cost of poor quality, we're also at a loss in determining the current cost of being in-flexible or less flexible than we would like.

The second major source of difficulties in financial justification is that the performance of new technology is often difficult to predict accurately. In fact, usually by the time a technology has been in the field long enough to generate "hard data," it's no longer new or state-of-the-art. As a consequence, in evaluating new technology we're often forced to make rough assumptions about numerous variables that will ultimately determine cost benefits.

The third source of uncertainty in justifying new automation is the most often overlooked. Long term, however, it may be the most significant. It has to do with all the changes that must be made in order to implement new technol-ogy initially, and all the subsequent changes that will be required to use the technology to its fullest.

In short, technology acts as a catalyst for change and, ideally, positive change.

From a financial-justification point of view, we're a long way away from being able to predict what these forced "improvements" will cost, what their payback will be, or even when they'll be put into effect. Often the need for these changes goes unrecognized as manufacturers concentrate on in-dependent "islands of automation" before addressing the larger picture.

But despite these apparent roadblocks, I believe that decisions to invest in new automation technologies can be reasonably justified, even though there are many unquantified intangibles. This can be done by supplementing tradi-tional procedures with a special analysis of one or two of the most important benefits of the new technology that are not given full value in the traditional approach.

For example, one of the major attractions of new automation technologies should be lower working capital requirements due to reduced inventory levels. Beyond the traditional cost-benefit studies of inventory savings, we should try to quantify additional cost benefits that reduced inventory will bring about in both upstream and downstream areas.

Upstream, for instance, design engineers will be forced to make greater use of group-technology manufacturing methods. Design and part changes will be more tightly controlled and thus better planned. This will reduce not only inventory obsolescence, but also direct manufacturing and assembly costs.

Downstream, smaller lot sizes will require tighter scheduling as parts are "pulled through" as they're needed. This will force assembly operations to be-come more efficient and will also reduce the levels of finished inventory. Overall, it's likely that new automation will cut carrying costs on a percentage basis as well.

By supplementing traditional cost-justification procedures with one or two special analyses of key elements such as inventory, quality, or flexibility, we'll often be able to tip the scales one way or the other. If it's in favor of the new technology, we can proceed with the assumption that the majority of the remaining intangibles and unknowns will equalize out or tend to be favorable themselves.

Of course, the assumptions imply some risk, but as we all know, no alternatives are risk-free, including that of doing nothing.

Daniel J. Meyer is vice president of finance/administration and chief financial officer for Cincinnati Milacron Inc.

15.

ALL FACTORIES ARE NOT THE SAME

Robert A. Becker

A brief review of manufacturing systems, processes, technology, facilities and personnel reveals that each factory is unique. Only when productivity programs reflect this factory-floor reality can they assume strategic importance.

The potential of productivity as a strategic variable is substantial, but that potential must be converted to performance. Strategy involves manipulating realities to attain defined objectives. To harness productivity in a strategic sense, we have to deal with it in operational terms, not in theoretical or general terms. This may be easier said than done.

From my vantage point, I see two groups intent on improving operational productivity: the manufacturing folks accountable for performance and their nonmanufacturing counterparts who would suggest a better way. Their backgrounds and perspectives differ. To draw a network analogy: while nonmanufacturing folks may have the expertise to devise a viable skeleton of beginning and ending events, only manufacturing can flesh out the real-world details of the activities in between. Success would be within their grasp were they to work together.

Wholehearted cooperation, however, has been the exception rather than the rule. In its stead we often find a barrier created by distrust, antagonism, and misunderstanding, with the protagonists disdainful of each other's expertise. This fosters superficial analysis and generalizations that, in due course, result in flawed programs that do little more than increase the friction.

The problem is best exemplified by the oft heard refrains, "All factories are the same," and "Manufacturing tends to overstate the complexity of its domain." Maybe so, if we observe from afar. But before meaningful strategies based on operational productivity can be developed, the spotlight must shift from questionable abstractions to the realities of the factory floor. At that level, where programs can be implemented and results achieved within a rational time frame, all factories are not the same . . . and to assume that they are voids protectiveness' strategic potential (and disparages manufacturing).

Unfortunately, this fact is not obvious to the outsider looking in or to the management trainee on temporary assignment, and that, in my opinion, is one reason why many productivity improvement programs founder or produce only marginal results. To bring this problem into focus, a brief review of current planning practice might be helpful.

When we strip away all of the program constraints and sophisticated techniques, a planning exercise can be reduced to three basic steps:

(1) Define current activities (A),
(2) Project future activities (B), and
(3) Develop a program to get from A to B.

Although there are three steps, most planning efforts today concentrate on steps 2 and 3, and grant step 1 only a superficial analysis.

Current activities are not completely ignored. Some form of preplanning or situation audit is usually conducted, or at least should be. My concern is whether the results are meaningful. This is just one more variation of the old saw about the right questions eliciting the right answers. Because the factory is a complex environment, asking the right questions requires considerable insight.

While the re-emergence of manufacturing as an important management discipline will doubtless force changes over the next decade, most generalists today have no experience on the factory floor as either workers or supervisors. They tend to be more familiar with activities that lend themselves to theoretical analysis than with those, like manufacturing, where the application of technology is largely empirical. Hence, communicating and interpreting observations can be difficult and hindered further by manufacturing's traditional reticence towards those perceived as outsiders. This haze surrounding manufacturing operations can understandably lead to erroneous generalizations about current activities. Let's take a closer look at several facets of manufacturing to see why this is so.

SYSTEMS

Some of the problems of manufacturing generalizations can be traced to fallacious extrapolation of macro-system concepts to micro applications. On a macro level, all manufacturing systems can justifiably be seen as fundamentally the same: each must balance the basic elements of materials, labor, technology, facilities, and cash flow. On a micro level, however, the mechanics for balancing those basic elements (what I call op-tech, the relevant operational technology) vary markedly depending upon the organization, product, and process. While generalizations can be useful in studying the principles of manufacturing systems, specifics are necessary for their application on a particular factory floor.

Generalizations would be more than adequate were we able to build and staff an optimum manufacturing facility from scratch. But, we seldom have that luxury. Our programs must contend with existing capabilities, and changes must be structured so as not to disrupt production. Since there are no inviolate rules, the operating systems we encounter have evolved along both formal and informal paths. This duality stems from rapidly changing demands placed on nonautomated manufacturing environments. Although formal manufacturing systems could conceivably be designed to cover all contingencies, they rarely are. So to keep the product moving out the door, informal systems spring up to bridge the gaps. Unfortunately, only the formal systems are defined by flow charts and standard operating procedures. The informal ones, having been created ad hoc, never are. The total system comprises two equally important parts; the formal one visible for all to see, and the informal one invisible except to those who anticipate its presence and know precisely where to look.

Even formal manufacturing systems cannot be taken at face value. They must be evaluated for substance. All too frequently a control system that appears perfectly acceptable on paper is inadequately supported by vague or incomplete processing definitions and inaccurate or inconsistent standards; only a mirage of effective floor control exists. In such cases, the formal system is either being made to work informally or is simply ignored, and manufacturing expertise is required to identify its flaws.

Informal systems further cloud the issue. Here, we must be prepared to ask those proverbial right questions. Like others intimately familiar with their tasks, manufacturing folks may not recognize their informal systems as such or realize their importance to the total system. Unfortunately, this has been a traditional area of friction, with manufacturing unjustly accused of obfuscation by those unfamiliar with its domain.

To compound the problem, informal systems are often viewed as symptomatic of poor management, incompetence, or worse rather than as pragmatic compromises that enable inherently inflexible formal systems to cope with the complex, rapidly changing manufacturing environment. So even if uncovered during an audit, these informal systems may be ignored or targeted for corrective action. But without them or their functional replacements, the total system becomes inoperable. Admittedly, in some instances, the intent of informal systems has been to subvert performance monitoring and controls, but in the main, those I've encountered in manufacturing have evolved to provide needed flexibility, to control costs, or to exploit the competence of specific individuals. Informal shop-floor scheduling systems are a classic example.

INFORMAL SHOP-FLOOR SCHEDULING

Job-lot scheduling is determined by part priority and constrained by the throughput capacity and technical capability of the various machines or work centers. If several machines are similar, a formal scheduling system may treat them as having similar capabilities. While logical, this is not necessarily correct. In practice, some parts will be queued awaiting open time of a specific machine even though a lower-priority part is running on a similar machine. Other parts may even be running on machines not specified in their routing.

This apparent disregard for formal scheduling can be the result of internal politics. On most labor accounting runs, performance is first tabulated by individual workers and then summed by responsible supervisors. Consequently, supervisors have a vested interest in how the system perceives the performance of their subordinates. If they have the opportunity, some supervisors may ignore priorities and assign easy jobs or those with loose standards to make their performance statistics look better. But manufacturing management fully understands the problems and pressures that are caused by schedule slippages and cannot be expected to tolerate such shenanigans for long. Usually there is a more logical explanation for disregarding formal scheduling.

Obviously, equipment conditions and operator skills do vary. Less obvious but often more important each machine has unique operating and vibrational characteristics, even machines that look the same. Specific parts have comparable idiosyncrasies. Because of these subtle differences, there is an optimum match between machine and workpiece which, in some cases, can spell the difference between consistent quality and expensive rework or scrap. Formal scheduling systems and data bases on which they depend rarely recognize machine, operator, and workpiece idiosyncracies to the degree necessary. Consequently, line supervisors must occasionally deviate from their master schedule to avoid wasting resources.

This massage of the master schedule is typical of manufacturing's pragmatic approach to problem solving. Theirs is a real world of imperfect materials, machines, and people. Time, cost, and design constraints dictate workable rather than ideal solutions. To manage effectively, flexibility commensurate with these parameters is required. Manual systems have this flexibility. They can be modified readily and informally to provide meaningful guidance for decisions made on the factory floor. Since results are the primary yardstick of performance, formal justifications and documentation are seldom warranted.

In supplanting any manual manufacturing system with a computer-based system, this working balance between operational parameters and flexibility, the mixture of formal and informal systems, must be recognized and maintained. This does not mean that the new system must be an automated duplicate to the old. However, if the new system does not incorporate the flexibility of the old, operational tolerances in terms of equipment, material, personnel, and quality will all have to be reviewed and adjusted to bring the system into balance.

PROCESSES

Just as manufacturing systems can be seen as similar, all manufacturing processes can be viewed as fundamentally the same—each process must balance the basic elements of technology, labor, and facilities. But once again, the operational technology, the op-tech, can vary widely.

In continuous processing, routing and processing parameters are designed into the facility to achieve volume, cost, and quality objectives. Once processing steps have been defined, preproduction effort is directed towards facilities design, equipment selection, erection, and start-up. Since processing is fixed before production phase-in, performance is tied directly to manufacturing engineering competence.

Job-lot processing, on the other hand, is often a joint effort between manufacturing engineering and the skilled workers and supervisors on the factory floor. It is structured around selected existing facilities. Operator skills are often pivotal. Here, it is possible to initiate processing with only tentative procedures. As work progresses and preproduction planning is found to be inept or superficial, changes in routing, operations, and sequencing can be introduced. When deadline pressures mount, manufacturing management, while burying the costs, can be expected to assign some of its direct labor talent and supervision to resolve the problems. So in job-lot processing, the fact that a part or product has been manufactured does not necessarily reflect manufacturing engineering competence.   This difference between continuous and job-lot processing becomes important when weighing productivity improvement strategies for specific organizations. Manufacturing engineering groups, although capable of supporting existing activities, may not possess sufficient manufacturing expertise to exploit the full potential of classical or computer-based factory automation concepts. As part of the overall assessment of current activities, it is important to evaluate their abilities.

Continuous processing problems indicative of weakness in this area—problems such as insufficient volume, low yields, erratic quality, and excessive maintenance costs—can be identified by overview analysis. But comparable job-lot processing problems may be obscured. Here, a detailed analysis by manufacturing specialists is necessary to ensure that new strategies do not rely on an unqualified group or individual for manufacturing technological support.

TECHNOLOGY

In recent years several of our basic industries have been roundly criticized for lack of foresight in not embracing new, more competitive manufacturing technologies. But productivity strategies must also separate substance from illusion within a given technology. Here again, manufacturing expertise is required to avoid the tempting pitfall of generalization.

First, we have to recognize that facilities and technology are not synonymous. State-of-the-art facilities or equipment do not indicate state-of-the-art technology, merely the potential. Those resources still must be utilized effectively. The sophisticated numerical control machining center is a typical example.

THE MACHINING CENTER

The inherent potential of the machining center derives primarily from its rapid precisely controlled movements and tool changes. On the surface, it would appear all that's needed to realize that potential is someone who can program it—define its cutter paths. But then, customers buy distortion-free parts to print and specification, not cutter paths. So in this regard, the bottom line, the machining center is no different than any other machine tool. It too must cope with workpiece distortion.

Distortion is the bane of metalworking. It results from changes in a workpiece's internal stresses, changes caused by processing. When a workpiece is unrestrained, lying on an inspection table for example, its internal stresses are in balance. During processing, however, when it is clamped or in a fixture, this balance can be disrupted by procedures that induce or relieve stresses, and almost all metalworking procedures do either one or the other. If this occurs, then when the restraints are removed the workpiece must physically change shape (manufacturing folks call the end result distortion) to bring its internal stresses back into balance. Consequently, a workpiece that conforms to print and specifications while still in a fixture or clamped to a machine table can, in fact, be scrap. So, while important machining parameters and tool positioning cannot guarantee an acceptable part. Something else is required, a successful processing concept.

Before actual work can begin, manufacturing must define, at least tentatively, the sequence of operations that it believes will produce an acceptable part after the processing restraints have been removed. This processing concept addresses fundamental manufacturing questions such as how to clamp and locate, where machining should start, how much material should be removed during each operation, how alignment will be maintained, and when or if to stress relieve. In effect, it expresses an organization's level of manufacturing expertise, its op-tech competence.

Detailed operation sheets and the related numerical control programs are written in conformance with the processing concept. The operational effectiveness of a machining center depends more on an organization's ability to develop a successful processing concept than on the center's ability to perform rapid, precisely controlled movements and tool changes. The machining center merely follows processing instructions and has no ability to develop the underlying processing concept. Unfortunately, its aura of sophistication may well convey that impression to the inexperienced observer.

As with facilities and technology, it is also important for us to differentiate between the future potential of manufacturing research technology and the current capabilities of factory-floor production technology. Many private sector organizations have internal manufacturing research and process development groups. Some are highly visible and even compete successfully for external contracts and funding. But while they may be of strategic interest, they are not a direct indication of factory-floor technology.

Manufacturing technology is especially difficult to evaluate because it is a composite of many interrelated factors, manufacturing factors. What you see is not necessarily what you get. But an accurate assessment is both tactically and strategically important; inexperienced observers are not appropriate candidates for the task.

FACILITIES

Facilities, like technology, can be illusory. We've all heard tales of equipment being run into the ground and of bailing wire fixes. Unfortunately, they're not fables. Such conditions do exist. We've also heard about those last-minute discoveries of production inadequacies, again, fact not fiction. But both records and appearances can be deceiving.

Data on facilities are available from many sources. Marketing may have a slick brochure, and MIS, a data base. Manufacturing, accounting and maintenance all have their lists. None of these sources, however, is completely objective. Sales wants to convey an impression of excellence to its prospects, manufacturing wants to justify new facilities, accounting is concerned about depreciation, maintenance has to substantiate its budget, and the folks on the factory floor want to get the job done with a minimum of aggravation. MIS knows only what it's been told. Consequently, the best we can expect to find is a depreciation listing of equipment by age or purchase date, a vague description of its capabilities, and a highly subjective estimate of its condition—hardly a sound foundation for near-term productivity programs. But is this important in a strategic sense?

Today's facilities may well be replaced before strategic plans are implemented or as a result of them. So, on the surface, a rigorous facilities analysis would seem to be of little value to strategic planners. Once again, however, appearance can be deceiving.

Like apple pie and motherhood, everyone's all for adequate care and maintenance of facilities, it's just that there are different definitions of *adequate*. Responsible managers can have divergent opinions on such subjects as what constitutes equipment abuse, whether preventive maintenance is boon or boondoggle, who should have day-to-day responsibility for facilities care, and how equipment procurement disputes should be resolved. The existing condition of facilities reflects these opinions. Therefore, even a brief review of facilities by an expert could help to realistically assess management attitudes that have a direct impact on productivity strategies.

PERSONNEL

In this cursory review of manufacturing, I've alluded several times to the key issue, personnel. In this country, we have traditionally emphasized individual initiative and contribution, not group effort. Our factory-floor competence derives primarily from worker and foreman skills. Even manufacturing engineering assignments, consistent with the empirical nature of manufacturing technology, are usually filled from the same labor pool and stress hands-on experience, not formal education.

Throughout the factory we can identify performance variables stemming from individual contribution. Tracing a manufacturing cycle from beginning to end, we encounter individual input every step of the way. These people are not automatons, and there are no universal standards against which to evaluate the quality of their imputs. Change and negotiation are common, with personal backgrounds, operational constraints, and internal politics all playing a role. The end result, be it a manufacturing plan, a performance standard, or a finished product, is frequently a blend of inputs of uncertain heritage. This means that, without manufacturing's assistance in interpretation, we cannot rely on functional or organizational charts, headcounts, job descriptions, or performance statistics to disclose where a factory's personnel strengths and weaknesses lie.

These must be identified because they are potentially crippling constraints to change. Today, it's difficult to hire highly skilled manufacturing personnel. Tomorrow, if our work force continues to deteriorate while concern about productivity grows, it may not even be worth the effort to try. But, within this grim prognosis lies opportunity. Organizations that anticipate the problem, define their manufacturing personnel requirements, and structure effective programs for meeting them, can make their productivity a significant strategic variable to be reckoned with by those who fail to act.

Admittedly, there is more to manufacturing than systems, processes, technology, facilities, and personnel. But I think that the point of my little expose of the myth, "All factories are the same!" is clear: all factories are not the same. Productivity improvement programs must be tailored to the unique needs of each organization. To do so, manufacturing folks and their non-manufacturing counterparts must work together. There is no viable alternative.

ADDENDUM

Since most of my published comments in recent years have dealt with integrated office automation planning and proposal analysis, I have intentionally focused solely on the factory. However, as I have long pointed out to office automation audiences, a similar case can be made that all offices are not the same. This takes on added significance today as interest shifts from isolated work-processing activities to integrated, broad-spectrum office automation, with its multifunction workstations and direct information access.

Except in those cases of production type assignments, the so-called back-room jobs in the financial industry for example, the office work environment is largely unstructured. As a result, while similar tasks are performed in all offices, their specific content and mechanics of performance vary widely.

Job descriptions for the typical office assignment are vague at best and may even be written to mesh with the requirements of a specific labor grade of actual job content. But then, incumbents, especially at the managerial level, bring different backgrounds and expertise to their office positions. They have different frames of reference for data interpretation, and different management styles. Therefore, they require different types, qualities, and levels of support. And, in return, they provide widely varying degrees of guidance or supervision to their subordinates. Consequently, there is no universally applicable office support system. Support must be tailored to the needs of the specific workplace, and so once assigned, the clerical worker, knowledge worker, or manager develops an informal routine to support his or her principal, personnel paperwork notwithstanding.

This effectively precludes generalized solutions to discrete office problems and again makes it imperative that we be able to ask the right questions and evaluate the substance of the answers. Frequently, only the workers themselves know the full scope of the support they provide and its tacit priorities. If we concentrate on office automation technology while neglecting the substance of the activities and personnel within the specific office whose productivity we aim to improve, we cannot expect our programs to succeed. As in the factory, those directly responsible for performance and those outsiders who would suggest a better way must learn to work together.

Part III
PERSPECTIVES ON MANAGING PRODUCTIVITY

16.
PRODUCTIVITY IS MANAGEMENT'S PROBLEM

Carlton P. McNamara

Much of the current problem of low productivity has been caused by management. Better allocation of resources is the key to changing a company's performance and to increasing overall management productivity.

It is virtually impossible to find a reasonably well-informed business person today who is not aware of the productivity problem in American industry. For the last ten years, productivity has clearly been the most widely discussed topic in business publications, management seminars, industry conferences, and executive offices.

Statistical evidence and unfavorable comparisons with Japan, West Germany, France, and Canada have underscored both the problem's severity and dire implications for the future. More recently, attention has been focused upon causation. How did we get ourselves into this predicament? What are the specific explanations for the productivity decline?

Although many industrialists, economists, academicians, and government officials have presented a plethora of theories for the "productivity crisis," two scenarios usually appear in most analyses. First, the present labor force supposedly possesses lower motivation, declining skills, and union-inspired uncooperative attitudes. This thesis is usually coupled with the deterioration of the American work ethic. Second, ill-conceived governmental taxation and regulation policies have reinforced the inefficient utilization of present company resources and prevented reinvestment in modern plants and new equipment.

Although these factors present natural targets for criticism, are they the actual causes? Are we not confusing culprits and scapegoats? And most importantly, do these explanations truly reflect today's business realities? The evidence is clearly not reassuring. Even in the most labor-intensive industries, direct labor accounts for only 7 to 12 percent of the U.S. manufacturing sales dollar. Labor productivity in the U.S. private domestic economy has in fact increased at a higher rate than in the overall economy since 1967. And no empirical study has ever shown a clear, positive correlation between the vast, bureaucratic regulatory industry and a valid productivity yardstick.

In rationalizing the productivity decline, worker performance and governmental interference do not provide the real answers. And yet consider where the major focus has been as both practitioners and academicians have asked, "How do we go about developing an effective approach for improving productivity?" Although 70 percent of today's work force is employed in white-collar and service jobs, the manufacturing shop has received a disproportionate share of both blame and corrective effort.

LOOKING UNDER THE ICEBERG

Corporate attempts to address the "how to" questions are increasingly pervasive—and misplaced. Not enough has been done by those who primarily caused the problem and who should now be carrying the ball—management. After all, who is entrusted with the responsibility for overall corporate performance? Who is most influential in shaping a company's future? Obviously, the answer is management. Yet, non-management productivity has received the lion's share of attention. This is why a subject of such widely agreed upon importance has been so resistant to positive change in actual practice.

In all the furor over productivity, why has so little concern been directed at managers? There are at least three obstacles impeding proper analysis of—and improvement in—managerial productivity.

First, there is the definitional problem. The executive job is filled with so many elusively qualitative and intangible nuances that it is very difficult to isolate the key performance ingredients of an effective manager. Some firms, understandably, have been hesitant to face the challenge of improving productivity in the absence of a precise yardstick with which to measure individual performance.

A second obstacle to improving managerial productivity is the traditional emphasis on administrative skills and practical experience. The underlying rationale is that when managers gain sufficient competence and exposure in these areas, they will become more productive. The problem with applying this rationale to top management is that if high-level executives did not already possess these capabilities, they likely would not have been promoted in the first place.

The third bottleneck can be described as the "success syndrome." Most top managers run a challenging obstacle course as they progress through their careers. The odyssey from functional manager and division president to group executive and senior management is usually fraught with competition, high stress, and substantial personal sacrifice. Not unreasonable, these managers possess a high degree of confidence in their ability, and their lofty positions confirm the perception of each that "I must have been doing something right or I wouldn't be here now." This self-assurance, working in combination with the awe accorded American management worldwide, hardly fosters self-analysis or examination. In the late 1960s, a report entitled "The Technology Gap" focused on why America led Europe in industrial productivity. The answer lay not in a better labor force or more capital investment, but in the quality of top management. Today, the all-important question is: Could it be better? The answer, in my opinion, is an unqualified yes.

The Secretary of Commerce has offered some rather biting commentary on the state of American management. At first blush, this blanket indictment of the managerial fraternity (by one of their own) may seem a bit harsh and overdrawn. However, there is growing support for this appraisal:

- W. Edward Deming, a respected statistician, has concluded that 85 percent of all productivity problems relate to management and only 15 percent relate to worker performance;
- Donald Frey, Chairman of the Bell & Howell Company, delivered a similar message at the Chicago World Trade Conference when he focused upon the 80 percent of sales revenue that is related to areas directly controlled by management;
- Hideo Sugiura, an Executive Vice President of Honda Motor Company, stressed that both product quality and workers productivity primarily depend upon a company's management system. He minimized the overall impact that a multi-billion dollar investment would have upon America's future competitive position in the automotive industry.

It is becoming increasingly clear that historical successes and long-standing habits have caused too many American managers to utilize their resources indiscriminately. The following typical manifestations of this phenomenon are all too familiar:

- Management control systems (especially inventory) tend to establish uniform procedures, resulting inevitably in over-control of the high-volume, low-value items and under-control of the important items;
- The organization of marketing and field sales forces often results in equal coverage of regions, districts, and accounts—independent of profit potential;
- Most financial control systems produce a voluminous amount of computer printouts concerning operating data, but only a small percentage of it is really necessary to monitor performance accurately and take corrective action;
- Many purchasing and accounts payable departments generally devote the same degree of time and effort to performing their respective functions—regardless of time, cost, or dollar obligations. The fundamental truth that underlies these real-life examples is that significant improvement in management productivity is being severely inhibited by a misallocation of available resources.

In defining management productivity as the real leverage point, the accountability for correcting problems is unquestionably assigned. Our central need is not to fine tune an existing management system with cosmetic improvements, but to change both the management-worker relationship and overall company culture. It is a management system problem of significant magnitude. As more firms conclude that declining productivity is a management problem, the inevitable pressure for reversing this trend will intensify. In responding to the productivity challenge, many present company programs are experiencing turbulent weather and limited success. While reciting a litany of corporate errors has a definite "Monday-morning quarterback" flavor, there is a far more important issue. What are the practical lessons and guidelines for future success that can be gleaned from these pioneering experiences and false starts?

WHAT IS NEEDED

Reviewing the productivity efforts of many corporations leads the examiner to at least five ingredients that are required to help ensure a more effective response to the productivity challenge.

LONG-TERM MANAGEMENT COMMITMENT

All successful company efforts for improving productivity have one element in common. Significant progress occurs when top corporate executives are personally willing to become a major part of the process. The chief executive officer and his team must thoroughly understand the nature of the commitment required, recognize the impact on their policy decisions, be prepared to overcome the inevitable resistance, and provide the necessary leadership. One of the first American managers to respond positively to the productivity challenge was Rene McPherson, dean of Stanford University's Graduate School of Business, and previously chief executive officer of the Dana Corporation. His unwavering support for overall cost reduction and productivity improvement was a major factor in his company's doubling its productivity within seven years. This management commitment must be for the long term.

Because productivity has been presented as a "national disease," there has been the inevitable tendency to search for a "Jonas Salk Vaccine." Where is that instant panacea? Every book and article produces a new set of catchwords and -phrases. Most of them focus on a quick fix or short-term payoff. The present "holy grail" is quality circles or quality work-life programs. While no one can refute the basic premise and potentially positive benefits of this technique, the initial U.S. experience generally demonstrates a clear lack of appreciation for both strategic timing and practical introduction.

For example, following what has become almost mandatory practice (tours of Japanese businesses), many American managers in hundreds of U.S. companies are experimenting with quality-control circles. But consider the following fact—very few of the more than fifty large Japanese manufacturing firms in the U.S. have yet extensively employed this concept. What is the reason? Perhaps it is a recognition that the implementation of quality circles is not the first step but one of the last actions taken in building a company culture that will support a firm's total and ongoing commitment to high product quality and productivity.

The experience of a large U.S. diversified energy-products company with implementing a quality-of-work-life program in their operations function dramatically reinforces the need for long-term commitment. Following an initial diagnostic phase to define major potential areas for improvement in management-union relationships, work conditions, and communications, a series of actions was planned. Over 75 percent of the recommendations were implemented in the first two quarters and all improvements were completed within the fiscal year.

Operations management immediately began to assess the impact of these steps by monitoring grievances, absenteeism, and MRB actions. While the initial results were quite favorable, there was no significant change by the end of the year. It was a classic example of both the Western Electric effect and of the need for an ongoing commitment to improve the manager-worker culture. The important lesson is that productivity (like profitability) is unequivocally the end result of many management decisions and organizational actions. It is not realistic to expect meaningful correlation between any new wondrous technique and overall company productivity.

A more positive example of long-term commitment for productivity improvement has been Lear Siegler, Inc. For ten years, this diversified company in aerospace/electronics, material handling/machine tool, automotive service products, automotive/agricultural, and commercial products has included productivity as one of its six major corporate objectives. Their actual program has been frequently cited as a model in numerous national publications. Each of their forty-five operating divisions has a productivity coordinator, and corporate management provides leadership, motivation, and encouragement and closely monitors the progress of all divisional programs.

Because the American worker has seen so many cure-alls, every new fad is greeted with understandable skepticism. The lesson is clear. There is virtually no substitute for an exhaustive and painstaking analysis of a company's overall management system. This effort must be led by top management and become a long-term commitment.

SELECTING THE "PRODUCTIVITY CZAR"

It has become the announcement to appear most frequently in a newspaper's business section—XYZ Company announces the appointment of a Director of Productivity. What happens in many companies is that the wrong individual is selected for a highly critical and exceedingly difficult job. The undistinguished track record and reputation of the person frequently causes a lack of credibility concerning the company's real commitment and forces the individual into a highly ineffective role. Many productivity directors are relegated eventually to being "traveling salesmen." While their efforts to sell productivity are commendable, they often have little or no effect.

The false starts of many companies suggest that the person must be highly respected, possess a proven track record, and have the unqualified support of the chief executive officer. It is not a job for the "weak hitter who is being kicked upstairs." Two companies that have successfully "matched the horses and courses" have been Tenneco and Boise Cascade. In both examples, the CEOs carefully selected experienced, senior executives to direct their eventually successful corporate productivity efforts.

COMMUNICATING THE NEED

A third factor in the demise of many embryonic productivity efforts is an overall employee perception that "this is just another company program" or a glorified suggestion box. What is really in question is the survival and competitiveness of some U.S. companies. The task of managing future growth with a potential scarcity of capital, raw materials, and energy sources coupled with an adversary management-union relationship is a formidable challenge. There must be the recognition that most large American firms are operating now in a business environment very different from that of the 1960s and 1970s. Competition in this decade and in the future is clearly on a worldwide scale and more intense than ever before. How can this really be successfully communicated? And what is an effective approach for introducing the overall productivity effort and implementing substantive improvement in a company's management system?

A large diversified corporation in the aerospace, engineering construction, and chemical business provides an excellent example. In responding to a real problem of ever-increasing managerial workloads, the chief executive officer chartered each operating division to improve its management productivity and specific patterns of resource allocation.

A top management off-site was conducted by the chief executive officer and his staff to introduce the basic concept, positive benefits, and need for practical implementation. Initial questions and doubts by the presidents of each company were brought into the open where they could be examined and answered. Genuine two-way communication was established between the corporate office and operating managements. Once the operating presidents understood the concept and need for reorienting their own thinking, they conducted similar sessions with their management teams. Functional heads then performed identical exercises with their managerial personnel.

Orientation of all affected company personnel was then undertaken because the eventual success of the project required a total commitment, from senior management to the first-line supervisors. An eclectic view was adopted toward the educational process, and a multidimensional program was established for every manager. The particular communications mix for each operating company was tailor-made, based upon considerations of cost, available time, number of managers to be oriented, depth of understanding required, background of key management personnel, and status of the management concept within each company. An important part of the project was a series of action items that were to be completed by all functional and departmental managers. Actual orientation programs included presentations by qualified corporate staff personnel, recommended in-house implementation guidelines, and iterative review sessions at each management level to help achieve necessary consensus.

The eventual success of this project generates a very clear lesson. Communicating the need for a meaningful response to the productivity challenge is a critical task. The same logical methodology that is indigenous to Procter & Gamble's product development process, IBM's market research on specific industry needs, successful performance of a large aerospace program, or General Electric's overall management system must be harnessed. Anything less will relegate the productivity effort to the back burner and limited success. It will be viewed with no more urgency and importance than the annual United Way Campaign or Savings Bond Drive.

NEED FOR A UNIFYING MANAGEMENT SYSTEM

It has become standard practice for newly appointed productivity directors in large multidivisional companies to spend their first months (if not year) traveling across the country and overseas to learn about present or contemplated divisional productivity programs. These directors usually encounter strong resistance to implementing a common methodological or corporate-sponsored approach because each division wants to develop a program most suited to its unique operations and industry. However, directors also (understandably) question why strategic business-planning systems can be established on a corporate-wide basis, but there cannot be a comparable management system at the operational level. It is a fact that many companies have recently begun to do a much better job of allocating resources on a business segment or macro basis; this is underscored by the plethora of strategic business-planning systems being implemented. The evidence is less satisfactory at the micro level—the resources available to individual managers and their organizational entities.

Even the more historically popular and heavily publicized planning systems, such as zero-based budgeting, which requires an overall reexamination and justification of the need for resources, still focus on the actual level of resources. They do not emphasize the strategic positioning or mix. Because the critical area of management productivity has not received the necessary emphasis, an abundance of either self-serving or ineffectual programs has often proliferated with very little positive impact.

What is clearly required is an overall philosophy and management system to help ensure a more rational and disciplined methodology for allocating managerial resources at the operational level. Strategic resource management is a proven and practical methodology for focusing management's attention and resources on the true results-producing activities. It is a natural complement to, and reinforcement of, a company's existing or contemplated strategic business-planning system. It also provides an overall umbrella for a firm's total productivity effort. If managerial resources are going to be allocated in a more strategic manner, the following action items should be implemented:

Defining Basic Mission. Although the fundamental question, "What business are we in?" is usually addressed at the strategic planning level, it has equal relevance for specific departments or functions. There must be a well-conceived and effectively communicated mission statement for every organizational entity. For example, a marketing function in an industrial products company contained both cost/pricing and contracts-administration capabilities. Although their supposed mission was the generation of profitable sales volume and future business opportunities, the actual character performed was both marketing and quasi-financial. A redefinition of basic mission and organizational reassignment of all non-marketing activities to the finance department eventually resolved a problem of resource dilution and unsatisfactory performance.

Determining Actual Contribution. A common error in most productivity efforts is the confusion of activity with accomplishment. The individual in preliminary design is frequently mistaken for being non-productive because he spends long periods of time in reflection. What is not appreciated is that this exercise often produces the best major breakthrough in new product design. The designer is contrasted with the staff assistant who is seen dashing around the plant, conducting studies, and requesting data from line management. The fact that the company is retrenching and that this individual is performing a multitude of make-work assignments to justify his own existence is lost on most observers. For resources to be allocated cost-effectively, there must be the determination of actual functional output. Without this step, there is not an objective baseline for validating present resource commitments or assessing future improvements. The well-publicized success of Intel Corporation in reducing cost by work simplification clearly refutes the notion that administrative output is not quantifiable.

Specifying Key Results-Producing Activities. Based upon the definition of basic mission and determination of actual output, all management personnel must identify their key activities. What really creates effective performance? What is high impact? High value? Specific criteria may include such variables as dollar impact, schedule performance, quality, historical experience, perceived results of a significant error, and common sense. The purpose of this effort is to delineate those activities that are critical to the successful performance of a specific department or function, and those that are less important.

Achieving Managerial Consensus. Agreement among all levels of management must be obtained to ensure a clear understanding of what is important and what is not. Unless an employee really knows what is critical to his boss and agrees with those priorities, it is difficult to refocus and shift resources in a timely and effective manner. Both management and their subordinates must understand and perform well those few critical activities that truly get results.

Comparing Historical Resource Mix. Operating budgets provide a key indicator for examining the level and mix of previous managerial resource allocations. Who has received the financial support, highly skilled manpower, managerial concern, and other resources? This assessment usually reveals a significant mismatch, with the few results-producing activities being undernourished and the remaining areas over-resourced.

Making Strategic Reallocations. Given the preceding steps, the appropriate modifications in resource mix should be made. Effective implementation requires structural, financial, and manpower changes. This action is not an exercise in window dressing but requires a major commitment to matching the best resources with the most important tasks. A parallel reduction in specific resources for the less important activities should also be implemented. This usually includes fewer or less skilled personnel, simplified procedures, streamlined systems, elimination of some tasks, and organizational restructuring.

Defining Expected Results and Acceptable Level of Risk. Agreement concerning desired performance targets in both the high-impact and low-impact areas should then be obtained. An important corollary of this overall process is agreement among all levels of management to accept a certain degree of risk concerning unsatisfactory performance in the less important areas. As one executive remarked, "If you want to achieve significant improvement in management productivity, you have to be willing to accept some shortfall in the non-critical areas without overreacting. This requires strong discipline or you revert to over-controlling the less important areas. A periodic audit of the low-value activities is the appropriate management tool in terms of both effectiveness and effort to minimize an out-of-scope situation.

Establishing Management Follow-Up. Finally, there has to be an ongoing effort at all levels of management to help ensure that this philosophy becomes a way of life. Although the basic concept is simple and easily understood, the implementation phase is more difficult because changes have to be achieved in long-established managerial habits and operational tendencies.

The successful implementation of strategic resource management provides four significant benefits:

- Meaningful and realistic short-term cost reduction opportunities,
- Increased management attention on true results-producing activities,

- Generation of additional discretionary resources for potential reinvestment, and
- Rational allocation of these resources to those few critical activities that are most important to effective functional performance.

The lesson is clear. Managers will truly raise their productivity only when their overall resources are strategically allocated and operationally positioned upon those tasks that produce both short- and long-term results.

BECOMING MORE PEOPLE ORIENTED

Although strategic-resources management is a proven concept for increasing management productivity and operational effectiveness, it must be complemented by a comparable commitment in the area of human-resources management. Too many companies have paid lip service to the critical and long-overdue need for improving the management process of its human resources.

A successful management response to the productivity challenge requires the basic recognition that people decisions—policies, promotions, pay, placement, development, and communications—are critical in the motivation of a company's work force. These actions are the "line-of-sight" that signals to all employees what management really wants, rewards, and values.

What is really required is a major commitment changing the way companies manage their employees, which may seem highly threatening to some present U.S. management personnel. However, the indisputable point is that there is substantial empirical evidence that successful and well-managed U.S. companies have either been people-oriented as a way of life for some time or are rapidly changing their management systems. A professional and enlightened approach to a company's human resources is no longer a luxury. Competitive pressures and socioeconomic forces have made it a necessity.

In converting the phrase—"more people-oriented"—from a desirable public relations slogan to an actual way of life, the following management-action items are required:

- Creation of appropriate organizational structures to ensure a more participative management environment (working and executive committees),
- Encouragement of self-managed work teams or problem-solving groups (quality circles),
- Timely validation of the salary structure,
- Significant improvement in the performance-appraisal system,
- Design of an effective management development program,
- Increased employee orientation and training programs,

- Generation of more management-subordinate teamwork through increased communication,
- Establishment of target employee improvement plans,
- Strengthening of the merit review process, and
- Evaluation/implementation of an employee gain-sharing systems.

There is comfort and apparent security in staying with a company's existing management system and always some risk in trying to change. But most U.S. managements no longer have the luxury of security. The "window of American business superiority" is already closing (if not temporarily shut) in the key industries of textiles, consumer electronics, steel, and autos. Because the competitive situation and overall business environment have so dramatically changed, responding to the productivity challenge must become management's most critical priority.

The challenge will require top-level commitment, long-term focus, new management concepts, and significant change in company cultures. The task will not be easy because there are no simple, quick answers and because the U.S. business community has a well-documented history of not responding to long-term challenges or problems. However, the fundamental issue of survival may prompt many previously complacent management teams to address and solve some very real problems in their present management systems.

Carlton P. McNamara is president of McNamara & Company, Inc., a Los Angeles-based consulting firm whose services include a specialization in management productivity.

17.
MISCONCEPTIONS ABOUT MANAGERIAL PRODUCTIVITY

Karl E. Weick

Too much emphasis has been placed on improving productivity through managerial thinking, analyzing and planning, and not enough has been placed on managerial action.

People have always wondered how to improve productivity. And people have always suggested lots of ways it can be done.   One of the more intriguing suggestions was made in 1818 by Karl Van Clausewitz, director of the General War Academy in Germany. Clausewitz said that there are four kinds of people, defined by combinations of two characteristics: energy and brightness.

First, there are the energetic and dull people. They should be driven out of any organization as soon as possible because they can do great harm.

Second, there are the lazy and dull people. You can take your time getting them out. They will not do much harm.

Third, there are the energetic and bright people. They should be staff personnel because they enjoy working and are smart enough to do it.

And fourth, there are the lazy and bright people, who should be executives because they are smart enough to know what to do and yet lazy enough to not want to do it.[1]

So Clausewitz's suggestion for improving productivity boils down to this: If you have dull people get rid of them. Get rid of them quickly if they have energy, slowly if they don't. Keep your bright people. If they have energy, put them in staff positions; if they don't, make them executives. Said another way, if you want productivity, worry more about how bright people are than about how energetic they are.

Managers seem to have taken this suggestion seriously, if some of their favorite mottos are any indication. Just listen to these six pieces of advice, all of which put the emphasis on thinking and planning:

- Think before you act;
- Look before you leap;
- Plan your actions;

- Keep it simple;
- Seeing is believing;
- Make good decisions.

What I want to suggest is that this kind of advice can actually reduce productivity. Each of the six maxims can backfire and provoke the very problems they are supposed to help you avoid because they put too much emphasis on thinking, too little emphasis on action. They give too much importance to being bright, too little importance to being energetic. I will illustrate this assertion by looking at three things managers do: analyze, plan, decide.

MANAGERIAL ANALYSIS

Many managers assume that analysis is a good thing and should always precede action. This assumption is captured in such phrases as "Think before you act" and "Look before you leap." Let's examine those assumptions more closely.

The best medical diagnosticians do *not* follow the sequence: observe symptoms, make diagnosis, prescribe treatment. Instead they follow the sequence: observe symptoms, prescribe treatment, make diagnosis. They can diagnose the disease they are treating only *after* they see how it responds to treatment, not before. That lesson has been lost on managers, who diagnose everything before they act. Rather than trust more action and less data, they ask for more data in the hope that sooner or later, everything will become clear. It never does.

Managers who act and watch closely to see what they have done understand their current situation more fully and are better able to take advantage of unexpected opportunities. The ones who are in trouble are the people who try to think everything through before taking any action. They are working with incomplete data because they don't know the details that they can discover only by moving about and doing things to see what response they get. People who act this way are sometimes criticized for being reactive and not taking enough initiative.

It's important to realize that there is nothing wrong with being a reactive manager. Being reactive provides a larger number of successes and failures, which makes you more adaptable and provides more occasions to learn. There's nothing wrong with responding to every straw in the wind. When you do this you remain extraordinarily current on what is actually going on. Many of the things you respond to will prove to be nothing but a flash in the pan. But some will not, and that's the point. Reactive managers play percentages and they do so by acting, not by trying to figure out what the pattern is in basically random activities.

Managers who act as if everything in their in-basket is important and contains an opportunity actually create a world that contains more of the opportunities that they presumed were there. Taking your in-basket seriously often creates opportunities that no one, including the sender, knew existed.

Thus, reactive managers, with a wonderful twist of irony, actually *create* a world that is more to their liking and more suited to their talents. By taking more items in the in-basket seriously, they set in motion activities that, in reality, change the next issue they get. The reactive manager, through continued responsiveness, gradually transforms himself or herself into a proactive manager who gets out ahead of the in-basket and controls what shows up in it.

I'm not at all surprised that managers are talking more about hands-on management. I read this as a growing realization that managers should get closer to the things they're analyzing so they understand them better. The more they are prevented from walking around the problem and seeing it for themselves, the more they are given models of it or abstractions of it or numerical symbols for it, the less well do they understand it and the more shaky their judgment is as a result. Their judgment is shaky, not so much because the problem is so large or so complex, but because managers are being forced to comprehend it in ways that distort what they see. The actual problem is broken up into numbers and ratios that represent it in cryptic fashion. When the problem is simplified this way, managers are not sure what the problem is. These doubts shake their confidence and they rely more on the opinions of others than they ought to; they trust the numbers more than they ought to; and they accept the "obvious" implications of the numbers more quickly than they ought to. All of this happens because managers forget that thinking occurs in the context of action. When they forget that, when they think without acting, they operate on a distorted view of the world and compound, rather than solve, their problems.

MANAGERIAL PLANNING

Analysis is often done in order to develop long-range plans under the assumption that planning is a good thing. Let's look at the manager as a planner to see how that assumption holds up.

Planning isn't nearly as crucial for productive action as people think it is. I can illustrate this point most clearly by recounting an incident that happened to a small Hungarian detachment on military maneuvers in the Alps. Their young lieutenant sent a reconnaissance unit out into the icy wilderness just as it began to snow. It snowed for two days, and the unit did not return. The lieutenant feared that he had dispatched his people to their deaths, but the third day the unit came back. Where had they been? How had they made their way? Yes, they said, we considered ourselves lost and waited for the end, but then one of us found a map in his pocket. That calmed us down. We pitched camp, lasted out the snowstorm, and with the map we found our bearings. And here we are. The lieutenant took a good look at this map and discovered to his astonishment that it was *not* a map of the Alps, but the Pyrenees.

Apparently, when you're lost, any old map will give you the confidence to go on. By extension, when you're confused about productivity, any old plan will do.

Plans are like maps. They animate people. And this is the most crucial thing they do. When people actually do things, they generate concrete outcomes that help them discover what is occurring, what needs to be explained, and what should be done next. Plans, even when they are wrong, are useful because they serve as a pretext to start acting. What managers keep forgetting is that it is the action, *not* the plan, that explains their success. They keep giving credit to the wrong thing—the plan—and, having made this error, spend more time planning so that they'll have more good outcomes. They are astonished when more planning improves nothing.

The basic point is, you can't make sense of any situation until you have something tangible to interpret. That something is the outcome of action. Consider the formula, "How can I know what I think until I see what I say?" The world of a manager is senseless until that person says something, until that person produces some action that can be inspected. People examine what they say, and only after they do this can they know for sure what they thought about a situation.

Too much planning can stifle action, but too much planning can also stifle seeing. When managers say, "Seeing is believing; I'll believe it when I see it," that is cause for alarm, not joy. The problem is, planners see much less than they realize. The best example of this error is Three Mile Island.

The operators at Three Mile Island had been trained to deal with design-based accidents (such as, if this pipe fails, reroute the coolant along this pathway). These problems had been seen before in simpler coal-based technologies, and people thought they could happen again, so they planned for them. What they did not believe in, did not plan for, and were not prepared to see, were simultaneous multiple failures, escalation of effects, and positive feedbacks that occur in more complex nuclear-based technologies. They weren't prepared to see synergism or to control it.

The key lesson of Three Mile Island for planners is found in the phrase, "Believing is seeing; I'll see when I believe it." People didn't see what was happening at Three Mile Island because their beliefs weren't complicated enough to comprehend the escalation that was occurring. An even more sobering thought is that it's doubtful humans can ever comprehend the ways in which effects can spread and amplify in elaborate, tightly coupled systems.

I want to emphasize that the issue here is not specific to the nuclear industry. Volcanic clouds, Social Security entitlements, infant nutrition, restarting the 1981 baseball season, psychological depression, and other matters can all have effects that are disproportionately large compared to the size of the starting conditions. Synergism is common in acquisitions, mergers, interlocking directorates, centralization, computer information systems; all can be viewed as building more elaborate, tightly coupled systems that are more complicated than anyone can comprehend. Our problem with productivity is *not* the Japanese. Our problem is that we are laying ourselves open to more Three Mile Islands. We are putting productivity beyond our control by lodging it in tightly coupled events that can escalate.

There are only two basic ways that a manager can deal with events that can escalate. The first is to become more complicated as a person, so that more of the complications in the events will be seen. The second is to make the events themselves less complicated by making their components more independent of one another.

People can gain some control over complex events if they complicate themselves so their personal complexity informs the events that occur outside them. When complicated people examine complicated events, there is a better chance that they will understand more of what is going on. This understanding, in turn, gives the person a heightened sense of control. It is not so much that they actually control the events, but rather that the events seem more manageable and people feel there is something they could do if they needed to.

The importance of this sense of control can be seen in a series of stress experiments. In these experiments, people were exposed to continuous, very loud aversive noise, which consisted of two people speaking Spanish, one person speaking Armenian, a mimeograph machine, a desk calculator, and a typewriter. While listening to this urban mayhem, these people did proofreading and worked on difficult problems. Half of the people were provided with a button that would enable them to shut off the noise, but they were encouraged to use it only if the noise became too much to bear. The remaining people had no such panic button. Those who had the button solved five times more problems and made significantly fewer proofreading errors than did the people who had no button. The amazing thing is that people who had the button *never once used it.* The mere knowledge that they could exert control if they wanted to was sufficient to reduce the effects of the stressful surroundings.

Complicated people often see options and explanations that the rest of us miss. We think there is no way out because we don't see much of the situation nor do we see how many skills we actually have to manage the situation. All of this information, which is more available to complicated people, helps them understand what is occurring. And that understanding acts like a panic button because it suggests both what they need to accept because it can't be changed and what they need to attack because it can be changed.

The second way to gain control over complex systems is to simplify them. The best way to simplify a system is to disconnect its parts so they don't affect each other.

A system with fewer interdependent events is a simpler system. It is easier to comprehend, easier to control. Things start and stop and that's it. The effects don't spread or amplify; they simply occur and people move on to something else.

A current trend in industry (for example, at 3M) toward smaller size units, more autonomy, more decentralization, and more self-determination creates simpler units that are easier to comprehend. At the other end of the spectrum is the equally popular movement toward computer systems where everyone is connected to everyone else by a terminal. Everyone can check up on everyone, and usually does. Furthermore, everyone is tempted to meddle and give unsolicited advice, which removes discretion.

The only way to handle this is to turn off the computer. That breaks a link. That decouples the system. That turns a tightly coupled system into a loosely coupled system. This method of regaining control actually is fairly common. It's precisely what the astronauts did in the Apollo 13 mission when they staged what some regard as the first strike in outer space on December 27, 1973. Mission control had been sending more and more directions, corrections, and orders to the astronauts; finally, Commander Gerald Carr said, "You have given us too much to do. We're not going to do a thing until you get your act in better order." He then shut off the computer for twelve hours, and the astronauts spent the rest of their day catching up and looking out the window to enjoy the spectacular views they had missed.

They regained control over their circumstances. And they reduced stress. They did so partly by complicating themselves—an astronaut who both disobeys and obeys mission control is a more complicated individual than one who merely obeys. They regained control, also, by simplifying their system—they cut off one whole set of demands.

The lessons of Three Mile Island and Apollo 13 allow us to make more specific the general argument that action has been slighted in favor of analysis in prescriptions about productivity. Productivity is improved not just by any old action. Two kinds of action are crucial. First, actions that complicate beliefs are important because, with more complicated beliefs, people see more when they observe complicated events. Second, actions that simplify events are important because they reduce the complexity of what people have to comprehend and manage.

MAKING DECISIONS

So far we've looked at the manager as analyst and planner, and now we consider the possibility that if managers want to be more productive, they need to make better decisions. To make better decisions, they have to be more reflective. That line of argument has serious problems.

Decisions are not so much episodes where managers convene to choose an action as they are small actions, such as writing a memo or answering an inquiry, that gradually foreclose alternatives. The decision is made without anyone realizing it or doing it. Thus the crucial activities for decision making are not prior, distinct episodes of analysis. Instead, they are actions that consolidate fragments of policy that are lying around, give those fragments direction, and close off other possible arrangements. The decision making *is* the memo writing, *is* the editing of reports. These actions are not preparations for decision making, they *are* the decision making.

It has been our mistake to assume that the quality of earlier decisions affects the quality of subsequent actions. That's not the place to look for an explanation of high-quality actions, because those decisions were never in place while the action was unfolding.

We have to look elsewhere than in the quality of the decision to understand high-quality actions and outcomes. We have to look at such things as willingness to improvise on the spot, the degree to which thinking is incorporated into the action itself rather than done apart from acting, the degree to which people act and pay close attention to the effects of their action, the extent to which people listen nondefensively to the feedback they get, their willingness to persist in what they are doing and to have several irons in the fire at the same time, and their willingness to tolerate a world in which they'll know what they've decided only after the event is finished and it's too late.

I don't think energetic, dull people are quite the problem Clausewitz thought they were back in 1818. Nor do I think that lazy, bright people are quite the solution that Clausewitz thought they were. I value being energetic more highly than Clausewitz valued it and I'm a bit more suspicious of brightness than Clausewitz was.

Being energetic is more important because analyses, plans, and decisions all turn out to be crucial largely because they animate managers to do things, which can then be examined in order to get a clearer notion of current opportunities. Being energetic not only gives you concrete data to inspect, but also imposes some order on events that otherwise unfold in a random manner.

Being bright is less important for productive action because people have limited ability to comprehend the escalating, tightly coupled systems they have created. Furthermore, people are not sufficiently bright to reconstruct actual systems based on abstract representations of them. To diagnose the reasons for low productivity, people need to have more detailed knowledge of what is actually going on than abstractions can provide.

If managers have only numerical data, they are unable to apply intuitive, nonlogical processes to it and they are also unable to reconstruct more detailed images of why problems might have occurred. As a result, they often conclude that they simply haven't tried hard enough, so they exert more effort. Numbers tempt analysts to conclude that they need to do more of the same, with more vigor. If they have been cutting costs, and the numbers still look bad, then they simply haven't been aggressive enough and they need to cut even more. The mystique of numbers lends itself to this more-of-the-same mentality. It does this because people who examine the numbers are unable to reconstruct the actual events that produce those numbers. The only way to get more accurate representations is to use different sets of numbers, first-hand observation, and intuition.

Becoming brighter may not help this process along nearly as much as becoming more active.

The warrant for this assertion is found in the debate between Richard Neustadt and Dean Acheson concerning whether presidents should be warned or given support when they are about to undertake controversial lines of action. Neustadt argued that presidents should be warned of the dangers and possible backlash that could occur from controversial decisions, whereas Acheson argued that presidents should be given support so that they take firm action that produces consequences.

"In a world of great complexity and poorly developed knowledge, it is inherently easier to develop negative arguments than to advance constructive ones. Uncertainty naturally allies with doubt, hesitation, delay. Fully warned presidents are likely to vacillate under counteracting pressures; their governments are likely to act incoherently. This, too, has its dangers, for there are some situations in which commitments must be established early, some for which the intrinsic problem is the *timely* discovery and resolute pursuit of larger purposes lying beyond immediate interests. In these situations the attempt to preserve options beyond the point where events will allow it can destroy the more attractive alternatives and can deliver the decision maker, whether individual or government, over to the control of a process he did not design, cannot direct. Some of the most serious issues generated by modern societies— including especially the handling of nuclear weapons—cannot be effectively addressed if serious action must await the outbreak of a crisis to become compelling. Precisely because the world is complex, there is need for men of vision, imagination, boldness, and dedication to give the nation concepts of its interests and theories of action when these are far from clear. These are the leaders, the confidence givers, and without them surely no government could manger very well."[2]

Or, more succinctly, "In order to act wisely, it is not enough to be wise."

Karl E. Weick is Nicholas H. Noyes professor of organizational behavior and professor of psychology at Cornell University.

18.
TEN WAYS TO MISMANAGE TECHNOLOGY

Therese R. Welter

> What goes on in corporate research labs may seem mysterious and un-
> approachable to all but the technologist. But if companies don't apply
> management principles to their technology, much of their R&D invest-
> ment may be wasted.

No company is immune to mistakes in handling new technologies. Companies ranging from Exxon to Cullinet Software have made their share. In fact,
the entire auto and computer industries have gone astray in this regard. Yet
successful R&D can pave the way along roads that would seem to be golden.
Unfortunately, the number of organizations that don't successfully reap their
R&D investments is surprisingly high.

In 1986, American companies spent $59.5 billion on research and develop-
ment. This year it's predicted that the figure will reach $63.8 billion. For an
individual manufacturer, this can represent anything from 2 percent to 12
percent of sales, says Donald Fiske, president, and Joseph Garber, investment
principal, A. T. Kearney Technology Inc., management consultants specializing in technology issues.

But in reviewing some 100 cases of technology problems across all industry
segments, the Kearney executives have found that the errors made have little
to do with technological sophistication. "In our experience we assessed that
one or more of ten fundamental errors lay at the heart of two-thirds of these
technologically troubled situations. [And] not one of these ten errors was a
technology problem," Mr. Fiske and Mr. Garber observe.

What else could they be? They were, in a word, all *management* problems.

And the Kearney executives have come up with a list of the ten most
common errors in managing technology.

1. INATTENTION TO THE MARKET

Too often, the failure to review the market at every step in a technology
project leads to disappointing market results. First of all, "you have to front-

end any product or technological development with a rigorous and structured piece of market research," says Mr. Garber. And it must not be designed to give you only the results that you want.

From time to time, he says, a company will develop very sharp, credible market criteria at the onset of a project. And this might prove, for example, that a product cannot be sold for more than $25. But as the project evolves, it becomes clear that it cannot be brought to market at that price, and so the price is raised to $27.

By the time it comes to market the product, it's three or four times the forecast price, says Mr. Garber, and no single person sinned; they just allowed themselves to drift away from the intelligence they'd gathered.

More generally, an organization must structure itself to bring the market into plans and programs so that they are market-driven rather than engineering-driven, notes Mr. Fiske. "Yet there's a mind-set in many companies—even if they think of themselves as being market-driven—to think more about what their customers *should* do as opposed to what their customer *will* do," Mr. Garber adds.

Management must also regularly reassess market assumptions. Despite the rosy forecasts of Atari and others, for example, the 1984-85 business slump in Silicon Valley was due, at least in part, to the downturn in the consumer market as the excitement of videogames wore off, they say.

"The consumer market is short-lived and faddish," says Mr. Garber. "Videogames were kind of electronic Hula-Hoops. They certainly didn't have the kind of sustaining value that warranted adding major production lines. Yet the folks who were pumping out silicon just didn't want to listen to the bearers of bad news."

2. IMPATIENCE

Allowing the "when" of a project to become more important than its "what" is a common but perilous management mistake, says Mr. Fiske and Mr. Garber. New-product or process development should be high on the list of issues about which top management should be most concerned. And corporate leadership must check and double-check that what is being done is being done *correctly*.

"Some business unit manager maybe gets to stand in front of the executive committee once a year for 15 minutes," says Mr. Garber. "And in the course of that 15 minutes he may say, 'We plan to have this product in the marketplace by this time next year.' When he returns to his division and the schedule starts to slip, he suddenly feels a lot of exposure, and he begins to think that maybe management will be happier if *something* happens even if it's not so good."

Instead of rushing to meet delivery dates or other constraints, while ignoring problems with the product, management should do as Ford did in delaying the Taurus and Sable, says Mr. Fiske. "Management actually delayed the delivery and sales of those cars even though it cost them a lot of money," he says. "But management said, 'We haven't got it right and we're not going to introduce them until they're right.'"

3. TOO MUCH, TOO LATE

On the other hand, there is sometimes the problem of a "passion for perfection," which can produce refinements to a product that go beyond anything the customer needs or even perceives. Since many technologies have windows of opportunity, a company that is putting too much into a product can easily miss its market.

"About a year and a half ago," says Mr. Garber, "I was working with a small technology start-up that had a superb local-area network product. It was clear to me that the product in its present state at that time solved 80 percent of the problems that its target customers had. But the technologist in charge wanted to spend another 18 months and something on the order of $5 million to solve the remaining 20 percent.

"That was madness," Mr. Garber claims. The company could have released its product in its imperfect form to solve most customers' needs, thereby making money for the additional R&D it needed to bring out a later version to solve the rest of the customers' needs.

Researchers sometimes feel personally challenged to bring a product out in its perfect state. But standards of excellence that the customer doesn't care about should not be pursued. "If it's not an important issue for the marketplace, and the product in its current form will satisfy the customers' needs, then don't tinker with it," says Mr. Garber.

4. THE WRONG TEAM

Typically, at least in Silicon Valley, say the Kearney executives, a group of very smart engineers is involved in new-product or process development. Though the group expertise is certainly crucial to planning, so are the requirements and limitations of other corporate functions that will be involved in delivering a new product—such as finance, marketing, manufacturing, and information systems.

Traditionally, new projects have moved sequentially through departments in the corporation. But the development of a new technology affects the operation of these other functions in unpredictable ways when they are not privy to the planning-and-development process. "So now we're saying it should be done in a parallel combination," say Mr. Fiske and Mr. Garber.

Any new project should be structured around a team of equals, with the team members speaking for the technology functions, as well as for marketing, manufacturing, financial, and so forth. This ensures that when a new product is launched, it is supported and understood on a corporate basis.

5. THE MANAGEMENT EXPECTATION GAP

The chief technologist of a [large] company once put this issue in perspective by telling us, "The bright young MBA who wrote our company's strategic plan expects R&D to violate several fundamental laws of physics this year," says Mr. Garber and Mr. Fiske.

Every manager has his own perspective, stemming from education, experience, and personality. And since no executive can represent both the business and the technical disciplines, it takes skill to bridge them. "The best executives recognize that it is their job to do so," says Mr. Fiske. That way, strategists and technologists are communicating their missions to each other.

Good executives also have an intuition for the market and can see the business as a whole. "[They] can look at a raw technology sitting in the prototype stage with the chewing gum and baling wire in a lab, and can see it translated into a product producing revenues in a marketplace," says Mr. Garber. "And equally important, they can see the steps that the new technology has to be taken through to get it out of the lab and into the factory, and then into the marketplace."

6. TOO MANY EGGS

In eagerness or because of a mistaken sense of synergy, a corporation may try to do too many things at once, thereby fragmenting its resources. In this case, "the corporate nest holds too many eggs," says Mr. Fiske and Mr. Garber. "A few hatch, [but] those that do are stunted and undernourished."

Back in the late '70s, Exxon illustrated this problem, says Mr. Garber. Because of "the 'windfall' results of its oil business, it found itself sitting on a ton of cash. Somebody in the corporate suite decided it was time to invest in non-oil, and Exxon became enamored with information technology. So it invested in a very large number of these things . . . and sat there waiting for the billions to roll in. Well, a year or two passed and the billions did not roll in."

When pursuing alternative technologies, a very clear distinction should be made when a company is entering a new arena, warns Mr. Garber. "Doing one thing very well is a lot better than doing a bunch of things—some well, some not well, or all of them fair," he says. "Once you develop scale and presence and capability in a market, then you can begin pursuing multiple opportunities. If Exxon had singled out the one or two good assets in its new portfolio, and worked on them, there might be something meaningful there today."

7. NOT INVENTED HERE

It's no secret that Japanese companies excel in seeking out alternatives to their own internal R&D. But "only a few American corporations have learned to do this well," say Mr. Fiske and Mr. Garber.

"What you sometimes see is an R&D department leader looking at a new project and saying, "My goodness, this is going to increase my responsibility, my staff . . . and my research facilities," says Mr. Garber. "If you then say, 'these things can be bought down the street' you've threatened that person."

"Too often, the R&D leader or the corporate development leader looks at internal development as a reflection on himself—that his R&D ought to be able to produce all technology." says Mr. Fiske. "He may say, 'Well, I've got a lab here and I've got to sustain it, and we can do anything here, so why should I go outside?'"

But management must weigh alternatives to internal development. The willingness to look to multiple sources for your technology development is important. Joint ventures, licensing, research organizations, and acquiring key technologies can be valuable options to reduce misspending on R&D.

8. TECHNOLOGICAL NOSTALGIA

Just as a person who dwells on the past may fail so see the promise of change, so do companies that hang onto old technologies or obsolete products.

"A technology whose time is up should be put to rest mercifully," say Mr. Fiske and Mr. Garber. "Milking a key technology to a lingering, painful decline weakens the entire corporate enterprise. Investing in improvements to products and processes destined for obsolescence pays poor dividends."

Mr. Garber cites Cullinet Software as an example. About ten years ago, when IBM announced the Standard Query Language (SQL) for accessing relational databases, Cullinet didn't move as aggressively as other database software companies in adopting the new architecture and SQL. Consequently, "they've really taken it on the chin in that market," he says. "They are in the position of playing catch-up now, for not having recognized that there was something new and different on the horizon."

This is quite common, says Mr. Fiske. Most organizations have gone through this at one time or another. "The auto industry and the computer industry have gone through it—when an innovator comes up with a new development, and the older organization misses the market while trying to maintain the present technology to extend its life."

9. READY, FIRE, AIM

This error occurs when a company launches into a new business without the necessary understanding of its technological foundation. Therefore, it is particularly prevalent among corporations that are diversifying. (Thus, Exxon is another good example of this.)

Just because a person is a good general manager doesn't mean he can manage *anything* and everything, notes Mr. Fiske. "A lot of management is based on strong intuition and a great deal of experience," he says. "And a lot of times [these are] not transferable. Different technologies have different drivers, different people, and different motivations. That's why many acquisitions just haven't worked—because management didn't understand the foundation of what they were acquiring."

As corporate strategies change, the proper talent must be in place to set and implement new courses. "It's not state of the art to decouple planning from implementation," says Mr. Garber. "You no longer have the excuse of saying, 'Hey, it was a great idea but the guys who implemented it messed up.' The person who does the planning and sets the direction has to have his feet held to the fire for doing the implementation."

A good way to test whether you *are* aiming before firing is to play devil's advocate, he says. "Early on in any new project, discipline yourself and your team to try to prove that the whole new idea is worthless and shouldn't be done—and listen objectively. This will do a lot to buffer you against the risk of a new development."

10. THE FRANKENSTEIN SYNDROME

Like Frankenstein's monster, a major technology project can turn into an enormous beast with a life of its own, which then becomes difficult to destroy, if necessary.

When the original parameters no longer fit your project and people are spending their time rationalizing why they no longer fit, a new technology is turning into a monster, says Mr. Garber. To avoid this, management should make frequent and informed checks on the technology, the budget, the timetable, the staff, and the dynamics of the marketplace.

An example of such a project was the RCA analog video compact disc, say the Kearney executives. "It made a heck of a lot of sense when it was originally thought out," says Mr. Garber. "But by the time RCA got ready to launch it, the world had changed profoundly with the takeoff of videocassette rental, which wasn't a major force when RCA did its preliminary research. So RCA was no longer in the position of charging $25 to compete with a $50 videotape. Now it was competing with a $2-$3 videocassette rental. But [RCA management] had so much momentum behind the technology that, even though they had the facts, they were reluctant to kill it."

It's painful to end a large project that has a long history behind it and hundreds of people, millions of dollars, and a lot of hope and aspiration tied to it. "But it's better to destroy a misaimed project than it is to let it out in the marketplace," says Mr. Garber. With the latter, "you're not talking about hundreds of people having their jobs on the line, but thousands; you're not talking about millions of dollars at risk, but hundreds of millions; and you're not talking about a small embarrassment, you're talking about front-page news."

19.
INCREASED PRODUCTIVITY
THROUGH EFFECTIVE MEETINGS

William L. Williams
Elaine Biech
Malcolm P. Clark

Ineffective meetings are a major source of lost productivity. Typical comments about meetings are "too many," "wrong people attending," "start late/do not end on time" and "hidden agendas." This article provides a training program designed to increase productivity through more effective meetings.

"The meeting has been cancelled!" Who hasn't breathed a sigh of relief at these welcome words and once again thought, "If I just didn't need to waste so much time in meetings!"

How much time *is* spent in meetings? Is it really wasted? "More than 11 million meetings are held each day in the United States."[1] "An executive spends 21 [hours] of a 40-hour work week in meetings, and over one-third [of the meetings], or six-weeks' worth of each executive's meeting year, are considered unnecessary by the people attending them."[2] We often complain but passively accept whatever comes our way. We accept the meeting climate our organization has inflicted upon its members. Lists in business magazines rank poor meetings as leading time wasters.

A framework for action to tackle this culprit was developed and implemented by a major federal research center as part of a plan to increase overall productivity. The plan draws from experiences in both the private and the public sectors and is readily transferable to most organizations.

BACKGROUND

The site of this project is the NASA Langley Research Center, established in 1917 as this country's first federal aeronautical laboratory. Currently it employs approximately 2,800 permanent civil-service employees and 1,650 support-service contractors. Almost one-half of the in-house employees are professional engineers and scientists.

While the Center was working to formalize its productivity improvement program, the Productivity Officer visited each division office to identify the most significant productivity issues. The myriad of daily meetings surfaced as a recurring theme. Interviewees were not interested in eliminating meetings, but rather in focusing on ways to improve specific aspects of the meetings and to increase their efficiency. Typical comments about meetings were "too many," "wrong people attending," "start late/do not end on time," "hidden agenda," and "a perception that if you are not having numerous meetings, you are not managing."

As a result of this perception, a detailed examination of the Center's meeting environment became a high priority. How do you capture existing practices and offer methods and procedures that will enhance their effectiveness? Would top management endorse an investment of time and dollars to address the problem? Where do you find the talents of an outside resource to help spearhead the effort? Who should attend any specialized training? These were just a few of the questions that surfaced.

Perhaps there were other organizations that had tackled this issue. A contact provided by the American Productivity Management Association (APMA) proved invaluable. A well-known U.S. producer of home-care products had recently completed a study on this topic. The management consultant who coordinated the study (and who also coauthored this article) was contacted. It was agreed that common threads of practice ran through the public-sector organization that could be tied to her private-sector experience.

Further, it was agreed that an organizational-development-systems approach would be used.[3]. A thorough needs analysis would identify the disparities between what is and what should be. This information would be used to determine the key changes that were necessary. The implementation phase would include designing a training program and materials, gaining top management support, and conducting the training for about 500 employees. The evaluation, which still continues, showed that the program has been successful.

NEEDS-ANALYSIS PHASE

After becoming familiar with the Center, the consultant analyzed needs by administering two different questions (see Figures 1 and 2). The questionnaires were designed to accommodate the collection of both objective data that could be measured and compared at a later date and subjective comments that would help to personalize the program's design and delivery. The questionnaires' design recognized the fact that individuals are both meeting leaders and participants. They were designed to cover activities that occur before, during, and after the meeting.

Figure 1
Questionnaire sent to participants in the training program
asks for opinions about meetings they attend.

MEETINGS I ATTEND

These statements address the meetings in which *you* are a *participant*. Please respond to them by checking the column that depicts the percent of time each occurs.

Prior to meetings I attend, I:

	0-20%	21-40%	41-60%	61-80%	81-100%
Am informed of my pre-meeting responsibilities	___	___	___	___	___
Receive an agenda	___	___	___	___	___
Am informed of the meeting objectives	___	___	___	___	___
Am informed of the time-line for the meeting	___	___	___	___	___
Feel my inclusion is appropriate	___	___	___	___	___

Comments:

The meetings I attend:

Start on time	___	___	___	___	___
Address most important agenda items first	___	___	___	___	___
Follow the established time-line	___	___	___	___	___
Remain focused on appropriate subject matter	___	___	___	___	___
Provide discussion of both sides of issues	___	___	___	___	___
Result in commitment to action	___	___	___	___	___
Accomplish planned objectives	___	___	___	___	___
End on time	___	___	___	___	___

Meetings I attend are productive when . . .

The percentage of meetings I attend which I consider to be productive is ___%.
I become frustrated with meetings when . . .

Following meetings I attend, I:

Receive a follow-up report	___	___	___	___	___
Receive appropriate meeting follow up	___	___	___	___	___

Additional comments regarding meetings you attend:

Figure 2.
Similar questionnaire asks for opinions about meetings
conducted by the participants.

MEETINGS I CONDUCT					

These statements address the meetings which *you conduct.* Please respond to them by checking the column that represents the percentage of time each occurs.

	0-20%	21-40%	41-60%	61-80%	81-100%
Prior to conducting meetings, I:					
Assign pre-meeting responsibilities	___	___	___	___	___
Send an agenda	___	___	___	___	___
Set observable, measurable objectives	___	___	___	___	___
Set a beginning and an ending time	___	___	___	___	___
Carefully choose who should attend	___	___	___	___	___

Comments:

When conducting meetings, I:					
Start on time	___	___	___	___	___
Address the most important agenda issues first	___	___	___	___	___
Follow the established time frame	___	___	___	___	___
Keep members focused on appropriate subject matter	___	___	___	___	___
Insure both sides of issues are discussed	___	___	___	___	___
Obtain commitment to action	___	___	___	___	___
Accomplish my objectives	___	___	___	___	___
End on time	___	___	___	___	___

Meeting I conduct are productive when . . .

The percentage of meetings I conduct which I consider to be productive is ____%.

I become frustrated with meetings when . . .

Following meetings I conduct, I:					
Distribute follow-up reports listing expected action	___	___	___	___	___
Follow up on unfinished business	___	___	___	___	___
Track progress of post-meeting responsibilities	___	___	___	___	___

Information I would like to receive to assist me in conducting more productive meetings includes:

The questionnaires were distributed to the Senior Staff Managers, each Directorate Head, every Division Chief, and a small sample of Branch Heads. One questionnaire focused on meetings that were attended by the individual; the other focused on meetings that were conducted by the individual. Ninety sets of the questionnaires were distributed and 78 were completed and returned. The 87 percent return rate indicated more than just a casual interest in the topic.

Several observations from the survey are worth citing. For "Meetings I Attend," a summary question asks the respondent to assess what percent are effective. The average of the 78 replies was 62 percent. Such a score on a report card would earn a grade of "D." On the responses from "Meetings I Conduct," that same summary question received an average rating of 75 percent or a "C." Even though the managers were generous in scoring their own efforts, those same meetings earned a lower grade from the attendees. The survey clearly revealed that considerable room for improvement existed, whatever the yardstick applied.

Each questionnaire provided space for written comments. About two-thirds of the 78 mangers took additional time to provide some personal observations. Some typical comments:

Meetings I Attend:

> One person rated meetings as 25 percent effective and commented, "Most are a waste of time." "What we need are less meetings, 90 percent are totally un-necessary," stated another, who rated meetings as 40 percent effective. "I seldom attend meetings which are not useful," comments the person who rated meeting effectiveness at 85 percent. "Frustrated when they have no clear focus or turn out to have no real relevance to work in my organization," was cited by one who said meetings were 60 percent effective.

Meetings I Conduct:

> "Would like information on how to reduce personal friction," one manager com-mented while rating meetings 80 percent effective. "People come late and not prepared," states another respondent, citing meetings as 80 percent effective. "Presented with problems I cannot solve," reported one manager who rates meetings 75 percent effective.

SURVEY TO EVALUATE ACTUAL TIME SPENT IN MEETINGS

A written questionnaire cannot provide all the information necessary for the effective design of a program. It is helpful to support the questionnaire with other sources of data if possible. The Center Director provided permission to review calendars of ten senior managers, including his own. The review was conducted to see how many hours in a two-week period each manager spent in meetings. The preview revealed that managers spent an average of 35 percent of their time in meetings. The figure was lower than was anticipated since most studies of managers at this level (no one below a Division Chief) showed at least a 50 percent involvement in meetings. The fact that the data were gathered from calendars could contribute to the conservative estimate. Unplanned emergency or spontaneous meetings may have occurred that were never recorded.

Together, the questionnaires and the calendar reviews provided a solid foundation to build upon. The comments expressed to the Productivity Officer during the Division Office visits were reinforced. The needs-analysis process often has a secondary benefit: it generates support, enthusiasm, and anticipation for the program.

THE PROGRAM DESIGN

The data and comments gathered from the needs analysis and the calendar review, plus the consultant's experience, led to the design of a slide presentation and preliminary participants' materials tailored to meet the Center's needs.

Several objectives established parameters for the program. The content and teaching methodology had to reflect the climate of the Center, maintain what was presently working, improve what wasn't, and introduce new ideas that were compatible with both. A topic like meeting skills can be sensitive, since it seems so basic. The fact is, however, that even through most people can cite any number of "good meeting practices," they don't practice them. The organization's meeting climate dictates what actually occurs. Therefore, if meetings always start late, most meetings' participants will arrive late.

The training was designed to accommodate as many learning styles as possible: lectures were short and accompanied by slides; group activities involved observation, experimentation, practical application, and idea generation.

• The program included a variety of activities: Self-assessment, a meeting quiz to determine what people know about meetings, agenda evaluation, meeting simulation, brainstorming ways to manage problem participants, discussion of obstacles to productive meetings, critical incidents, and practice in writing meeting objectives.
• The program encouraged a transfer of learning back to the workplace: a simple agenda/follow-up report system was developed; job aids (such as the meeting preparation guide) were provided; meeting evaluation forms were to be used after the training session to measure progress; and participants wrote memos to themselves (mailed back one month later) and to their supervisors about changes they were going to make in their meeting behavior.

- The program was personalized for the participants and the Center: lectures and participants manuals were punctuated with statistics and comments gathered during the needs analysis; ample opportunity for sharing of personal views, ideas, and expertise was built into the design; real-life problems were incorporated; and an action plan at the end of the session allowed personal goal setting.

TRAINING MATERIALS

The training materials were designed to address not only what occurs during the meeting, but also the activities that are necessary prior to a meeting to ensure organization and those activities that must take place after a meeting to guarantee that action will occur. Three items were produced: a Participant's Manual, a slide presentation, and a Trainer's Guide.

The Participant's Manual is an 8 1/2 x 11-inch booklet that is used in several ways. First, it includes a format for taking notes during the slide presentation or other discussion. The left half of the page identifies key concepts and the right half is blank for note taking. Second, activity pages are included with room to practice new skills or to list ideas. Third, samples and examples are provided. Fourth, job aids are a part of the booklet. Some are designed to be torn from the book for easier use. Fifth, the booklet is meant to be used as a resource after the training session. In addition to the examples and job aids, pages of information, checklists, processes, and time-saving tips are also included.

The Participant's Manual is sprinkled with cartoons, graphics, and sketches to add eye appeal. Funny but pertinent quotations are sprinkled throughout, such as the Murphy's Law that states. "Those who have the shortest distance to travel to the meeting will usually arrive late."

High-quality slides provided a mixture of people-in-action shots and concept/information slides. The slides were shot in a studio setting rather than on-site to save time and cost. The objective was to provide a visually stimulating training tool to accompany the lectures. The slides are graphically appealing and help to clarify the message.

The Trainer's Guide includes instruction pages for each activity, text of the lectures, masters of the participants' material, and special trainer materials. The instruction pages include the materials and equipment needed, the amount of time, the lead-in statement, step-by-step instructions, and comments that address possible changes and cautions for the facilitator. The lectures are typed on one-half the page so the facilitator can add personal examples or note changes.

The special trainer materials include masters of all auxiliary material, such as special handouts, the roles for the meeting simulation, and the action plan. Also included are such trainer aids as a pre-workshop preparation list that identifies everything that must be done from two weeks before the training session to one month after it.

The training program was dubbed "Gold Nuggets and Gravel." This theme expresses the belief that the network of meetings was pumping a lot of gravel through the system and the attendees would have to sift through that gravel in order to find a gold nugget from time to time.

PILOT CONDUCTED TO TEST DESIGN

A pilot training session was conducted to test the preliminary design, obtain organization input, and generate other ideas. A one-day session was attended by a representative mix of supervisors and managers from each Center directorate. The training staff who would conduct the program were also a part of the session led by the consultant.

The first of the pilot session was to have the supervisors, managers, and training staff participate in the training session as it was designed and to use the preliminary participant materials.

Following this, the participants were asked to critique the activities and materials and to suggest options to increase the effectiveness of the training program. For example, a key portion of the training pivoted around a meeting simulation exercise. A topic for the meeting needed to be identified that would be as real as possible. In addition, roles needed to be refined that would represent typical problem roles that most often existed at the Center. It was also agreed the length of the session needed to be adapted to fit the schedule at the Center. These and other suggestions were used by the consultant to modify the program.

The third step of the pilot session was to generate other ideas related to the meeting's topic. Small groups brainstormed areas such as meeting time-saving tips (hold stand-up meetings), creating program attention (newsletter articles), ways improved meetings can increase productivity (train those in the highest management levels), incentives for change (traveling trophy), and tools needed to encourage change (train the secretaries).

One of the most innovative ideas came out of this last step. Each supervisor would receive a copy of a Supervisor's Handbook with numerous examples and situations contributed by the operating supervisors who helped create the material. A secondary benefit of the pilot session occurred when the participants became advocates for more effective meetings within their respective directorates.

The pilot session was successful, and the next step was to secure approval from the Center Director to begin training.

BRIEFING FOR THE DIRECTORS

A two-hour overview was given to the Director, Deputy Director, and each Directorate Head by the consultant and the Productivity Officer. The purpose of the session was to provide the following:

- A summary of the needs-analysis data
- An overview of the program
- Insights into the attitude toward meetings at the Center
- An opportunity to discuss needs, changes, support, and endorsement
- A timetable for the future of the program.

A recommendation that all local supervisors attend a training session scheduled for each directorate was approved. Eighteen sessions were conducted by the Training Branch. The importance of the program was underlined when each of the Directorate Heads made a point to participate in the training with their subordinate supervisors.

TRAINING

Training for the trainers who would conduct the sessions gave them an opportunity to ask questions, to try out activities, to become more familiar with the features and benefits of the Trainer's Guide, to understand the objectives of each activity, to gain some tips for presenting the information or conducting the activities, to acquaint themselves with the slides and the Participant's Manuals, and to gain confidence before beginning the training schedule.

Approximately 340 of the Center's 375 supervisors attended the training sessions. One of the participants stated that the Center has a large number of technical specialists, contract monitors, and functional experts, who are not supervisors but who conduct many meetings. He felt they would also profit from such training. To meet this need, a session was advertised and offered for non-supervisors, and 120 attended. This session was also videotaped and is available for those who missed the training or who have just recently become supervisors.

The scheduling and follow-up activities are important segments of meetings that are often the secretaries' responsibility. A special session was given to all the directorate and division-level secretaries at the Center to ensure that these key personnel were program participants.

ASSESSMENT OF THE IMPACT OF THE TRAINING

About six months after the last training was conducted, a request went out to each division for comments on the benefits of the program and the problems yet to be addressed. The comments received are shown in figure 3. In general, these comments showed that the program has increased the productivity of meetings significantly. The principles and concepts that were cited included adopting a specific meeting format, preparing an agenda, establishing time-lines, obtaining commitment to action, and tracking follow-up progress. In

---

Figure 3.
Sample responses after participants have completed
the training course in productive meetings.

Six months later, the Productivity Officer sent out a follow-up request to all divisions asking for their responses concerning the impact of the effective meeting training. A review of these responses provides the following typical observations:

Structures Research Division Chief: "The most apparent impact of the subject training is the adoption by the Division Office of the proposed meeting format. Recent meetings conducted at external sites went well as awareness of the subject training led me to datafax to the participants an agenda, responsible persons, and anticipated action items."

Assistant Division Chief, Central Computing Facility: "I have asked each Branch Head to provide follow-up comments about the training course, their comments are enclosed."

"I believe this seminar was helpful in planning better meetings through the preparation of an agenda and your helpful hints for sticking with the agenda and time limits. I have personally found this useful."

"The course was effective in that it raised the matter of conducting meetings to a higher level of attention among managers.

"I think the training course heightened my awareness of the time wasted in many meetings. Most of our meetings do have an agenda and a general guideline for the length of the meeting. I think the course was a good one and have no recommendation for other items which should be covered."

Structures Research Specialist: "I have been able to reduce the number of meetings by approximately 50 percent."

Electronics Research Division Chief: "I believed the training increased my awareness, the techniques needed to accomplish where reinforced."

Management Operations Division chief: "One change I made to the Division weekly staff meeting was to eliminate the automatic weekly staff meeting . . . in the past we have sometimes held the meeting even though there was little or no information to discuss with the employees."

---

many cases productivity was increased by eliminating unnecessary meetings: a simple principle, but one often ignored.

FUTURE ACTIVITIES

Several additional activities are planned at the Center to keep attention focused on the program:

a. The role of Center support contractors, approximately 1,650 total, is increasingly emphasized. Offering the training to contractor supervisors is envisioned.
b. Each year the Center selects approximately 30 new supervisors to replace turnover or to fill newly created positions. Offering the training to each of the new supervisors is being considered.
c. Each conference room at the Center may have a plaque mounted in a prominent place like this:

> Effective Meetings
>
> • Prepare agendas
> • Start/end on time
> • Stay on track
> • End on a positive note
> • Assign action items.

CONCLUSIONS

Evaluations after each training program, follow-up evaluations, and general enthusiasm and support indicate that the program met the goal to increase productivity through more effective meetings. We believe that the success was a result of using an approach that was grounded in sound organizational development theory and that applied the conditions for successful change efforts.[3,4]

In discussions of this program with people from many organizations—public and private sectors, profit and nonprofit, large companies and small, manufacturing plants and service providers—all indicate that problems are similar and that what is needed is a plan for initiating a program and maintaining support for it. Perhaps if meetings become more effective, employees will be less joyous and even disappointed when they hear the words, "The meeting has been cancelled!"

REFERENCES

1. Michael Doyle and David Straus, *How to Make Meetings Work* (New York: Berkely Publishing Group, 1976): 4.
2. Robert Half, "This Meeting Will Come to Order," *Time,* December 16, 1985: 50.
3. Karl Albrecht, *Organizational Development* (Englewood Cliffs, NJ: Prentice Hall, Inc., 1982): 135-38.

4. Richard Beckhard, *Organizational Development: Strategies and Models* (Reading, MA: Addison-Wesley Publishing Company, 1979): 96.

William L. Williams is productivity officer, NASA Langley Research Center. Elaine Biech is president and managing principal of Ebb Associates, Portage, Wisconsin. Malcolm P. Clark is head of the Employee Development Branch, NASA Langley Research Center, Hampton, Virginia.

20.

MANAGERIAL PRODUCTIVITY: WHO IS FAT AND WHAT IS LEAN?

Leonard R. Sayles

> Efforts to increase productivity need to focus more on managerial work. Many organizations have been careless in creating additional hierarchical levels without having the means to measure managerial productivity. Managers create work—they can be very busy while their contribution to organizational effectiveness is minimal, even negative.

The latest recession finally brought top management attention to managerial productivity. In fact, this is a major problem that has been ignored for decades. Its sources are several.

- Managers (and professionals, staff, and technical personnel) create work—for themselves and others. They can be very busy and their contribution to organizational effectiveness minimal, even negative.
- It has always been easier to assume that anonymous workers can be unproductive, but managers, almost by definition, do everything they can to further the interests of the firm. Yet, as I have argued so frequently, managerial output is far more difficult to measure than worker output.[1]
- Most organizations have been careless in creating additional hierarchical levels. The costs are enormous in slower decisions, frustrating on the part of motivated employees seeking a decision, and supporting this "fat around the middle."
- Management control systems and appraisals ignore the most important responsibility of a supervisor, regularizing work flows, and therefore work flows don't get regularized.

JOB ELABORATIONS; MAKE-WORK FOR EXECUTIVES

As I have explored in various field studies, the typical description for a manager allows the creation of activities which call for additional effort and staff and which may not contribute to the objectives of the firm.[1]

For example, a department may be created to improve the cost effectiveness

173

of data-processing services (DPS) in response to growing management uneasiness over the rate of increase of automation costs. Over time the new DPS department can shift from analysis and recommendations (a traditional staff advisory task) to periodic review of a variety of technology decisions in data-processing units as well as operating units needing those services. These audits can absorb a great deal of time both of the new unit and the departments being appraised. Beyond this it would not be unusual to have DPS request that they be allowed to sign off on a variety of decisions that affect data processing and even to be part of committees and task forces created to make new computer technology choices. Increasingly, redundancies would grow between the computer professional in line departments and DPS, and these would produce conflicts that would require more DPS time and personnel. More experts would be brought in, and the departments being served (read threatened) would have to add additional personnel to hold their own against the encroachments of DPS's specialists.

It is not difficult to conceive of the exponential growth in managerial time (surely not performance, however) devoted to the activity being created by an elaborating DPS unit. To make matters worse, the coordination problems created by new specializations like DPS frequently result in still new specialists being added to solve the cooperation difficulties created by the original unnecessary increased specialization.

SPECIALIZATION AT WORK

In fact, growing specialization in management is perhaps the most important source of productivity problems. Rarely is systematic attention given to the total cost of adding any new specialist or specialized unit. Yet each new unit creates the need for many coordination activities, which drain managerial time of existing departments and can create the need for more staff, more managers, and then still more coordination problems.

POORLY DESIGNED REWARD SYSTEMS

The kind of positive feedback loop just described also occurs when reward systems ignore coordination and stress compartmentalized specialization.

For example, a publishing company had a books division and a magazines division that facilitated each work other's work—particularly in the flow of ideas from well-received magazine articles to acquisition editors in books. As management began stressing small-group profitability, the flow of ideas and assistance dried up. To restore lines of communication, a liaison office was created. It, in turn, explored what each department could do for the other. To help its work, it requested certain reports from both books and magazines, which added to those workloads. In fact, the liaison office was needless, as was its growing staff, since historically books and magazines had been eager to share ideas and provide mutual assistance. But top management effectively discouraged this cooperation and then sought to recreate it in a structurally expensive fashion. It would not be hard to imagine the added workload created by formalizing liaison leading to the addition of liaison specialists in books, and so forth.

HIERARCHIES TEND TO GROW TALLER

Levels multiply in organizations for many reasons; whatever the reason, the impact on costs is negative. Many organizations have managers with one subordinate because at some point it was important to create a promotion for someone. Or because of poor coordination, basically due to ineptly structured work, a given manager can't handle all the interventions required by the faulty work flow. The unit is broken into two parts to provide closer managerial attention. When this occurs in many places, the number of managers increases to the point where a new level is necessary to maintain reasonable spans of control.

The more useful response is to analyze the work flow and assess the sources of the disturbances requiring managerial intervention. With smoother, more consistent work flows, less managerial attention is required, and the number of managers can be reduced; eventually the number of levels can also be reduced.

Many companies have discovered that just by simplifying approval systems (who must be consulted, sign off and approve budget changes, purchase orders, design modifications, and so forth), the total quantity of managerial time gets reduced, and fewer managers and fewer levels result.[2] In the bargain, a great deal of managerial time formerly devoted to dealing with the problems created by slow, multilevel approval seeking can now be devoted to more productive work.

THE NEED FOR SELF-MAINTAINING WORK FLOW SYSTEMS

The real test of middle- and lower-level managers is the degree of regularity, predictability or routinization of the work flows under their direction. Few, if any, formal or informal appraisal systems consider this key criterion. Short-run organizational performance is directly a product of the regularity of work flows. When managers identify breakdowns or interruptions in the flow, it is their primary responsibility to seek human or technological "fixes" to improve coordination. The ideal is each individual in the flow responding to and complementing the work of those preceding and succeeding them in a self-maintaining system. When the manager has to intervene or when special expediting procedures or staff intervention is required, that is the signal that some greater managerial initiative is needed to solve a structural problem (in contrast to fruitless administrative procedures).

Ideally, this is what should occur. In a financial-services organization, a data-processing supervisor realizes that every other Thursday is very stressful. Almost all her efforts must be devoted to expediting data processing required by accounting. When the bottleneck appears to be reports coming in late from another department, the supervisor negotiates an agreement with that feeder department to send one of her people over to help accumulate the data in exchange for assurances that it will be sent on Tuesday not Wednesday. Also, some of the data will arrive in semi-processed form; with only a slight change in one of the programs, it can be run as is. The result is the elimination of a significant deviation in the work flow.

Rather than modify the division of labor continually, most managers simply introduce more procedures and people and pressures to assure that their work gets done. Such remedies increase overhead. The managers are working hard but fruitlessly because the underlying work flow is less productive, and they are wasting their own and staff time.

There is no way to increase managerial productivity without measuring the capacity of managers to increase the self-maintaining character and routinization of their work flows. This is the heart of managerial responsibility. Control systems need to measure deviations from regularized, self-maintaining systems in exactly an analogous fashion to the statistical measure of quality. Managers who must intervene constantly to maintain the system are incurring double cost: their time and the cost of the interruptions itself.

COPING WITH UNANTICIPATED TECHNICAL PROBLEMS

Of course these are work flows that cannot be regularized; new product development is a good example. Any new product or service will be plagued with a wide and unpredictable variety of start-up problems. It is easy to forget how many such bugs have been eliminated over the years in existing products: the ideal material begins to deteriorate with heat; two parts, given the slightest variation in dimension, interfere with each other, a particular fabrication process that worked perfectly with a similar product will not consistently produce acceptable quality in the new product.

What is important to management is not the ability to predict these problems; many can't or won't be predicted, no matter how well planned the change process or how careful the testing. Rather, what is critical is the managerial response to the problem. Two typical reactions are fatal to the long-run success of a new venture and waste time and injure managerial productivity by misdirecting managerial attention. They are polar opposites: assigning blame and glossing over problems.

The first fatal reaction is to presume blame and to seek the culprit. The temptation to find a scapegoat is strong when an unforeseen problem is delaying delivery of an initial order for a new product or service, raising cost way above estimation and threatening the very reputation of the fledgling venture's performance. The venture management or established corporate management may panic, fearful that optimistic projected targets of sales or costs aren't being met, and seek to place blame and punish those who have made a mistake. A number of deleterious consequences follow from this "management by autopsy."[3]

Fearing retribution and seeking to avoid prosecution, each individual or unit seeks to prove its work or plan is not the source of the problem. "If everyone else had done as they should have, the problem wouldn't have occurred," is the party line. Further, everyone knows that agreeing to change one of their specifications or procedures will be equivalent to admitting guilt. Thus, just when there should be some looseness in the organization and everyone should be trying to cooperate in making the whole project work, each is defending his own turf. The number of committee and task force meetings will be huge.

Ideally, this is what should occur: A new extruder is not producing the finish that was anticipated. However, if the next process in line can add one additional step to their work procedure, that level of finishing can be achieved. However, that extra step will increase labor costs, require a change in their budgeted allowances, and, at the outset, it will slow their output. This will create some problems for the sales staff seeking rapid installation in the first customer's premises. A whole series of trade-offs involving compromises and adjustments among several units and consultants with the customer must take place with the final plan reflecting the larger interests of the project and not the special and local interests of any of the participants.

This type of rolling adjustment and change in specifications is a constant in new-product development, but it won't take place when the participants fear that concessions will be held against them or are an admission of guilt. Such concessions are discouraged whenever management presumes that no such problems will arise if there is careful planning in the first place and that, if they do, someone goofed in the original designs and ought to be penalized: a ritual bloodletting.

Alternatively, in their haste to get early sales and installations, new-product managers seek to ignore or gloss over early difficulties. Often they rationalize that every new product is defective and that difficulties can be solved by retrofitting either on the customer's premises or at the end of the line. Such tactics discourage early customers, demoralize staff, and accustom the entire new venture to less-than-perfect quality and poor standards. The start-up period is crucial for identifying flaws in materials, methods, or the design itself, and if not solved at that stage, they will haunt and possible destroy the credibility of the new venture at a later stage.

Ideally, this is what should occur: I witnessed how NASA handled the development of a new satellite. After a failure occurred, every manufacturing stage and component was examined. Through meticulous record keeping and analysis, the agency was able to determine that the component that had failed had been assembled in a specific location during the afternoon of a particular day when a truck had been parked near a duct leading to a clean room. The truck's exhaust had produced particles that interfered with the performance of a finely turned electronic part. As a result of the investigation, the air-circulation system was improved and no vehicles were allowed near the building.

Thus, successful new-venture management involves being sensitive to and being able to track down every unanticipated problem but without seeking to punish culprits or to rush through faulty products.

THE BOTTOM LINE

There is no simple way to spot a fat organization: hard-working managers (unlike workers) may be unproductive or, worse, by making nonwork for everybody else. What is required are detailed work-flow assessments and studies of what given managers do with their time. Such analysis enables the organization to identify empire-building job elaborations, and imperfections in technology and reward systems that are creating needless demands for management time. As it is most management job descriptions are next to worthless for checking whether a manager is doing constructive or destructive work.

The organization keeps adding staff on the presumption that unresolved problems or new problems require another specialist. Little attention is paid to the real future cost of that specialist as the activity becomes embedded in the organization and the specialist moves from being an aide or advisor to being a check and a control.

To control the multiplication of managers, organizations need to be built from the bottom up, from the careful design of work flows to the addition of staff only to facilitate flows.[4]

REFERENCES

1. Sayles, Leonard, *Leadership* (New York: McGraw-Hill, 1979).
2. Sayles, Leonard, *The Complete Book of Practical Productivity* (New York: Boardroom Books, 1983).
3. Burgelman, Robert and Sayles, Leonard, *Inside Corporate Innovation* (New York: Free Press, forthcoming).
4. Chapple, Eliot, and Sayles, Leonard, *The Measure of Management* (New York: Macmillan, 1961).

21.
THE MANAGEMENT CLUB: A QUALITY CIRCLE FOR MANAGERS

Jan P. Muczyk
Robert E. Hasings

Many authorities argue that poor management is at the heart of the productivity problem. Since traditional means of improving management seem to be falling short of their goal, the authors propose the establishment of voluntary management clubs whose members would explore solutions to their company's specific problems.

Declining productivity is a major problem in the United States. The grave implications of this unfortunate trend have been recognized by most people, and fingers have been pointed at numerous culprits: inadequate capital investment due to counterproductive taxation policy and inadequate savings rate; insufficient expenditures or research and development; overregulation by the federal government; decline of the work ethic; growth of union power; additions to the work force (more younger workers, women, and minorities); the evolution from a manufacturing to a service economy; a short-run orientation; increasing crime rate (especially by employees); alcohol and drug abuse; and a number of lesser villains—such as the changing family structure.

A cause that is not mentioned in this list may, however, be the most important one—poor management. It is our considered opinion that poor management is not only the most important reason for the decline in productivity, but also underlies the other contributing factors enumerated above.

Fortunately, American management recognizes that it is the principal cause of the productivity decline. In a survey conducted by *Productivity*, a monthly newsletter, about 80 percent of the top managers at 21 concerns cite "poor management" as the key reason for lackluster productivity. A third of the managers responding to this survey say that their organization has put an executive in charge of productivity improvement.[1] In another survey, 236 top-level executives representing a cross-section of 159 U.S. industrial companies conceded that management ineffectiveness is by far the single greatest cause of declining productivity in the United States.[2] Although recognizing a problem and appointing someone to correct it are favorable signs, productivity can only be increased through the practice of good management by supervisors, managers, and executives at all levels of the organization.

EXISTING STRATEGIES AND THEIR LIMITATIONS

Organizations employ numerous strategies for developing supervisors, managers, executives, and staff personnel. They have tuition-reimbursement plans for a variety of degree programs, and send people to seminars, symposia, and colloquia. They employ consultants and in-house training staffs to assist in management development. They encourage organizational members to join and participate in professional organizations and they create in-house libraries that house books, monographs, and journals relating to the state of the managerial art. Some organizations, such as the big eight accounting firms, have training units and centers which provide comprehensive course offerings, and require the employees to go through the courses in a prescribed sequence. Yet, poor management practices continue to plague many, if not most, organizations.

The traditional strategies suffer from a number of limitations. First, not all employees avail themselves of the development opportunities that the employer provides. One can argue that the persons who need management development the most are the ones who use the traditional strategies the least. Second, much of what employees are exposed to in degree programs, seminars, conferences, and management development programs offered by consultants and in-house trainers is either unrelated or marginally related to their immediate and near-term job needs. Therefore, the employees are not motivated to invest more effort, and they go through the learning experience as passive participants. Third, a significant amount of material presented in degree programs, by consultants, and in seminars is so general and abstract that the necessary transference of what is presented to the job never takes place. Fourth, new ways of doing things are seldom encouraged and reinforced on the job because frequently the superiors are not exposed to the same learning process. All too often management development consultants are viewed in the same manner as the common cold: Just wait a while and they (and their proposed new methods) will go away.

It is generally conceded that colleges of business administration do a good job of training staff specialists or technicians, but are seriously deficient when it comes to producing effective managers. It is no coincidence that foreign students in U.S. colleges of business administration concentrate in technical areas such as finance, accounting and operations research, and eschew management. Consequently, the burden of training good managers falls on the employer. The challenge is especially important because never before has the United States been confronted by a superior managerial technology, as is the case with the Japanese system of management. Historically, the advantage in this arena has been ours.

THE MANAGEMENT CLUB APPROACH

A management club is a voluntary organization created by employees interested in improving their managerial skills. The members meet regularly, typically once a month, for the purpose of exploring some facet of management that is of interest to all or many of the members. Everyone from first-level supervisors to top executives is eligible to join. The discussion leader could be a knowledgeable person from the organization or an expert from outside the organization.

The management club is not a novel idea, of course, and as with all management development approaches, its success depends on how well it is implemented. However, valuable lessons can be gleaned from the clubs that are operated successfully.

IMPLEMENTATION PRINCIPLES

Some firms have management clubs that are restricted to senior executives and invite distinguished persons to speak on a variety of social, economic, and political issues. That, however, is not the kind of management club that we have in mind. Although there is no one way to establish the type of club that we are recommending, adhering to certain principles should increase the likelihood of success.

Voluntarism. We know of no way to force people to learn unless they are motivated to do so. Individuals who are forced to join will merely go through the motions and begrudge the time that is devoted to the management club. Thus, membership in a management club must be voluntary.

Motivation. This can be accomplished by involving top executives and addressing issues that are perceived by organizational members as being relevant to their work and career progress. Lower-order participants will commit their time and energy to an undertaking if executives and their immediate superiors are actively involved with issues that are central to the day-to-day administration of the organization. Initiating a management club is a delicate matter. It is most convenient for the top executives to do so, but if they take the lead, the club could be perceived by lower-order participants as a top-management forum. The initiative should come from other members of the organization with the encouragement and facilitation of top management.

Ownership. All members of the management club should have an opportunity to nominate topics for the management club agenda. If executives or club officers monopolize the agenda, the sense of ownership on the part of everyone else will be diminished. Consequently, an instrument, such as a monthly survey, should be created to identify the issues that are foremost in the minds of club members. Executives should also take turns suggesting issues that are important, affect the entire organization, and haven't been suggested by others. In fact, the chief executive officer can use the management club as the appropriate vehicle for disseminating the corporate philosophy that provides general direction to the organization. A discussion of the importance of a corporate philosophy can be found in Ouchi's provocative and topical book, *Theory Z*.[3]

The agenda for each working session of the management club could be selected by a program committee, which could also solicit agenda topics from organizational units that are not participating.

Shared Investment. Club meetings should be held partly on company time and partly on employee time. This arrangement is suggested to discourage those who would attend simply to avoid work. Meetings should take place once a month. The financial burden of the club should be borne by the organization. If club members wish, the working sessions of approximately three hours could be followed by an optional dinner or a cocktail hour. This would permit an opportunity to continue informal discussions regarding the topic covered during the working session, and facilitate social interactions between persons from different levels of the organization and different departments.

Decentralization. For a management club to achieve its potential, size must be considered. If the club is permitted to become too large, it will become unwieldly. A multiplant firm should encourage the formation of a management club for each plant. The medium-sized and small organization probably can benefit the most from the management club concept.

Follow-up. Needless to say, some of the critical issues raised during a working session of the management club cannot be resolved during one, or even several sessions. Therefore, follow-up is essential to translate talk into action. Otherwise, discussion will simply raise expectations, which, in turn, can cause considerable frustration and dissatisfaction if they are unfulfilled.

A number of follow-up strategies can be pursued. Task forces or committees could be created to implement new policies, procedures, methods, practices, or whatever else is needed. These task forces or committees are not creatures of the management club. They must be constituted officially by managers in the formal hierarchy who possess requisite authority, and they should be chaired by respected individuals. The task forces of committees should be provided with the necessary resources to complete the task and should operate under realistic time tables. Finally, they should be accountable to the managers who created them and expected to finish their tasks on time.

When in-house expertise is lacking, consultants could be retrained to facilitate the discovery of solutions or to assist with the implementation of a solution emanating from the management club. It may very well turn out that consultants will be better received when they are brought in to assist organizational members with a significant need that the members identified rather than at the apparent whim to top management.

We are not recommending that changes be initiated in every instance through task forces, committees, or consultants. The management club should not be used as an opportunity for retaining consultants to address most or even many of the issues that surface during the management club meetings; the hazards inherent in being over-consulted are recognized by an increasing number of managers and employees alike. In most instances the formal hierarchy possess sufficient resources to effect a change. The management club serves as the vehicle for identifying the need and obtaining a consensus regarding the action that needs to be taken. It certainly would be a good idea to provide the membership timely feedback regarding the projects that have been initiated as a result of the efforts of the management club. This could be accomplished at the beginning of each management club meeting.

Evaluation and Modification. A management club cannot be artificially grafted onto the management subsystem of the organization. It must be fused in such a way that it becomes compatible with the needs and idiosyncrasies of the organization. Toward that end the management club should be started on an experimental basis, carefully monitored, and modified until it is perceived by its members to be a valuable management development tool. Although top executives should take the lead regarding the continuous monitoring and evaluation of the management club, inputs from all members of the club should be given consideration. Once a year a working session of the club could be devoted to the topic of improving the usefulness of the club. To facilitate such an evaluative session, club officers could collect information from members through informal discussions, anonymous surveys, or a suggestion box, analyze the data, and present the summary to the membership for discussion.

It would be unusual for a management club to become a resounding success overnight. Integrating the management club with the specific needs of the members and the management development efforts of the organization requires patience and continuous effort. It is reasonable to expect at first a certain amount of skepticism toward the idea and proforma participation. However, if the involvement continues at a superficial level after a trial period of two or three years, the club should be permitted a quiet demise.

ISSUES DESERVING ATTENTION

The number and variety of specific problems that plague organizations preclude the presentation of an exhaustive list of topics worthy of consideration by management clubs. Nonetheless, we feel compelled to identify the salient issues that we consider to be prime candidates for deliberation and action by management clubs.

Examining the Role of Staff Departments. The purpose of staff departments is to serve line departments, not the other way around. Many organizations have bloated staff departments and have too many of them. By trying to justify their existence and growth these staff departments frequently create work for line personnel that is marginally related to the principal mission of the organization, thereby making it more difficult for line to attain its objectives. Therefore, care must be exercised to insure that the management club does not become a stage for the self-interests of the sundry staff departments. The edge that Japanese products enjoy ensues mainly from superior manufacturing processes and better management of operating personnel. If U.S. firms are to compete effectively, they need to make major improvements in these line functions.

Establishing a Connection Between Performance and Rewards. The sad truth of the matter is that in many organizations with productivity problems the below-average, average, and above-average employees at all levels of the organization receive the rewards that these organizations have to offer in about the same amounts; this applies to non-unionized organizations as well. Therefore, the extrinsic incentives for performing at high levels are absent from the workplace. If executives who lead their firms into bankruptcy are paid hundreds of thousands of dollars, how much would they be worth if their firms made a profit?[4] We must be mindful that incentives must approach a motivational threshold in order to have significant impact on performance. Workers will take their pay in the form of leisure rather than exert maximum effort for an extra five or ten cents an hour. We have much to learn about motivational thresholds from Lincoln Electric. In 1983, Lincoln Electric employees received on the average a $22,000 bonus on top of their regular compensation. For that kind of incentive, employees will work harder and smarter.

Creating Reliable and Valid Performance Appraisal Systems. Most performance appraisals are not worth the paper on which they are printed. This state of affairs is not due to a lack of knowledge, but to a dearth of effort. Unless organizations implement performance evaluation capable of identifying high, average, and below-average performers, then these organizations simply cannot reward performance in a differential manner.

Engendering Greater Employee Involvement and Commitment. The contemporary worker possesses different values, attitudes, needs, and expectations than his or her forebears. He or she expects much more from a job than just a paycheck. Consequently, the modern worker needs to be managed differently from previous generations of workers. Toward that end, the modern employer should experiment with participative decision making, quality circles, job enrichment programs, participative goal-setting programs, and shared ownership, such as Employee Stock Option Plans.

Providing Greater Job Security. If the employer expects greater loyalty and commitment from the workers, then the employer must reciprocate. To make it possible for more employers to guarantee their employees greater job security, employers must operate with a lean work force to begin with, and the federal government must pursue policies that create economic stability. Otherwise, a boom or bust approach to the economy will make job security commitments practically impossible for most employers.

Encouraging Better Education and Training. A young person entering the work force today can expect to retrain three or four times before he or she retires; that is how rapidly the world of work is changing. What we need then are retrainable employees. It is imperative for us as a society to improve our educational institutions and for each organization to improve its training methods. It is no coincidence that the Japanese worker is better educated and better trained than the American worker.

Providing a Satisfactory Juridical System. Organized employees benefit from a grievance procedure negotiated at the collective bargaining table. Unorganized employees frequently have no one to turn to except the personnel department (hardly a neutral instrument), when disputes and grievances occur. In other words, the employees are at the mercy of the hierarchy. Voluntarily installing grievance procedures that produce swift resolutions and are perceived as being impartial will not only be a positive step toward obviating a need for a union, but also should improve morale as well.

Improving Labor/Management Relations. It is instructive to point out that the percent of unionized workers in Japan and West Germany is larger than that in the U.S. The difference between the countries is the way in which the labor-management relationship is conducted. A modicum of progress is being made now in this arena because of recurring recessions and acute foreign competition. However, this progress must be continued even after the economic recovery for a permanent rebound in productivity to take place. One thing is for certain—collective bargaining agreements must establish a connection between compensation and productivity.

Establishing Discipline. It would certainly be desirable if all motivation-related problems could be solved through quality-of-work-life programs, such as job enrichment, quality circles, and participative decision making. However, in numerous organizations, productivity problems result from a general breakdown in discipline; absenteeism is high, coffee breaks excessive, reject levels intolerable, instances of insubordination too frequent, and disregard of rules, policies, and procedures commonplace; establishing the requisite discipline is the logical solution.

Adopting a Long-run Orientation. American managers place too high a premium on quarterly, semi-annual and annual performance measures such as net profit, rate of return on investment, market share, and other indicators. Such a short-run orientation is frequently counterproductive. The benefits of a long-run orientation have been clearly illustrated by the so-called "Japanese miracle."

Continually Improving and Refining Specific Management Practices and Procedures. A study at a large U.S. firm revealed that 30 percent of the worker's time was wasted because of work-scheduling problems alone. No one really knows how much of the worker's time is wasted when one takes into account all the inefficient management practices. A senior vice president of another large U.S. firm made the following observation:

a. Managers are not sufficiently sensitive to the critical importance of accurate, timely sales forecasts in manufacturing detail. Hence, they don't anticipate well, are unresponsive to customer needs, and miss changes of strategic significance.
b. Managers frequently have insufficient data to make the routine but critical decision of what to produce, when, and how many.
c. American business systems give insufficient attention to reducing purchase and manufacturing lead times. As a result, American businesses lack flexibility and fail to achieve high levels of service to the customer.
d. Many managers do not have a full appreciation of nonfinancial performance standards and, as a consequence, they let them slip and deteriorate.[5]

We know of a number of firms in our city alone that are still using standards developed through time and motion studies conducted at least twenty-five years ago. In the interim, the jobs have changed to the point that there is no longer a relationship between what people are paid and the value of their work.

The management club is not being proposed as a substitute for the formal and informal management training efforts sponsored by the firm. Furthermore, it should not be perceived by managers as an excuse to avoid coaching and on-the-job training of subordinates. Neither should managers wait for a needed change to emanate from the management club. The club should be viewed as another avenue for voluntary self-improvement activity. To realize its potential it must be viewed by participants as being instrumental to improving their job-related skills, facilitating solutions of work-related problems, and enhancing their careers.

The managerial challenge facing most firms is threefold. One, how does the organization motivate managers to upgrade their managerial skills on a continuing basis? Two, how does the organization make available to executives, managers, and supervisors the best and most recent in management theory and practice? Three, how does the organization relate the state of the art to the immediate and pressing needs of its members? We believe that a well-designed, implemented, and maintained management club has the potential to supplement in a meaningful way and at a modest cost the extant organizational strategies for meeting the threefold managerial challenge.

No doubt many executives, managers, and supervisors have valuable ideas that they are reluctant to share or introduce for any number of reasons. Many observers of the industrial scene are convinced that if organizations could somehow motivate their members to volunteer their ideas and implement them, significant benefits would accrue to the organization in the form of increase in productivity, quality of products and services, and quality of work life.

Ideas are inspired through attending conferences, reading a book or journal, or pursuing a degree. More likely than not, ideas are generated through work experience and insight. The management club affords a convenient vehicle for disseminating the information and having it discussed, evaluated, and even implemented.

The management club also provides a stage for able and motivated junior managers to gain visibility beyond their immediate work group and supervisor. The opportunity to observe and interact with junior supervisors and managers provides an added incentive for senior executives to become involved regularly in the management club.

It is possible that a management club can, over time, create a value system in the organization that encourages and rewards experimentation, sharing of ideas, receptivity to new ideas and practices and scanning the environment for useful information. We would anticipate that such a climate will eventually filter to the bottom of the organization and alter the way first-level supervisors relate to their to their subordinates.

The multifaceted problems that bedevil our economy were a long time in the making, and solutions will not surface overnight. Progress will have to be made on the many fronts that we identify in the introduction. Many of the solutions will come easier and quicker if all employees are involved in the identification of problems and the search for solutions. Without straining the imagination too much, a management club could evolve into a quality circle for executives, managers, and supervisors. In fact, that is the real payoff.

REFERENCES

1. The Wall Street Journal, January 6, 1981: 1.
2. Arnold S. Judson, "The Awkward Truth about Productivity," Harvard Business Review, September-October 1982: 93-97.
3. William G. Ouchi, Theory Z (New York: Avon Books, 1981).
4. Carol J. Loomis, "The Madness of Executive Compensation," Fortune, July 12, 1982: 42-52.
5. A. William Reynolds, "What Can We Do About Productivity? A Management View," The Gamut, Fall 1980: 58-62.

Jan P. Muczyk is a professor of management at Cleveland State University in Ohio. Robert E. Hasings is also a professor of management at the same university.

22.
WHITE-COLLAR OVERHEAD

Lester C. Thurow

Though computers have made office work more efficient, the number of white-collar workers has increased. Despite all the talk of downsizing, management hasn't seriously begun to attack the problem of bloated executive and office staffs.

The growth of private productivity has gradually but persistently declined from 3.3 percent per year between 1948 and 1965 to 0.7 percent per year between 1978 and 1985. In 1985 productivity growth essentially stopped at +0.1 percent for the entire private economy and −0.3 percent in the non-farm business sector of the economy. The most recent trends seem as ominous as those in the past two decades.

After the first OPEC oil shock, productivity growth fell everywhere in the industrial world as attention was focused on energy rather than labor-saving investments, but in the late 1970s and 1980s there has been a sharp rebound in the rest of the industrial world that has not occurred here. Our major industrial competitors have productivity growth rates four to six times those in the United States. Something specific within the American economy is causing slow productivity growth here but not elsewhere.

From the point of view of traditional neoclassical economics, the decline in productivity growth is a major mystery. Productivity growth can decline because of deterioration in the quality of labor itself or because of a deterioration in the quantity or quality of physical capital, natural resources, and technology. But economic analysts cannot find declines in the quantity or quality of these inputs large enough to explain the observed decline in the rate of growth output relative to inputs. Often inputs have, in fact, risen rather than fallen. Investment in plant and equipment, for example, has risen from 9.5 percent of the GNP between 1948 and 1965 to 11.1 percent of the GNP between 1978 and 1985. As a result, after all the economic analysis is completed, the slowdown remains substantially unexplained.

Some have suggested that this unexplained slowdown may be produced by such factors as a deterioration in the American work ethic. But this is simply to convert an economic mystery into a sociological mystery. Why did the work ethic deteriorate? There is also little independent evidence to confirm a deterioration in work effort.

Even if the quantity and quality of inputs could explain most of the decline in productivity growth, however, economics would still be left without a recommendable cure. If a market system of individual rational choice leads to a decline in the quality or quantity of economic inputs, so be it. Change can be recommended only if it can be shown that this decline is caused by some market imperfection rather than by free choice, and no one has suggested a market imperfection that can explain those deteriorations in the quality or quantity inputs that have been found. As a result, the deterioration in productivity growth is like sex between consenting adults. It's nobody's business.

Let me argue, however, that the decline in productivity growth is only a mystery if one accepts the blinders imposed by conventional economic analysis. The standard economic approach assumes that social institutions take care of themselves in the sense that economically efficient social institutions automatically drive inefficient social institutions out of the economy. Thus, at every point in time the economy is full of efficient social institutions. The same is true when it comes to the habits, customs, and goals of firm managers. Managers cannot be systematically or persistently wrong. If they were, they would be inefficient, and inefficient managers would be systematically weeded out by efficient managers. As a result, no one ever asks whether something might be wrong with management. The question isn't asked because in conventional economic theory it's impossible for anything to be systematically wrong with management.

Instead of looking at changes in the quantity and quality of labor, capital, natural resources and technology, let's approach the problem from the point of view of the occupational structure of the economy. As mentioned, productivity grew by 0.7 percent per year between 1978 and 1985. Over that same period, the number of blue-collar workers on American payrolls declined by 1.9 million, or 6 percent, while real output was rising by 15 percent. If one produces 15 percent more with 6 percent less, one has had a 21 percent gain in productivity, or an annual growth rate of 2.8 percent. When it comes to blue-collar productivity, America has had a world-class rate of growth.

But American firms were simultaneously adding 10 million white-collar workers to their payrolls, which represented a 21 percent increase. Now, if one needs 21 percent more employees to produce a 15 percent gain in output, one has had a 6 percent fall in productivity. And since there are currently 58 million blue-collar workers on American payrolls, this decline in white-collar productivity wiped out much of the gain in blue-collar productivity.   If one adds service workers (excluded in the previous data) and remembers that many of them indirectly work for American industry, then white-collar productivity becomes even more central as an explanation for declining national productivity growth.

Viewed from this perspective, what America has is not a general productivity problem but an office productivity problem. The American factory works; the American office does not. Why?

Productivity comparisons with the rest of the world reveal the same problem. Studies of the relative cost of producing an automobile in different countries, using the Ford Escort as an example, show that 40 percent of the Japanese cost advantage is due to lower white-collar overhead in Japan than in the United States.

Such studies have led to a lot of talk about reducing white-collar overhead in American industry, but no action. According to the most recent data the problem is, if anything, getting worse. In 1985 real output rose by 2.1 percent. Yet the number of executives and managers on American payrolls rose by 5.6 percent and the number of what the Department of Labor now calls "administrative support staff" rose by 3.5 percent. Why should the administrative support staff of U.S. industry have to rise almost twice as fast as output, and why should the number of executives have to rise almost three times as fast? "Down-sizing" is much talked about but seldom done when it comes to white-collar overhead.

This situation is even more puzzling if one remembers that the United States is supposed to be in the midst of an office automation revolution and that investments in office automation have accounted for a large fraction of total business investment in recent years. New technology, new hardware, new software, and new skills are all going into the American office, but negative productivity is coming out. Why?

If one seriously asks why office productivity is falling while investments in office productivity are rising, one has to confront a set of beliefs and attitudes about American management that are left out of conventional economic analysis.

These have to do with power (American bosses exist to boss); style (a good boss should know everything and, in principle, have the knowledge to make all decisions); institutions (most middle-level managers get paid based on the number of people who report to them); peer pressure (it is harder to fire those who directly work with you than those at a distance); and beliefs (if the system is based solely upon individual effort, there is no need for group motivation, voluntary cooperation, or teamwork). None of these appears in what economists call "the theory of the firm." They simply aren't important when it comes to efficiency.

Take the proposition that the best boss is the boss who has the most knowledge and can intelligently make the most decisions per day. In the business press, bosses such as Harold Geneen of ITT were held up as models. They supposedly knew more about middle-level management's job than the middle-level managers themselves, and they were famous for making thousands of rapid decisions. Geneen was the prototypical boss who bossed. He was the macho manager whom lesser managers should emulate.

Although such beliefs may have long existed, most managers could not implement them without the technological office revolution that is now under way. Previously, bosses had to defer a certain amount of decisionmaking to those on the scene; there was no feasible way for them to know what they had to know to make good decisions. But with the onset of new technology and the office revolution in the '60s and '70s, bosses could get a lot more information more rapidly. Bosses could do a lot more bossing.

To do so, however, they had to build enormous information bureaucracies. Information could be obtained, but only at the cost of adding a lot of white-collar workers. And if there was an improvement in the quality of decision-making for all of the information that could now be moved up the corporate hierarchy, the positive effects on output were smaller than the huge number of extra information workers that had to be added to they system. Information was moved faster from place to place, but productivity fell.

The problem is graphically seen in accounting. While the total output rose by 15 percent from 1978 to 1985, the number of accountants on American payrolls rose by 30 percent—from 1 million to 1.3 million. Though computers made accounting more efficient, that efficiency was used not to reduce the number of accounts but to increase it as the frequency and types of accounting multiplied. Old accounts that used to come every three months were ordered up every day. Whole systems of new accounts that had been impossible to calculate were invented and implemented (management information systems, cost accounting, inventory control, financial accounting). Yet there was no evidence that these new accounts, with their increased frequency, improved decision making enough to justify their cost. In fact, as the data cited above show, there was clear evidence to the contrary. Power and style, however, called for ordering up all of those accounts, and it was done.

The economy is rife with such examples. Banking enjoyed not just a computer revolution in accounting but a robot revolution in dealing with its customer—automated teller machines. Yet employment in banking went up faster than its real output, and productivity fell.

Beliefs about how one "should" operate are important, because they condition what we do. Consider the conventional medical rule of stopping treatment: "Do no harm." As long as there isn't very much technology to treat an illness, it doesn't cost much to invoke every available procedure up to the point where it actually starts to harm the patient. But if new advances come along and present us with a lot of very expensive techniques that have very marginal payoffs, the same rule can become very costly. So it is with "Know everything." As long as the technology to implement that stopping rule does not exist, it isn't very harmful. But when technology comes along that in principle makes it possible to know everything, that rule becomes socially very expensive and leads to the need for a very large number of white-collar workers to keep that information system working.

Those with efficient stopping rules will eventually drive those with inefficient stopping rules out of business, but the process may take a long time. Despite international competitive pressures from foreign firms with lower white-collar overhead, American firms, as we have seen, are still adding white-collar overhead much faster than they are adding output. Beliefs about the "right style" change very slowly.

Factors of power emerge, because to do away with those white-collar workers is to delegate decision-making powers to those on the spot who have the necessary information, though lacking the benefit of an information system. To do so is to become a boss who does less bossing. But this is contrary to one's conception of one's own role. No one became a boss to do less bossing. But to do bossing requires more information.

Japanese managers have moved decentralization and participatory management from the utopian dream into the mainstream of efficient enhancement. American managers have been laggards rather than leaders in this effort. Why?

Consider shop-floor inventory control as it is done at the end of the shift on the Toyota assembly lines. Letting assembly-line workers do inventory control increases the variety of their tasks and may thereby increase their motivation to do a good job. The major efficiency gains, however, are not to be found in motivation among these blue-collar workers but in the fact that their activity permits the complete elimination of a staff of white-collar workers and the information system that is necessary to support their activities.

Efforts to allow shop-floor employees to directly purchase equipment, rather than using purchasing agents, has a similar payoff. Motivation may increase when workers want to prove that their purchasing decisions were good ones, but the real efficiency gains are to be found in reducing the number of industrial engineers and their supporting staffs, who used to be responsible for such purchasing decisions.

Traditionally, American plants have had "locked" numerically controlled machine tools, while the Europeans and Japanese have had "unlocked" numerically controlled machine tools. The difference between locked and unlocked tools is whether blue-collar workers are allowed to change the programming (unlocked) or whether only white-collar programmers are allowed to change it. In the latter case, the machines are locked to prevent blue-collar workers from altering the system.

Efficiency would seem to be all on the side of the unlocked machines. A large staff of white-collar programmers does not have to be maintained and information system does not have to be developed so that blue-collar operators can tell white-collar programmers that something has gone wrong, and downtime is reduced because the program corrections can be made instantly, without waiting for the white-collar programmers to show up. But most American firms have opted for locked machines.

The issue seems to be one of power and control. With a locked machine, management has more control and can set the pace of work. Locked numerically controlled machine tools were, in fact, sold as devices for capturing the initiative on the pace of work from assembly line workers and increasing management control. In the words of *Iron Age*, a respected trade journal, "Workers and their unions have too much to say in manufacturers' destiny, many metalworking executives feel, and large, sophisticated FMSs [Flexible Manufacturing Systems] can help wrest some of that control away from labor and put it back in the hands of management, where it belongs." If control is the issue, locked machines may dominate unlocked machines. But if enhanced productivity is the issue, then it is clear that unlocked machines should dominate.

In addition to the loss of power and control with shop-floor inventory control, shop-floor purchasing, and unlocked machine tools, managers in the American system face a direct reduction in their own salaries if they become efficient and reduce white-collar overhead. What manager is going to make such a shift in functions when he and his peers get paid based on the number of workers who report to them? To take actions to make the firm more efficient is to reduce one's own salary. It is also going to reduce one's promotion opportunities, since a reduction in white-collar employees will reduce the number of bosses necessary to manage the system. When faced with a current and future reduction in one's own prospects, very few people are going to enthusiastically support any such shift in the standard operating procedures of American industry.

Or consider word processors and the failure of office automation to yield the predicted gains in productivity. Not even in the companies that make office computers can anyone show hard data that using such machinery pays off with higher productivity. The source of the failure is to be found in the interaction of a number of institutional realities. As with shop-floor inventory control or shop-floor purchasing, management salaries are reduced when white-collar employees are eliminated.

But even more important to efficiency, office automation requires major changes in office sociology. The efficient way to use word processors is to eliminate secretaries and clerks and have managers type their own memos and call up their own files. But a personal secretary is an office badge of prestige and power. No one wants to give up that badge. To shift to the new technology also requires managers without good keyboard skills to go through a transition period during which they look clumsy and get work done more slowly than when it was being done for them. Few bosses can maintain their prestige, power, and self-respect while looking clumsy in front of their subordinates. As a result, they will order the assembly-line people to shift from human to robot welding, but they will not order themselves to shift from human to computer typing and filing.

Here again, the boss who is willing to make such changes faces a lower wage rate for himself, but, even more important, he feels the peer pressure not to fire those who are close to him in status. If those like you can be fired, you can be fired. No one likes to be reminded of that fact of life; as a result, American industry is much more ruthless when it comes to eliminating blue-collar workers than white-collar workers. Almost every American firm has a vice president for factory productivity; almost no American firm has a vice president of office productivity. In the 1981-82 recession, 90 percent of the firms that laid off blue-collar workers laid off not one white-collar worker.

In the American system, to fire managers below you is to open up the possibility of being fired by managers above you. A good illustration of the problem is to be found in the American armed forces. There are as many generals and admirals today, with two million troops in uniform, as there were in World War II, with 12 million troops in uniform. Why? The answer is simple. What general or admiral wants to reduce the opportunities to become a general or admiral? If the existing generals reduce the number of middle-level officers, there would automatically have to be a cutback in the number of generals, since you can't have a system with more generals than colonels.

In Europe and Japan, where managers' salaries are more seniority-dependent (that is, not so dependent upon merit or the number of people reporting to them), layoffs are very rare, and reducing white-collar overhead is not seen as such a personal threat as it is in the United States. Paradoxically, in the United States the real threat of firing managers ends up producing a system in which there is little real danger of a manager being fired because of improvements in efficiency.

In experiment after experiment with participatory management, the problems have been found not among workers or in inefficient production but among middle-level managers who feel threatened. Because they feel threatened, they block experiments with new, more efficient forms of production. The personal dangers in the American system are not imaginary. Personal rationality intervenes to prevent social rationality and social efficiency from being achieved.

Productivity gains are dependent upon the development as well as the use of new technology. The pattern of research and development in American firms differs from that in Japan and Europe in having more new-process R&D and less new-product R&D. Both ultimately end up producing higher productivity, but new-process R&D at any given time has a bigger effect on productivity than new-product R&D, since every economy is more heavily weighted toward old products than new products. Ultimately, new products are more important than more efficiency in producing old products, but new products are much easier to copy from the competition than new processes. One can buy a product and "reverse-engineer"; one cannot buy a new process and see how it is made.

This structural difference, however, is not caused by American stupidity. It is endemic to the structure of organization. New processes require that one change old, established ways of production. This requires managers who can manage people and persuade them to shift efficiently to new processes. If people were interchangeable parts—the view inherent in much of American management and economics—such shifts would present no special problems. But people aren't interchangeable. Sociologically, it is far easier to set up a new plant for a new product than it is to change production processes in old plants.

In a system that pays people for the skills that they use at work and fires them if improvements in efficiency make them superfluous, new-process technology is threatening to the incomes and employment of both workers and managers. General unenthusiastic support (foot-dragging) can quickly turn a profitable new-process technology into an unprofitable one.

Compared with the inherent difficulties of new processes, mergers look like the easy route to economic success for both the firm and its managers. The firm expands in old markets without having to adopt new technology, and managers whose salaries are keyed to sales get a big bonus when sales rise as a result of a merger. But for the society as a whole, mergers do not lead to more productivity, while new-process technology does.

Here again, what is rational at the micro level is not rational at the macro level. But in an economy based on the principle that the engine of economic change is individuals operating at the micro level, no one has a responsibility to insure that all of the micro activity does, in fact, lead to improvement in macro efficiency.

Standard operating procedures have a strong hold on the human mind. A Wang executive recently told me about an incident in which the company investigated a Wang Taiwanese facility that had much lower production costs than an American facility even after correcting for wage differences. They found that the differences could be traced to a lot of small standard operating procedures in the American facility, such as the provision of a telephone for every white-collar worker.

No one is terribly expensive, but private phones for thousands of white-collar workers add up to an important cost. Most white-collar workers make very few business calls each day, and could easily use a central phone bank. Extend the telephone example to other areas, and one is talking about a significant saving. But the change isn't made, because to do so would require a confrontation with those standard operating procedures.

If one thinks of the recommendations for replacing today's wage system with a bonus system like that of the Japanese, for replacing profit maximization with value-added maximization, or for eliminating the fast track for young managers, a believer in neoclassical economics will tell you that none of them could possibly enhance productivity growth. That is not something he has to investigate empirically; that is something he knows.

People are paid in accordance with their marginal productivity, and how one writes the check—hourly, monthly, or partly in the form of a bonus keyed to some measure of performance—is irrelevant. Human workers look only at the bottom line—the total sum that they are being paid—and aren't going to be affected by the institutional means whereby that sum is delivered to them.

Whether a firm is organized as a profit-maximizer and hires and fires workers to maximize those profits, or as a value-added maximizing partnership in which partners aren't fired as soon as sales decline, is irrelevant to the ultimate efficiency of the enterprise. Efficiency depends upon the quality and quantity of inputs and not upon the institutional forms of organization. A society that fires its redundant labor, rather than having to increase sales in order to absorb redundant workers, should, if anything, be more efficient, since workers are more rapidly moved into the open labor market when supply and demand allocate them to new activities.

A society that learns to take advantage of differences in talent at every career stage should also be more efficient. The firm that quickly promotes what seem to be promising managers onto the fast track (the American pattern) should have an edge over one that keeps managers working as a cohort with roughly the same pay and rotation of jobs, and doesn't start the fast track until managers are in their 40s (the Japanese pattern).

But from the perspective of what might be called economic sociology, motivation, voluntary cooperation, and teamwork make a difference. The willingness to provide those key factors may well depend upon the way in which people are paid.

The neoclassical man is not worried about unemployment and will not resist technical change to avoid it; he realizes that other jobs are easily available in the open market. But actual human beings may fear unemployment and resist technical changes that threaten to throw them out of work. In neoclassical theory, having a compatriot on the management fast track does not lower the work effort of those not on the fast track, but if may well do so in the real world. Why should anyone work hard if it is already obvious that he doesn't have a chance to make it?

When it comes to that famous bottom line so beloved of economists, it makes a great difference which of these economic theories one believes.

Lester C. Thurow is Gordon Y. Billard professor of management and economics at the Massachusetts Institute of Technology.

23.
SELLING QUALITY TO THE TROOPS

Thomas M. Rohan

> Everyone pays lip service to the importance of quality, but undertaking the kind of institutional change that can make the difference in implementing a successful program is among the toughest of corporate challenges.

In 1986, while browsing in a bookstore the manager of a Cleveland aircraft parts plant spotted a paperback copy of *Quality is Free* by Philip Crosby, the highly successful Florida consultant.

Since his plant had been experiencing a higher-than-normal parts rejection rate, the manager was intrigued. He bought the book, was impressed with its message, and ordered several hundred copies, which he distributed to his employees.

He not only urged them to read the book but also announced that, on the following Monday, the plant would begin to operate under the Crosby system.

A bit presumptuous, certainly. But he isn't the first executive who's assumed that all you have to do to improve quality is to decree, "It shall be done." One company president, it's reported, bought 15,000 copies of the Crosby book to give to all employees—and later complained that "nothing happened."

Quality professionals cringe at such half-baked implementation efforts. "It may seem difficult to believe, but many U.S. managers simply don't know how to implement a quality-improvement plan in their operation," observes Dr. Myron Tribus, director of the Center for Advanced Engineering Study at the Massachusetts Institute of Technology.

"Many executives have told me that they just can't get their programs going." Dr. Tribus says. "They realize that they must do something different, but they don't know what. And it is totally unfair that, in most instances, top management hasn't done its job but the guy at the bottom gets the blame."

A disciple of Dr. W. Edwards Deming, the internationally known Washington-based consultant, Dr. Tribus adds: "it is a deadly serious business and, unfortunately, a lot of people may wind up out on the street —and their job shifted overseas—because their bosses don't know how to run quality programs."

"I'm beginning to sound angry like Dr. Deming, but it is tragic. And I am furious about it."

COMMITMENT NEEDED

Often the missing ingredient is *commitment* to the program—*at all levels*. Too frequently, quality programs originate when a top executive reads a book on the subject—or gets an ultimatum from a major customer. Or perhaps when the company loses a big order because of quality problems.

But while everyone pays lip service to the importance of quality, undertaking the kind of cultural change that can make the difference in implementing a successful program—and institutionalizing it—are among the toughest of challenges.

One of the biggest obstacles is the difficulty in convincing middle management that there really is a problem—and that top management is serious about solving it. If middle managers aren't sold, then how can a CEO expect the production troops to take the quality message seriously?

"Many upper-level managers have opted for a road that can properly be called 'exhortation only'." says Dr. Joseph Juran, chairman of the Juran Institute Inc., Wilton, Conn., and a long-time apostle of quality control. "This road consists of using skillful propaganda to arouse awareness among subordinates that quality is important. But the implied goal is vague, not specific."

Executives who take the sloganeering road typically rely on such themes as "Do It Right the First Time," says Dr. Juran. "But the middle managers on the receiving end of the exhortations are seldom enthusiastic about the approach."

Mr. Crosby, who has trained some 12,000 people at his Quality College in Winter Park, Florida, and branches around the world, says that executive attendees are told up front that in order to implement a program, they must first admit to employees that quality is a management problem, that it hasn't been managed correctly, and that it will take the efforts of everyone in the organization to change things.

"The question for employees always is whether management is serious about it," Mr. Crosby says. "Most managers have been through a series of management programs which quickly die off."

"For management, the challenge is to get rid of the notion that it will be quick—like learning a new dance or technique. We tell them flat-out that it will take five or ten years to make a complete change in a large organization—and perhaps two or three years in companies with a few hundred employees.

"You are talking about changing the culture of a company. This covers a broad spectrum—purchasing, finance, administration, personnel, accounting—not just manufacturing. It can be traumatic for many people because we are teaching quality management, not inspection."

"You must get top executives on board to get any results," agrees Dr. Charles Holland, president of Qual-Pro Inc., a Powell, Tennessee-based consulting group. "You must teach them and middle managers—and other employees as well—the philosophy and the statistical techniques. You work first on the manufacturing activities, since most people can easily apply the concepts there. Then you expand it to other activities and it just cascades.

"But management must first create the environment. And if the middle managers aren't convinced, the program will not go anywhere."

GETTING THEIR ATTENTION

So, how does top management go about convincing middle managers and production workers alike that it is serious? Most authorities agree that a good kickoff is important—a major public event or ceremony in which top management makes a commitment.

One Silicon Valley firm closed its 2,000-worker plant for a day and held a barbecue in the parking lot to launch its program. Others have invited top consultants like Mr. Crosby and Dr. Deming to speak to their employees.

But what if the employees still aren't convinced that serious problems exist? Some companies have answered that question by letting workers discover the truth for themselves.

At General Motors Corp.'s Lordstown, Ohio, assembly plant, 20 hourly workers were taken off their assembly-line jobs for several months and instructed to simply walk around the plant and inquire about quality problems. Their mission: To find out what happened on the assembly line that affected quality—and to solicit worker suggestions.

United Auto Workers representatives initially were suspicious that management was setting up a "spy ring." But once the purpose had been explained, union officials cooperated. The walkers' "unproductive" time represented a financial investment by GM, a company spokesman notes, but the solutions that emerged from the program dramatically raised the plant's quality rating.

An increasingly popular tactic for convincing workers is to send them to customers' plants. In one classic case, General Electric workers who build drive motors in Erie, Pennsylvania, visited an Ohio steel-mill maintenance shop. What they heard there was more than they'd bargained for.

At one point, a burly maintenance worker told the motor builders: "So you guys are from GE? I'd sure like the meet the S.O.B. who drills the mounting holes for these damm motors you send us. Every one is off-center and I have to redrill them. It's a bitch of a job!"

As it turned out, the hole-driller was standing right there—red-faced at the gales of laughter that erupted from his coworkers.

For months, the mounting hole problem had resisted solution, despite a flurry of letters between vice presidents on both sides. But, following the embarrassing encounter, the problem disappeared overnight—and GE's rating on the steel-mill's vendors' list rose several notches.

NUMBERS THAT TALK

Sometimes, hard numbers will do the trick. At least that was the case at GM's large plastic-molding plant in Adrian, Mich.

"The prevailing attitude in a plastic-molding plant," says quality assurance manager Ed Opie, is that there is no real scrap or waste because we can reshoot our mistakes. So everyone thinks that scrap doesn't matter. We just regrind that scrap and use it again."

But research by Mr. Opie indicated that the financial loss on plastic that had to be reground, repacked, and reused, came to $2 million a year—2 million pounds at a dollar a pound. As a result, the 1,300-employee Adrian plant was rated by GM as one of its least efficient.

Using hard numbers like these—which previously weren't available—plant manager Fred Meissinger was able to convince middle management and workers that a major quality program was needed. Within ten months, regrinds had been reduced to a yearly rate of 122,000 lbs, for an annual saving of $1.8 million.

The Adrian plant is now near the top in GM's rating system.

KEEP AT IT

Another way to convince workers that the front office is serious about quality is to maintain top management's visibility in the program. "In the 1960s and 1970s, top executives were mostly financial and production experts," notes Dr. Armand Fiegenbaum, president of General Systems Co., Pittsfield, Mass., and a pioneering consultant in the field.

"We are reaping some of the fruits of that era with our quality problems of today," Dr. Fiegenbaum says. "It was rare for top executives to get involved with quality control—and eyebrows were raised if you did. It was rarer still for any quality-control official to make it to top management.

"Today, with the emphasis on managing quality, you need direct personal know-how and involvement in manufacturing by top executives to get the cooperation of the people who have to carry out the program," he stresses. "If they walk through the shop two or three times, there's no impact. But if they walk through 40 times, and ask questions about quality and talk to workers about quality problems and solutions, the people start to get the message."

One top executive whose questioning led to results is Ronald Borrelli, president of Zehntel Inc., a Walnut Creek, California, maker of electronic circuit-testing and production equipment. Acting on a gut feeling that quality could be improved, he instructed managers to ask employees what they were hearing from customers—and to ask customers what they thought of Zehntel.

The answers surprised some company managers. "About 80 of our 300 people are in contact with customers—and I was aghast at some of the things they knew or found out," confesses Ralph Roe, vice president for manufacturing. "For one thing, we found complaints that our testers began to 'whistle' after a few months of service and the noise annoyed users."

The problem was traced to a rubber seal in the frame that joins circuit boards with probes in a vacuum. Air leaks in the seal caused the whistling noise, which was eliminated by using a new compound.

"The interesting thing is that once our employees heard of the problems in quality or service, they pitched in to help. And, because of top-management attention, they were solved quickly."

POPCORN LESSONS

Many experts insist that quality-management programs will be more successful if top executives get a 'feel' for the system by getting hands-on experience. Joiner Associates inc., a Madison, Wis., consulting firm, makes executives at client firms operate a simulated 'popcorn factory' to help them get that feel.

Typically, Joiner sends a two-man team—a statistics expert and an organizational development (OD) expert—to set up and implement programs for clients. "We try to blend the two types of management skills, and make para-statisticans and para-OD types out of them," explains Dr. Kevin Little, an associated at Joiner. "They get hands-on experience because the statistician shows them how to do statistical experiments and use control charts. And the para-OD gets the people in the organization to use the system, rather than try to sabotage it.

"The popcorn factory is great for giving managers the 'feel' of the system by actually walking around and collecting data," Dr. Little says. "It also helps us to determine who is interested and enthusiastic—and who isn't."

At the Juran Institute one company ran two groups of managers through training courses on quality management. The first group simply watched eight hours of videotaped courses featuring Dr. Juran. The second group viewed the tapes and then participated in hands-on project.

After six months, reports Dr. Robert E. Hoogstoel, vice president of the institute, the participants were surveyed. The first group's interest in quality had largely stagnated, while the hands-on group had progressed.

STATISTICAL OVERKILL

While most specialists agree that it is important to have a strong quality-control plan in place—including statistical process control (SPC)—many feel that quality-control programs often overemphasize the statistical approach.

Dr. Deming, for one, maintains that quality improvement requires a change in the corporate culture from the top down. And, he contends, if managers and workers get bogged down in the mechanics of SPC, a program will die.

Many consultants even object to using the word "program," since it tends to convey that the effort has a finite time span. They feel that quality consciousness should become ingrained and efforts continually improved.

Some companies, Juran Institute's Dr. Hoogstoel reports, are now making quality improvements a permanent fixture in the business-planning process, ensuring that it will continue regardless of the personalities involved. During planning sessions, quality-improvement goals automatically appear on the agenda.

Dr. Fiegenbaum at General Systems, who helps companies design and start up SPC programs, emphasizes. "Quality must be sold within an organization as a total way of doing business—not some Fourth of July flag-waving. There must be a clearly defined umbrella organization and structure—including task forces—to manage and maintain it."

As a graduate student at MIT 35 years ago, Dr. Fiegenbaum authored a book, *Total Quality Control,* which is now in its third edition and has been translated into a dozen languages. He maintains that, in many operations, the absence of good quality-management programs is tantamount to subsidizing a "hidden plant" representing 15 percent to 40 percent of total productive capacity. This hidden plant is occupied with reworking, retesting, reinspecting, and rejecting output.

Organizations with strong quality-control programs have been able to convert these "hidden plants" to more profitable use—adding 5 to 10 cents per sales dollar in positive cash flow.

TURNAROUND

A well-implemented program can even turn a company around. Dr. Holland at Qual-Pro recalls that one company—DeRoyal Industries Inc., Knoxville, Tennessee—was thinking of closing several of its six plants about three or four years ago. The 700-employee company, which makes some 3,000 types of medical supplies and orthopedic devices, was losing business to larger competitors like Johnson & Johnson and American Hospital Supply.

Among the problems discovered by Peter DeBusk, DeRoyal's president and founder, was that the wrong material was going to the wrong manufacturing department at the wrong time far more often than was reasonable. So Mr. DeBusk called in Dr. Holland and, with his key managers, worked out a plan of action.

First, Mr. DeBusk met with all the managers and laid out the problems: increasing costs and rejection rates and growing competition. "I also talked to the workers in groups and found that they were as aware of the problems as I was," Mr. DeBusk says. "When they learned that I was sincerely interested in helping to solve them, they flooded us with suggestions."

With Dr. Holland's guidance, an elaborate training program in Dr. Deming's management and SPC methods was launched. Production also became more automated with bar-code readers, computerized order-entry and dispatch systems and automatic inspection and monitoring.

"It has worked fantastically well," reports Mr. DeBusk. "We're not closing anything now."

In fact, productivity has jumped 250 percent, he notes, and annual sales are up by 60 percent or more. "We recently signed a $50 million contract with the Voluntary Hospital Assn.—which exceeds our total sales in 1982.

"It has all resulted from thinking of the process as a total system."

Part IV
AUTOMATION AND INNOVATION: CAUSE AND EFFECT

24
THE INNOVATION TRAPS AND HOW THEY CAN THWART TECHNOLOGICAL LEAPS

Anthony Warren

> The ways in which companies apply innovation in technology and management are important factors in determining their success in the years ahead. Therefore, an understanding of the pitfalls that often obstruct innovation can help companies make the best choices for their futures.

Given today's intense competition at home and abroad, U.S. corporations face important decisions about which technologies to invest in and what management tools to develop. How companies apply innovation in technology and management will determine their success in the years ahead. However, an understanding of the pitfalls that often obstruct innovation can help companies make the best choices.

First, it is important to differentiate between *innovation* and *invention*. Invention could be described as the creative assembly of existing technology to make a product, usually before there is a need for it. Examples include: penicillin, the jet engine, and lasers. Generally, years pass before profits can be derived from inventions.

Innovation, on the other hand, is an assembly of existing science or technology to meet a specific need. It focuses on the short- and medium-term and does not require major breakthroughs in techniques. Innovation requires selecting items from existing know-how worldwide and combining them in a unique way to gain an advantage over existing products or processes. Examples of product innovation are: the Apple computer, radial tires, and the Sony Walkman cassette tape recorders.

The process of innovation extends into areas beyond technology. A new way of marketing a service or organizing a business requires innovation. Bringing securities trading to the average consumer at local savings and loan offices is just one example of innovative marketing. Behind this marketing approach are the computer and the telecommunications technology that make it possible.

THE 'S-CURVE'

In deciding which technologies and methods to invest in to ensure future competitiveness, companies should be aware of the up-and-down movement of the "S-curve." Most technological and managerial developments can be described by this curve, which measures effectiveness in terms of investment versus benefits. In the early 1950s, for example, transistor technology lingered at the bottom of the curve while the electron tube rode at the top. However, large amounts of money were required to obtain increasingly smaller increments of performance from the tube. Therefore, conditions were ripe for a new technology that could satisfy market demand—and the transistor began to climb up the curve as the tube fell.

The S-curve applies to many different situations. In business it describes product performance and development, product costs, product life cycles, production technology, and even company culture—for example, Texas Instruments' move from entrepreneurial to mature to defensive. This inevitable working of the S-curve "throws" corporations to the top and then pushes them back down again. Because the curve affects all parts of business, companies should try to keep different functions—such as external marketing, manufacturing methods, and organizational structure—in phase so that one complements the other.

TWO CHOICES

Keeping the S-curve in mind, in today's increasingly competitive global marketplace there are two choices available to a company. One strategy is the "Best Game in Town," which means doing what everyone else does—only better. Examples include IBM's entry into the personal-computer market, where company size and product engineering are important; Johnson & Johnson's baby powder, where brand recognition, quality, and image have paid off; and Far East copies of consumer products, where cost has won the day. If companies choose to play this game of using derivation technology, they must recognize the risks for the future and make sure that they have a lean and aggressive organization that can fight hard.

An alternative strategy is "Buying Tickets for Next Season"—or taking a quantum jump. In this case, the rules of the game are altered and the advantage is gained by learning to play sooner than your competitors. Examples of quantum jumps include the progressions from incandescent to fluorescent lights, locomotives to aircraft and vacuum tubes to integrated circuits.

AVOID THE TRAPS

But the quantum-jump strategy holds many traps. One is *The Success Trap*. When a business appears most successful it should begin doing something else.

The "S-curve" dictates the wisdom of this move. However, it is difficult to avoid the success trap because conventional management-information systems often indicate short-term well-being and U.S. managers tend to work for rewards in the short term rather than planning the next generation of products. The problem is to persuade the board of directors to invest in new areas when they are confronted with demands for extra capacity for existing profitable products.

THE ACCOUNTING TRAP

Accountants tend to be too cautious and too conservative on long-term projects, favoring the low-risk point of view because the high-risk approach is extremely difficult to calculate accurately. This represents a trap because the way to make a business grow is to take risks.

When weighing an investment in a new area, companies use the conventional discounted cash-flow analysis, which relies heavily on accurate forecasts several years into the future. But, clearly, these are difficult to make. Furthermore, a part of the net present value arises from the *terminal value* of the investment. This is usually biased toward fixed assets rather than the total marketable value of the business which, while difficult to quantify, could be much higher. For example, if one invested today in the development of a growth hormone for cattle, the capital investment would be relatively small. But, if it became successful, the total market value of the business generated could be much higher.

THE INVESTMENT TRAP

If the major costs of a business relate to fixed assets, it is very difficult to switch to a new technology. The steel industry is a perfect example.

THE MARKETING TRAP

Companies typically judge themselves against what their competitors are doing. However, their vigilance can turn into a dangerous myopia if they fail to look at potential competitors in other sectors. For example, Senco Products Inc., Cincinnati, became a leading supplier of surgical instruments by moving laterally from its established business (staplers for furniture) into skin staplers.

THE ORGANIZATION TRAP

Mature businesses often develop strong vertical structures designed to milk their "cash cows." However, innovation requires strong horizontal lines within a company. The reason: successfully exploiting an opportunity requires a recognition of the opportunity by all functions within a company. This will help prevent a company from falling into the classic organizational trap in which marketing people decide what product *they* think will fit, the engineering people decide what product *they* think will fit, and the operations people have to try to accommodate both of them.

THE INCEST TRAP

As a successful company begins to regard itself as a world expert in a particular area, it tends to stop looking outside the organization for new technologies or ideas. The danger in this was confirmed in a recent study by the Sappho Study Science Policy Research Unit at England's University of Sussex. The study showed, among other things, that companies with the best track records for staying ahead also make the greatest use of external resources.

THE TIME TRAP

Each product has a "window of opportunity"—a time span during which it can yield the greatest returns. But the ever-increasing pace of technological change means that these "windows" are opening and closing at a faster rate. Not getting an early jump can mean missing an opportunity. On the other hand, products can be introduced *too early*. An example: the home videodisk introduced in the early 1970s in Europe by Telefunken and subsequently in the U.S. by RCA. The "window" closed in the late 1970s with the emergence of videotape technology.

SUCCESSFUL INNOVATION

Avoiding some of these traps through astute technical innovation has helped a number of companies remain competitive. For example, the investment trap was avoided when a match manufacturer put garden seeds on the tips of its cardboard matchsticks. With little added investment, the company moved into an entirely new area with a new and attractive product.

The organization trap was avoided by a clock manufacturer that designed a new electric clock with so few moving parts that robots were not needed for its assembly. Instead of development engineers designing the clock in isolation and then handing it over to the manufacturing people, they worked as a team—sharing responsibilities in every stage of the project. This was a case of taking advantage of horizontal ties.

In choosing a plan of action, a company should determine where it stands and where it is headed, and then develop an appropriate strategy. If it opts for derivation technology—that is, playing the same game as its competitors—then it should focus on developing a lean organization, use innovation to improve its manufacturing operations, and be prepared to fight hard.

But if this game seems too brutal, it may be wiser to channel innovation toward exploring new territory.

But, first, identify the traps.

Anthony Warren is chairman of PA Consulting Services Inc., Princeton, N.J., an international technology and managerial consulting firm.

25.
INNOVATION AND TURMOIL

William W. Myers

All new systems require innovation. Even if they are replacing existing systems, they use new hardware, software or programming techniques. Disorder and confusion usually accompany such changes but there are steps that can be taken to minimize the turmoil.

Designing and implementing new systems should follow an orderly process. After all, we now have many tools that help the systems analyst to design and manage projects. However, one of our trainees who was working on her first new system said "Do all new systems have so many changes during development? I always feel so confused." (Her training program was so much more orderly.) My answer was "yes," but I could not explain why that was true. In fact, for every new system that I designed, a time came when I wondered if things would ever come together. This was a startling revelation. Was this caused by sloppily used design tools and poor programing, or was it due to the nature of systems?

All new systems are inventions. Even if they are replacing existing systems, they still use new hardware, software, or programming techniques. New systems must be much more productive, provide more information or do more work. Procedures will be changed to meet new user needs. All of this requires innovation.

NATURE OF SYSTEMS WORK

Innovation means change. It also means creating something that did not exist before. It is up to the project leader to foresee as many of these changes as possible and plan for them. Even with the best of planning, there will be some disorder and, at times, some confusion. There are reasons for this:

1. The world changes! Things that have nothing directly to do with the project change. The company may be purchased by another company, laws may change, management could change, etc. Of course the chances

of these things happening are somewhat remote, but they are not under the control of the analyst.

2. The champion leaves! All projects need champions—a person in the user community that has a personal interest in seeing that it is successful. When this person is no longer connected with the project, the project suffers. At this point, someone on the project team must carry on until a new champion can be found. Hopefully, the project has more than one champion on the user side.

3. The users learn more. The number of changes to the original design will increase as the users become more knowledgeable. They will see things that they want to change slightly. They will also see many things that can be done. The project leader must be very careful here. If a lot of new items are added to the project, the project may never be implemented.

   The project leader must also be careful not to reject everything. Each request must be analyzed. Items that make the system easier to use and require little time to program, probably should be added to the system. Others that have merit should be saved for future enhancements. The analyst should consider these future enhancements when finishing work on any uncompleted portion of the system. However, nothing should be added that would require a large amount of rework.

4. Large number of variables. As the project progresses, a person is introduced to a large number of new variables. First of all, you must learn the user's jargon. Familiar words may have a whole new meaning. Databases may have hundreds or even thousands of fields. There are personal adjustments for both you and the users. You may be working with a lot of new people, both in the user community and on the project team. The environment itself is probably new to you. It's no wonder things are confusing.

WHAT CAN ONE DO?

There are things that one can do to relieve stress and reduce confusion. This is true for analysts, project leaders and programmer trainees.

1. Never, never lose sight of the ultimate goals! Become obsessed. Make sure that everything that you do moves you one step closer to the goal. However, don't be discouraged if something fails the first time. Just learn from it and try something else. After all, only the last test counts (the one that works and will be used).

2. Do something! Produce tangible results as soon as possible, even if it is only one data flow diagram or one working screen in a program. There is a time to stop talking and to start producing.

3. Don't try to be perfect. Once you have completed a task, show it to the

users, and make the requested adjustments, then stop. Perfection is not necessary, assuming that you have already done an excellent job (shoddy work is never excusable).

4. Write it down. Document. Keep a notebook of all your ideas. Include notes from meetings, conversations with friends. Write down anything remotely applicable to the project. This is over and above any normal documentation that you would do for the project.

5. Visit users often. Go to their workplace. Keep them informed at every step in the project. You will both develop confidence as you become accustomed to each other. Be aware of the environment during these visits. It may change. Once, in a manufacturing operation, a conveyor line was installed between the operators and the spot where I planned to put terminals. It would have been both expensive and embarrassing to have made this discovery after the terminals have been installed.

6. Prototype where possible. Prototyping can help you to work through the logistics of a program or system. It works well even if the system is being installed on another machine without the prototyping language.

7. Ask for help or advice. Ask an expert if there is one. If not, explain what you are doing to someone with a general background in the subject. Sometimes, you will find your own solutions by explaining your problem to someone else. This organizes your thoughts. However, make sure that you have tried some tangible solutions on your own first. Don't become a pest.

8. Always go home at night with a success. Set one or two intermediate goals daily that can be met if you exert some effort. You will feel better about yourself and your project after a series of small victories. It is surprising how much can be accomplished in a short period of time by using this method.

9. Leave the project at work. If you take things home, they will hang over you like a cloud and you will feel guilty if you don't work on it. That causes burnout. Besides, the subconscious mind can work on problems much better if you are thinking about something else. Frequently, the solution to a problem will be obvious the next day.

10. Keep learning. Read technical journals, even if only the advertisements. Study things that are generally related to the user's areas of interest. For example, if you work for an insurance company, study insurance, how it is created, marketed, financed, managed, etc. The knowledge may not be directly useful on the current project, but it will be useful sometime in the future. However, do this on your own time. Doing it at work can be another form of procrastination. These are steps that an individual can personally take to reduce his/her own state of confusion and frustration. However, life becomes better for the project team as a whole as the project team learns more. More knowledge of the user's area and the technical side provides a firmer base to work from. Even though the

outside environment is constantly changing, the broader knowledge base provides the needed stability. The team will develop confidence as this base grows and the team will handle changes faster and easier.

CONCLUSION

Disorder and confusion accompany any new undertaking, be it a college research paper or development of a state-wide communication network. It is not your fault! Follow the steps outlined here and things will work out all right.

William W. Myers is a systems engineer with EDS.

26.

THE PROMISE OF AUTOMATION

Mike Lewis

Automation provides long-term improvement in quality and consistency of product, but companies considering an update of their manufacturing techniques face a number of obstacles.

Picture a factory of the future: Hundreds of robots swarm across the factory floor busily performing all the tasks needed to manufacture widgets. Nowhere in the vast plant is a human being to be found. But at a control panel hundreds of miles away, a sole human technician monitors the performance of this plant and a dozen others like it.

For some people, this image of the future might be a dream; for others, a nightmare. Regardless, the people who are bringing automation to manufacturing processes say it is unlikely ever to come true.

As a matter of fact, the great advantage of automated manufacturing is not even reduced personnel costs, according to the engineers and manufacturing executives who have brought high technology to plants around the country. Typically, labor accounts directly for only about 10 percent of manufacturing costs, even in nonautomated plants, explains Robert B. Erskine, who heads General Electric Company's production management.

For all the talk of robot's displacing blue-collar workers, robotics represents only a minor portion of automation. Erskine says GE has, at most, 2,000 robots, compared with a manufacturing work force of 350,000. "The robots perform a vital function" by freeing workers from potentially dangerous or mind-numbing tasks, he says, but "the idea of lots of little robots running around is absurd."

If personnel costs are not a major factor, what are the benefits to companies climbing aboard the automation bandwagon?

Short-term payback is one consideration, of course, but most companies are thinking of long-term gains. Says Charles Duncheon, vice president for marketing at Denver-based Fared Robots System, a three-year-old firm that designs and installs automated factory lines: "The biggest payback, so far, is quality consistently and capacity consistency."

"Quality is much more important" than personnel savings, GE's Erskine agrees, "as is the inventory reduction and flexibility" made possible by precision equipment that can adjust a plant's production rapidly to match even minor changes in the marketplace.

With the advantage that automation offers, why aren't all companies updating their manufacturing techniques?

When the National Electrical Manufacturers Association surveyed senior managers at its member firms, 73 percent of the companies responding said the biggest obstacle to automation was not hostility to it but rather lack of knowledge among design and engineering staffs. The second biggest difficulty was lack of appropriate software—for programing, for communication among sophisticated machines, for computer support.

Another study, this one of middle management engineers by the Institute of Industrial Engineers, drew a less rosy picture of the acceptance of automation. More than half of the industrial engineers who responded identified major people-related obstacles to improved productivity through automation. They included failure by management to understand how improvements can be achieved, as well as insufficient staff to direct changes aimed at improved productivity and to measure the results. The engineers also cited the inability of labor and management to work toward common productivity goals.

Nearly half the industrial engineers predict that another country—most likely Japan—will surpass the United States in productivity in 10 years. Less than 30 percent expect the United States to remain the most productive industrial nation for another 10 years.

Training engineers and operators to design and maintain high technology equipment is, nearly all manufacturers say, a great challenge.

More and more of the burden of training workers will have to be assumed by industry, says Homer J. Hagedorn, who specializes in organization and human-resources issues for Arthur D. Little, Inc. the Cambridge, Massachusetts-based consulting firm.

Because automation is a continuing process with frequent improvements in technology, Hagedorn says, companies that automate must constantly train and retrain workers.

"There aren't any schools that know how" to provide that kind of training, he says, adding that there is no reason to expect the federal government to spend large sums on such training. Individual companies will thus be left with the training burden.

Hagedorn predicts that nearly every manufacturing company will make a substantial financial commitment to training. Some training programs, he says, will be run in-house, but others will be run by equipment manufacturers and suppliers—who may find training a lucrative service—and by firms specializing in training.

The decision to automate is seldom made by the manufacturing executives who see the need for automation most directly. Because of the costs of automation—not only for equipment but sometimes also for redesigning products for ease of manufacture—the executives who make corporate strategy must be evolved.

"That's one of the serious internal problems," says the National Electrical Manufacturers Association's manager of automated systems, William C. Rolland. "We've got to train senior accountants and the top people to understand" that expensive equipment for automation can be upgraded in the future, for re-use in even more sophisticated systems. The flexibility that automation provides, Rolland says, can make a three-year payback period cost-efficient in industries that have traditionally expected a one-year payback.

The principal tax benefit from automation is the investment tax credit, with an effective rate of 8 percent, and depreciation over five years. Additionally, nearly all states have depreciation allowances for business equipment.

A number of companies in electronics and other industries have moved production to Asia, drawn by low labor costs. But many firms are now looking at automation as an alternative to offshore manufacturing.

Priam Corporation, of San Jose, California, a maker of disk drives for computers, has decided automation is the answer. The three-year-old company produces a full line of Winchester disk drives that it sells to computer manufacturers for $2,000 to $3,000 per unit. Priam generated $63.4 million in sales last year and had to decide how to expand its production facilities.

It considered moving its factory to Asia, but because product life cycles are short and getting shorter, Priam wanted to keep the plant near its engineering and pre-production staffs, so information could be shared more easily. That meant keeping the plant in the Silicon Valley area, near company headquarters, even though labor was expensive and rather scarce.

The solution was to take the company public in June 1983, "and we currently have about $46 million on the balance sheet," President William J. Schroeder says. With that liquidity, the company could build a $10 million, 142,000-square-foot plant near its headquarters.

Because of market conditions, Schroeder says, the company has produced only 150 to 200 disk drives a day since moving into the new plant early 1984, despite a projected capacity of 1,200 a day. Priam is, however, reducing the time formerly required to make a $3,000 disk drive.

The process of making Priam a fully automated manufacturer is a long way from completion. It is several years and perhaps another $10 million away, with automated workstations and an information management system yet to be added.

Schroeder says the idea is to position the company for a future in which what he calls "glorified garage shops," in Silicon Valley and elsewhere in the United States, will compete against highly automated Japanese firms.

In Priam's industry, U. S. manufacturers at the low end of the disk-drive business are "beating a path overseas" to Singapore, Hong Kong and Puerto Rico, Schroeder says. But his direct competitors—those making more expensive drives—are automating to keep production near their engineers and their customers.

Investing $10 million "may be peanuts to General Motors," Schroeder says, "but it's an awful big number for Priam." That big number, he says, is an investment he expects will pay off in improved ability to compete with Japanese companies.

And, multiplied many times as other companies automate their plants, those dollars could pay off handsomely in much stronger and more competitive American industry.

27.
DOWNSIZING YOUR COMPANY TO MEET NEW REALITIES

B. Charles Ames

You can wait—probably in vain—for the "good old days" to
return. Or you can restructure your company to prosper despite a
smaller sales base, emphasizing its current strengths and
developing new ones.

I am not optimistic about a recovery in the foreseeable future that will restore
sales volumes in a number of basic industries to their pre-recession levels. Many
capital-goods marketers are likely to suffer for a long time because of excess
capacity in so many basic industries and because smart manufacturers are improving productivity without significant additional capital investment.

Other traditional markets have been greatly diminished in size as electronics
and software replace many mechanically based products and systems—and as
substitute, or improved, materials prove more cost-effective.

Also, cost-containment programs have halted growth in many markets and
intensified the competitive environment. When you add the growing impact
of foreign competition, it is clear that the market opportunities that many
domestic companies enjoyed through the 1970s will not exist in the 1980s.

Many companies that once were star performers are now likely to be
marginal performers—or even fail to survive without major changes in strategy
and operating methods. To be successful, they will have to restructure
themselves for a smaller sales base or at least a demonstrably slower rate of
growth than in the past.

In our company's case, we first need to figure out how to earn a respectable
profit on about $200 million of volume in our traditional businesses, in con-
trast to the $400 million-plus volume we enjoyed in 1980 and 1981. Next, we
have to figure out how to get a larger share of a smaller pie or recover the capital
employed and take the business into new markets with more attractive
opportunities.

ROADBLOCKS TO CHANGE

Restructuring means dismantling an infrastructure that was put in place to support a business that no longer exists and gearing the business to the realities of the marketplace. It means abandoning old plants, moving away from high-cost labor situations, dropping certain products or technologies, breaking apart and combining organizations and functions, achieving major breakthroughs in product design and/or process technology, entering new markets or market segments, and acquiring new products or diversifying into entirely new business areas. While the idea of restructuring is not difficult to understand, there are several roadblocks that make it difficult to get this job done.

The first is a reluctance on the part of many managers to face the real facts about their traditional markets and businesses. Managements in far too many companies are still waiting for the effects of the recession to disappear and for business to get back to normal. In many cases, this is simply not going to happen. The demand changes that have occurred in many markets are structural—not cyclical—and it is silly to expect any kind of a dramatic recovery that will restore demand to former levels. It is understandably difficult—and may be impossible—for managers who have built the business to accept the fact that their market has leveled out at 30 percent to 40 percent below prior peaks, or that big chunks of it have been irretrievably lost to new competitors and/or technology. The key question is whether the managers who built a business are emotionally capable of downsizing it to deal with the realities of current market conditions.

The second roadblock is inadequate attention to the importance of being fully cost-competitive. Managements in many companies do not yet realize (or are not willing to admit) that they are not cost-competitive and that they are going to lose as a result. It should be obvious that you cannot be cost-competitive with:

- Product designs that have not been changed for a decade;
- Plant, equipment, and manufacturing methods carried over from World War II.
- Labor costs that are out of line with those of competitors;
- A manufacturing process that chews up working capital beyond sensible guidelines;
- Structured cost built up during the years when price increases covered indiscriminate staff additions.

You can have the most innovative, brilliant, hard-working management team in the world and the most ingenious marketing strategies; but if you are saddled with a lot of baggage from the past, such as old product designs, plants, equipment, organizations, and work habits, there is no way to be fully cost-competitive.

The third roadblock is a bureaucratic approach to managing the business in a way that resists change and frustrates the entrepreneurial spirit. This roadblock manifests itself in at least three ways.

One is the tendency of large multidivisional companies to build large corporate organizations that are bloated with a lot of high-paid staff and redundant group and middle-management people. I am very suspicious about the *real* contributions of any large corporate marketing, corporate public-relations, corporate advertising, corporate manufacturing, corporate planning or corporate development group. I have heard just about all the arguments that can be made to justify these activities at the corporate level, but I simply don't buy them. As far as I am concerned, all these activities should be handled by line management.

Of course, any company of size has to have some staff to fulfill its legal and financial requirements. But this can generally be done with a small group. In our own case, we cut our corporate staff from 120 people to 38, and I think this number may still be too high.

A second manifestation of this problem is the excessive layering in many organizations that separates senior management from those on the line who are actually doing the work. As a general rule, I think that whenever you have more than four or five layers in an organization, there is probably something wrong. I doubt that any senior manager can really know what is going on when he is that far removed from the action.

SMALLER CHUNKS

The third manifestation is the tendency of many companies to organize and manage their business around big chunks with a decentralized top-down approach. Any business is better off if it can be managed around a number of smaller discrete profit centers. At Reliance Electric we went from five to 100 discrete profit centers. At Acme-Cleveland we have moved from five to 20, which in my mind is still not enough. Managing around small discrete profit centers encourages entrepreneurship, avoids middle-management "drag" that slows organizations and decisions, provides a better basis for planning and control because someone with clear-cut responsibility is on top of everyday problems, and helps uncover more strategic options because more people are thinking strategically about what they can do to accelerate the profit growth in their particular business. The argument against this approach is: "Divisionalization is too costly." But it doesn't have to be. Profit-center responsibility can be assigned to an individual without going to a divisionalized organization.

The fourth roadblock is an overdependence on old or "me-too" products that don't begin to measure up to current competitive offerings. Many products contributed nicely when the demand curve was moving upward and capacity was strained, but now they simply are not competitive. Given the accelerating rate of technological change, the opportunities to maintain a viable business around these products is diminishing. For example, look at Acme-Cleveland's twist drill business. How can we expect to maintain our traditional high-speed cutting tool business—even though the tools themselves are fully competitive with those of other manufacturers—when carbide tools, lazer applications and surface coatings to extend wear life are rapidly chewing up a large portion of our market opportunities?

The final roadblock is a lack of drive, urgency, and competence in sales and marketing groups that have become conditioned to earning a living by simply taking orders. The high inflation rate of past years allowed too many sales and marketing personnel to look good in terms of increasing sales dollars. It didn't take much skill or effort to ride the demand curve upward in the late 1970s, and a lot of dollar volume was generated through price increases. Too many sales personnel still are trying to get by on personal relationships and loyalties, which really don't count for much in today's market when customers are pressuring for lower prices and better value.

MARKETING FUNDAMENTALS

Overcoming these roadblocks and gearing the business for profit growth in the face of diminished or slower market growth requires emphasis on marketing fundamentals that somehow seem to have been forgotten by many managers.

The first requirement is an organization geared to the more-demanding conditions of today's competitive environment. Most of the organizations I have seen evolve during the 1970s are too top-heavy, overstructured, and overstaffed to be effective—and too costly to be competitive. Reshaping the organization means management has to push hard for the right answers to questions like:

1. Is the organization properly structured around products, markets, or functions in light of what needs to be done?
2. Are corporate staff costs reasonable (anything over 1.5 percent of sales should be challenged)?
3. Does some individual have an assigned profit-and-loss responsibility for each important business segment? Do any of the segments represent a disproportionate amount of the total business?
4. Is the ratio of results-producers to support staff at least 3-to-1? Can some functions be combined, eliminated, or farmed out?
5. Are there any one-over-two, three, or four situations in the structure? Are there more layers than necessary?

These may be obvious questions. But they are not asked frequently enough—or in a significantly challenging way—so that a change from the status quo is seriously considered.

FACT OR FOLKLORE?

The second requirement is for management to insist on getting the real facts. Very few managers are sufficiently tough-minded in searching for the facts, analyzing them, and then presenting them as a basis for their conclusions and recommendations. Many purported "facts" fall into categories like the following:

- *Folklore Facts* that have grown up with the business and have never really been challenged. For example, "We are a low-cost producer." This claim may not stand up when you ask, "Compared with whom?" or "At what volume levels?"
- *Assumed Facts* that are assumptions about the future, but not facts. For example, that the market will grow at a certain rate or that competitors will react in a certain way. What is the basis for the assumption? What happens if it doesn't hold up? What are the contingency plans if the assumptions change?
- *Reported Facts* that tend to be given unwarranted validity simply because they have been published by some association or industry "expert." How valid or complete is the source?
- *Half-True Facts* that have a certain element of validity to them but are misleading. For example, "The market has grown at an average rate of 10 percent a year over the last five years." This may be a true statement, but it is misleading if, five years ago, the market dipped to an unusually low level and much of the 10 percent growth was simply a case of catching up.

The third requirement is a thorough understanding of the profit economics for each product/market business. At a minimum, understanding the profit economics of the business requires one to know the following:

1. How many dollars of assets are committed in each stage or step of each product/market business (e.g., R&D, materials, plant and equipment, finished stock, post-sale support)?
2. What is the fixed/variable cost relationship for each product/market business—that is, for each dollar of sales, how many cents are attributable to "bedrock fixed costs," how many to structured or discretionary costs, and how many to out-of-pocket costs?
3. How do costs and profits change with swings in volume?
4. What is the break-even point at current volume—and what actions could be taken to bring that break-even point down should potential volume decline?
5. What is the rate of incremental profit on each added increment of volume? What are the volume points at which new increments of structured costs must be added?

WAY TO START

A net profit-and-loss statement (after all allocations) and a balance sheet for each product line is an essential starting point for generating this kind of information. I doubt that very many managers have this information readily available. Most accounting systems are not designed to provide it; and accountants will argue that you can't get the information because many products run on the same machines, a lot of indirect costs can't be allocated, and so on.

I say, "Baloney!" Shared fixed and indirect charges are serious problems, and they are difficult to attach as a "lump." They must be broken down and assigned to a discrete business unit, even if it is done arbitrarily, so that a manager with hands-on responsibility can argue about fairness and whether there is value received for the costs involved.

The fourth requirement is to segment markets in different ways—and to a far greater degree than typically was done in the past. The traditional way to segment most markets is around standard SIC codes, but this isn't particularly helpful. These cuts tend to result in product segments, not market segments. Moreover, they represent such gross cuts of a market that they are not useful in making intelligent marketing decisions.

If you slice an overall market that appears to be unattractive into small enough segments, you can generally find one or more that present a much better opportunity for profit growth. Second, it is wise to assume that some competitors, particularly smaller ones, are going to segment the market, find the attractive segments, and capture market share from the companies that have not geared up to match them.

The final requirement is to make a hard-nosed assessment of the strategy for each product/market business in light of the many structural changes that have occurred in the marketplace. Any company that's pursuing the same strategy today that it did 24 months ago is probably on the wrong track.

Strategies must be market-focused to overcome the product emphasis that restricts thinking and actions in so many companies. For example, our new way of looking at our drill business is to say that we will help customers make holes in the most efficient way—not simply sell drills. This approach takes us well outside our traditional products and technology into lasers, fluid cutting systems, and carbides.

TIMESAVERS

A few key questions can avoid a lot of wasted time arguing about "can't win" strategies:

1. Is the strategy designed to serve specified markets, as opposed to simply selling products.

2. Do the target markets offer attractive growth opportunities?
3. Is the cost/profit structure attractive?
4. Is the plan based on unique advantages over the competition? Does the strategy revolve around distinctive product features, programs, or other unique advantages that provide a competitive edge?

If these questions can't be answered positively, don't waste much time arguing about the plan's viability.

B. Charles Ames is chairman and chief executive officer of Acme-Cleveland Corporation. He is the coauthor of Managerial Marketing: The Ultimate Advantage.

28.

GAIN SHARING: DO IT RIGHT THE FIRST TIME

Michael Schuster

Gain sharing can be introduced for any number of reasons: to make labor costs reflect the economic conditions of a business, to transform manager-employee relations and to boost productivity levels, to name a few. This article examines the four keys to implementing a successful plan.

Senior managers and economists show increasing interest in the concept of gain sharing—or passing on the benefits of increased productivity, cost reductions, and improved quality through regular cash bonuses. Where it was once considered a last-ditch effort to save a company from financial collapse, today gain sharing is introduced for any number of reasons: to make labor cost reflect the economic conditions of a business, to transform manager-employee relations, and to boost productivity levels, to name a few.

At its most effective, gain sharing can do all those things; consequently, it can genuinely improve a company's financial standing. Unlike individual incentive and profit-sharing programs, it is not expensive to administer nor does it require disclosure of sensitive business information. However, the effectiveness of gain-sharing plans varies a great deal. There appear to be four keys to success: defining the plan's strategic objectives, devoting sufficient resources to feasibility assessment and plan design, commitment to the concept at all managerial levels, and effective implementation.

The concept is not new: the Scanlon Plan—the oldest of these plans—has been on the American scene since the late 1930s. Rucker Plans first appeared in the 1940s. Although they began as attempts to save companies from imminent disaster, by the 1950s many plans reflected a broad philosophy and a changing relationship with unions—specifically, a commitment to cooperation and improved use of human resources. During the 1960s, interest in productivity sharing waned. Interest has resurfaced over the past fifteen years in response to several factors: declining productivity growth rates, erosion of position in world markets, a perceived need to improve the quality of work life, and an inability to continue to pass along to end users increases in compensation costs. A 1984 article by ex-UAW president R. E. Majerus reflected the renewed interest; it suggested that both employees and unions wanted to explore the notion of sharing productivity gains.[1] Although the idea was originally considered applicable only in manufacturing environments, gain sharing is also catching on in the not-for-profit sector, particularly government agencies and health-care organizations.

This article is based on research conducted at over sixty American and British firms in union and nonunion settings.[2] It focuses on the benefits of gain sharing, but also draws on knowledge gained from unsuccessful examples. The negative findings are of particular importance, since the downside of gain sharing has gone largely unreported in the business press. The article provides a framework for deciding whether gain sharing is appropriate for an organization, and guidelines for implementation that will reduce the risk of failure.

STRATEGIC BASES FOR GAIN SHARING

Gain sharing should contribute to the achievement of one or more strategic objectives. The plan's success will depend in part on how well defined the objectives are, and on whether the plan design reflects those objectives.

In some companies, particularly Scanlon Plan firms, gain sharing reflects a broad philosophy of management. It is used to increase employee identification with, and commitment to, the organization by providing opportunities to participate in decision making and to share in financial gains. In these firms, the opportunities for employee involvement appear to be just as important as the actual cash bonus. One interesting study of Scanlon Plan firms found that hourly employees and supervisors believed the plan improved morale and commitment; it was *senior managers* who believed most strongly that the plan improved the company's financial standing.[3]

Other firms introduce gain sharing for entirely different reasons. It some companies it is used merely as a management tool to increase productivity. In these cases, the application of gain sharing is most likely to be short term. There is little concern about whether it continues beyond an initial one-to-three-year period.

Some firms use gain sharing as a vehicle for organizational change and development. They have found that financial rewards can be an effective inducement to change long-standing attitudes and behavior, thus revitalizing older and more mature facilities.

Still other firms find that gain sharing is an excellent way to relate employee compensation to organizational performance. In these firms, annual pay increases are modest, but employees receive sizable bonuses in years when business conditions are good, and little or no bonus in poor years. One firm we studied had had a gain sharing program since 1968. In years when the business did well, bonuses exceeded 20 to 25 percent of earnings, while in poor years there were few, if any, bonuses. This approach is receiving increased attention from economists, who argue that it would help firms to be more competitive by making labor costs more sensitive to economic cycles, thus reducing inflation, and would reduce unemployment during recessionary periods by lowering the cost savings for layoffs.[4]

Yet another application occurred during the recent round of concession bargaining. A number of companies and unions agreed to institute gain-sharing plans to offset concessionary reductions of wages and benefits. Higher productivity, cost reductions, and improved quality were used to generate bonuses to compensate employees for reduced wages.

A significant number of firms use gain sharing as a replacement for, or an alternative to, an individual incentive system. These firms found that their existing individual incentive systems were costly and often dysfunctional, but thought their employees needed some form of economic incentive. Consequently they introduced gain sharing, believing that the group bonus would be easier to administer and would encourage more positive employee work behavior.

Thus, from a strategic perspective, senior executives may be motivated to adopt gain sharing merely as a method of compensation, or as the basis for a far-reaching organizational transition—or as anything in between. These distinctions are vital, since they affect the successful design and implementation of the gain-sharing plan. Our studies indicate that organizations that approach gain sharing strategically and incorporate it as a management philosophy are most likely to be successful. Tailoring the plan to the company's environment, rather than accepting an off-the-shelf approach, also increases the probability of success. These findings argue for a careful analysis of both the decision to introduce a gain-sharing program and the logistics of its design and implementation.

INTRODUCING GAIN SHARING

Too many organizations make serious mistakes by attempting to introduce a gain-sharing plan without proper study and analysis. These firms can find themselves with plans that do not work. Or worse, they can pay considerable bonuses to employees without verifiable increases in performance.

As indicated in Figure 1, the gain-sharing process involves six important steps. Managers should expect to spend between six and eighteen months to assess, design, approve, and implement a plan.

Step One: Initial Seminar. Ideally, the process should begin with a seminar for senior managers that explains the history and structure of gain sharing, its benefits and risks, and the problems involved in designing and implementing a plan. Although the concept itself is not new, it represents a substantial change

Figure 1.
Institution of a Gain-Sharing Plan

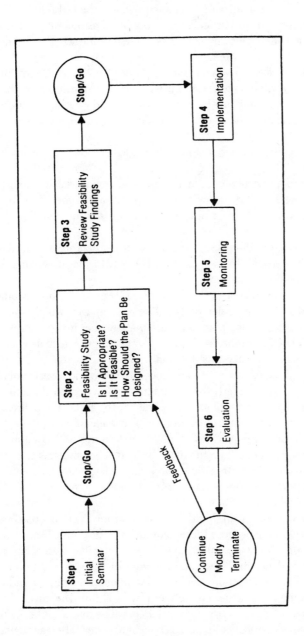

for many companies. As such, it is best if key decision makers are fully informed. Many companies make the mistake of sending one to two people to
general seminars on gain sharing. It is far more cost effective and educationally
sound to conduct a smaller in-company program where the full focus of the
discussion can be on the particular organization. The outcome of the seminar
and subsequent deliberations should be to determine whether or not a full
feasibility study is warranted.

Step Two: Feasibility Study. Assuming there is top management interest, a
feasibility study will help to determine whether gain sharing can contribute to
the achievement of the firm's business objectives and whether the organization
is a good candidate. The study should address three critical issues:

1. Is gain sharing appropriate from a strategic business and human-resources
    perspective?
2. Are the proper structural, human-resource, managerial and financial con-
    ditions present? If the answers to (1) and (2) are in the affirmative, then
3. What is the appropriate design for the gain-sharing plan?

The first issue was discussed at the outset; the others are discussed in detail
later on in this article. In the answer to (1) or (2) is negative, an alternative
approach should be considered.

Step Three: Review Feasibility Study and Plan Design. Once the feasibility study
is completed and a plan design proposed, senior managers will decide either to
implement a gain-sharing plan or to terminate further investigation. The information derived from the feasibility study should provide management with
the data it needs to make this decision.

Step Four: Implementation. Companies often expend considerable effort
designing a plan, particularly the bonus formula, but neglect the implementation process. This is unfortunate, since the key to success is employee understanding, along with both supervisory and managerial acceptance. Several
companies have developed very innovative training and communications
materials that enhance commitment to the plan. The implementation process
should also include addressing related human-resources issues, such as
managerial style, union/management relations, and renewed efforts at
managerial training.

It is best to start the gain sharing at a point during the year when employees
have a reasonable chance to achieve a bonus, especially if the firm's production
cycle is uneven. Doing this will establish the creditability of the plan, promote
employee confidence and trust, and generate high levels of interest.
on a monthly basis to ensure that it is developing as expected and that the
formula is being calculated accurately and fairly. During the initial year, many
managers and employees have substantial questions that must be addressed in
order for the necessary organizational changes to occur. Thereafter, absent unusual circumstances, gain-sharing plans require less frequent examination.

Step Six: Evaluation. Many gain-sharing plans die out in the first five years, often unnecessarily. A formal evaluation after two or three years will reveal whether any strategic objectives have been met—and may point the way to intelligent revisions. Often business conditions have changed, new managers have come on the scene, new objectives must be incorporated into the plan, or the bonus formula requires a substantial overhaul. Following an evaluation by an outside consultant, one firm revised its plan to include nonhourly employees and instituted a new approach to measurement. This plan is now more successful than it was before.

FEASIBILITY

The most complex of the steps above is the second, which encompasses feasibility assessment as well as actual plan design. When determining whether a productivity gain-sharing plan can effectively be installed in an organization, the following factors should be taken into consideration. With the exception of the measurement issue, however, *no single issue* should operate to eliminate consideration of gain sharing.

Performance and Financial Measures. In order for gain sharing to succeed, the company and its employees must believe that the bonus formula is reasonable, accurate, and equitable. Ideally, the formula requires good financial and operating reporting systems with a history of validity and stability. It is preferable to have two measures. The first will measure the bonus, and the second will validate the bonus as an accurate measure of company performance. In any organization, there will be someone who asks, "What are we getting for the bonus dollars we are paying out?" Hard data with which to answer such questions is essential. In one instance, we used an output-per-hour measure as a check on a gain-sharing plant that used a labor-to-sales ratio to determine the bonus. The measure correlated nicely and it was concluded that bonuses were being paid on the basis of real productivity gains.

If there is not a reasonably good measure upon which to base the gain sharing, then the organization should not attempt to install a plan. An alternative approach to the relevant strategic objective should be considered instead.

Plant or Facility Size. The best wisdom on plant size is that facilities with less than 500 employees are ideally suited for gain sharing, while those with over 2,000 are not. Gain sharing also can be very effective if there are between 500 and 1,000 employees. With more than 1,000 employees it becomes difficult, but not impossible, to manage a plan. Here the quality of the management team and its commitment to the concept are the most important factors. Any facility with more than 2,000 employees is a more risky candidate. Nonetheless, there are examples of successful plans with more than 3,000 employees in multiple facilities. In sites with more than 1,000 employees, management should be aware that greater resources will be needed to implement the plan, that progress may be slower, and that considerable effort may be needed to overcome resistance to change.

Type of Production. Plants with highly mixed types of production will find it difficult, but not impossible, to introduce gain sharing. Diverse product lines make measurement more intricate: as output shifts from high-labor-content products to lower-labor-content products, a bonus can be created when none has been earned, and vice versa. For a firm that seeks to reward employees for productivity increases, this is a very important consideration. If a firm seeks to reward employees when the performance of the *business* is strong, it becomes less of a concern because the bonus will be determined differently.

Work-Force Interdependence. Highly integrated work forces are good candidates for large group gain-sharing plans—and very poor candidates for small-group plans. In situations where departments or shifts work independently, gain sharing can be more difficult to install. In these instances, the potential exists for small group or combined group and plant structures.

Work-Force Composition. Many work forces do not need or would not be motivated by financial incentives. There is a famous study of secondary workers who did not respond to the monetary incentives and employee involvement offered through gain sharing.[5] In another case, the average worker was fifty-three years old, already had very good pay and benefits, and had met major financial commitments (homes paid for, children through school, etc.). This facility was not regarded as a good candidate. In instances similar to these, other human-resource strategies may have more motivational potential than gain sharing does.

Potential to Absorb Additional Output. Most firms that introduce gain sharing experience an initial increase in productivity of 5 to 15 percent. (In one case in our study, the initial increase in productivity was 40 percent.) In order to avoid payoffs, the company must be able to capture this productivity gain. Some companies have solid backlogs of orders, others use their attrition plan, and some reduce scheduled, but not as yet announced, overtime. One firm accurately forecasted that it could acquire a higher volume of business on the basis of expected cost reductions made possible through gain sharing.

However, where increased productivity leads directly to layoffs, gain sharing should be approached with great caution. In survival situations, this issue becomes less of a priority for obvious reasons.

Potential for Employee Efforts. In determining the feasibility of gain sharing, it is important to consider the degree to which employee efforts can contribute to the success of the business. In some highly automated situations, employees' ability to contribute through additional work efforts or ideas may be very limited, so gain sharing may have minimal impact.

Even in considerably automated facilities, gain sharing may be valuable if employee effort can be expected to result in improved equipment use. Managers in these situations argue that even here a substantial employee contribution can result from operating the capital equipment to the fullest extent. Consider one case we encountered in which employees began to stagger normal and lunchtime breaks to keep equipment operating. Thereafter these same employees recommended higher machine speeds, which required more effort on their part. If management had attempted to introduce these changes in the absence of gain sharing, there would have been overwhelming resistance.

History of the Facility. Many plants have a long history of unsuccessful human-resources programs, and gain sharing may be seen as just another short-lived management effort to get more out of the work force. Other facilities have a history of problems and a lack of management credibility. In these situations, considerable credibility building may be needed before a gain-sharing plan becomes feasible.

Present Organizational Climate. Gain sharing can be used to improve the climate and culture of an organization, but some minimally acceptable level of trust must be present at the outset. Employees develop positive attitudes toward gain-sharing plans when there is organizational trust, group attitudes supportive of the concept, and supervisory acceptance.[6] A lack of trust suggests that the plan should be postponed until the situation improves. In one unsuccessful case, management was unable to properly communicate the goals and objectives of the plan because its communication lacked creditibility. The plan never got off the ground.

Union-Management Relations. It is easier to install gain sharing in a nonunion environment. Where a reasonable relationship between the company and the union exists, union involvement gives the program greater credibility—and generally the union is an active partner in program installation. In difficult union environments, it might be advisable to pursue other strategies before considering gain sharing.

The presence of a union is not the key factor, but the *attitude* of management and union leaders toward cooperative efforts is critical. It is important to note that the general design of the plan is an excellent topic for problem-solving negotiations and that there are many issues in which union input can be very useful. However, the gain-sharing formula is best arrived at by third-party experts.

Capital Investment Plans. It is not advisable to install gain sharing in an environment where unusually large capital investments are planned; these change the capital-labor ratio and make gain-sharing measurement unreliable. Substantial new investments should be made before gain sharing is introduced, particularly if the investments results in a work-force reductions. Most formulas are capable of capturing incremental capital improvements; they become part of the historical relationship upon which most plans are based.

Facility Management. It takes a good management team to make gain sharing successful. Well-managed operations usually are prepared for employee involvement and have taken many of the management initiatives needed to make steady productivity improvements. If site managers are having difficulty managing the business, adding gain sharing is not likely to improve the situation. It requires at least one key effective manager on-site to act as the gain-sharing catalyst.

Higher Management Support. Managers who introduce gain sharing take a risk, particularly when there is steady turnover of higher management personnel. Organizational support for the concept is needed to make it work most effectively. Continuity of management, or at least management philosophy, is a basic requirement.

A careful analysis of the factors cited above will allow a company to determine if gain sharing is likely to be successful. It is not necessary that the organization qualify on all counts: with the exception of reliable measurement capabilities, none of the others should be considered knockout factors. However, if several fail to support gain sharing, or if the measurement factor cannot be met, a program should not be attempted unless there are overwhelming business arguments for the concept—as can sometimes occur in wage-concession situations.

DESIGNING THE GAIN-SHARING PLAN

The key differences among gain-sharing plans evolve from varying philosophies, ways to measure productivity, and provisions for employee involvement. *Rather than use standard applications, or "canned" programs, managers should adopt plans tailored to their own situation.* In this way, they can use the best features of each program.

Answering the following questions will define a company's stance vis-a-vis the three key issues.

1. Which groups of employees should participate in the gain-sharing plan?
2. How much employee involvement should there be and under what ground rules? How can the employee involvement best be structured?
3. How should the bonus be measured?
4. How often should the gain sharing be measured?
5. What other human resource strategies should be employed to effectively complement the plan and maximize its effectiveness?
6. When should the gain sharing begin?

Employee Participants. Some managers are willing to share productivity improvements, but become concerned when the gain sharing includes personnel outside the factory, for example, clerical and professional employees. This is a philosophical question. One view is that gain sharing should be applied only to factory employees, with a measure of productivity reflective of factory efforts only. Another view suggests that efforts by all employees are required to make a business unit successful, and, therefore, a measurement system must be designed to reflect the performance of the larger group. A variation of the second view is that some form of financial participation by all employees makes organizations more effective.

Those firms seeking to achieve major cultural change will include all employees, since that strategy's message is that all employees must work together to achieve the organization's objectives, and therefore all participate in the gain sharing. At a minimum, when designing a plan for factory employees only, I believe it is a mistake to exclude first-level supervision, since this "divides the team" and creates an issue of whether it is in the supervisor's interest to support the program. With the exception of the Scanlon Plan, most plans are used almost exclusively with hourly employees. The Scanlon Plan generally includes all employees, except for those who already participate in some other corporate bonus opportunity.

Either approach can work well, so long as senior executives make a conscious choice, communicate that choice to employees, and stick with it. One company designed its program to include all hourly and salaried employees in order to promote a philosophy of organizational cohesion; later, it abruptly removed all white-collar employees from the formula. Thereafter, no bonuses were earned and the factory employees, believing management had manipulated the bonus formula, gave notice through the union to terminate the plan. A residue of ill will continues.

Employee Involvement. Employee involvement also differs from one plan to another. Some plans contain no provisions for involvement at all; others allow for department-level committees as well as a high-level employee-management steering committee. (Firms with active employee involvement teams or quality circles that add gain sharing later are similar to Scanlon Plan firms in their level of employee involvement.) The key to success appears to be that the level of employee involvement reflects the strategic objectives of the gain-sharing plan itself and is consistent with management philosophy.

Because it has been studied so extensively, the Scanlon Plan can offer important insights about the ways in which employee involvement affects gain sharing's usefulness. Many of the Scanlon Plans that are unsuccessful fail because management does not recognize that the plan is something more than a committee structure and a bonus-sharing program; rather, it is a highly developed philosophy of management. In firms with successful Scanlon Plans, managers focus on the value of the individual. They recognize the contribution of each member of the organization, encourage decentralized decision making, and seek each employee's identification with the company's goals. To foster the concept that employees should take more responsibility, Scanlon committees are authorized to spend limited amounts of money to implement each project they work on. This strategy seems to pay off: the amount of employee participation in firms that retain the plan is higher than is those that do not.[7]

Managers in more traditional environments may find that other forms of gain sharing, with less emphasis on employee involvement, are physiologically better suited to their situations. Gain-sharing plans can be effective in either context. The important thing is to install a plan that is consistent with the facility's dominant philosophy, or the philosophical direction senior managers would like to take. If managers expect to achieve substantial organizational change, they must design plans with substantial employee involvement. However, they must be realistic about the genuine commitment to, or capacity for, change. One firm installed gain sharing and structured it with potentially high levels of employee participation. Unfortunately, most decisions in the organization were actually made in a highly autocratic manner. In this environment, the shop-floor-level committees became paralyzed because supervisors were unable and unwilling to make decisions. The employees soon became disenchanted with the process.

The degree of involvement tends to determine the role that managers and supervisors play in gain-sharing plans. If a considerable structure for employee involvement exists, supervisors play a key leadership role. Managers are expected not only to be supportive of the process, but also to provide their expertise when requested. The implementation of gain sharing requires considerable management training and development. Those firms that lack confidence in their supervisors, or with managers unwilling or unable to become active in this process, should consider gain-sharing plans with less employee involvement. Again, the Scanlon Plan experiences shed light on the relationship between managers' attitudes and the success of the program. Retention of the plan seems to be related to manager's confidence in the capabilities of their employees.[8] Managers in firms that *dropped* the Scanlon Plan believed rank-and-file workers demonstrated less dependability, initiative, long-range perspective, and willingness to change, and had less judgment, sense of responsibility, pride in performance, and alertness. Whether these attitudes say more about the managers, or their employees, is not clear: it is abundantly clear, however, that these circumstances make constructive employee participation unlikely.

Even if a gain-sharing plan includes no opportunity for direct employee involvement in decision making, complementary participation programs are not precluded. In some organizations, there are existing opportunities such as labor-management committees, quality circles, or ad hoc employee participation teams. When fitting gain sharing into existing programs, it is important to remember that money is a powerful motivator, and that the gain sharing and other employee opportunities must be complementary. An example demonstrates this point. One organization, which had installed quality circles after long controversy, went on to introduce gain sharing. Unfortunately, no care was taken to ensure that the two programs did not diminish each other's effectiveness. The gain-sharing plan actually *penalized the group* for time spent in quality circle meetings. Within six months, the quality-circles program had ceased to function.

Measurement Issues. Gain-sharing plans use both financial and nonfinancial measures of productivity. These are most often developed following an analysis of historical data going back over a period of two to five years. Some firms develop historical data on several potential measures to assess the one that will operate the best. Great care must be taken in designing the measurement for the bonus. My advice to firms considering gain sharing is that if you can not satisfactorily measure it, do not do it.

The most common financial measures of productivity are the relationship between sales value of production and labor costs (Scanlon Plan), or between production value (sales value minus cost of goods sold) and labor costs (Rucker Plan). These measures can be adapted and modified. Hence one firm using a labor-to-sales ratio also used cost-of-quality to sales and operating supplies to sales ratios. Gain sharing was thus measured as productivity plus or minus quality plus or minus operating supplies. Another firm that included a large number of engineers and designers in its plan added savings on warranty costs to its added-value measure. The financial measure of productivity have great educational value in spurring employee understanding of business fundamentals, but require firms to disclose information that might be considered proprietary and therefore confidential. Financial measures tend to closely parallel overall firm performance.

Nonfinancial measures of productivity include output per hour (units/hours of labor), output per hour plus or minus a measure of quality (called Productivity and Waste Bonus Plans), and engineered time standards, absorption of indirect hours, and actual hours worked (Improshare plans). In Productivity and Waste Bonus Plans, improvements in productivity can be enhanced or reduced by improvements or deterioration in quality. Another approach combines Group/Plant concepts. Productivity is measured on a departmental/shift basis. Gains are shared in a formula in which a portion is allocated to the group, with the remainder to a plant bonus pool. The Department of the Army has developed a gain-sharing plan to motivate and reward civilian employees. In this plan, performance standards are used to determine "earned hours" of production, which are compared with direct labor hours. In the present economic environment of declining prices and margins, nonfinancial measures present more risk, as firms could pay a bonus for certifiable increase in productivity while simultaneously losing money.

It is important for firms to find the measure of productivity that best fits their situation and correlates with the strategic objective of the gain-sharing plan. One firm that did not do so instituted gain sharing in two plants that were undergoing substantial price competition at the same time that inflation was causing materials, supplies, and regular labor costs to increase. Although there was a substantial productivity increase, these factors meant that very few bonuses were paid to employees. As a result, employees felt aggrieved and both plants later experienced sixteen-week strikes. Employee understanding of the plans proved to be very limited.

Time Frame for Measurement. The most commonly used measurement period for gain sharing is one month. Many firms have recently moved to quarterly measurement because this tends to create more stability in the measurement process and avoids severe month-to-month fluctuations. A small number of firms use six-month measurement periods, but the longer time will tend to reduce the motivational impact (although the actual bonus payments increase with the longer period).

There are many firms that measure weekly, often using a four-to-six-week rolling average, which relates to the manner in which individual incentives are calculated and paid. I do not recommend this approach. First, these firms include the bonus with the regular paycheck. It is best to pay the bonus by separate check so as to differentiate performance from regular earnings. Second, the rolling average lessens the variability in earnings and therefore is less effective from a motivational perspective. And third, many employees do not understand the concept of a rolling average.

Other Human Resource Strategies. Most gain-sharing plans require a considerable training and communications effort connected with program installation. In addition, firms taking a broad view of gain sharing will use the installation period to effect even more substantial changes in human resource programs, policies, and initiatives.

One firm used the occasion to require all operating managers to go through an assessment center for diagnostic purposes. The result was individualized training and development programs to upgrade the quality of management. Other firms used gain-sharing introduction as the occasion for ending outmoded human-resource policies such as individual suggestion programs and attendance reward programs. (Attendance is rewarded in gain sharing, since the size of an individual employee's bonus is a function of the number of hours worked.) Yet another firm terminated a flex-time program that had been the subject of considerable abuse. Other companies have seen gain sharing introduction as a chance to change the style of management and relations with the union, to expand skills-based training, or to reexamine job design and staffing levels.

The basic point is that, at some firms, gain sharing becomes the centerpiece of human-resource management strategy. When this is the case considerable planning goes into assuming that gain sharing is supplemented by a coherent, integrated HRM program. Those firms that are less ambitious may still find a need for some compensatory human-resource activity to meet the minimum conditions for establishing a gain-sharing plan.

Gain-Sharing Start Date. It is best to begin gain sharing at a point in the firm's calendar when activity is normally high, to give employees an opportunity to achieve good results. Many firms that began plans in the middle of a financial year found it useful to operate the first year of the plan as a short year, in order that subsequently the gain sharing could operate in concert with the financial year.

A WORD OF CAUTION

Favorable publicity in the popular press reflects the fact that firms using gain-sharing plans can achieve sizable performance and employee relations benefits. Nonetheless, there are pitfalls, and executives considering gain sharing should move carefully.

Many plans do not survive beyond the first several years, or create serious problems that might not otherwise have arisen. Often these difficulties are avoidable. It is important for firms considering gain sharing to examine their philosophy, goals, and business objectives. Thereafter, a plan incorporating a structure and measurement system can be designed that fits the business unit. One very important factor is that firms should avoid using a canned program, and instead design one specifically geared to the situation.

Too many firms introduce gain sharing as a separate program rather than as part of an overall strategy of human-resource management. Thus, they fail to see the relationship between the gain sharing and other human resource programs. Others fail to consider the long-term implications of the program.

Companies should determine whether gain sharing would contribute to realization of intermediate-range (three-to-five-year) business objectives. Next, through a feasibility study, firms need to determine whether it would be appropriate to install gain sharing. If appropriate, a plan must be structured that is congruent with the organization's dominant values and characteristics. A measurement system that accurately and equitably conceptualizes its operations must be formulated. Finally, executives need to get behind the program and identify a member of their staff that can provide the leadership to make gain sharing a success.

REFERENCES

1   R. E. Majerus, "Workers Have a Right to a Share of Profits," *Harvard Business Review*, September-October 1984, pp. 42-50.

2   See M. Schuster, "The Impact of Union-Management Cooperation on Productivity and Employment," *Industrial and Labor Relations Review*, 36 (1983): 415-430; M. Schuster, "Union-Management Cooperation: Structure, Process, and Impact" (Kalamazoo, MI: W. E. Upjohn Institute for Employment Research, 1984).

3   P. S. Goodman, J. H. Wakely, and R. H. Ruh, "What Employees Think of the Scanlon Plan," *Personnel*, Spring 1972, pp. 22-29.

4   D. J. B. Mitchell, "Gain-Sharing: An Anti-Inflation Reform," *Challenge*, July-August 1982, pp. 18-25.

5   T. Gilson and M. Lefcowitz, "A Plant-wide Productivity Bonus in a Small Factory: Study of an Unsuccessful Case," *Industrial and Labor Relations Review* 10 (1957): 284-296.

6   P. S. Goodman and B. E. Moore, "Factors Affecting Acquisition of Beliefs about a New Reward System,"*Human Relations* 29 (1976): 571-588.

7   J. K. White, "The Scanlon Plan: Causes and Correlates of Success," *Academy of Management Journal* 22 (1979): 292-312.

8   R. A. Ruh, R. L. Wallace, and C. F. Frost, "Management Attitudes and the Scanlon Plan," *Industrial Relations* 12 (1973): 282-288.

Michael Schuster is associate professor of management at the School of Management, Syracuse University, and the director of the University's Employment Studies Institute.

29.
GROUP EFFECTIVENESS:
WHAT REALLY MATTERS?

Gregory P. Shea
Richard A. Guzzo

We know far too little about managing groups, partly because research about group task effectiveness has not kept pace with the increasing importance of group performance. This article explains how managers can set groups up to succeed.

Quick, name an organization that does not use any groups. If you are tempted to name one, then consider this definition of what constitutes a group: a set of three or more people that can identify itself and be identified by others in the organization as a group.

The importance of formal groups in organizations matches their prominence. The complexity and turbulence facing so many organizers lead to increased specialization and temporariness; this movement, in turn, fosters more participative management in general and a greater reliance on groups in particular. How *effectively* groups are used has a decided impact on organizational performance. According to Peters and Waterman, small groups are "quite simply, the building blocks of excellent companies."[1] Nonetheless, we know far too little about managing groups, partly because behavioral-science research and theory about groups and group task effectiveness have not kept pace with the increasing importance of group performance.[2] This article presents a framework for thinking about groups as well as a way of "taking their temperature."

WHAT MATTERS?

We do not really know. Most of what academic experts say about effective management of groups comes from one of two traditions: laboratory studies of examination of group dynamics. The laboratory studies number in the thousands; typically they involve college students performing highly structured tasks with total or virtual strangers for a very limited amount of time. Consequently, as Hackman points out, "The major contextual influence in the laboratory . . . is the *experimenter.*"[3] Subtleties of intra- and interpersonal relations are carefully studied, while "in the interest of good experimental practice some of the variables that may most powerfully affect what happens in groups are fixed at constant levels, *thereby making it impossible to learn about their effects.*"[4] So, while these studies frequently concern effectiveness or productivity, generalizing from them is difficult at best.

Regrettably, the work on group dynamics is not much more helpful. These examinations often concern the full range of phenomena that occur in groups almost without regard for any connection between a given phenomenon, like member openness or satisfaction, and group performance. A manager is left to sift through a variety of ideas about improving group process, and given little guidance about what process improvements will actually affect performance. Indeed, reviews of various types of group process intervention report no consistent relationship between group performance and interventions aimed at improving interpersonal relations.[5]

We believe that real-world, real-time group effectiveness is what matters and that it boils down to the production of designated products or the delivery of contracted services, per specification. Our review of the academic literature on groups, and our own experience, leads us to suggest that three variables are especially important in determining group effectiveness: task interdependence, outcome interdependence, and potency. These variables both influence group performance *and* can be influenced by members and supervisors of groups. Thus they warrant special attention by academics and practicing managers alike.[6]

Task interdependence is the degree of task-driven interaction among group members. Group members may work in parallel, having little or no contact with one another, perhaps not even seeing their work combined. Research and development groups occasionally operate in this fashion, as do some staffs. Alternatively, group members may work in sequence, with one member completing part of a task and passing it along to another member. Larger organizations tend to have some groups that operate this way. Finally, group members may have to interact frequently in order to do their work, as is often the case for task forces, focus groups, or employee-involvement teams.

Outcome interdependence exists when task accomplishment by a group yields consequences that are important to and shared by some or all group members—for example, pay, time off, and recognition. The "outcomes" are bestowed by people other than group members, usually a supervisor or senior manager. They may be rewards or punishments; they may include pay, promotion, skill acquisition, exposure, or survival; and they may be distributed in a variety of ways, for example, cooperatively or competitively. Outcomes do *not* include any benefits derived from within the group, such as social interaction.

Clearly, the degree of outcome interdependence varies widely from group to group. Some organizations provide rewards to workers contingent on their group's task performance, while others do not. Toyota, for example, recognizes quality-circle performance with both monetary rewards and companywide, even national, acknowledgment;[7] many U.S. firms do not reward quality-circle performance similarly.[8]

Potency is the collective belief of group members that the group can be effective. This belief depends on group members' sense that they have what they need to succeed—for example, training, skills, talented members, money, time, access to key organization members, and feedback about group performance. Potency tends to be closely linked to performance; if the group has received positive feedback about performance to date, it tends to believe it can be effective henceforth. Additionally, task interdependence and potency are linked: increases in task interdependence provide members with more opportunity to see and therefore to evaluate one another's skills. The converse also holds; changes in the group's sense of potency affect how group members organize their task interdependence. Figure 1 summarizes our theory.

WHY IT MATTERS

How these three issues are handled affects group performance significantly. No group will sustain effective performance in the absence of outcome interdependence. The *degree* of outcomes—the importance or meaningfulness of the rewards and punishments resulting from group performance—is particularly important. So is how the outcomes are distributed: how equally and how competitively.

To perform effectively, groups also need at least a minimal belief in their own efficacy. If, for instance, members of a task force know that they are the fourth group in six years to address a particular problem, and no one can remember seeing any of the members of previous task forces recently, and no one can identify any improvement in the resources made available this time around—then most people will concentrate on trying to get off the task force, rather than on the problem at hand. This group has been set up to fail.

A third issue facing the members of any group is how they should act toward and regard one another: How involved should I be in your work and should you be in mine? Should we be involved as colleagues or as competitors? Too often groups receive mixed messages in this area. For example, if the task requires considerable interacting among team members (e.g., joint decision making) and outcomes are important (e.g., bonus pay) and yet competitively distributed (e.g., only one person receives a bonus), then the stage is set for counterproductive behavior by group members. The task requires members to cooperate, the outcome makes them want to do well, and the distribution of the outcome makes them want to look better than other group members. In other words, undercutting each other can become more important than group success. The amount of interaction required makes it easy for members to inhibit one another's performance, either actively by sabotage or passively by not cooperating. Conflict between task interdependence and outcome inter-

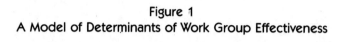

Figure 1
A Model of Determinants of Work Group Effectiveness

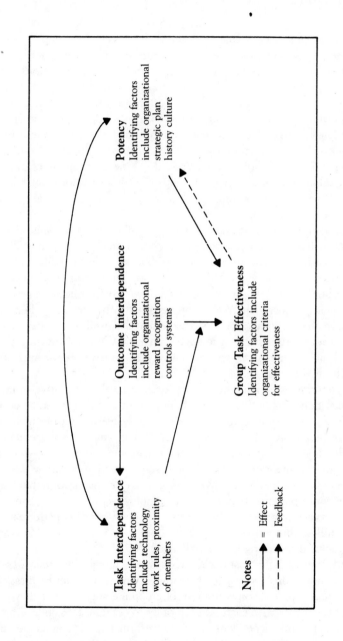

dependence, like insufficient outcome interdependence, can set a group up to fail.

WHAT TO DO

Any time a manager assigns a task, he or she sets employees up to succeed or fail. Setting groups up to succeed requires thinking carefully about three issues.

First, does the group have a clear charter? Supervisors and subordinates are more likely to succeed when they know what success looks like. Groups—particularly managerial ones—often resist the notion that they can spell out what constitutes a good job, but with encouragement they can usually list the few key tasks that they must accomplish. Participants in our research note that defining the group's goals helps them to focus and to notice their interdependence. As one manager said, "I never thought of them [his managerial subordinates] as having group objectives, only individual ones, but they do have things to accomplish as a group. I have to think about how to manage them as a group."

Second, the supervisor and the group members need to determine what resources will be required and whether those resources are available. There are obvious practical reasons to establish this, but the issue has a direct impact on how group members *perceive* their work, as well. Their motivation often depends on the belief that what they are doing is worthwhile and that it can be done. Seeing a clearly chartered group, staffed with people who believe that they have the necessary skills and experience as well as the demonstrated support of key organizational members, matters. So does knowing that the feedback about their work will most likely be positive. A winning attitude comes from winning.

An important side issue here is the desired level of initiative from group members. Believing both that a job is important and that it can be done can easily lead group members to behave more aggressively. They pursue ideas and complaints far more vigorously. Such a change may impress management if, for example, a sales force learns more about customer preferences—but it may distress management if the sales force starts pressing to know why those preferences are not being met. We worked with one organization that installed a group bonus plan for its rank-and-file employees, who then began to push their supervisors more about two issues: the supervisor's job performance and his/her follow-through on suggestions from group members. Motivating a group includes preparing to be challenged.

Third, the manager must decide what type of group is wanted. If cooperation, teamwork, and synergy really matter, then one aims for high task interdependence. One structures the jobs of group members so that they have to interact frequently with each other in order to get their jobs done. Important outcomes are made dependent on group performance. The outcomes are distributed equally among group members. If frenzied, independent activity is the goal, then one aims for low task interdependence and large rewards are distributed competitively and unequally.

Most important, managers should not give mixed messages about how much group members should collaborate; this is frustrating and time-consuming. Either task interdependence and outcomes interdependence should be lined up, or else group members should have the opportunity to do this themselves. One upper manager spoke to us of his frustration with his staff; he claimed each acted as if his were the only business unit in the company. Subsequent discussion revealed a fairly high level of task interdependence (frequent staff meetings and some required joint decision making) *and* large bonuses dependent solely on individual business unit performance. The degree of task interdependence called for cooperation, but the lack of outcome interdependence precluded anything more than courteous neutrality. His subordinates were making a logical, although possibly unconscious, adjustment to their boss's mixed messages. The upper-level manager needed to decide what he really wanted from them—close teamwork or optimization of individual business unit performance—and then line up the messages he sent.

Managers can use the framework of task interdependence, outcome interdependence, and potency to diagnose how well existing groups are likely to do. These variables help to "take a group's temperature." For example, lack of cooperation among group members *may* reflect personality conflicts. It may also reflect poorly structured outcome interdependence or a poor fit between outcomes and task interdependence. Apparent lack of motivation by group members *may* reflect member laziness, but it may reflect the conviction that they have been set up to fail. A question or two may reveal, for example, that top management failed to respond to group member requests for support on the project. The members then concluded that their charter was a farce, the spoken commitment of top management a charade. They felt impotent and acted accordingly.

Similarly, pressure from group members to change job descriptions, or policies and procedures, may be a response to a change in outcome interdependence, not a reflection of some inherent orneriness. A new-found group aggressiveness might reflect a change in potency or, again, a change in outcomes that makes group performance more important to members than ever before. Often when organizations alter compensation systems, for example, they do not consider the behavioral implications. To misread the reasons for changes in behavior is to invite wrongheaded "correction" of group members for patterns that the organization may have precipitated. Acting on those misreadings will hinder effective group performance by giving mixed messages.

Two additional issues merit comment. First, the group management style that this theory suggests is facilitation, but with a specific focus and willingness to intervene. By concentrating on the key variables presented here, managers can allow groups to succeed. Supervisors should guide, direct, and, above all, monitor their group in light of task interdependence, outcome interdependence, and potency.

Second, if the group believes it, then it's real. The supervisor needs to comprehend and address group opinion. If, for instance, a group does not believe that any important outcomes depend on its performance, then the manager should change the perception, either by explaining what does depend on group performance or by identifying outcomes that would matter more to group members and making some of them dependent on group performance.

We designed a study to begin testing our theory about the determinants of group effectiveness. Its results follow.

A CASE IN POINT

The setting was a large national retail corporation with more than 900 outlets. Corporate management was exploring ways to increase sales. Clearly, exogenous variables like store renovation, advertising, and corporate pricing, let alone the economy as a whole, affect sales. So too do salespeople—through their presentation of themselves and the merchandise, product knowledge, feedback to management, and helpfulness to one another. Management believed that increasing group incentive to sell would increase both sales and service by increasing salespeople's customer orientation and cooperativeness. Consequently, the sales force went from being paid an hourly wage to being paid an hourly wage plus a group bonus. The bonus depended on sales gains in the current calendar month over sales for that month in the preceding year.

Generally, salespeople in a given store area (e.g., housewares) made up the groups, but occasionally areas were combined. Stores posted both weekly sales performance figures for each group and a monthly sales summary. Actual bonuses depended on the percent of sales gain and the hours worked by a group member; in other words, the bonus was distributed relatively noncompetitively. Each person could earn an hourly bonus that ranged from a few cents to over a dollar for each hour worked in a month, depending on the size of the team's sales gains. No financial penalties existed for sales losses. The weekly sales-figure postings meant that groups received continual feedback regarding their opportunity to earn bonus money.

We examined the effects of this change by administering a questionnaire twice, a month before the bonus plan went into effect and again six months later. At the time of the second distribution, we conducted interviews and collected corporate sales data. The sample at time one included 13 stores with between 150 and 250 employees. Stores were nominated by district management subject to store manager approval. The sample, while not random, was intended to be representative except that no unionized stores were included. Questionnaires were distributed to employees at work and were returned, anonymously, to a drop-off point, where they were collected and sent to the researchers. The company had an established history of conducting employee surveys.

The vast majority of the 435 salespeople who responded at time one were women; 75 to 80 percent were full-time employees. The number of members in the sales teams ranged from 4 to 24; the average was 9. All teams reported to a first-level manager, 61 of whom also completed questionnaires. At time two, the sample of stores was the same and the response rate within stores was again around 75 percent. Eleven stores returned surveys that, in total, included 360 salespeople, 62 first-level managers, and 44 upper-level managers. We will concentrate here on the data collected from sales personnel.

The questionnaire contained structured and unstructured items designed primarily to measure task interdependence, potency, and, to a lesser extent, outcome interdependence. Items were built into scales for a variety of behaviors that included facilitating each other's work and blocking each other's work, as well as actual selling. We also included an internal measure of customer service to complement the external measure of sales gains or losses for the first three months under the team bonus plan.

The findings generally supported the theory presented above. More specifically, the study demonstrated the importance of outcome interdependence. The team bonus plan represented a major change in the degree and type of outcome. During the seven-month period of this study, sales gains corporation-wide averaged approximately 28 percent. At the work group level, outcome interdependence increased significantly and marked changes occurred in the patterns of work interaction among group members.

The internal measure of group performance, namely, member evaluation of customer service being provided, showed the predicted links with outcome interdependence. More specifically, higher customer service was significantly correlated with greater outcome interdependence and with a stronger sense of potency. A check showed that supervisory perceptions of customer service lined up well with group member's perceptions.

A second group level measure of performance, gains in sales, was not found to be related to the hypothesized causal variables. That is, the difference in sales gains from group to group did not correlate in a statistically significant fashion with total changes in task interdependence, outcome inter-dependence, and potency. This nonfinding merits comment, especially in light of the corporationwide sales gains and other results supporting the theory posited above.

At least three explanations suggest themselves. First, the impact of systematic change in outcome interdependence may have overwhelmed adjustments made by individual groups, at least in the short run of seven months. The organization had altered outcome interdependence for all groups and had done so in such dramatic fashion that individual group adjustments in outcome interdependence paled in comparison.[9] Second, at the group level, changes in customer-service behaviors and not in sales figures may be a more appropriate measure of group performance. Customer-service behaviors are substantially more controllable by group members than is the amount of money customers spend—group members can provide good service and not make a sale. Thus, customer-service behaviors may better measure the effects of the hypothesized causal variables at the group level, since sales figures can reflect the impact of external factors (for example, economic conditions, company advertising practices, competitor's tactics). Interestingly, sales gains were weakly *negatively* correlated with ratings of customer-service effectiveness. Third, some things other than the corporationwide change in outcome inter-dependence may have precipitated all or nearly all of the 28 percent sales gain.

A noteworthy finding concerned the relationship between potency (the collective belief of a group that it can be effective) and how effective the group actually is. Potency related strongly to group performance as measured by customer-service behavior both at time one and at time two, as predicted. This finding, together with other findings, indicated that potency is a con-temporaneous, immediate determinant of a group's effectiveness.

Both expected and unexpected findings regarding task interdependence emerged from the study. We expected—and found—that the patterns of inter-action established by a group appear to be related to its sense of potency—in this case, the more interaction, the more potency. What we did not expect was the extent of the change in task interdependence within sales teams. The degree of change suggests that sales teams exercised substantial discretion in determining their patterns of interaction at work, enabling them to adjust to such changes as a new pay plan.

The change in the degree of task-driven interaction among group members was not random. It changed in systematic relation to potency and outcome interdependence, as predicted by our theory. We regard task interdependence as malleable, especially when the group's work is not highly constrained by technology. Not surprisingly, then, the sales teams of this study did not work under strong technological constraints and their patterns of interaction did change over time.

Other data from this study shows a change in blocking, facilitating, and producing behaviors. Evidence provided by group members and their managers suggests that blocking behaviors declined during the study, while facilitating and especially producing behaviors increased. In other words, as predicted, rewarding whole groups for focusing on sales coincided with some decrease in group member's blocking or hindering each other's work, as well as an increase in mutual assistance and producing/selling.

The behaviors, in turn, affected overall team performance. The greater the extent to which group members interfered with each other's work, the smaller the average sales gains. Similarly, the more they "facilitated" or "produced," the higher their customer-service rating. One would expect such findings in a retail store setting, where a large degree of task-driven interaction occurs. In settings where team members work independently, the relationships between these behaviors and effectiveness would be weaker.

We also investigated the extent to which groups were responsible for work-related decisions (for example, how to display merchandise) and found that involvement in decision making systematically varied with a group's sense of potency. Whether the involvement causes potency or vice versa is unclear. It may be that groups believing in their own efficacy take on decision-making responsibilities, or it may be that involvement in decision making helps develop a group's sense of efficacy. The connection between these two variables deserves further investigation.

By way of a summary, a prototypical high-performance group in this study had several characteristics. Members believed that they could be effective. They were decidedly less likely to interfere with or block one another's work and were more task interdependent than were less effective groups. They also took more initiative, both with customers and with management.

IMPLICATIONS

This study's findings generally support our theory and, like the theory, have practical implications. First, group managers should attend closely to the degree and type of outcome interdependence. Large changes in this area seem to produce genuine behavioral and performance changes. A number of managers might do well to rethink the messages they are *really* sending and to consider the effect of these messages on group performance. Second, managers should focus on enhancing group potency. Training, availability of needed resources and feedback can all enhance a group's sense of efficacy. So too can increased task interdependence, depending on member competence, and ability to develop new task-related skills. Third, managers should expect groups to establish their own patterns of task-driven interaction. Since different patterns can prove equally effective, managers may want to give groups latitude in this area. Finally, supervisors should attend carefully to performance measurements. One alternative is to use multiple measures of performance (for example, sales and customer service). Less comprehensive measures often leave both group members and their supervisors confused about goals and expectations. This confusion diminishes group effectiveness.

REFERENCES

1   T. J. Peters and R. H. Waterman, Jr., *In Search of Excellence* (New York: Harper & Row, 1982).

2   D. Gladstein, "Groups in Context: A Model of Task Group Effectiveness." *Administrative Science Quarterly* 29 (1984).

    J. R. Hackman and C. G. Morris, "Group Task, Group Interaction Process, and Group Performance Effectiveness: A Review and Proposed Integration," in *Advances in Experimental Social Psychology* 8, ed. L. Berkowitz (New York: Academic Press, 1975).

    I. D. Steiner, *Group Process and Productivity* (New York: Academic Press, 1972).

3. J. R. Hackman, "The Design of Work Teams," in *Handbook of Organizational Behavior*, ed. J. W. Lorsch (Englewood Cliffs, NJ: Prentice-Hall, 1986).

4. Ibid.

5. R. Kaplan, "The Conspicuous Absence of Evident That Process Consultation Enhances Task Performance," *Journal of Applied Behavioral Science* 15 (1979): 346-360; R. W. Woodman and J. J. Sherwood, "The Role of Team Development in Organizational Effectiveness: A Critical Review," *Psychological Bulletin* 88 (1980) 166-186.

6. A full explanation of this theory appears in G. P. Shea and R. A. Guzzo, "Groups as Human Resources," in *Research in Personnel and Human Resources Management*. Vol. 5, Ed. K. Rowland and G. Ferris (Greenwich, CT: JAI Press, 1987).

7. R. Cole, *Work, Mobility, and Participation* (Berkeley: University of California Press, 1979).

8. G. Munchus III, "Employer-Employee Based Quality Circles in Japan: Human Resource Policy Implications for American Firms" *Academy of Management Review* 8 (1983): 255-261; G. P. Shear, "Quality Circles: The Danger of Bottled Change," *Sloan Management Review*, Spring 1986, pp. 33-46; F. Thompson, *Quality Circles* (New York: AMACOM, 1982).

9. Sales gains and customer-service behavior appear to capture different dimensions of performance, since they do not correlate significantly with each other, and in addition each does correlate significantly with different types of selling or service behaviors. The relation between these two performance measures warrants further exploration, as do the conditions under which sales gains are the best indicators of team effectiveness.

Gregory P. Shea is adjunct professor at The Wharton School, University of Pennsylvania, and a principal of the Coxe Group. Richard A. Guzzo is associate professor of psychology at New York University.

30.
DOES AUTOMATION NECESSARILY MEAN AN INCREASE IN PRODUCTIVITY?

Ralph L. Kleim

> Many managers think that employee productivity and company profits
> will increase through automation. As a result, "office automation fever"
> runs uncontrolled through many corporate headquarters while no one is
> asking the key question—will automation *really* lead to increased
> productivity?

Despite the upturn in the economy, management in American businesses
are struggling to increase productivity through office automation (OA).
Through automation, many managers feel employee productivity will increase
and, consequently, profits. As a result, "OA fever" runs uncontrolled
throughout many corporate headquarters without really asking a simple question—will automation *really* lead to increased productivity?"

THE REASONS FOR AUTOMATION

Because the country is moving from an industrial to a service economy, the
demand for reliable and current information has become critical. And the need
for such information grows annually. Over 325 billion documents, for example, currently exist in American business offices, and some experts estimate
that figure will grow about 20 percent a year. Automation is seen as a cost-
effective way to collect, compile, and distribute that information.

In addition, many managers feel pressured to automate an office for another
compelling reason—skyrocketing office expenses. In 1980, office expense cost
U.S. businesses approximately $800 billion and that figure increases annually
since the salaries of clerical, managerial, and professional employees are moving ahead of inflation. To compensate for this rise in compensation, many
managers purchase and install automated systems believing an increase in
productivity will result, thereby offsetting rising office expenses. They see

automation, too, lessening or eliminating unproductive and labor-intensive activities, like telephone tag, nonessential meetings, and collecting information.

Because the need for rapid collection and distribution of information exists and because office expenses are increasing annually, many corporations invest huge sums of money into automated systems, including word processors, electronic mail, electronic calendaring, microcomputers, teleconferencing, and facsimiles. In 1980, shipments of office technology in the United States totalled $9.9 billion and experts estimate that figure will at least double by 1985.

A FALLACIOUS ARGUMENT

No doubt, automation does increase productivity under certain circumstances. Spreadsheet programs for microcomputers can expedite the laborious task of compiling financial reports. Word processors enable the rapid production and revision of official correspondence and other documents. Teleconferencing can lessen or eliminate "wasteful" traveling time for professionals and managers. Electronic mail permits employees to have rapid access to information that would ordinarily take days even weeks, for them to receive. And electronic calendaring enables employees to efficiently schedule meetings. But using these systems does not necessarily mean a bona fide increase in productivity.

Just because an employee uses automated equipment to distribute or produce information does not not mean an increase in *real* productivity. Many office automation experts believe, for example, that automation will increase productivity at least 25 percent. But what goes into an automated system does not necessarily mean what comes out is useful, productive information. The old saying "Garbage In, Garbage Out" that is attributed to data-processing systems is just as applicable for office automation.

Take word-processing systems. These can enhance productivity if used properly and efficiently. Often, however, these systems are misused in several ways, such as producing unnecessary documents and creating a flood of useless information. What could normally be handwritten and reproduced on a copier, for example, is submitted to a word-processing operator who takes time to input the information, produce a copy for each recipient, and mail the documents. Under such a circumstance, the question to ask is: Is it more productive to just write a short memo or to have it "word processed?" The answer is obvious.

Or take electronic mailing. Theoretically, electronic mail systems can be used to send important messages quickly and efficiently. While that is often the case, employees sometimes misuse and abuse the system. Many times, clerical and professional employees send unproductive messages to destinations, known as "mailboxes." Many messages request answers to questions that could have just as easily been answered by referring to a nearby procedure or manual. Or an employee may send a message requesting the proper attire for a forthcoming golf game. Obviously, these are two extreme examples. However, they illustrate that not everything produced on an automated system is actually productive.

Whether an office uses specific technologies or a mixture of technologies to automate an office, management should measure productivity in terms of the quality of material produced, known as *actual* productivity and not just quantity, known as *nominal* productivity. Hence, the real question is whether automation contributes directly and efficiently to the productivity of a system. More paper or extensive use of a system does not necessarily equate to actual productivity.

PREPARATION IS THE KEY

Automating just for the sake of it does not, therefore, necessarily result in actual productivity. While in most cases automation will increase productivity quantitatively, managers should avoid the common misconception that a casual relationship exists between bona fide productivity and technology. That relationship is tenuous at best.

So what can management do to ensure automation will result in actual productivity?

Perhaps the most important step is to concentrate less on the "how's" of processing documentation and information and more on the "why's" and "who's." In other words, management must conduct an extensive business analysis of the environment *before* automating an office to determine requirements. That means ascertaining who will need access to the automated system and under what circumstances. In addition, management should prioritize documents and other informational requirements on the system.

Next, management should establish quality-control measures to ensure that all documentation produced by the system is relevant, useful, and complete. That means implementing measures to periodically review all documentation created and stored in the system. Many times, for instance, employees store correspondence or reports no one really needs. That can mean ineffective utilization of memory capacity and the wasteful use of labor and paper. The ultimate consequence, of course, is an increase in office expenses. Occasionally, a review of what exists on file should be conducted to ensure no irrelevant or outdated material is being produced or distributed.

Finally, management should prepare for automation. That means preparing people to use the system before it arrives. Often, people misuse technology for only one reason—they do not understand how to effectively use it. Many employees see automated systems, like word processors and microcomputers, as space-age toys. For hours, they play with the equipment and produce a less than adequate product. The recipient of the document ends up saying something like: "Gee. This is great. But it's not what I need." The result is a misallocation of manpower and loss of actual productivity.

Therefore, management should help employees learn to use an automated system effectively. It can do that in three ways.

1. Documentation. Developing user procedures and manuals enables employees to have ready access to information not only on operating an automated system but also using it effectively. Documentation can provide, for instance, guidelines to help employees determine the priority of documentation and other informational requirements under varying circumstances.

2. Personnel. Management should reassess personnel requirements before introducing a system. This will ensure that a properly skilled staff is available to use the system. If the clerical, professional, or managerial staff lacks the appropriate skills, it could use the new system for simple tasks that could be more effectively and efficiently done manually. At the same time, the staff could be doing more time-consuming and difficult tasks manually when automation would prove otherwise more efficient and effective.

3. Training. To use the system properly and productively, managers should have their staff trained before the system arrives. This enables employees to know in advance how to effectively use the technology once it arrives. Without prior training, many employees will experiment with the system, which can only result in wasteful "trial-and-error" tasks and lessen actual productivity for a considerable time period. The training should be application-oriented to ensure the users to effectively use the system.

SUMMARY

Automation does not guarantee effective production of documentation and other forms of information. But it does provide the means for doing so. Making automation a very productive experience requires preparation by management. That means determining information requirements and prioritizing them from the very first. In addition, management must develop users documentation, reassess personnel requirements, and implement a serious training program. Otherwise, management will find itself with employees working with toys rather than tools.

Part V:
EVOLUTION IN THE WORK ENVIRONMENT

31.
A TEAM APPROACH TO COST CUTTING

Richard Ludwig

> One dollar in cost reduction is worth more than one dollar in sales. Below are some suggestions for implementing an effective cost-reduction program.

One dollar in cost reduction is worth more than one dollar in sales! This is a strange statement for a CEO to make to his organization, but I've made that statement many times—and because it has been proven, our management and employees believe it. Consider the fact that an average company makes about four and a half to five cents profit after taxes on each dollar of its sales—perhaps nine to 10 cents before taxes. But if a company reduces its cost by one dollar, that full dollar finds its way into profit before taxes.

It is not that sales are unimportant, because obviously, no company can exist without them. But it is axiomatic that an organization in business to make a profit will have some level of sales and cost reduction. This can be the difference between mere survival and profitability. The impact of an effective cost-reduction program can be dramatic. If you believe this, it's time to start looking for a system to reduce and control costs.

CREATIVE MANAGEMENT

Any "good" manager with a degree of creativity can look at his operation and change something—or things—to reduce cost. The difference between a good manager and an excellent one is the ability to focus the people reporting to him or her on accomplishing the task that must be accomplished. It is one thing to react to financial difficulty by embarking on a cost-cutting spree because the company is in trouble; it is quite another to provide for cost reduction as an organized, planned, ever-present factor.

With these thoughts as background considerations, the Lavelle Aircraft Company developed a system that enlists the efforts of all employees on cost reduction. The system has some of the elements of the highly touted Japanese quality circles, but with important variations that make it uniquely American. It incorporates the use of teams, goals, incentives, rewards and recognition. Lavelle has used the system since 1981 with positive results.

The theory behind the program is that teams of knowledgeable, dedicated people who are given goals and incentives are willing to change their methods and, thus, reduce costs. Now that Lavelle has had the program in effect for five years, the company is pleased with the results.

The cost improvement (CI) organization was established by creating teams of six people. Each team is cross-functional—one might have a production control specialist, a marketing person, an engineer, quality assurance person, a finance person and a shop supervisor, for example. Each team is required to select its own captain and recording secretary. One manager from the president's staff is selected to be the project leader on a rotating basis for one year. Three of the staff managers are assigned two teams each and the vice president of finance is given the responsibility for analyzing the approved projects for savings.

ESTABLISHING GOALS

At the beginning of each fiscal year, the company-wide cost-reduction goal for the year is set. This, over the past five-year period, has been about 10 percent of the budgeted overhead cost. The total savings target is divided by six, so that each team has one-sixth of the total as its goal for the year. That value is again divided by six so that each team is given that amount as its goal for a two-month period. Over the past five years, the goal ranged between $9,000 and $12,000 for each two-month period.

The teams are asked to meet at least once every two weeks on company time, and they are free to meet whenever else they think it is necessary to help them meet their goals, either on or off company time. At the first meeting each year, they select their captain and recording secretary by a method of their choice. These names are given to their team manager and publicized. Then, the teams are asked to brainstorm about possible projects.

This is not a suggestion program. The team members are not permitted to merely suggest that an action be taken. They must be the actual change agents, and demonstrate initiative to get their projects incorporated in order to receive credit for a cost reduction. They must do things like obtain cost-tradeoffs information, prepare presentations for management, convince the engineering staff to change manufacturing planning, talk to suppliers or in some other way effect the change.

In order to avoid potential conflicts when two teams have an identical or very similar idea for a project, a rule was adopted that control of the project goes to the first team registering the idea the earliest with the project manager. However, a team may trade away a percentage of its project to get help from an individual or another team. Suppose, for example, a team without a tool designer proposes to reduce the cost of fabrication of a part if a tool is redesigned—a task requiring engineering support. Their captain can approach the captain of another team and offer a percentage of any savings for his or her help.

TEAM PROJECTS

After the teams have identified their projects and laid the groundwork, they turn in a one-page report stating that their project has been implemented and is ready for approval and financial analysis. These reports are then brought to the CI board and, if approved, are turned over to the finance department for evaluation. On the date of approval, the team is credited with the savings. The finance department usually has their analysis completed within a week so that there is little lag in notifying the team of its standing.

If the team's aggregate savings credited for a two-month period meets or exceeds the goal, each member of that team receives an award whether or not he or she contributed in the award period. When we first started the program, we awarded $50 gift certificates at one of three or four stores of the individual's choice. Because of the success of the program, we now use $100 gift certificates, and the top team for the year shares a larger award of up to $1,000.

Lavelle has had savings each year from a low of $228,000 (3.1 percent of sales) to a high of $738,000 (12.1 percent of sales) as a result of this program.

A caution worth noting is that the full value of the savings doesn't always find its way to the bottom line. This is because there are two classes of savings. At Lavelle, they are called "hard savings" and "soft savings." Soft savings are the type that eliminate work, but because there is no reduction of human resources, there is no measurable saving at the bottom line. Instead, the labor becomes available to do other things. This is differentiated from hard savings, which reduce the use of material, permit using less expensive discarded items, or provide a similar method, which does reduce costs and increase profits.

WINNING SUGGESTIONS

Another important benefit comes from the suggestion program. All employees not on the CI program are eligible for suggestion awards. In the past, there was great difficulty with these programs because supervisors fought suggestions. There was some belief among the supervisors that suggestions were really criticisms. Suggestions were stacked up, evaluators didn't respond, and as a result, employees were disenchanted with the suggestion program.

Now, however, any person on a CI team who has a direct report on the suggestion program gets credit for suggestions that are implemented. This creates a win-win situation, rather than the win-lose situation we had before. Consequently, there are now more suggestions and there is no backlog.

As important as the savings are, there are other benefits from the CI program, including the following:

- increasing the awareness of all employees to the importance of reducing costs;
- fostering teamwork between departments;
- providing an outlet for recognition of ideas;
- development of leadership potential in all employees (also, increasing management's ability to identify those with leadership potential);
- creating a little competitive "fun" in an activity that can be onerous and can cause friction between management and employees; and
- enhancing communications.

As with any program, there are also potential problems and pitfalls which must be considered. These include those pitfalls listed below:

- insufficient leadership attention (the "I don't have time" syndrome);
- team members' lack of support;
- team size too large—or too small;
- personnel assignment and reassignment to teams;
- teams or people unwilling to share ideas; and
- some people spending too much time on cost improvements to the point where regular work suffers.

Leadership, of course, is the most important element needed for the program's success. The top person must establish the program, push for its implementation, monitor results, provide the incentives and provide visibility to those who provide significant contributions.

Without the interest and dedication of the top person, the program will not succeed. He or she must force the management team to make the program work and must not allow statements like "I don't have time." A more useful argument is "If I have time, so does everyone else." After the program shows results, this argument will disappear.

Richard Ludwig is president of Lavelle Aircraft Company, Newtown, PA.

32.

WHAT WENT WRONG
WITH QUALITY CIRCLES?

Gopal C. Pati
Robert Salitore
Sandra Brady

Can an organization recover from a negative quality-circle experience to learn and reintroduce the concept? Ironically, for the success of the program's bottom-up philosophy, it has to start from the top. The president must set the proper tone, create trust and confidence and make a commitment to a people philosophy.

This above question was pointedly asked by management of Lake Financial Corp., a major metropolitan banking institution, in the early 1980s. The company, which instituted the quality-circle groups to improve efficiency, communications and team spirit, and in turn to boost the company's profits, discovered a short time after the start-up of the program that it was in need of professional consultation.

In 1983, the company participated in a series of intensive state-of-the-art training sessions as part of a total organizational development strategy. Nine groups, composed of supervisors and staff, wanted to breathe new life into their participative management or quality-circle groups.

One part of the training dealt with stages of group development. Members asked how the stages and phases of group development applied to them, and about the overall experience with their respective group meetings before this educational exposure.

Participants used such words as *nuisance, a joke* and *very unproductive* to describe previous meetings. Some said there were no ideas generated during the sessions, which were dull, boring and lifeless. The participants felt there was a lack of emotional involvement, and that they really didn't understand what they were supposed to do or accomplish. Additionally, most workers agreed they were too intimidated to speak.

One group progressed farther in its evolution than the others. Although the members had the usual doubts and fears, eventually they moved into a stage in which members brought and discussed ideas during each meeting. The group did submit and receive approval on two suggestions, but their energy was drained. They felt more effort was being spent coming up with new ideas than discussing them.

A natural response for Lake Financial at this point might have been to cut its losses and move on to the next management fad. However, the time was right to dissect the experience and redirect its efforts toward revision and renewal.

The company wanted to find out if a group that goes through this process without proper training could be retrained to revitalize the faltering program.

It discovered the answer is yes. Today in the United States, establishing quality circles is a multimillion-dollar business, yet the company discovered that the program could be set up for pennies.

Most organizations do not have the luxury of time and resources for experimentation. Therefore, before attempting to introduce a quality-circle program they should consider such issues as:

- Creating a culture for productivity
- Where and how to create the necessary culture
- How to eliminate or minimize possible supervisory backlash and resentment
- How to select group members
- Training, and who needs it
- Reward structures
- Who and how to select a facilitator.

It's important to remember that timing is all important. Do not start a quality-circle program if the organization is not ready for it. Lake Financial, for example, considered starting its program several years earlier than it did, but top management recognized that a great number of employees as well as management were accustomed to an authoritarian management style in which the boss gave the orders and the subordinates implemented them.

The company prepared for the program for nearly four years. Yet, in spite of years of preparation time, employee apprehension still existed. Its first and biggest challenge was to overcome the apprehensive feelings of the group.

ESTABLISHING A SUCCESSFUL CULTURE STARTS AT THE TOP

The philosophy, program and objectives must be created and articulated by the president, chairman and CEO. It's important for the invitation to come from the top and not from human relations because most employees are most comfortable with a top-down management style. Ironically, for the success of the program's bottom-up philosophy, it has to start from the top. The president must:

- Set a tone that says he or she will listen and act
- Create trust and confidence by example
- Make a commitment to a people philosophy as a way to improve company profit and a means to ensure job security.

At Lake Financial, the prime mover was its chairman, an entrepreneur who liked taking risks and rewarding others who followed his lead. The first step he and his management committee, consisting of five senior officers, took after listening to the managers was to change some policies and procedures that blocked progress. First, the annual polygraph examination and the time clock were eliminated. After that, the managers and the employees were convinced of the company's sincerity and commitment to the program, and they began to trust their management.

Those changes came about after the committee established a line of two-way dialogue through regularly scheduled meetings. A theme of company survival for profitability, with an emphasis on job security and supervisory training, was repeated continuously.

Lake Financial, in addition, recognized the possibility of supervisory backlash or resentment caused by such a program. Therefore, the senior vice presidents and officers were instructed to *listen* to their supervisory personnel. During these discussions they let the supervisor know they were not expected to be perfect, and that upper management recognized there were policies, procedures and other structural issues over which the supervisors had no direct control. Direct conversations and suggestions on how to correct problems were encouraged.

Issues were resolved daily during regularly scheduled departmental meetings and one-on-one confidential counseling. Additionally, supervisors and managers were kept informed through a new program that alerts the managers first, before it's communicated to the employees in general.

The bank also initiated an ongoing supervisory- and management-development program. Thus, at the time the quality-circle concept was systematically introduced within the organization, every manager and employee was exposed to a one-day seminar on the subject. Because the trainees learned that group involvement made everyone in the organization more successful, the program was accepted as a way of life, not an additional headache to be endured.

The company soon discovered it is very important for each member to join voluntarily. Industrial and government leadership must realize that not everyone needs or wants to participate in company policy planning or problem solving. There should not be a stigma attached to those who do not want to participate in a group.

The initial membership at Lake Financial was termed compulsorily voluntary. Because the chairman wanted full cooperation, each employee was obligated to participate in his or her respective department's and office's group. Although some got involved to avoid stigma of being considered disloyal and quietly endured the pain, others began to enjoy the experience.

More importantly, one key objective—the emergence of a team concept—was achieved. Co-workers talked with, not just down to or at, each other. The employees were building a foundation for good morale and teamwork.

Today at Lake Financial, participation is voluntary. Immediately after its employees attended the most recent training sessions, the company asked for volunteers. Although a dozen were expected to rise to the challenge, 44 employees submitted their names for consideration. The welcome yet unexpected problem of too many volunteers was solved by asking some to serve as regular members and others as alternates. The remaining were placed on a waiting list.

Lake Financial learned an important lesson from the experience: There is a lot of creativity in an organization that can be tapped, provided it's done in a spirit of cooperation and care.

After the selection process, it was determined that participants needed training and education in group processes as well as in technical areas, such as problem-solving skills.

To appreciate what was involved in the process, every member of the Lake Financial organization first went through a very basic program. The approach was sold not as a program but as a contribution of efforts to build an attitude. The quality-circle training component was only one part of the company's overall educational development effort. It was presented as a part of an overall strategy to improve teamwork.

Emphasis was placed on the fact that participative management did not mean a democracy was being established or that employees would run the company. Employees would have input in day-to-day decision making, which would improve the quality of work life by working together for better customer satisfaction and employee job satisfaction.

Group creativity and problem solving was emphasized next. Members were told not to expect instant results from the initial meetings; things were to evolve gradually. As a result, quality measurement techniques, considered too advanced, were not mentioned during initial training. Although advanced training in statistical methods, fishbone techniques and flow charting was important, they found it was necessary to the success of the program to first create a unit that works and feels like a team.

Lake Financial's group members soon discovered nobody was fired when they voiced an opinion. In addition, they began to see the role of leadership and communication in problem solving. Supervisors encouraged coworkers to attend meetings. Alternative members attended the deliberations if a regular member was unavailable. As a group they learned the basics about working for and with other people.

A SYSTEMATIC STRATEGY TO INTRODUCE AN INVOLVEMENT EFFORT

1. Level with the CEO about the organization's current state of management and employee thinking.
2. Consider an involvement program, even in an authoritarian environment, but be sure the style is modified as the group matures. Do not wait until all managers' styles are changed throughout the organization to introduce such a program.
3. The CEO and senior officials must be models for change in implementing constructive ideas.
4. Make the program voluntary.
5. In the beginning, provide group members with solvable problems. Be prepared to change structures, policies and procedures. Keep objectives simple.
6. Emphasize that these are not complaint sessions.
7. Communicate and educate every person in the organization about the program. Emphasize that group members need support.
8. Establish a climate of care and feedback.
9. Involve line people and make them leaders of the group whenever possible.
10. Provide additional training to complement quality-circle training. Introduce the concept as an ongoing process of good supervision.
11. Provide confidential counseling.
12. Involve experienced operations employees in the program.

Because of the program, Lake Financial learned a lot about its employees and what they needed and wanted.

About its ESOP program, for example, the company discovered the employees wanted to contribute without a mention of immediate financial reward. Basically, the employees were interested in recognition, such as acknowledging good customer service and the fact that the employees had a stake in reshaping the company philosophy and its operating practices.

The company, realizing the importance of back patting, bragged about its quality-circle members. In one issue of the company newsletter, the president issued a statement of commitment, reaffirming his conviction and support for the program. This, in addition to other gestures, bolstered the morale of each employee in the organization.

It's imperative that the facilitator be part of line management. He or she must be experienced in and understand the entire organization, including its structure, procedures, functions and jobs. That individual must also have credibility, sensitivity and operational experience. Cutting across department barriers and eliminating red tape must be almost second nature to the facilitator.

If the program is solid, with commitments from its facilitator, members and management, the program could go on indefinitely. New people should be encouraged to replace those who are ready to relinquish their positions. Involve all levels of employees to ensure the success of the program, which, more importantly, ensures heightened levels of morale and productivity in the organization.

Gopal C. Pati is a professor of management of industrial relations at Indiana University Northwest at Gary. Robert Salitore is a senior vice president of human services with Bank One, Merrillville, IN. Sandra Brady is a management major and research assistant to Gopal Pati.

33.
THE EIGHT BARRIERS TO TEAMWORK

Robert E. Lefton

> When it comes to teamwork, there's no known limit to what people can achieve. When things are really clicking and collaboration is at its best, the word "teamwork" has real meaning. But this happens only when teams avoid the eight barriers to effective teamwork.

Certain words appear to catch on for no discernible reason and become fashionable almost overnight. Everything anyone reads contains the latest buzzwords, and people can't seem to get through a sentence without it. Yet the word's very popularity turns it into an instant cliche whose original meaning becomes obscured.

Personnel management has its share of words in vogue; the latest is "teamwork."

The implication is that if professionals in human-resources development can promote teamwork within their organizations, positive results are certain to follow. Employees will obviously achieve better results by collaborating than by working independently. Interaction—synergy—will provide something extra: the insights, ideas, solutions and directions that result from working as a team.

It's a sound concept and certainly one that should work, but, unfortunately, it often fails to materialize. If teamwork is to be more than just a popular buzzword—as obsolete tomorrow as it is chic today—it is necessary to examine why it doesn't always work.

Why don't teams synergize all the time? During the last two years, I've worked with the top teams in 26 major US corporations, 22 of them on the *Fortune* 500 list. Time after time, eight problems have prevented synergism. Any group that genuinely wants to produce that something extra should be aware of these factors.

1. *Breakdown in Probing.* If there's one thing everyone on a team should know, it's how to probe, how to elicit information. Yet remarkably few people do know, probably because probing is very rarely taught in our schools and colleges. The assumption is that people naturally know how to ask questions and dig for information.

    Even top executives frequently do a poor job of probing. In meetings, they rely on the three probes that actually elicit the least information. Closed-end probes ("Do you buy that?") usually evoke a yes or no response, but not much more. Leading questions ("You want people to think we're stupid?") answer themselves but don't produce any new information. And brief assertions ("Go on") may not tell you anything worth hearing.

Communication experts have identified a total of eight probes. So five probes—open-end and neutral probes, pauses, summaries and reflective statements—do produce sizable amounts of information. Strangely, however, only about 10 percent of managers consistently use these five probes that are essential for getting to the heart of things.

Why is this such a big deal?

No team is likely to synergize if it doesn't get to the core of the issue. Complete and accurate information is indispensable for credible problem solving. Since complete and accurate information is rarely presented spontaneously, it has to be uncovered. That takes skillful probing.

2. *Promotional Leadership.* A promotional leader leaks his or her own ideas to subordinates before they've had a chance to state theirs. ("I think we ought to revamp the entire plan, but right now I'd like to hear what you think.") Nothing will do more to stifle discussion and squelch candor. Once people know what the boss thinks, the whole discussion is likely to shift in that direction.

Promotional leadership isn't necessarily deliberate. Many team leaders simply blurt out their views without considering the consequences. They unintentionally choke off discussion. But team leaders often use promotional leadership as a subtle means of ensuring that no real discussion takes place. They can make a show of open-mindedness, while guaranteeing that the discussion won't get out of hand. ("I'm absolutely convinced we should close down the Eureka operation, but of course we won't do it until you've had a chance to speak your minds.")

3. *Intra-team Conflict.* Synergistic teams aren't always cautious. They don't sit around making safe, inoffensive remarks. They argue, they debate, they say things openly and honestly; they tell it like it is. But through it all, such a team functions as a unit.

Once the members of a team start pushing their own separate goals or agendas, however, desynergism is sure to result. As soon as private agendas displace the team's goal, candor disappears, probing becomes a way to put other people on the defensive, debate becomes dissension, teamwork disappears and one-upmanship takes its place.

4. *Insufficient alternatives.* A team that wants to make decisions with something extra in them should consider all the options before deciding on one. That seldom happens.

Teams usually explore only a few of their choices because they don't take the time to prepare and they're not ready to list all the options. And many teams feel uncomfortable with brainstorming, although it's essential to generating options.

These teams object on the grounds that brainstorming produces too many crazy ideas, too much talk, too much wasted time. But the truth is that exploring alternatives isn't just talking, it's a way of making sure the group winds up with the best idea instead of merely a good idea. What's more, the team that takes action instead of talking may end up wishing it hadn't moved so quickly. Taking action is fine, but it's usually best to do so after deliberation.

5. *Lack of Candor.* I've never known a synergistic team that wasn't consistently candid.

    People are most likely to generate fertile, productive ideas when they first have all the information they need or as much of it as they can get. On a team, that means everyone must level with each other—tell all they know about the subject at hand without distortion or evasion. Candor means *full* and accurate disclosure.

    Two problems usually interfere with candor. One is that people have personal reasons for not being open and honest. They may be afraid of hurting someone's feelings, so they may withhold information, or they may want to put someone on the spot, so they may embellish the information. Either way, candor goes out the window.

    A second problem is intra-team politics. Employees may hold back or distort information because it seems like the expedient thing to do. Fear can make most people particularly evasive. Many managers have explained their failure to divulge information by saying, "It seemed safest to keep my mouth shut." It may be safe, but it won't be synergistic.

6. *Pointless Meetings.* Unless a meeting has a clear-cut objective, nobody can tell whether it's synergistic or not. But a startling number of meetings either have no objective at all or such a vague goal that nobody's sure what it is.

    The solutions are simple: eliminate unnecessary meetings, and do a thorough job of planning the necessary ones.

7. *Lack of Self-Critique.* Most teams fail to do regular, systematic critiques of themselves; their operations, strengths, weaknesses and areas needing improvement. These teams take teamwork for granted.

    What every team needs is an institutionalized critique—a critique built into its activities so it can't easily be avoided. Time must be set aside and a format developed so the team learns from and profits from every meeting.

8. *Failure to Cycle Downward.* This is crucial. Many a good decision has died because the team failed to cycle it downward—explain it to all the people whose collaboration will be needed to make it succeed. A decision made at one level thus may never filter down to lower levels, even though those levels are indispensable to the decision's success.

This explains why managers sometimes scratch their heads and say, "I don't know what went wrong. We had a great idea. Everybody was excited about it. But nothing seemed to happen after that. Somewhere along the line, it just fizzled."

When it comes to teamwork, there's no known limit to what people can achieve. When things are really clicking and collaboration is at its best synergy does occur, and the word "teamwork" has real meaning. It can happen. It does happen. But only when teams avoid the eight barriers to organizational teamwork.

Robert E. Lefton has consulted and conducted seminars for numerous US and European corporations in management development, organization development and sales training.

34.
WHY EMPLOYEES STAY IS MORE CRITICAL THAN WHY THEY LEAVE

Charles L. Hughes
Vincent S. Flowers

> Progressive management should try to improve employee retention by reinforcing positive reasons for staying, while at the same time making it easier for people who are staying for negative reasons to quit. Turnover *quality*, as opposed to turnover *quantity*, might improve.

Many personnel executives spend a great amount of time and money investigating the causes of employee turnover, particularly through exit interviews. The objective is to find out why people leave. If a company can identify the reasons for terminations and departure, the theory goes, it can remove some of the causes for employee dissatisfaction. There are, however, two shortcomings with this traditional practice:

- It looks at only why people quit. Why not also look at the reasons others stay? The reasons why people stay are just as important as the reasons for leaving. One individual may stay in a job for the same reason another leaves.
- Exit interviews also assume there is a correlation between job dissatisfaction and turnover. A low turnover rate presumes that employees are happy and consequently productive; this is not necessarily the case. The mere fact an employee stays is not as important as *why* that person remains.

To get a more integrated view of work-force stability, a study of more than 400 employees in three different companies investigated the reasons employees stay and proper ways to encourage retention. This went as far back as 1973.[1] Since that time studies of the attitudes of tens of thousands of employees in more than 500 organizations elicited similar results. From anonymous questionnaires and selected interviews this is the picture that emerged:

Why do employees stay? Employees tend to stay where they are until some

270

force causes them to leave, in other words "inertia." As in physics, a body will remain as it is until acted upon by an external force.

What causes inertia? Two factors inside organizations and two outside make people stay. Job satisfaction and satisfaction with the working environment produces the internal inertia and is directly affected by the positive or negative correlation between the employee's personal value system and that of management.

A disparity between personal and organizational values reduces the desire to stay, while compatibility between these two values increase the desire to stay.

The external factors increasing inertia include perceptions of other job opportunities and personal and family reasons. Some employees stay because they like the schools or the neighborhood, but what if both of these deteriorate and become less appealing? Other job opportunities become more attractive.

Other employees report they stayed in an unpleasant job because they could not leave the community in which they or their spouse was born and spent all of their lives. Despite low job satisfaction, they stayed.

Want to stay versus have to stay? Progressive management should try to improve retention by reinforcing positive reasons for staying, while at the same time making it easier for people who are staying for negative reasons—negative to both employer and employee—to quit. Turnover *quality*, as opposed to turnover *quantity*, might improve.

Improving employee retention will be more effective over the long run than the ordinary, negative approach of simply reducing turnover. The key is improving attitudes about the work itself, supervisor competence, confidence in the fairness of management, work group cooperation, consistency in treatment, feedback about performance, opportunities to get ahead and other positive aspects that relate to the work context. Work content factors—those aspects of the job inside the organization—include pay, benefits, facilities, attendance rules and other environmental aspects.

External factors include outside job opportunities, the community, financial obligations, family ties and even the annual weather patterns. As a result of the combinations of external and internal factors influencing employees' job decisions, employees can be identified as one of four types:

Turnovers are not happy with their jobs, have few external reasons to stay and will leave at the first opportunity. Employees may not start out in this position, but a gradual erosion of their inertia causes them to slide into this area.

Turn-offs are candidates for union, employee relations and productivity problems. These employees have negative attitudes about their jobs and stay because of golden handcuffs. They may feel they are too old to start over again and are locked in by benefit programs and high rates of pay. Productivity may suffer.

Turn-ons have positive attitudes and remain with the company almost exclusively for reasons associated with the work itself. From management's point of view, as well as the individual employee's, this is the most desirable situation.

If management actions lower attitudes and the positive, work-related reasons to stay, turnover will probably jump. Because the turn-ons are not affected by environmental factors, they will not stay without continual job satisfaction.

Turn-on-plus employees are likely to stay for the long run because they have work and environmental satisfactions. A short-term drop in satisfaction does not lead to resignation. If attitudes drop permanently, however, these employees become turn-offs. This does not raise turnover, but increases employee relations problems.

The traditional approach to measuring and understanding terminations has focused on turnovers. These employees generally represent a small percentage of the total employee population, therefore, emphasizing retention efforts on them exclusively ignores the reasons the majority of the work force stays with the company. Employers wanting to improve their working environments should stop assuming exit interviews are providing a meaningful picture of why other employees stay.

An anonymous attitude survey was used to identify where employees fit in the matrix, Figure 1, of "having to stay versus want to stay." This survey covered 20 factor-analyzed statements to which individuals could respond "Agree, disagree, ?, not sure." It explored job satisfaction, supervision, management, advancement, working conditions, pay, benefits, communication, performance expectations, job security, favoritism, use of skills, work-group cooperation, rules, freedom to do the job well, plus an item on whether the individual had looked for another job during the past six months.

Simply, correlations between each attitude factor and whether the individuals were looking or not looking to terminate from their company were sought. For example, if they are satisfied with any factor, but looking to terminate anyway, they are classified as "turned-on" by that factor, but "not locked in." Conversely, if individuals are "dissatisfied" by any of the attitude factors and not looking for another job, they are "turned off" by that factor or factors *plus* they are "locked in." If an individual is "satisfied" with any factor and "not looking" to quit, then that factor, or factors, "turn on" but don't "lock in" that employee.

Consequently, there are three reasons employees stay: two positive (want to, and want to plus have to) and one negative (do not want to, but have to). None of these shows up as a turnover statistic and none gets an exit interview. In short, sometimes companies have lost many people who are still with them. So it is why people stay, not just why they leave that must be considered.

EMPLOYEES' VALUES SYSTEMS SWAY EMPLOYEES' JOB DECISIONS

In looking at attitudes, what stimulates some individuals drives others crazy and vice versa. It's a matter of each individual's value system. Not everyone

Figure 1

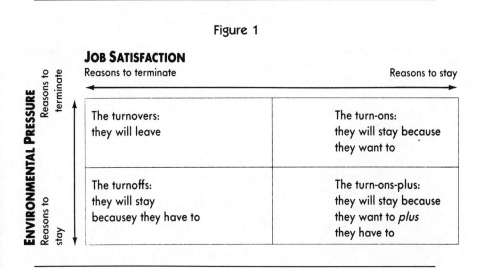

JOB SATISFACTION

	Reasons to terminate	Reasons to stay
Reasons to terminate	The turnovers: they will leave	The turn-ons: they will stay because they want to
Reasons to stay	The turnoffs: they will stay becausey they have to	The turn-ons-plus: they will stay because they want to *plus* they have to

ENVIRONMENTAL PRESSURE

finds the same satisfaction from the same work. Some prefer a variety of tasks and others prefer routines. Some want a participative management style and some truly want to be told what to do and make no decisions. Some seek promotion and some prefer to stay where they are.

These individual differences in value systems are not unusual. People are dramatically different in their values for working and often hold quite different values than upper management for working. Research has easily identified situations in which two individuals occupy similar jobs with the same supervisor, the same pay and benefits, working conditions and so on. But one employee was satisfied and one was dissatisfied—by the same things. One may be looking to leave and the other looking to stay. Therefore, it is necessary to add another dimension to determine what keeps people in a job—value systems.

To capture these individual differences, a second part was added to the survey that studied employees' attitudes—an analysis of an individual's value systems. This is accomplished by an instrument that measures six different aspects of value systems.

Tribalistic. Characterized by a strong focus on a group leader (chieftain) and his or her benevolent autocratic style, this person desires a routine, non-decision-making job. Pay and benefits security is essential, and this employee works most effectively under a paternalistic management style. Family values are strong and advancement is not essential to job satisfaction. A compatible work group is necessary. The future is short-term and the inertia to stay is strong.

Egocentric. Characterized by rugged individualism and pervasive negative assumptions, this employee responds to authoritarian leadership. Tending to be suspicious of management, this type of person is often disruptive and a chronic complainer. He or she likes tough jobs, with a tendency to challenge the supervisor for control; however, this employee displays no sense of ethics or fair play.

Conformist. Characterized by the traditional work ethic, this employee is loyal to causes and organizations if he or she believes in what they stand for. The employee prefers highly structured situations, detailed tasks, written instructions and unchanging patterns. Judgmental of right and wrong, he or she will persevere despite adversity and expects others to conform and work hard for the future.

Manipulative. Characterized by materialism, achievement, and the need for success and advancement, this employee is goal- and career-oriented. She or he seeks status and is an inveterate game player. While trying to manipulate others for his or her own financial gain, this type of employee plays to win by gaining titles and controlling others. Planning ahead for every aspect of life this employee is constantly trying to influence and sell others on what to do: money is the scorecard.

Sociocentric. Characterized by a high degree of concern for other people and social causes, this employee places humanistic ideals foremost, and cooperative, non-conflicting work groups are preferred. Harmony among people is essential for this type of person to support the peer-group focus, but the employee will persist in unpleasant situations if it is helpful to others. He or she is distrustful of manipulative people and sensitive to feelings and moods.

Existential. Characterized by individuality in action and behavior, this employee has a high concern for intrinsic work satisfaction over money or promotion in and of themselves. He or she is outspoken on beliefs, but quick to change if appropriate; learning and self-development are paramount needs. This type of person will not tolerate routine tasks or simple answers. This employee provides his or her own leadership and is flexible and adaptive in behavior and language style.[2]

Research indicates tribalistic and egocentric employees usually stay at their jobs because they are locked in by external factors. That is, they cannot leave because they have no place to go, regardless of whether they like their current situation. They show a high degree of inertia and so remain where they are—whether they're satisfied or dissatisfied.

Consequently, a company can have low turnover but that does not by itself illustrate whether employees are staying because they want to or because they have to. It is necessary to look at attitudes to find out. The internal organization reasons to stay are primarily pay and benefits more than intrinsic work satisfaction and management style. Thus, low turnover proves nothing but low turnover: *why* they stay is the key.

Conformists and sociocentric employees were about equal on internal and external reasons to stay. They stay because they cannot leave and they also stay because they want to. The internal reasons to remain with their companies were pay and benefits *plus* intrinsic work satisfaction and appreciation of the management style of the organization. In short, they stayed more for tradition-al reasons.

Sociocentric and conformist employees show a classical balanced pattern familiar to human-resource people. They stay with a company during short-term difficulties and dissatisfaction. In these instances, then, a company can have low turnover, but high dissatisfaction. To presume morale is high because turnover is low is a serious error. That is why they seek union representation rather than quit.

Manipulative and existential employees stay almost exclusively because of positive reasons. They are far less vulnerable to being locked in. Their turn-ons come mainly from positive motivation relating to their working situations and seldom from external factors.

Manipulative employees stay primarily for factors relating to advancement and pay, whereas existential employees stay mainly for intrinsic work satisfac-tion and to use their skills and abilities. They pay little attention to external factors and keep their resumes up to date so they can leave quickly if they become dissatisfied.

THE QUALITY OF EMPLOYEES RETAINED SUPERSEDES THE QUANTITY LOST

From the analysis of value systems it becomes apparent that quantity of turnover is not as important as is the quality. Is the company keeping the people it needs for the future? Exit interviews with those who leave provide little information about reasons the others stay. To find that out employers must ask those who stay why they choose to do so. To keep them, employers must reinforce the positive aspects of their employees' reasons for staying and eliminate the negative aspects of jobs.

Because many people stay because their value system tends to lock them in, it's in everyone's interest (except labor unions') to search out and eliminate the negative aspects that turn off those value systems and accentuate the positive aspects of the work. For those employees whose value systems demand a posi-tive environment and are not locked in by negatives or the external factors, the positive must be accentuated as well as the negative eliminated. The following seven-step process identifies ways to accomplish this.

Step 1. Accept that value systems of employees may be quite different than those of management. Not everyone in the company sings off the same song sheet. What satisfies one group may likely turn off another and vice versa. Realize and accept that it is not a matter of who is right and who is wrong, but that there are dramatic differences.

Step 2. Be willing to look at employee-relations policies and procedures from the perspective of who is on the receiving end of the process, not on the design end. The right policy for pay, attendance, promotion and the rest is what works best for the people in the organization, not what is preferred by the personnel department or upper management.

Step 3. Ask people why they stay, either through a survey or in interviews, and listen carefully. Ask them their opinion or attitude about a particular policy or management practice and be willing to redesign it so it matches a prevalent value system.

Step 4. Communicate whatever policies the company has in a language style that is compatible with the employees' value systems. Learn to listen in a style befitting the employees' value systems and respond accordingly. Ask the supervisors how to do this. They are closer to the employees and probably already know how their people think.

Step 5. When hiring and placing employees, consider the value systems of the stimulated people who stay and match the new people to their value systems. Try to fit new employees naturally to the company's internal environmental value system. Avoid hiring people whose value systems resemble those employees who are locked in and turned off.

Step 6. Always remember that eliminating the negatives and accentuating the positives is a process, not a program. Employee involvement in the process is key; always fully involve supervisors before anything is changed. People are more likely to believe in what they help create.

Step 7. Think about why you stay, yourself.

REFERENCES

1. Flowers, Vincent S., and Hughes, Charles L., "Why Employees Stay," *Harvard Business Review*, July-August 1973.
2. Hughes, Charles L., "If It's Right for You, It's Wrong for Your Employees," *Personnel Administrator*, June 1975.

Charles L. Hughes is the cofounder of the Center for Values Research and served as corporate director of personnel for Texas Instruments. Vincent S. Flowers is the cofounder of the Center for Values Research and served as assistant dean of business at North Texas State University.

35.
THE TEAM THAT WORKS TOGETHER EARNS TOGETHER

K. Dow Scott
Timothy Cotter

Group incentive programs boost productivity, promote innovation and inspire teamwork. However, most managers recognize that certain conditions must be present for rewards to elicit desired performance.

One major objective of compensation programs is to motivate employees to perform if not excel at their jobs. Numerous programs for linking an employee's pay with his or her job performance have been tried since Taylor introduced his now-famous piecework incentive system. The assumption that some or all of an employee's pay should be tied to individual performance as a means of obtaining the desired work behaviors is a well-accepted concept in compensation today.

Lawler, Locke, and others have provided substantial documentation that, in situations where pay is related to individual performance, employee motivation is increased and the tendency for turnover is centered among poor performers. In fact, based on a rigorous examination of the empirical literature, Locke concluded that financial incentive programs were more effective motivators than were goal setting, job enrichment, and participation programs. Lawler has not only shown that pay is highly valued by employees, but also that employees prefer performance-based compensation systems to general increase programs.

A POPULAR METHOD

In recent years, merit pay programs have become the predominant method for motivating and rewarding job performance. A 1976 Conference Board report indicated that 88 percent of the companies surveyed had a merit pay program for at least some of their employees. Typically, merit pay is an incentive program where an employee's salary is reviewed and adjusted based on

277

individual job performance. Where pay ranges are established, movement from the minimum to the maximum of the ranges is based on performance as opposed to seniority. Usually, an annual organization-wide merit budget is developed and divided among the various departments. Individual managers then distribute the monies based on an assessment of the subordinate's performance. Performance is traditionally evaluated on the basis of employee traits, employee behaviors, or employee attainment of preestablished goals (Management by Objectives).

However, for reasons articulated by Meyer and Hills, many managers have become disenchanted with paying for performance. These criticisms have been directed toward the technical feasibility of rewarding individual performance as well as toward the undesirable consequences that may result from the installation of incentive programs. Unfortunately, when problems with paying for performance are discussed, the arguments are often reduced to the pros and cons of traditional merit pay programs, as typified by Lawler and Meyer's exchange of letters in *Organizational Dynamics*. However, there are other alternatives, and as a result, one does not have to accept or reject the pay-for-performance concept based on the strengths or weaknesses of the individual merit pay approach.

We believe that group incentive programs (GIP) represent not only a viable alternative for linking pay to performance but also may be superior to individual merit pay programs (MMP) in many situations. In this article, we briefly define and describe GIPs, then compare the GIP to the MPP in the context of specific organizational conditions. Finally, we examine the issues that must be considered for determining which incentive system (if any) will produce the best results.

GROUP INCENTIVE PROGRAMS

In this context, a group incentive plan (GIP) refers to a pay-for-performance system that measures and rewards the performance and productivity of employees in work units. Group incentive plans range in scope from a small group of employees working against performance standards developed for their unit, to all employees of an organization receiving some financial reward based on company performance. However, group incentive plans generally may be described in terms of three major categories.

First, there are small group or work-unit incentive plans. In this category, performance standards, similar to those used for individual incentive plans, are established and rewards are allocated on group performance—not individual performance—against the standard. For example, a logging crew is rewarded for the amount of board feet of lumber produced, rather than each individual being rewarded for performing his or her task in the logging operation regardless of how much he or she produces.

The second major type of group incentive plan is the productivity improvement program. Under such a program, the primary goal is to improve organizational efficiency by encouraging innovative ideas and teamwork. Typically, employees from all levels of the organization participate in a process that develops and processes recommendations for improving organizational efficiency. Financial rewards are based on cost reductions, usually in the area of direct labor.

The Scanlon Plan is an example of a productivity improvement program. Committees are formed to elicit and evaluate employee suggestions for productivity improvements. Cost savings are determined by comparing the historical cost of labor to output (ratio) with the current labor cost to output. If the current cost is lower per unit produced, then the difference (dollars saved) becomes a bonus pool. The company's share and a reserve for future deficits (when current labor costs per unit are higher than the historical level) are deducted and the rest is divided among employees. The Rucker Plan, Kaiser-Steel program, and Improshare are also examples of productivity improvement programs.

The other major type of group incentive program is profit sharing. The employer rewards employees at some predetermined rate based on the profitability of the enterprise. These payments may be made directly to employees at regular intervals or withheld until the employment relationship is terminated, usually at retirement. Typically, only top-level executives participate in profit-sharing programs because they are believed to have the major influence on profits.

CONDITIONS OF SUCCESS

Most managers recognize that certain conditions must be present for rewards to elicit desired performance. Lawler has provided a succinct list of these conditions, which can be used to compare the advantages and disadvantages of individual merit pay programs (MPP) and group incentive plans (GIP).

1) Important rewards can be given and tied to performance.
2) Information can be made public about how rewards are given.
3) Superiors are willing to explain and support the reward system in discussions with their subordinates.
4) Rewards can vary widely, depending on the individual's current performance.
5) Performance can be objectively and inclusively measured.
6) Meaningful performance appraisal sessions can take place.
7) High levels of trust exist or can be developed between superiors and subordinates.

It is often argued that a MPP may not provide a reward important enough to motivate performance. Because of competing needs for resources within the organization and competing pay objectives (for example, cost of living allowances, longevity increases, and across-the-board increases), the total money invested by organizations in merit increase programs is often insufficient to motivate employees. In addition, the number of people who must share this budget increases in relationship to management's ability to attract or develop qualified and motivated employees.

Theoretically, a GIP should have the same constraints placed on the total budget for incentive pay as do merit programs. However, a GIP is often more closely associated with the productivity and profits of the operation. As a result this budget is designed to be flexible, based on organizational productivity rather than being a fixed amount that must be divided among high performers, as is common in a MPP. For instance, the Scanlon Plan provides a bonus pool that is the difference between budgeted labor costs and actual labor costs. As a result, the financial rewards are paid only when employee suggestions reduce the total cost of labor. Because the reward program does not increase labor cost and, in fact, may reduce them, it is easier for management to justify increased incentive payments.

In addition, peer recognition represents an important reward that a GIP can stimulate more effectively than a MPP. As Roy noted, individual incentive systems can foster rate restriction among production employees. Because merit pay budgets are limited, employees realize that high performers are going to receive a larger share of this budget. This realization will create mixed feelings at best toward the high performers. However, under a GIP, high performers are going to contribute to rewards obtained by all coworkers, which will certainly increase the value of the high performers to the members of the work unit.

FURTHER COMPARISONS

Under a MPP, the reality of pay ranges and the need to maintain internal equity must be recognized. The better an individual performs, the more quickly he or she will move to the top of the pay ranges, whereas under the typical merit increase program, further increases (except for structure adjustments) cannot be given without distorting the pay structure.

This problem does not exist under most GIPs because incentive pay is given outside of the formal pay structure. In other words, each time the incentive pay is earned, payment is made, but the base salaries of employees remain unchanged. To further distinguish between incentive pay and base pay, many GIPs require that separate checks be issued to employees for their incentive payments.

High rates of inflation often have a negative impact on MPPs. Given realistic constraints on the organization's ability to provide pay increases, there is considerable employee pressure to preserve "real wages" by granting "merit money" to all employees regardless of actual performance.

Another related problem is the temptation that managers have to manipulate the MPP because merit pay is often the only portion of total pay that they control. For instance, the manager may give a large merit increase to an average systems analyst because tight labor market conditions make the systems analyst difficult, if not impossible, to replace.

GIPs are more difficult to manipulate than are most MPPs, where supervisor ratings are often subjective and may not be subject to meaningful scrutiny. Typically, GIP performance standards are explicitly developed before the program is implemented and represent specific measures of output of the department or organization. Although inflationary and labor market pressures will still exist, these pressures will be directed toward having the compensation department adjust the pay system, rather than toward supervisors who may react to these pressures on a case-by-case basis.

PERFORMANCE AND PRODUCTIVITY

The ability to assess performance and productivity accurately is essential for any type of pay-for-performance program. The validity of performance appraisal programs (rating scales, checklists, essays, person-to-person systems, MBO, and combinations of the above) is being placed under increased scrutiny, as is evident by the court cases where discrimination concerning performance evaluation is alleged.

The assessment of performance for a MPP is often made by a supervisor who receives little training and is subject to intentional and unintentional bias. In fact, it is often not in the supervisor's best interest to provide an accurate assessment of the subordinate's performance. On one hand, low rating can induce a hostile reaction from the subordinate and may invoke questions concerning the supervisor's ability to select or manage employees. On the other hand, a high rating may increase the subordinates demands for pay increases and "advancement opportunities" within or outside the organization. In either case, the supervisor increases the possibility that he or she will lose a valuable subordinate. Thus, it is no surprise that performance appraisal programs suffer from the tendency to rate everyone the same. Although approaches are available to counter these problems, the cost of program implementation and maintenance are heavy.

As most managers are aware, for many jobs it is extremely difficult to develop defensible measures (quantity, quality, timeliness, and cost) of individual job performance. However, measure of output for group efforts may be more explicit. For instance, an operating unit usually has such performance measures of profitability, return on investment, labor costs, waste, quality, etc., that are already available because these measures are needed to manage the operation.

Finally, from a performance measurement point of view, group incentive programs provide an administratively less cumbersome approach. Rather than developing measures for each position and appraising each individual's performance, only work units need be evaluated. Thus, a GIP can usually appraise results more frequently (often monthly) than the annual appraisal that is common for MPPs. Performance feedback can be done more frequently without substantially increasing the cost of the incentive program. The major disadvantage of this approach is that, with increased unit size, the individual's perception of his or her impact on unit performance may decrease.

Even if these technical problems of utilizing a MPP can be overcome, the desirability of using MPP to link pay-to-performance can also be questioned. As Deci points out, merit pay may have negative effects on self-esteem. Giving large increases to a few individuals is going to communicate to the majority of employees that they are, at best, average. The effect on morale and actual job performance has not been tested, but psychologists say expectations have a major impact on behavior.

Increased competition can also be a double-edged sword. Competition among employees for limited rewards may motivate people to perform at higher levels, but this competition may also lead to hostilities, distortions of communications, negative perceptions of others, and decreased interaction. Furthermore, it becomes irrational for employees to help each other, for by doing so, they jeopardize their own chances of receiving a large merit increase. Finally, one must ask if merit pay, which directs rewards to selected individuals, represents a sound method of enhancing productivity in large groups.

However, GIPs are designed such that cooperative behavior is encouraged. Employees can feel good about the total group efforts rather than comparing themselves with each other. Because performance reflects on the entire group, it is in the best interest of groups to help poor performers to improve. Finally, a GIP communicates to employees that performance is determined by the interdependent efforts of the work group.

A FEASIBILITY ANALYSIS

Although merit pay programs can be excellent motivators of job performance under certain conditions, group incentive programs represent a viable alternative of rewarding performance for organizations that are unwilling or unable to reward performance on an individual basis. However, organizational objectives, organizational structure, and the work itself must be examined before determining the appropriateness of a MPP or any variation of a GIP. The following major issues should be considered in making this decision:

Size of the incentive unit. The incentive unit can vary from the single employee under an individual merit pay plan to every member of the organization that participates in a profit-sharing plan. Unit size represents trade-offs between the cost of developing, collecting, and reviewing performance data for the smallest unit (each employee) as opposed to a few large units, and the tendency of employees to believe that the larger the unit the less influence they have on performance and productivity. The organizational structure must also be considered because it influences the perception of work unit (team) autonomy and determines whether the efforts of the group affect performance and productivity.

Time span between performance feedback and rewards. Psychologists have found, in most cases, that the shorter the time span between effort and reward, the better. However, providing more immediate feedback must be weighed against the administrative costs, the size of the reward (more frequent rewards are necessarily smaller), and the natural work cycle that provides the performance indicators.

Selection of performance measures. Several criteria must be considered when selecting performance and productivity measures: 1) the cost of generating the data: 2) the meaningfulness of the measures to employees in the incentive unit; and 3) the impact that the performance indicators will have on organization operations (you get what you measure). It has been our experience that these measures should be constructed from currently used measures and be relatively easy to understand. As employees develop an understanding of productivity, more complex formulas can be developed to better reflect the relationship between employee contributions and outputs.

Reward amount and distribution. The reward certainly has to be significant enough to motivate increased performance and production has to justify the extra cost (including both the incentive pay and program administration costs). One of the problems with merit pay is the difficulty in determining the value to the firm of increased performance. However, the value of the program is easier to evaluate under a GIP, as can be illustrated with the Scanlon Plan. The rewards distributed to employees are generated by actually reducing labor costs. Each month employees receive the same percentage of salary or wage reward although the actual dollar amounts vary.

Program coverage. Consideration must be given to those employees who directly affect productivity. Support people should not be included as they indirectly effect productivity; support people should not be ignored, however. For instance, buyers may not directly affect the productivity of the unit, but if the materials are not available when needed or are not of the quality necessary to get the job done, productivity problems will result.

Program manipulation. Of course, the incentive program must be administered such that employees cannot gain without performing in the desired manner. The ability to manipulate the system is increased by the number of evaluators and the subjectivity of the measures.

Program communication. It has been our experience that not enough time is spent communicating the essential elements of the incentive program to employees. According to expectancy theory, motivation will occur only if employees perceive a link between effort they exert and performance, and a link between performance and desired outcomes. The linkage between performance and productivity and rewards must be clearly established if the program is going to be successful.

PROBLEMS OF SUCCESS

Too often managers don't completely consider the ramifications of an incentive program that works. Yet employees are going to realize that by becoming more productive they will be faced either with increased opportunity if there is an expanding market for the organization's products or services, or the number of employees needed will be reduced. Organizations that have fallen into the latter category must be able to assure employees that their jobs are secure. One U.S. organization provides a lifetime employment guarantee for those individuals who can figure out ways to do away with their own job. When a reduction-in-force is required, this organization relies on attrition. In either case, employees must understand how additional production and efficiency will be handled or rate restrictions can result.

Although we have pointed out a number of inherent limitations in merit pay programs and we believe that GIPs offer a viable alternative for linking pay to performance, organizational conditions will dictate which type of program will be most beneficial. In fact, these approaches are not necessarily mutually exclusive. Such incentive programs as the Lincoln Electric Plan have both group and individual rewards. Furthermore, there has been a movement in management theory and practice to reduce the discrepancies between blue-collar and white-collar employees. The "all salaried" approach is a popular management program designed to reduce this discrepancy by putting blue-collar workers on the same salary schedule and by giving them some of the same benefits that salaried employees enjoy (paid absences, no time clocks, flexible schedules and so forth).

We believe that interests and values can be more closely aligned by including both groups in the same incentive program rather than by using the traditional merit approach for salaried employees and length-of-service or piece rate systems for hourly employees.

Finally, we suggest that more thought be given to the design and implementation of incentive programs for technical, professional, and managerial employees because these are the employee groups experiencing the fastest growth. With a productivity crisis facing our nation, improved job performance is a necessity. Regardless of one's individual preference—merit pay or group incentive program—rewarding performance and productivity is essential because, as most managers are well aware, "you get what you pay for."

K. Dow Scott is an assistant professor, Department of Management, Virginia PTI, State University, Blacksburg, VA. Timothy Cotter is a vice-president in The Sullivan Group, Dearborn, MI.

36.

JOB MATCHING BRINGS OUT THE BEST IN EMPLOYEES

Ann Coil

The most satisfied and productive employees are those who are appropriately matched to their jobs. This article presents a four-part model to help identify an employee's preferred skills and working style, providing managers with a positive way to monitor and evaluate productivity.

The most satisfied and productive employees are those who are carefully and appropriately matched to their jobs. An appropriate and productive job match means that the primary tasks of a job enables the employee to use his or her strongest and preferred skills.

Although an employee may possess a range of skills that can be exercised when needed, each individual also possesses skills that he or she prefers to use over others. These are skills that come most easily and naturally to the individual and are responsible for his or her most satisfying and successful accomplishments. Preferred skills are sometimes referred to as "motivated" skills because individuals will gravitate to tasks and situations that allow them to use their preferred skills.

Furthermore, employees who are given the opportunity to exercise their strongest and preferred skills will be valuable assets to the company, enhancing its prospects for having increased productivity, higher levels of employee retention, and lower levels of absenteeism.

Thus, job matching is a skill a manager needs both to effectively recruit and to manage employees. The ability to understand the specific skills and working style required for a position is vital. A good manager will use job-matching skills every time he or she delegates duties, forms work teams, hires, fires, evaluates, and promotes.

The model in Figure 1 is designed to assist managers in identifying employees' specific and preferred skills. The model is essentially a problem-solving cycle since each category represents a cluster of related skills that must be performed if a problem is to be solved, a task completed, or a project brought to fruition. For example, if a new personnel policy needs to be instituted:

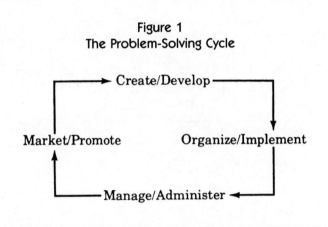

Figure 1
The Problem-Solving Cycle

Create/Develop

Market/Promote   Organize/Implement

Manage/Administer

1. The need must be identified and the policy must be *created*.
2. Once the policy is created, the details must be organized so the policy can be *implemented*.
3. The implementation becomes part of the department's larger responsibilities and must be *managed and administered*.
4. Finally, if the policy is to be accepted by those at all levels, it must be *marketed and sold*.

MODEL OF SKILLS, STYLES AND ROLES

Each category consists of sub-skills that describe specific activities one performs in completing a phase of the project. For example, to *implement* an idea, one usually selects tasks to be done, prioritizes tasks, schedules the work, and follows up details.

The four categories in this model are major, or overriding, clusters of skills that delineate the critical phases in the completion of a project. These categories have their counterparts in the major functions of an organization, represented by different departments or divisions of a company: research and development (*Create/Develop*); operations (*Organize/Implement*); management (*Manage/Administer*): marketing and sales (*Market/Promote*).

When applied to individuals, these categories capture four distinct working styles that also define roles an individual plays: the *Creator/Developer*; the *Implementor*; the *Manager*; the *Marketer/Promoter*. It is important to recognize that successful people use all of these skills and play all of these roles to some degree. Most people, however, prefer to play one of the roles more than others. The role that an employee is most eager to assume is indicative of that individual's preferred skills and working style.

CREATORS AND DEVELOPERS

To create and develop involves the generating of new ideas, the developing of new plans, the devising of different and better ways of doing things, or the creating of a better product or service. For example, "creating" in a working environment can take the form of: 1) developing a new procedure for constructing performance evaluations; 2) designing a new strategy for defining and describing a product or service to customers; 3) devising a different structure for determining a department's goals and objectives; 4) designing new forms or formats to gather and process information and streamline procedures; and 5) creating new programs or services for customers or clients; or 6) conceiving and designing a company or department newsletter.

Creators/Developers derive greatest satisfaction from creating ideas, projects, approaches, and techniques where none existed before. They get gratification from the surge of feeling that comes when a new project, idea, or product is born. Creators become bored and restless when they find themselves trapped in a maintenance role. (See Figure 2 for more examples.)

A good example is the director of a new program who conceives the idea for a new program and willingly suffers the trials of testing, modifying, and adjusting the program until it is healthy and successful. At this point the challenge to the Creator is over. The efforts necessary to maintain the program are not as rewarding or stimulating as developing the program, and the Creator begins to search restlessly for a new challenge.

Creators and Developers are found in all departments and at all levels of the organization, whether it be the secretary or administrative assistant who is always creating new procedures and forms to increase efficiency or the executive who is always developing new directions for the business to take.

IMPLEMENTORS

To implement an idea or project, a program involves the planning and coordinating of activities, tasks, people, and materials to bring an idea to fruition. In a sense, implementing is the practical application of the Creator's creation; the Implementor attends to the specific details and coordination of the plan.

Examples of typical implementation tasks include: coordinating and planning a seminar or presentation; organizing and managing a new employee-benefit program; coordinating training sessions in three new branch offices; overseeing and implementing a new management-by-objectives program in all departments of an organization; and coordinating the training and use of word-processing equipment, etc.

People who are Implementors find the task of thinking of new and different ideas, approaches, and projects a burden. They prefer to work with someone who can relieve them of the major responsibility for creating and, instead, give

Figure 2
Creators/Developers

Creators/Developers are innovative people who generally:

- need a degree of quiet time in which to create and think
- prefer longer periods of time to develop their ideas
- like to work with a small group of other stimulating people in brainstorming and creative sessions
- have a vision of the future, the end product, or the project
- become restless and bored in a position that requires maintenance of a project, goal, etc.
- tend to think long-term and are more concerned with the future and less concerned with day to day details
- dislike detail work, except when analyzing the abstract creative details that compose a part of the creative plan
- prefer to work with someone who likes to implement and will help the creator with the coordination of details
- have many interests and, therefore, find it difficult to concentrate on any one project or activity for extended periods of time (months and years)
- derive satisfaction from fantasizing, thinking, and reflecting
- tend to be somewhat idealistic and abstract

Possible Limitations

- coming up with more ideas than can be implemented
- creating ideas that others of dissimilar thinking and working styles cannot understand, assimilate, or implement
- spending too much time on creating and reflecting, and not enough time on actively implementing ideas

---

them the general and broad outlines of a project, program, or task. (See Figure 3).

The Implementor finds it easy and rewarding to systematically and efficiently plan and organize all the elements that are required to see a project to its end. Project management involves many implementing skills. Implementors are most satisfied when they have a tangible product or practical results from their efforts. They find too much contemplation and reflection a frustrating and unrewarding task.

Figure 3
Implementors

Implementors are task-oriented individuals who generally:

- like a great deal of variety to their day
- like to keep active and busy physically as well as mentally
- like to move around and have flexibility
- prefer short-term projects with tangible results and outcomes
- prefer to work with a Creator and Developer who establishes the general parameters of a project
- are most interested in the application and utility of an idea or project
- are more interested in the short-term results and day-to-day activities
- can work alone to implement a project or plan, although they may not prefer to
- enjoy attending to and following-up detail
- derive satisfaction from the organizing and ordering of tasks, materials, and details
- tend to be practical and pragmatic

Possible Limitations

- impulsively rushing to implement an idea without taking into consideration long-term ramifications
- Being too shortsighted, focusing only on the immediate and day-to-day details without sufficient consideration for the whole picture
- focusing on the immediate and concrete results without sufficient regard for the intangible effects and outcomes, such as the emotions and politics that might surround a situation

---

MANAGERS

"To manage" is a broad concept with many definitions. Traditionally, managing has meant assuming responsibility for the work of others. In the model presented in this article, the skill of managing involves leading and directing others, establishing goals and objectives, making important decisions, and coordinating people, activities, and resources. (See Figure 4.)

A good Manager will understand the process and steps involved from initial planning to final implementation. Management incorporates creativity and

Figure 4
Managers

Managers are leaders who generally:

- need to have an impact on the direction and development of a group or organization
- like variety and flexibility in their work
- work well, and even thrive, under time and environmental pressure
- are skilled at juggling many activities at one time
- prefer to delegate details to other
- see the whole picture
- need to work with others and are sensitive to the needs of others
- can work with people at all levels of the organization

Possible Limitations

- theoretically, an effective manager would not suffer from extremes of preferred skills or working style
- the primary responsibility of a manager is to orchestrate the organization's people and activities in such a way as to maintain a balance between possible extremes in goals, functions, working styles, roles, and activities according to the organization's needs

---

implementation and marketing, but goes beyond them. A Manager plans long-term, establishes direction, and must interact with others at all levels of the organization.

A person who enjoys managing derives satisfaction from being in control, making decisions, having the opportunity to impact the direction and development of an office, department, division, or organization and its workers. Managing, more then creating and implementing, requires interpersonal skills. A Manager can be described as someone who likes to make "to do" lists for others. A natural Manager is sensitive to the strengths and needs of the worker and is able to guide and direct an employee to well-suited tasks and responsibilities.

A Manager enjoys exercising leadership skills. He or she who prefers to manage will become bored and restless with positions or responsibilities that are focused and narrow in scope. To be challenged and satisfied, this person needs to be responsible for leading a group or organization toward established goals. Managing requires an individual to see the large picture, predict future trends and needs.

MARKETERS AND PROMOTERS

To "market, sell and promote" as it applies to the operation of an office, department, division, or organization means to lobby for an idea, a person, a project, a procedure, product, or a plan in order to get it accepted. Acceptance may be sought from coworkers, a manager or supervisor, upper management, vendors, or clients.

Effective sales requires the merging of three major abilities: communication, teaching, and interpersonal skills. Communication skills enable the seller to clearly and succinctly present an idea. Teaching skills are important in educating the buyer about the value and use of the idea. And interpersonal skills are essential in dealing with the feelings and emotions of the potential buyer. (Marketers are good listeners and read between the lines to detect the real message, concern, fear, or interest that isn't always clearly stated. See Figure 5 for more examples.)

Marketers are extremely focused on an end goal and usually persevere in their efforts to reach that goal. They prefer relatively quick resolutions. For the Creator, the satisfaction lies in the process leading to the resolution. For the Marketer, the satisfaction is in seeing how quickly one can reach a resolution and actually achieve a result. He or she has a great sense of immediacy and urgency and will tend to be concerned with short-term goals.

Marketers/Promoters are generally highly motivated and enthusiastic individuals. They derive great satisfaction from having a pet project or idea to support. Marketers like a lot of activity and variety in their work. They are people-oriented and can deal effectively with a variety of personality styles and characteristics.

Their real skill, however, is the ability to appropriately select and match particular features of an idea to the specific needs and interests of the buyer. For example, a manager trying to gain acceptance of a new personnel policy finds he is meeting some resistance from a supervisor. The creative and effective Marketer recognizes that the supervisor is plagued by an overload of paperwork and is aware that the policy, if properly used, will streamline this harried supervisor's processing of forms.

APPLICATION OF THE MODEL

An understanding of the concept of preferred skills and working styles and the ability to identify them in employees can help a manager in many ways.

Writing and Interpreting Job Descriptions. According to Richard Irish, author of *If Things Don't Improve Soon I May Ask You to Fire Me,* [1] job descriptions are frequently a "hopeless muddle of peripheral and nonessential requirements." Too often they never consider the one or two highly important skills that are essential for the position. A job description that delineates the category of skills and style required for success in the job provides the employer with clever

Figure 5
Marketers/Promoters

Marketers/Promoters are goal-oriented people who generally:

- prefer to have a high degree of interaction with people
- like variety and flexibility in their tasks and responsibilities
- prefer a relatively unstructured environment
- become restless and dissatisfied when expectations and end results are vague and intangible
- are more interested in the utility and practicality of an idea or project because it makes it easier to sell
- deal well with or can withstand rejection
- adjust easily to a variety of situations and people
- are most comfortable working toward specific goals
- are tasks oriented

Possible Limitations

- being so goal-oriented that they neglect subtle steps and consequences leading to the goal
- keeping so intent on the selling that they give insufficient attention to the creation and development of new ideas, plans, and projects
- promoting and selling a concept before it has been sufficiently thought out and proven to be viable
- going ahead with a concept before the mechanisms are in place to deliver the product, service, idea, or project

---

criteria for the initial decision to hire and facilitates ongoing evaluation of job performance.

Recruiting and Hiring. Effective recruitment and hiring is essentially good match making; that is, matching the tasks and skills required for the job with the employee who not only has those skills but prefers to use those skills over others. For example, if your production department frequently needs to set up prototype lines, you will be better served by hiring a supervisor who has a preference for conceptualizing and planning new systems.

Delegating. Knowing an employee's preferred skill and working style can help you better select the appropriate people for new projects, tasks, and assignments. Someone with marketing and promoting skills would be most appropriate for presenting new policy decisions to supervisors and managers in other departments. A Creator/Developer would thrive on an assignment to develop a proposal for a new employee-assistance program.

Forming Work Teams. Employees with complementary skills will form more effective work teams. A team of all Creators will generate excellent ideas, but may be less effective in bringing those ideas to fruition. A team of all Marketers may have prospective buyers all primed and ready, but there will be no product to sell.

Since this is a problem-solving model that describes a productive sequence of activities, an ideal work team would be composed of a Creator, Implementor, Manager, and Marketer. If four such creatures are not available, there needs to be the recognition that the people composing the team will need to play some of these roles, at least for the duration of the project. In some cases, it is possible for one person to play more than one role, particularly if the two roles incorporate this individual's first and second skill preferences.

Career pathing. Richard Bolles[2] cites research indicating that 70 percent of the American working population is under-employed. This means that 70 percent of the people working are not using their highest and preferred skills and are relatively unchallenged and unrewarded in their work. American business is not getting its highest level of productivity from these employees. Attention to preferred skills and working style of employees can assist managers with career pathing that will increase employee satisfaction and company productivity by matching a person's most finely honed skills to the right job.

UTILIZING PREFERRED SKILLS

Identifying the preferred skills of a valuable employee can aid the manager with the nature and timing of promotions. Knowledge of these skills can also tell the manager whether or not he or she should promote the employee. The next rung in the corporate ladder is not always the position that will be most rewarding and satisfying to the employee.

For example, companies often promote technically competent people into management positions because of their high performance, despite the fact that some of them do not have the skills nor the inclination to manage. A better career path may be a lateral transfer to a different department that affords new opportunities to exercise underused preferred skills. In one such case, a woman who was a successful supervisor of a large clerical staff transferred to the training and development department, which allowed her to deliberately and consistently use preferred teaching skills that she had used only sporadically as a supervisor. From this lateral move, the woman advanced in the company.

Another career pathing option is to enhance and expand a current position by adding or substituting tasks and responsibilities better suited to an employee's preferred skills. An example is the chemist whose solitary research and development activities were reduced and replaced with more responsibilities for customer service. This job refinement took advantage of his preferred communication and interpersonal skills and his ability to deal with customers in trouble-shooting problems with the company's product. The customers benefited, the company benefited, and the employee was happier and more productive.

The preferred skills model describes roles, functions, and skills that operate in every work group, department, and organization. An efficient, self-scoring guide based on the model enables managers and employees to assess preferred skills and working style. This knowledge gives managers a positive way to monitor and evaluate performance. It provides a specific, concrete vehicle for leading, directing, redirecting, delegating, and promoting. It makes managing more manageable.

REFERENCES

1. Irish, Richard. *If Things Don't Improve Soon I May Ask You to Fire Me* (New York: Anchor Press/Doubleday, 1975).
2. Bolles, Richard Nelson. *What Color Is Your Parachute?* (California: Ten Speed Press, 1972).

Ann Coil is a managing partner of Coil, Ballback & Slater & Associates in Santa Ana, California.

37.
TEAM BUILDING WITHOUT TEARS

Paul S. George

When Americans care about something, they count and measure it. A company that cares about teamwork measures it, evaluating the movement toward improved cooperation and collaboration on the job. Here are some simple ways to keep score and improve the team at the same time.

Team building is in. From Japanese and American models of corporate excellence, management has learned that productivity and profitability are closely tied to how employees work together, and they're rushing to invest millions of dollars in the latest training programs on teamwork.

Big name consultants from the worlds of athletics and the military collect equally large fees by giving seminars and workshops on teamwork and related concepts. One work group after another is engaged in training retreats full of structured experiences and exercise intended to mold various individuals into smoothly functioning groups. Additionally, the popularity of in-house organizational development specialists is on the rise once again.

And with it all comes the tears and tinker toys. Managers shed tears at the lamentable lack of teamwork among their subordinates and at the dollars they seem forced to commit to building a team.

Subordinates cry over the time devoted to simulations, exercises and activities that may or may not be related (as they perceive it) to the activities for which they are regularly paid. Employees also seem forced into risk-taking interpersonal situations that, in true encounter-group style, produce enough heavy emotion to leave a river of tears and regrets in their wake. And, of course, the big name consultants cry all the way to the bank.

In a manner that resembles the sensitivity-training days of the late '60s, many managers believe real team building requires tears. Effective work groups are thought to result only from expensive, time-consuming, high-risk, encounter-group style experiences in which oracular consultants lead groups through carefully designed artificial exercises.

It is possible to agree that team building is absolutely necessary, but that it's also possible to accomplish, in large measure, without the tears and tinker toys thought to be an inevitable accompaniment?

Employees who work together frequently and intensely, or who should, need to see the world in somewhat similar ways. They need to view themselves as important parts of an important group, as cogs in a gear. And they need to like and trust each other to the degree those feelings make work more pleasant and productive.

But it costs a lot of time and money to teach employees about team building. Or does it? Although sensitivity training may be the answer for some, it's not always necessary to engage in life-wrenching, emotional confrontations to move toward those goals. Additionally, team building does not have to cost so much it brings tears to the eyes of everyone.

Human beings have engaged in team building since the beginning of time. As a result, most of us possess a fairly effective, commonsense understanding of how to create a climate in which persons come to like, trust and work well with each other. The ways we do this are so much a part of the common legacy of civilized societies it may seem unnecessary to discuss them. Yet, the fact is that many often ignore the commonsense, basically free methods for team building without tears.

What are some tearless team-building strategies that might be pursued by managers interested in developing work relationships? The following is a checklist that is useful in assessing both the current status and avenues for improvement in group teamwork.

Lip service is not sufficient. Teamwork must be the expectation for employees' conduct. Improved interpersonal relationships with the members of the work group must be part of every agenda. It should be understood and accepted that teamwork is necessary for the survival and prosperity of the group. Improvement in teamwork and team building must be intentional and perceived as a perennial goal.

COMMITMENT TO TEAM BUILDING MEANS KEEPING SCORE

When Americans care about something, they count and measure it. A company that cares about teamwork measures it, and the movement toward improved cooperation and collaboration on the job is evaluated. There are some simple ways to keep score and improve the team at the same time:

Enjoy It. Does the group take time and make the effort to have fun together?

Fun is essential to both individual and group strength and health, and it is possible to work at team building while enjoying it. Because having fun together is one of the most effective ways of building bridges and bonds between people, there are almost as many ways of having fun as there are different groups.

Sharing meals together is one of the most common ways different groups enjoy time together. It includes getting the group together in the lunchroom and arranging special mealtimes. Sharing meals together is a traditional American team-building effort that goes back to the frontier days, when sharing meager foodstuffs with others was a way to show trust and care for the other person. It still works that way today.

Fortunately, there are as many reasons and opportunities for sharing meals together as there are weeks in the year. It can be as simple as rotating responsibility for bringing in the morning donuts, or it can be a monthly breakfast cooked by members of one team group for the remaining members of the unit, division or the whole company. Even though this is one of the easiest and almost completely tear-free team-building tactics, don't leave it to chance. A systematic operation, where responsibility is shared is the fairest and most effective approach. If your unit can't find time to share meals together, under any circumstances, it's time to assess the unity and spirit in the organization.

SHARED LAUGHTER AND TEAM SYMBOLS ARE SIGNS OF ONENESS

Laughter is another tearless team builder that builds understanding and empathy, essential ingredients to group cohesiveness. Simple techniques work well, such as daily calendars with humorous stories, pictures or words hung on the walls of the entrance hall or over the time clock. Little things provide the laughter that permits people to enjoy their time together. Jokes that are not at the expense of one race, sex or ethnic group can be shared to prompt healthy happy laughter.

Post cartoon, quips or notes on bulletin boards. Humorous ceremonies and rituals, such as roasts and awards ceremonies, also build bridges through laughter—a lesson the Japanese learned very well. Shared laughter is a sign that bridges are building between persons and that communication is possible within all ranks of the hierarchy.

What seems like silly or sentimental exercises to some eases interpersonal friction for others. Adults enjoy such occasional and simple traditions as secret Santas in which names are exchanged for inexpensive gifts before the Christmas holidays. Special recognition for birthdays, from brief acknowledgments to the team's guest at lunch, is one way to distribute positive strokes at low cost and even lower risk. It may be worth at least one try before deciding the ideas would never work. And, they don't cost a thing.

Symbolize It. Webster's dictionary says a symbol is a material object representing something, often immaterial. Teams and teamwork are, of course, immaterial. Symbols signify the existence of teams as well as help create the sense of unity and togetherness that knits teams more closely together. Trademarks, logos, mottos and other indicators of product lines and company efforts do more than advertise the company or product; they advertise a joint effort. Company jackets, T-shirts, coffee mugs, luggage tags, even stationery and business cards bearing the company symbol can be modified for a particular subunit of the company to declare the intentions and aspirations of the group. Symbols legitimize, by their existence, efforts to realize their declared aspirations.

Athletic teams, primitive tribes, military units, religious organizations, Scottish-clans and others have known of and used the power of symbols for centuries. Crests, coat-of-arms, totems, insignias, flags, signs, banners and badges have inspired pride, loyalty, courage, sacrifice and commitment in every culture and subculture on the globe.

Modern institutions in America subscribe to such ancient trappings even today, and most of these team-building efforts are extremely small in terms of money and tears. Although it may appear your team has no symbols because there is nothing to symbolize, it's more likely no one has taken the initiative to do it.

In addition to the physical symbols of team life, there are social symbols, such as symbolic group activities, that also identify and build team unity. Many groups use rituals, ceremonies and recognitions to accomplish team-building goals inexpensively. Awards and banquets recognizing teams rather than individuals are natural team-building times.

Organize a ceremony announcing the successful introduction of a new product or effort that was the result of a team effort. Regular monthly rituals identifying the team of the month or calling attention to the progress of every team or bringing staff members together for a "state-of-the-team" meeting let members know there is a group unity that spans time.

Along the lines of physical symbols of unity and group pride, a row of pictures on a special wall portraying past and present teams and members presents visible testimony to the existence of team effort and spirit.

Such simple, and some might even say sentimental, techniques as team scrapbooks containing photos and other momentos of team life portray a group that cares enough about its life to document its history. Scrapbooks should record the team's or entire company's activities, not just the CEO or the stars in the corporation. New video technology provides an inexpensive and fun way to chronicle the life of the team, to be played back later on special occasions.

Organize It. Just like most primitive tribes, modern work teams require a territory in which to live and work together. Members of a real team require common tasks, workstations and schedules. When team members are separated by distances that are difficult or impossible to overcome, teamwork and effective relationships become vulnerable to a different set of pressures.

Physical proximity is an important ingredient, yet if it's absolutely impossible for workstations to be located adjacent to one another, a team planning room, lounge or dressing room can help. Decorate these areas differently from others in the building and add a few amenities, such as a coffee pot and a refrigerator, to provide an informal atmosphere for team members at the beginning or end of the day or break time.

If space limitations make working or planning together an impossibility, arrange for the team to have break times together. This makes up for some difficulties that distance or lack of space present. If common break times are impossible, try to organize training and development opportunities so the team can participate as a unit.

Overnights or day-long trips that put people together for extended periods, such as in the same car, may build wholesome relationships. The same principle can apply to team membership in professional or trade associations, which provide a good opportunity for positive, off-site interaction.

Loosely coupled teams, such as members of a university department faculty or sale force, take extra effort to organize because of their job schedules. It's necessary to organize a monthly meeting in which team members engage in some simple but structured sharing about their individual activity and how it fits in with the mission of the department or the division.

Sharing can be organized around personal updates as well as business news. Weddings, births and other occasions that generate great personal meaning can be acknowledged on a regular basis without detracting from the power they add to the individual's life outside the workplace. Furthermore, many workers want to share the highlights of their lives with those they work with and to stay informed on at least the highlights of coworkers' home lives.

Japanese managers spend a great deal of time on the informal approach to team building, much of which happens after hours. Because our culture and our values are different than those of the Japanese, it's unlikely Americans will engage in informal team building as it is done in Japan, but we can do things our own way.

American workers may not want to spend long hours away from their families to build a work team, yet it's possible to bring families together in a way that strengthens relationships at work. In addition to having the boss or the team over for dinner, there are sporting, civic, religious, aesthetic and patriotic events that can be attended in family groups.

Intramural sports and games, such as volleyball and bridge, can lead to tournaments that provide limitless team-building opportunities. These and other activities build bonds between workmates as well as families.

MAKE IT CLEAR EVERYONE IS A LONG-TERM MEMBER OF THE TEAM

Team building and attrition work against each other. Relationships and productivity respond positively to long-term interpersonal relationships and each suffers when work groups, families, military units and athletic teams play musical chairs in relationships.

Organize individuals so they see themselves spending the foreseeable future together as a team, which usually leads to greater degrees of interpersonal commitment. This encourages workers to build their own teams.

The promise of permanence is important; no amount of money or time spent on formal team-building efforts make up for shredding interpersonal fibers by upsetting and separating the team too often. Organizing teams with an eye on a long-term membership goes the extra mile toward natural team development.

Personal styles that mesh well are important components of an effective team. If styles fit well from the beginning, formal team building is less necessary in the later stages of team life. Every minute spent in the early stages of the team to ensure compatible personal styles pays big dividends in productivity at later stages. Using such personality inventories as the Myers-Briggs Type Indicator makes good sense.

For compatibility, it's critical to involve team members in the recruitment and selection process of new members. Inform potential members of the team's life and mission, which may encourage incompatible candidates to withdraw gracefully. Likewise, warm welcomes and effective induction of new members hastens their commitment to the team.

Eliminating unnatural and unnecessary signs of institutional hierarchy also comes under the rubric of organizing for tearless team building. The concept of the team implies a sort of equality that is undermined by conspicuous inequality.

Make it clear that everyone is on the same team. Avoid practices that make it obvious that some managers are on the first team and others are part of another.

There will be problems if, for example, one group of managers is served lunch on fine china by white-coated waiters, while to other group eats from paper plates and cups in the break room. Several other glaringly obvious signs of hierarchical inequality also doom any team-building effort.

Reserved parking spaces, privileged office locations, executive bathrooms requiring the fabled key and many other signs of status may reinforce the efforts of the few, but they undermine the morale of the many who are denied. Most companies that work at day-to-day team building downplay or eliminate such unpopular signals that say some are more equal than others.

Modifying the hierarchy provides opportunities for participation. Rotating important and unimportant responsibilities as well as leadership roles on a regular basis convinces teammates that each person is an important group. Also, encourage team decision making if their work lives are affected.

For many decades social psychologists have known that teamwork results are highest whenever the group has a common mission, or a subordinate goal. This is a shared goal that goes beyond and is more important than petty squabbles. Groups seeking improved teamwork, without tears or tinker toys, find that the time devoted to clarifying and highlighting the subordinate goals of the team is time well spent. Therefore, it would appear, unity of purpose is the main distinguishing characteristic of successful management teams.

Model It. Perhaps the most effective way to encourage the emergence of effective teamwork is by example. Self-disclosure by the leader who reveals important information about ideas and feelings relevant to the work of the group, in appropriate ways and circumstances, encourages others to participate. And it's this type of interpersonal sharing that builds the bonds that neither tears nor tinker toys can build.

Mutual trust, respect, warmth, common goals and the feeling of group oneness are crucial to effective team operations. It's nearly impossible to permanently build such attributes into the life of teams through short-term, one-shot workshops. The basic components of teamwork result from a concerted and commonsense effort to make team building a daily goal of the group's members.

Studies of close group relationships reveal that the construction of a shared reality in the minds of the members and a common way of seeing and valuing their work is the essence of effectiveness.

Paul S. George is a professor of education and human resource development and a consultant to various educational groups.

Part VI
THE PRODUCTIVITY CHALLENGE: MEASURING, MONITORING AND OTHER BARRIERS

38.
PRODUCTIVITY GAINS STILL PEOPLE-DEPENDENT

Sheldon Weinig

Productivity increases cannot occur without committed employees, especially engineers. In order to develop committed employees, American industry must adopt employment security.

The retention of any semblance of international competitiveness in the United States will require a marked reversal of the sluggish productivity gains posted by our manufacturing sector in the last few calendar quarters.

The effects of capital cost, corporate taxation, and tax incentives on productivity in the U.S. have all been considered by our leading economists.

While not minimizing the impact of these financial factors, productivity increases cannot occur without committed employees, especially committed engineers. The human dimension is often forgotten in the productivity equation as computers and automation dominate our thinking. Yet, computerization and automation result from human effort, and their successful operation in the desired flexible manufacturing environment is highly people-dependent.

NEW WORK FORCE

Developing committed employees, while never easy, may be more difficult in the future. Managing human resources in the next decade will present different challenges for corporations, and yesterday's methods will be mostly anachronistic. The traditional work force of the past, whose main focus was salary and salary-equivalent benefits, and whose members found strength as part of a collective group that rarely *intellectually* challenged management, has been replaced by a non-docile, individualistic, provocative, and creative body of mixed gender, mixed language, and mixed work objectives.

Yet, corporate America must rid itself of the illusion that technical superiority is an American birthright. We believed that our high-tech creativity could not be challenged, let alone equaled. This belief is no longer valid. And Americans are finally beginning to understand that it can be invented *there*. In fact, the greatest danger to our society is that many Americans no longer believe that it can be invented *here*.

Clearly, improvements in our technological and manufacturing position are highly dependent upon the contribution of the engineering profession. To compete in today's global marketplace, we must improve the attitude, effectiveness, and number of our engineers.

If I were beginning a new technological enterprise today, my plan would be: Innovate in the United States, engineer in Japan, produce in South Korea, and sell like hell all over the world. (Please note where I would do the engineering.)

Roughly 7 percent of all college graduates in the U.S. are engineering majors, whereas in Germany and in Japan the total approaches 40 percent. The numbers do not reflect how bad our situation really is. Nearly 100 percent of graduating engineers in Japan practice their profession. In the U.S. fewer than 60 percent of our engineers are still practicing five years after their graduation.

For example, engineers are the single largest category of MBA candidates in this country. Many engineers go into sales because they perceive their monetary rewards as practicing engineers to be insufficient. Others go into medicine, law—anything, as long as they don't have to pursue an engineering career.

And yet, despite the shortage of engineers in the U.S., thousands of them were laid off in 1985 when the electronics and computer industries experienced one of their periodic economic downturns. We are the only Free-World nation that uses layoffs as a counter to the vagaries of economic business cycles. Employment security must be adopted by American industry, especially technology firms that must retain their core engineering and technical talent.

MENTAL EXERCISE

I believe employment security is a fundamental requisite to developing employee commitment. But it is only one part of the overall human-asset-management fabric. Companies must make significant investments in the education of their not-to-be-laid-off employees. Thus, an enlightened educational program is also required. "You pass, we pay" is my program. Our employees may take any educational course, related or not to degree matriculation or job improvement. Granted, this approach doesn't meet with Wall Street acclaim. Companies may provide gyms, or support baseball and bowling teams, without any need to justify their activities. But not so with education.

However, educational programs provide exercise for the brain. I would hope this would be of equivalent value to a company as well-toned muscles.

Moreover, when industry cyclicality occurs, causing economic downturns, wages in many companies are immediately frozen. Given choice of stick or carrot, in tough times we throw away the carrot and use only the stick. In many cases, this has proved disastrous. In short, wage increases must be performance-based. For those who excel, be it in good times or bad, reward them generously.

Some pundits defined employee commitment as "high productivity, low turnover, and a better chance of avoiding death at the hands of the Japanese." I have no argument with that definition.

Sheldon Weinig is chairman of Materials Research Corporation.

39.
MEASURING R&D PRODUCTIVITY

Richard Pappas
Donald S. Remer

Productivity is usually defined as the ratio of an output to an input. While R&D may have measurable input, the output is often intangible and difficult to quantify. Flexible measurement techniques are needed to attack the problem of R&D productivity since the R&D function itself is so flexible.

Measuring the productivity of an R&D organization is extremely tricky. Productivity is usually defined as a ratio of an output, like number of cars produced on an assembly line, to an input, like the wages paid the workers. While R&D may have a measurable input, the output is often intangible and difficult to quantify. This is further complicated because the return from an R&D department may not be realized for one to two decades, which means the time lag is much higher than in factory measurements. Furthermore, many researchers believe that this kind of measurement may be counter-productive, since the mere act of measurement could reduce R&D productivity. Nevertheless, companies continue to evaluate R&D with the crude methods available as they desperately look for more effective, quantitative methods.

After reviewing the literature, we divided the R&D evaluation techniques into three general categories: (1) quantitative, (2) semi-quantitative, and (3) qualitative.

Quantitative techniques usually follow a specific algorithm or predefined ratio to generate numbers that can be compared with other projects and past experiences. In many cases, this involves having key managers rate different aspects of the effectiveness and importance of the project using probabilistic weighting factors. These numbers are then combined using a rigid algorithm, as described later in this article.

Semi-quantitative techniques are basically qualitative judgments that are converted to numbers. These techniques differ from quantitative techniques in that no attempt is made to use a sophisticated formula to compile the data, though techniques like averaging are sometimes used to simplify the output.

Qualitative techniques are intuitive judgments. We will not analyze qualitative techniques in detail because our survey was aimed at quantitative methods, and because little has been written about qualitative methods.

Qualitative techniques are, however, in widespread use today. In our literature search and interviews with some 20 experts, we found that people using today's measurement methods do not accurately define what stage or research they are attempting to measure. This is a major flaw, not only in current efforts to improve techniques to measure R&D productivity, but also in the application of the methods already in use. The problem is that R&D has so many different stages, and that no single measurement technique is best at each stage. Thus, we propose the system show in Table 1, where each of the three evaluation techniques described earlier are compared with the research stage to which they are best suited. Understanding this simple figure is imperative before a useful analysis of R&D may be attempted, since it reflects the current areas where quantitative measures are most applicable.

The R&D stages can be defined as:

1. Basic Research—directed to the search of fundamental knowledge.
2. Exploratory Research—to determine if some scientific concept might have useful application.
3. Applied Research—directed to improving the practicality of a specific application.
4. Development—engineering improvement of a particular product or process.
5. Product Improvement—directed to changes for a product or process that can increase its marketability, reduce its cost, or both.

In basic research, a quantitative method is less applicable because the output is often too abstract. Thus, most companies use a qualitative method based upon the intuitive feel of managers to evaluate basic research. But, on the other end of the scale, product improvement usually has a more quantifiable output that is more easily modeled by a rigid algorithm. As a result, quantitative techniques used today are usually aimed at this stage of R&D, though it is generally not explicitly stated.

Between these two extremes, there is a mix of techniques used, but often the semi-quantitative approach proves to be the most useful. Applied research usually does not produce an output that is readily quantifiable. For this reason, the rigid algorithm of a quantitative technique is usually not applicable given today's state of the art. However, often the output is not as abstract as basic research, so that it is possible to assign quantitative values to qualitative judgments. Thus, the best measurement technique for this R&D stage is one where the evaluations of persons near the projects are quantified, i.e., a semi-quantitative technique. Therefore, as a concept filters through the different stages of R&D, all three evaluation techniques could be used as shown in Table 1. However, it should be noted that this is a *general* trend, and exceptions are possible.

Table 1
General Uses of Evaluation Techniques

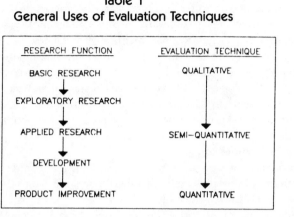

THE INTENT OF PRODUCTIVITY MEASUREMENT

Whether R&D professionals like it or not, the productivity measurement that management seeks is bound to be used to allocate salary raises and bonuses. These rewards may not only be personal, but they may dictate which projects are funded, which is perhaps of more importance to the R&D scientist. Thus, the measurement will provide incentive to produce those outputs that top management deems necessary.

But before R&D productivity is ever measured, top management must first *decide what they expect to get* from their research center, and, second, *what is the intent* of the productivity measurement system. Some research centers are nothing more than glorified technical service centers, because they are being evaluated on a short-term basis rather than long-term payouts.

This philosophy is reflected in the measurement techniques used today. The current algorithms for quantitatively measuring R&D can only model incremental improvements rather than the dramatic breakthroughs. If management runs its business based upon only quantitative measures, then R&D would be rewarded better if they concentrate on product improvements, which are outputs that can be more easily quantified. But this incentive is in reality short-sighted, because it is the breakthrough technologies that can propel a business to more fruitful horizons.

Incremental improvements can be very useful, but there is a point in the life of a technology when the time and money spent on another incremental improvement could have diminishing returns.

Recognizing when the returns for a technology are diminishing is the basis for an analysis technique of R&D projects proposed by Richard Foster at

McKinsey & Co.[1] Foster claims that technological progress proceeds along an S-shaped curve when a plot of effort versus performance is drawn. The slope of this curve is considered to be R&D productivity, and its peak occurs at the midpoint. The idea here is to follow the S-curve of a technology until this peak is reached, and then switch to a new technology and a new S-curve. This has the advantage of never expending high effort for small gain in a mature technology. Thus, to improve R&D productivity, a business should concentrate on technologies that have the most technical and economic potential, and recognize when it is time to move on to a new technology. Of course, the difficulty here is knowing when to switch technologies, but it is clear that Foster believes that the most productive research centers will provide many different opportunities to pursue.

Former director of research at Cyprus Research, Larry Ferreira, told us he agrees with this philosophy, but with a slight twist. He claims that to survive, businesses must *"renew"* themselves. He defines renewal as being equal to profits plus depreciation, and strategies should be built around maximizing renewal. The function of R&D, then, is to establish new technologies and ideas to renew the entire business, not to be a technical service center. In fact, Ferreira's R&D department was so good at producing new products and opportunities that the president at Cyprus once told him to slow down. His reply was simply that he had constructed a "candy store" of products so that top management had a complete array of "candy" to try, provided that the time was right. Thus, both Foster and Ferreira agree that the intent of R&D should be to provide the company with many possibilities for renewal, and that measurement of R&D should motivate scientists to that end.

Unfortunately, measuring those developments that achieve the goals and objectives of the company can be the most difficult, and herein lies the problem with today's measurement methods.

QUANTITATIVE TECHNIQUES FOR MEASURING PRODUCTIVITY

1. Benefits. Management wants to have numerical data to help them with their decisions. The reasons are obvious—numbers are easily compared, both between companies and historically within a company. Thus, management hopes to make *better decisions* with a quantitative measurement of productivity, since they would be able to tell whether R&D is becoming more or less productive. These measurements would also help management allocate funds and resources, and provide insight to selection for future ventures.

Another advantage of the quantitative techniques is the valuable information that will be discovered during the quantification process. First, the goals and direction of the R&D department must be understood. Then, the development of a quantitative measure requires exploring the communication lines and idiosyncrasies of the R&D department. An analysis like this on an R&D department is rarely done.

Quantitative techniques will probably never develop to the point where a generalized formula fits all stages of research in all fields. On the contrary, it is this *tailoring* of the measurement process that makes the rigid quantitative methods so attractive.

2. Problems. Forcing the efforts of an entire R&D department into a rigid formula is not practical or desirable given today's state of the art in quantitative measurement of R&D productivity. There are subtle differences between projects. How can one project that searches for fiber optics applications be compared with another that finds methods for better fiber optics materials? The ramifications of each are far different, and quantitative methods can falsely treat each project alike. Furthermore, quantitative methods are not sensitive to the subtle differences in work effort by individuals on a project.

Another major problem with quantitative techniques is the unavoidable time lag in judging the effectiveness of an R&D project. Roland Mueser, supervisor of innovative studies at Bell Laboratories, believes that a time lag of 7 to 19 years is about average for an R&D endeavor. If that is true, then estimating the future potential of an R&D project is like predicting the stock market 19 years from now! But quantitative techniques are only useful to management if they can measure current productivity, not what it was like 10 years ago.

R&D is difficult to measure quantitatively. Typically, productivity measurements can best be made on *repetitive tasks* as opposed to one-shot, creative ones. But the work performed in R&D does not appear repetitive to the casual observer. The authors believe that research should be directed to finding models that relate a common thread of repetition in the creative development of ideas, as outlined in the earlier diagram. Until that is found, quantitative techniques will continue to monitor those tasks that are most repetitive, i.e., incremental product improvements. Unfortunately, these algorithms do not consider breakthrough ideas, which are one of the greatest benefits from R&D.

3. The Business Opportunity Concept. The business opportunity concept is a quantitative technique for the measurement of R&D productivity that is presently being used at Borg-Warner and has been discussed in articles by Donald Collier of Borg-Warner and Robert Bee of DuPont.[2,3] The measurement system used at Borg-Warner actually combines all three techniques mentioned earlier, namely quantitative, semi-quantitative, and qualitative. The semi-quantitative portion is discussed in the next section.

The business opportunity concept is based upon the premise that the objective of research is to generate opportunity. Thus, research productivity is measured in terms of the amount of opportunity generated. Efficiency is then measured in terms of opportunity generated per dollar expended, since a more efficient R&D organization will generate opportunities at a minimum cost. This method is used to evaluate opportunity of entire projects that have "transisted"—that is, R&D has completed their efforts as prescribed by another department at Borg-Warner, so it is in a transitional phase. Thus, the business opportunity concept cannot be used to evaluate individual participants in a project, but rather rates their collective efforts.

To determine a new technology's business opportunity four steps are followed:

- Estimate the market for the newly developed technology.
- The customer's total cost to accomplish the function is then estimated, assuming that the best present alternative to the newly developed technology is used. This will establish how much a customer might be willing to pay.
- Using the customer's cost as a ceiling, a price is set on the newly developed technology by working backward.
- Annual income resulting from sales of the new technology to the entire market is calculated, using the hypothetical price.

The annual income generated is the business opportunity that a specific development might realize. It is unrealistically high since capture of the entire market is unlikely, but is has been useful in making project comparisons. Furthermore, a return-on-research index can be constructed by adding together the annual income for each project and then dividing by the total cost of operating the research unit. This index can be used to make year-to-year comparisons.

Gee uses a rigid formula derivation to illustrate just how this technique can work. A simple example provided by Collier more easily describes the idea. It begins with the assumption that a new development is 10 percent more efficient than the best competitive unit, though it can be manufactured for the same cost. First, the market is estimated at 4665 units sold per year. Then, the savings from the higher efficiency of the new device are estimated at a present value of $14,200, using a discount rate of 12.5 percent over 20 years. Also, it is estimated that the current units yield an average profit of $6,200 per year. Thus, the price that a customer would be willing to pay to break even would be $14,200 $6,200 = $20,400. Finally, assuming the new development draws the entire market, the business opportunity would be 4665 x $20,400 $95 million.   In a conversation with Dr. Collier, he stated that the business opportunity concept is still hampered by problems. The biggest of these is the fact that marketing has not been able to accurately estimate the markets where a new development might serve. Marketing apparently does not understand enough about the customer's needs. However, Collier maintains it is not the wrong approach, they just need to obtain better marketing data. He did note that this system is only used to judge incremental improvements, and the few breakthroughs they find at Borg-Warner are still measured in strictly qualitative terms. Thus, the system at Borg-Warner appears to follow our earlier outline.

There are several other limitations to the business opportunity concept. For instance, the method contains only economic considerations, while other qualities such as aesthetics or convenience are ignored. Therefore, this particular system is more feasible for the industrial market than for consumer products. In addition, Schainblatt points out that there is no relationship between the value of a business opportunity created by a new development and the difficulty of achieving that new development.[4] Finally, Borg-Warner's system is not sensitive to the length of time spent on the project, so the results may balloon in some years when several projects "transit," and tailspin in others even though the R&D department has been just as productive.

4. *Program Value Method.* A good example of a quantitative technique to evaluate R&D programs was reported by Schainblatt.[4] The value of a program is based upon four different factors:

- Potential Annual Benefit. This is defined as the annual pretax income that will result from successful commercialization of the R&D program output. Financial benefits from R&D programs are estimated by their ability to be marketed as a new sales item, their applicability to be added on to existing items, or their ability to reduce costs. In each case, these financial benefits must be estimated separately.
- Probability of Commercialization Management attempts to rate how well the R&D projects fits with overall strategic plans and long-term goals. A low fraction might be assigned if the technology has low interest level in business, while a high fraction would be attributed to a project that would be immediately fruitful.
- Competitive Technical Status. This probabilistic factor attempts to recognize the historical and scientific significance of the project. For example, a project that has had continued historic significance and is ahead of competitive activities would rate a high probability, but a project that is an alternative to more promising solutions would yield a low fraction.
- Comprehensiveness of the R&D Program. This factor discounts those projects that may aim at part of the potential benefit. For example, a program that is targeted to a general area of opportunity and only has vague connection to the potential annual benefits is not very comprehensive. Thus, high-fraction comprehensiveness projects are perceived as having direct benefits for the entire problem.

The calculation of "program value" follows this algorithm:

1. Estimated annual new or projected sales for complete product
2. Estimated annual cost improvements
3. Potential annual benefit = (assumed percentage of line 1 that represents average incremental pretax income plus 100 percent of line 2)
4. Probability of commercialization
5. Competitive technical status
6. Comprehensiveness

7. Program Value = line 3 x 4 x 5 x 6
8. Total program value is summed over all businesses or products
9. A discount factor can be incorporated depending on the number of years to potential annual benefit

The authors of the program value method know that the values generated are only rough estimates, and they only treat differences in *order of magnitude* as being significant enough to help with decisions regarding their R&D program mix. Thus, it does not seem relevant to use the program value to measure productivity. Rather, this method was presented to show how one company uses probabilities to help quantify the qualitative judgments of its managers.

5. Other Quantitative Methods. Many companies have used the "bean counting" approach to quantitatively measure the productivity of their R&D personnel. This involves keeping records of patents, technical publications, or honors and awards from peer groups. For the high achieving R&D person, this might seem to make some sense. But so much of industrial research is carried out at a project level that counting patents or publications might be misleading. Also, much of today's research involves software, which, as of now, is very difficult to patent. In addition, some companies do not apply for patents because they feel they are better protected by keeping their research results a secret.

Furthermore, professionals are more prone to publish minuscule contributions if the number of publications is used as a measure of productivity. We interviewed a medical researcher who said that rather than publish three or four results together, he publishes each one separately so as to impress his funding sources. He has done research at three different organizations and he found this to be the standard method for reporting medical research. This researcher happens to do quality work, but he "plays the game" in order to have more publications.

Roland Mueser at Bell Labs suggested using *citations* of publications as an indicator of productivity. The fact that others had cited an R&D person's publication may show contribution to the field. However, this indicator could not be used exclusively since many researchers do not publish or may be working on proprietary matters.

During technical innovation as a new technical event like an invention, discovery, or theory that has proved to have practical utility, Mueser believes that technical innovation, unlike patents and publications, can be defined to gauge the results of all kinds of scientific and engineering work. Thus, counting technical innovations has been used at Bell Labs to measure fundamental research and product development.[5]

Dundar Kocaoglu, professor of management at the University of Pittsburgh, suggested the development of *models* of the R&D department to help with the measurement of productivity. He is working on a way to combine control theory complete with feedback and delays to model the R&D function. The advantage of this approach is that a degree of understanding will result from studying the characteristics of R&D before it is modelled. Nevertheless, successfullly modeling an R&D department appears to be a monumental task.

Another quantitative technique by Michael Packer of MIT suggests the use of a productivity information system that allows management to choose specific criteria that can be plotted for easy evaluation.[6] This method appears to be quite promising because it stresses the need to present the productivity measurement in a useful format. The algorithm involves using a factor analysis to convert both objective criteria (like the number of patents) and intuitive indicators (like an undisputed reputation) into the underlying abstract concepts that managers use to evaluate R&D productivity (for example, "quality" vs. "quantity"). The factor analysis allows the output of R&D to be plotted according to these abstract concepts, and a trend analysis can be done to show the optimum positioning according to management's collective attitudes. The strength of this technique is the fact that management can easily adjust the plot with subjective inputs much easier with a plot than they can with hard numbers. However, this method could suffer in that it chooses specific criteria based on current objectives and assumes that they can apply over time. Since managers' attitudes and objectives tend to shift, it seems unfair to base R&D's productivity against criteria that could be unstable. This is a common problem in quantitative methods, though this method might still prove to be a valuable tool.

Five other methods to measure productivity as found by Schainblatt are summarized in Table 2. The location where every method is being used is not revealed because of promised anonymity. This list, when coupled with the examples described earlier, gives a good cross-section of the kinds of quantitative techniques now being used, even though it is not all-encompassing. Note that the examples we have presented range from the complicated algorithms presented before to the simple ratios in Table 2. Nevertheless, each of these methods has problems that seem unavoidable. They are too rigidly defined to incorporate the broad spectrum of activity in an R&D department, and in some cases, such as the first in Table 2, would serve to irritate rather than motivate R&D professionals. It appears that the underlying problem of all quantitative methods is that they have attempted to quantify R&D using, in our opinion, poor models. Thus, it seems logical that research be directed in the area of improved model building so that quantitative measurements will be more accurate. A start for this modeling approach might be the use of the simple concept we outlined in Table 1.

SEMI-QUANTITATIVE MEASURING TECHNIQUES

Semi-quantitative techniques appear to be among the best methods for evaluating R&D productivity. The subtleties of different projects are not lost through the use of formal algorithms because the evaluation process is performed by assessors who are located near the project. Basically, this

Table 2
Some Quantitative Methods Used in Industry Today

Methods	Disadvantages
Oil company counts outputs like flow sheets, cost estimates, and drawings; standards were developed, and complexity factors assigned. (This is engineering and not R&D.)	Staff using it questioned the meaningfulness of the output: method obtrusive to professionals.
Comparative analysis and trends; science panel judges quality & impact of discoveries; use indices like number of analytical tests per professional to measure trends of developmental research.	How can different projects be rated on the same scale? Some projects may need more tests than others.
Figure of merit = (pre-tax profit over last 5 yrs)/ (R&D expenditure); used in trend analysis for pay increases.	Assumes changes in sales are due to R&D expenditure, and that marketing, etc. has no effect on those sales.
Measure productivity increase due to investment in labor-saving equipment and instruments.	Assumes R&D just conducts tests, does not consider impact of improvements on business.
Quantitatively rate by patent attorney (for technical excellence) and by VP of R&D (for relevance to business); then check with (costs of R&D/(goods produced) and (patents)/(professional).	Patents can be misleading, goods produced are dependent upon many other departments; VP ratings are semi-quantitative.

technique asks people close to the project to write down what they think, and it is these opinions that are then quantified according to different rating factors. These numbers may be crudely manipulated; for instance, by averaging them so that a condensed output may be provided. Thus, management has a number that they can readily use for comparison, as opposed to a purely qualitative statement.

But semi-quantitative techniques are not without their limitations. Often people can be swayed by bandwagon effects in making their qualitative judgments. Furthermore, using numbered scales can always be misleading since some people believe there can never be a perfect "10" while others think everything is perfect. Thus, relative differences in qualitative scaling can distort the output if these measures are incorrectly combined.

Discussion of several different examples and their problems will help to illustrate why we like this approach.   *1. Borg-Warner.* The semi-quantitative technique used at Borg-Warner was described by Donald Collier.[2] This system is used with the business opportunity concept described earlier. While the business opportunity concept analyzed the R&D efforts according to a specific algorithm, this semi-quantitative measure describes how well the research department met the agreed-upon objectives according to qualitative judgments.

At the end of each year, the "customer," or other division within the company, compares the actual R&D performance with the initial objectives brought to R&D, and rates the effort on a scale from 0 to 3: "0" means that the objectives were badly missed; "1" means the project overran time and cost; "2" indicates the objectives were met; and "3" is assigned to a project that exceeded the stated objectives or completed them well below the budgeted expenditure of time and money. This rating is then multiplied by the money spent on each project, and finally normalized by the total amount spent on R&D. Thus, a performance rating can be generated for each project for comparison and from year-to-year for historical trends analysis.

Borg-Warner uses these ratings to help determine annual bonuses. They believe this system has helped to improve the quality and clarity of the objectives for each project by encouraging better communication. The method has provided incentive to R&D staff not to overrun time and cost. The company believes productivity has improved as a result of using this productivity measurement.

However, this and many other measurement techniques are too strongly related to the estimates made prior to the project. Thus, the measurement is not of productivity, but rather of how well R&D can estimate its own abilities. Collier claims that his R&D workers are "perennial optimists," but it has been our experience that if someone is faced with making more money by meeting objectives, he tends to set his objectives lower. This is especially dangerous in a R&D environment where original thought and personally risky ventures should be encouraged rather than thwarted.

Nevertheless, this example is typical of many semi-quantitative methods. Note that no formulas or obscure ratios are used, just the qualitative judgments of those nearest the work have been asked to assign numbers to their opinions.

2. The Union Carbide Questionnaire. At Union Carbide, an annual "R&D Categorization Questionnaire" helps to evaluate the research efforts. This questionnaire, as described by Whelan, is the result of several years of work to establish definitions of different kinds of projects that are understood and accepted by both management and R&D personnel.[7] The intent was to avoid good-bad connotations so that each active R&D project could be categorized fairly. Ratings are provided annually by line managers in charge of typically $1-$5 million in R&D funding.

Union Carbide has found it useful to convert the responses to each question to dollar average rating. The average response is weighted by the project funding. Since responses generally fall within a continuum from a defensive to an offensive posture, it is helpful to define this common scale as one in which zero represents defensive and one represents offensive. These defensive to offensive (D/O) averages are reported with the detailed data. Further condensation has proven helpful by combining selected D/O averages into composite indices. For example, Union Carbide numerically analyzes historical trends by combining the D/O averages for the sections on the questionnaire that judge the purpose, stage, type and organizational implication for a project as well as the two ratings of success probability.

This system has several advantages. First it is possible to ascertain the relative amounts of corporate R&D effort being devoted to *high risk versus low risk* projects. In addition, the profile serves as a *communication tool* between R&D and corporate management. Also, *trend analysis* of R&D posture reflects the R&D response to corporate goals as well as the impact on budget variations on R&D objectives. Finally, this method incorporates analysis of *all types of research*, from basic research to product improvement.

However, this measure does not necessarily measure productivity, but rather converts the impressions of line managers to numbers as they perceive how their workers are performing. Experience has shown that quite often line managers can distort the truth to impress their superiors or can be misled by their subordinates. In addition, line managers in R&D sometimes lack the qualifications necessary to rate each project. Thus, this method is limited because the sample may not be broad enough.

3. *The Peer Rating Approach.* Quite simply stated, a peer rating system merely asks all project members to evaluate themselves and one another on some quantitative scale. A supervisor then correlates the data and condenses it to some grading factor. The system has worked quite well in evaluating the participation of students in industrial-funded projects at Harvey Mudd College, and it might be applicable to an R&D environment in several ways.

Obviously, R&D professionals could be asked to rate each other. But they could also be polled as to their opinions about the type of tasks they think they should be doing and how well they perceive other projects are doing. Naturally, it is expected that this kind of information would be compared with a supervisor's own appraisal. Thus, this is not just a personal evaluation, but a project rating as well, which could be used to measure the productivity of an entire division.

The advantages of a peer ratings system are numerous. First, the subtle differences between people and projects are certainly highlighted by peer ratings. It seems that true breakthroughs might surface faster as well, since peers can recognize the value of an idea before it is reduced to the layman's term of top management. This would also occur without ignoring the benefits of significant incremental improvements. Thus, it seems that many of the problems of quantitative techniques can be avoided using peer ratings.

Another important benefit of the peer rating approach is the added understanding management can obtain about their own employees. In R&D departments, the seemingly unproductive, purely creative individuals sometimes make the most fruitful discoveries. Sometimes that "unproductive" person is a "gatekeeper"—the kind of person who always answers everyone else's questions, but never seems to have time for his own work. These types of individuals might be weeded out in a strictly quantitative method. However, a peer rating system will alert management to these extremely valuable R&D professionals.

Peer ratings will also help in managing R&D. It is management's responsibility to formulate the right mix of talents on a research project. If management knows more about the strengths and weaknesses of each professional, it stands to reason that a better mix could be achieved. For example, one of the authors recalls that the Jet Propulsion Laboratory could have used this kind of information when a new supervisor was hired for a group of three world-class mathematicians whose only drawback was their inability to communicate. The previous supervisor had extremely good communication skills, so the mix was very good. But the new supervisor was not as effective because his skills in communication were not as good as his predecessor, and the talents of these mathematicians were not fully used. A peer rating system would have encouraged management to locate a communicator to work with the mathematicians, or improve the communication skills of the new group supervisor.

A peer rating approach is not without its problems. In R&D, there are occasionally those individuals that work on their own project by themselves. There are also individuals who work on many projects at once. Thus, there is an immediate problem to assess just who is to evaluate whom so that a valid evaluation may be generated. In addition, individuals in one project may have limited or no knowledge of certain other projects because of secrecy requirements. This means that the secret projects will have a more limited sample of evaluations.

Often it is claimed that people cannot accurately rate the performance of their peers. But a study done at the Air Force R&D Laboratories shows that professional colleagues are suited to evaluate the innovativeness and productivity of researchers' output.[8] The experiment asked 2, 3, 4, or 5 people to rate their peers on a scale from 1 to 9. After applying various mathematical tests to their data, they concluded that peer ratings of R&D people are both *reliable and valid.* They also found that those individuals who were classified by their peers as innovative were generally productive as well.

Another problem with peer rating is the aggrandizement effect. This is the hypothesis that a rater will almost always rate his own ability or output higher than others would have rated them. For example, it is mathematically implausible to have 40 percent of all mathematics departments in the top 5 percent, but if they are asked individually, they will all certainly claim that they are. A study was conducted to test for the aggrandizement effect in 55 sets with six organizations per set. The organizations range from Camp Fire Girls to insurance associations. It was found that the raters overestimated the prestige of their organization eight times as frequently as they underestimated it, and net overestimation could be discerned in every one of the sets.[9] Our experience in using peer ratings at Harvey Mudd College to evaluate students substantiates this study. But we have found that aggrandizement can be minimized by eliminating an evaluator's rating of himself.

A peer rating system as applied to an entire R&D department could be a disaster if it were not handled correctly. Careful consideration should be given as to just how the peer ratings are administered and how the results are presented. Promoting the feeling that everyone is evaluating you at all times might stifle communication that is vital to the success of an R&D organization.

Laurie Larwood, professor of psychology at Claremount McKenna College, suggests the use of the Delphi Method to develop an effective peer rating system. The Delphi method has been used for years to determine the best strategy for a business to pursue by interviewing prominent people in the field. The results are then combined and reviewed by top management, and a new set of questions for the experts is filtered through. This process is reiterated until some focus has been determined. Presumably, this technique eliminates the "band wagon" effect of a brain storming session. Prof. Larwood believes this technique could be used to help find out what criteria the R&D personnel would like to be rated on, and how. In addition, the questionnaire could be formulated so as to include those aspects that professionals feel are important to the well-being of a project and an entire R&D organization. It is hoped that a valid questionnaire would result from this stage, one in which the majority of professionals would find effective.

Overall, the peer rating approach seems to have met with general approval from several of the experts we interviewed in the course of this study. According to Kocaoglu, an R&D department at Westinghouse Electric is happy with its peer rating system, which involves having each of the 16 professionals rate the strengths and weaknesses of each other, the organization, and the mix of R&D projects that were adopted.

Peer ratings appear to be better than most other semi-quantitative techniques. Most other rating systems use only the supervisors of R&D, or some outside specialists in the field. In fact, one of the authors worked for a large company that ranked each employee based upon ratings of their supervisors, not by peers. We believe both systems should be used and the results compared. Differences between the two should raise important, subtle questions about how R&D is run and where it is going.

Semi-quantitative techniques seem to attack the problem of R&D productivity measurement better than quantitative techniques. They deal with the measurement on a more flexible level because the R&D function itself is so flexible. However, given time and research into new techniques of measurement, this current trend could change.

In sum, a great deal of research needs to be done to discover better ways to measure the productivity of R&D. Since so many different intangible factors come into play, perhaps an integrated group of individuals might be able to make significant contributions. A team consisting of scientists, psychologists, economists, engineers, and management scientists would be necessary to formulate a better model to evaluate the R&D process. For instance, the Claremount Colleges, and Harvey Mudd College in particular, have all of these elements represented in a contiguous area so that the work could proceed smoothly. We are interested in pursuing such an endeavor. As this kind of research progresses, measuring R&D productivity may become a valuable tool to guide and motivate R&D organizations.

REFERENCES

1. Foster, Richard N., "Boosting the Payoff from R&D," *Research Management*, January, 1982.
2. Collier, Donald W., "Measuring the Performance of R&D Departments," *Research Management*, March, 1977.
3. Gee, Robert E., "The Opportunity Criterion—A New Approach to the Evaluation of R&D," *Research Management*, May, 1982.
4. Schainblatt, Alfred H., "Measuring the Productivity of Scientists and Engineers in R&D: A State of the Practice Review," The Urban Institute, Washington, D.C., May, 1981.
5. 1980 IEEE Engineering Management Conference Record, "What is Technical Innovation?" by Roland Mueser, Catalog #CH1603-0.
6. Packer, Michael B., "Analyzing Productivity in R&D Organizations," *Research Management*, Jan-Feb., 1983.
7. Whelan, J. M., "Project Profile Reports Measure R&D Effectiveness," *Research Management*, September, 1976.
8. Stahl, Michael J. and Joseph Steger, "Measuring Innovation and Productivity—A Peer Rating Approach," *Research Management*, January 1977.
9. Caplow, Theodore and Reece J. McGee, *The Academic Marketplace*, Doubleday & Company, Inc., Garden City, New York, 1965, pp. 88-90.

Richard Pappas is a regional sales engineer at Hewlett-Packard. Donald Remer is the director of the Energy Institute and the Oliver C. Fields professor of engineering at Harvey Mudd College.

40.
CHALLENGING TRADITIONS

John Teresko

Strategic manufacturing calls for evolving appropriate production and management systems, capitalizing on available options, developing new supplier relationships and becoming leaders of change—not keepers of the status quo.

No longer can companies be content to merely relegate manufacturing to a passive role in corporate strategy. If American-made products are to retain their lucrative U.S. markets—and succeed in the global market-place—management will have to ensure that the manufacturing function fulfills its strategic potential. Properly done, it can give a manufacturing company a competitive edge in a variety of ways—from improving quality to reducing break-even points to providing the flexibility required for success in today's marketplace. But it's not a question of applying a quick fix, and it won't be painless. For one thing, it will mean scrapping the old, comfortable ways of running a business. Strategic manufacturing calls for evolving appropriate production and management systems, capitalizing on available options, developing new supplier relationships, and becoming leaders of change—not keepers of the status quo.

What is the role of manufacturing in a business? Until recently it was simply to implement strategy that other corporate functions, such as finance or marketing, had devised. Too often, it was, and still is, considered as a stepchild—and an afterthought.

However, given the manufacturing technology options such as CIM (computer-integrated manufacturing) that are now available, manufacturing's role is changing. It should be at least on a par with the other functions in defining organizational goals and strategies.

But for manufacturing to attain the necessary credibility and status to fulfill such a role, some old traditions will have to be broken. The first is the cultural "chestnut" that manufacturing should play no more than a reactive role—catering to the whims of the "real" driving forces. For examples, marketing searches out what the customer wants. Finance decides how much to invest to make the product the customer wants. And manufacturing simply listens and obeys—or tries to.

In this scenario, manufacturing management in effect abdicates its responsibility for defining how its production prowess could be made more competitive. Characterized by weak communications links with top management, such a manufacturing organization is likely to be saddled with old and neglected manufacturing systems, and equipment—and, worse yet, no appropriate plans for developing a strategy keyed to long-term corporate purposes.

True, reactive manufacturing-management teams did fare well following World War II. Encouraged by the stability that the comfortable status quo provided, managers became administrators, eschewing the discomfort of continual self-improvement; unions sought—and found—new ways to carve bigger pieces of the pie; and domestic competitors were lulled into no more than minor skirmishes over market share.

All of that, however, was before the offshore competition discovered the U.S. market. Now under attack and finding itself extremely vulnerable, U.S. manufacturing must undergo major changes if it is to survive.

BREAKING TRADITIONS

Fortunately, survival is possible, but only at the expense of outdated traditions that to some extent have kept management operating in the dark ages of manufacturing. Some of the familiar are:

- Maintaining inventories on a just-in-case basis rather than paring them to just in time.
- Having labor check its brains at the time clocks rather than realizing that labor can be part of the solution—just for the asking.
- Chasing labor around the globe rather understanding the total cost picture.
- Realizing that, when justifying the cost of capital equipment or measuring the benefits of automation, the accounting model has its shortcomings.

It was in such an environment of change in 1985 that General Motors Corporation broke with tradition in creating Saturn Corporation. It was to be an organization with the lofty goals of implementing a high degree of advanced manufacturing technology, installing a new corporate culture, and creating a paperless corporation.

By the fall of 1986, when GM scaled back its investment in the Saturn experiment, some observers thought that Chairman Roger B. Smith had abandoned this American dream, a vision he had once hailed as "the key to GM's long-term competitiveness, survival, and success as a domestic producer."

But while he has trimmed back the initial capacity and the total investment, he has not rescinded his vow of driving the first Saturn off the assembly line. Mr. Smith turns 65 in July 1990—one month after production starts.

To the "administrators" in American management, GM may appear to have failed in its attempt to break with tradition. But to real corporate leaders—and Mr. Smith is mightily trying to be one—GM has already succeeded, because it recognizes the need to break out of the old mold.

20 PERCENT FAILURE RATE

The automotive industry is not the only sector that needs to break with tradition. Another sector facing the same challenge—and that's more representative of the national problem—is the auto-part suppliers.

Confronted with the restructuring of their primary market as the Japanese automakers move in with their own long-term supplier arrangements, the U.S. auto suppliers will either have to break with some traditions or close up shop, believes Edward L. Hennessy, Jr., chairman and CEO of Allied-Signal Inc., Morristown, N.J.

While change is creating difficulties, Mr. Hennessy believes that it also is opening up many opportunities for those that are preparing for the rigors of global competition.

Mr. Hennessy believes that breaking with some traditions will result in Allied-Signal's reaching $5 billion in automotive-supply sales in 1990. "And I'm convinced that the prospects can be very bright for other suppliers that take the same route."

Mr. Hennessy says the first and most important step for suppliers is to establish new relationships with their customers—in this case, the automakers. "The auto industry's drive for improved productivity and quality is already leading to greater collaboration between suppliers and manufacturers," he says. "And before too long, this new partnership will largely replace the traditional alignment of manufacturers and suppliers put together in the early years of this century."

The second priority, he says, is to continue to internationalize operations. "We must be able to guarantee our customers rapid deliveries anywhere in the world."

COMMITMENT TO TECHNOLOGY

The third priority, he contends, is a commitment to advanced manufacturing technology—computerized manufacturing that is both integrated and flexible.

Mr. Hennessy describes his ultimate goal as "a computer network that integrates all the business and manufacturing functions at our 78 plants, 25 engineering centers, and 28 business offices. It will also be able to link our operations with those of customers and suppliers, thereby creating a complete product-development, manufacturing, and distribution system."

Why is Mr. Hennessy so obviously putting his manufacturing strategy at the center of his corporate strategy? Consider the benefits he anticipates for automation at the company's Bendix Brake Division, South Bend, Indiana. Beginning in 1987, that operation is scheduled to start sending electronic-engineering data directly to five computerized machine centers located at a St. Joseph, Michigan, plant. Expected benefits include halving program-writing time through the use of automated programming, reducing setup time by 75 percent because of the manufacturing flexibility of the machining centers, and trimming tooling and fixturing costs by 60 percent by using flexible locators and clamps.

In breaking with old traditions in manufacturing, Mr. Hennessy expects to encounter severe challenges. "One of these is making the right decisions about what stages of production should be automated—considering the capabilities of available technology as well as the payback. But the major challenge is that most of our people have little experience with the complex technologies we're adopting. So we're spending a lot of time analyzing our prices and training our people."

BASKETBALL TO FOOTBALL

Offshore competition, of course, is a major stimulus for the tradition-breaking process at Allied-Signal. But the need to break with the past pervades virtually all segments of American business.

"The rules are changed—it's almost like going from basketball to football," asserts Robert L. Callahan, president of Ingersoll Engineers Inc., Rockford, Illinois. "The new rulebook reads like this: If you're going to stay alive and stave off foreign competition—or at least stay even with it—you've got to do three things.

"First, American manufacturers are going to have to take a lot of money out [cost reductions] of manufacturing—an awful lot. We say 30 percent but we've had some clients [manufacturing firms] ask for 40 percent in order to compete with the likes of the Japanese, Taiwanese, and Koreans. Second, we can no longer get by with the traditional approach to quality. Not only will we have to do it more cheaply, but also with a vast improvement in quality—and 90 percent quality improvement isn't a bad number, and it's achievable," emphasizes Mr. Callahan.

"Finally, when it comes to delivery, the new rules indicate that U.S. managers will have to do from two to ten times better."

NONTRADITIONAL COMPETITORS

Mr. Callahan stresses that American manufacturers have allowed themselves to be lulled into viewing their competition as just like other

American manufacturers, playing by the same old American rulebook. "Before the current round of foreign competition, an American firm never undercut another firm by 30 percent. Maybe 10 percent—but never 30 percent. We are so bound by traditional approaches, so used to competing with people who didn't want to compete very hard, that we have built a lot of fat into our manufacturing."

Because of all the "fat" Mr. Callahan's recommended remedies don't start with computer-integrated manufacturing, but with simpler approaches—such as straightening out the flow of materials into the plant and out to the customer. He sees a need to throw out a passel of other American manufacturing traditions. One, the outcome of the spaghetti-like material flow in American plants, is the obsession with lift trucks moving materials from one place to another.

"Wouldn't redesigning the flow be easier and more effective?" he asks. "Inventories are another tradition that needs to be broken. Instead of just in time, the American way is just in case."

Next on the list of traditions to scuttle is the use of so many foremen to manage all the "stupid" people out on the shop floor. "Its almost as if we asked the workers to leave their brains on the time clock in the morning and pick them up when they ring out in the evening," Mr. Callahan quips.

Mr. Callahan also reacts harshly to the great tradition of the American accounting system. "In addition to being known for producing bad, unusable information, our accounting systems require so many accountants that American companies wind up spending five to ten times as much as their Japanese counterparts to keep the books. What's worse, we've never been in a company where you couldn't find piles and piles of accounting reports filled with spurious information that nobody uses or cares about, yet they continue to be produced."

He doesn't see traditional U.S accounting systems helping much in the area of capital equipment justification, either. "This requires predicting cost reductions and carefully measurable cost items, when the truth is that most benefits [for manufacturing technology] are largely unpredictable or hard to measure."

Mr. Callahan's list of traditions to be challenged include:

- Trying to inspect quality into the products.
- The boss-versus-workers syndrome.
- Labor standards in the shop that are adding cost rather than controlling them.

"We have huge corporate and divisional staffs that are second-guessing, double-checking, and generally redundant. We have purchasing departments whipsawing vendors instead of trying to get in bed with them—for the mutual benefit of everybody."

DRAMATIC SAVINGS

He repeats: "There are two steps needed to play by the new rules: Straighten out the flow, and get rid of as many traditions as you can." For an oil-pump maker, these actions reduced throughput time—from order receipt to time of shipment—from 25 days to two days. "The effect on inventories of course is that inventories turn over much faster—what used to be five turns is now 30. The inventory reduction is from $14 million to $5 million."

Other savings come in the elimination of a lot of material-handling costs, and reductions in total hours per unit and in on-time delivery. All of this, he points out, is the payoff from making the simple, low-tech corrections that must precede CIM. Without this simplification, Mr. Callahan quips, adding technology would only give you the capability of producing scrap faster.

Mr. Callahan claims that the benefits accrued to the pumpmaker from the simplification steps are not unique. He cites the experience of an automotive tailpipe manufacturer: "By straightening out the flow and dumping some traditions, throughput time was reduced from three weeks to four hours."

Such results—even before CIM is implemented—suggest that we *Han* play by the new rulebook.

But how did all that fat get there in the first place? It was basically built on the past successes of American manufacturing, says Mr. Callahan. "The flow problem—which seems to be a product of decades of haphazard, evolutionary, unplanned, sloppy growth—is really a result of successive waves of market stimulus. Every time they [American manufacturers] expanded, flow tended to be adversely affected. Soon, flows became spaghetti-like. And, if you tour American manufacturing plants, you'll have to conclude that it must be a tradition."

WHERE'S THE PROBLEM?

Mr. Callahan is amused by the great American problem-solving tradition. "We are in love with spending 90 percent of the time solving 10 percent of the problem. Consider the typical cost-reduction approach. In a manufacturing plant we still tend to flog the hell out of the direct labor on the shop floor. But nobody worries about the other 90 percent of the cost equation—and that is where the flow money is!"

Mr. Callahan also casts a critical eye on management productivity. "Having too many layers of management seems to be an American tradition. Most of our businesses are routine—automotive pumpmaking for example—but tradition dictates eight levels of management. Overseas, they're doing it with half that."

MOST POPULAR TRADITION

Mr. Callahan claims that the most popular American manufacturing tradition is the make-buy decision that sends work offshore based on what he calls Mickey Mouse allocations of overhead.

"It's tantamount to giving up," he says in explaining what happens: "The offshore competition comes in way below the American price. The U.S. maker, devastated, sends its work to another country.

"The U.S. company gets a lower production cost, but it could have had the same cost reductions here if management had attacked its flow and traditions problems," Mr. Callahan asserts.

DISTRIBUTION, NOT LABOR

The fallacy in chasing cheap labor is that, for most products in today's markets, it just isn't the competitive tool it appears to be.

"Distribution costs, not direct labor costs, are going to be the determining factor as to where the products of tomorrow are going to be produced," says manufacturing consultant Hal Mather, president of Hal Mather Inc., Atlanta. He observes that distribution costs (moving raw materials and products) are increasing at a faster pace than the costs of manufacturing goods.

That's significant, he adds, in that emerging technologies will have far less potential for reducing distribution costs.

MANUFACTURING COMING BACK

"Although the export and import of goods is at its peak right now," it's going to decline and will be replaced by the concept of producing near the market," predicts Mr. Mather. That means foreign competitors are already manufacturing in the U.S. or are in the process of building manufacturing plants here. By one count, the Japanese alone have more than 600 plants in the U.S.

Mr. Mather rhetorically asks: "If they were mighty competitors from their overseas plants, just how much tougher are they going to be when they're just down the street from you?" If offshore sourcing still sounds like a desirable way to gain competitive advantage, why are overseas competitors setting up shop next door to us—with none of the "great" American manufacturing traditions?

The question for American management is: If the offshore competition can successfully manufacture here, why can't we? Mr. Mather feels it's only a matter of time—when the direct-labor content becomes insignificant enough.

As an example, he cites a client of his, Philips' Lamp Works, a European marketer of television sets. "They used to make black-and-white television sets in Singapore. They sourced all the components locally, produced the sets in Singapore, and the shipped them to Europe, a major market. However, with only 45 minutes of direct labor per set, it's no longer profitable and the company now produces the sets in Europe. With only 1.3 hours of direct labor in the production of their color TV, it won't be long before that, too, is produced in Europe."

Some products will be repatriated sooner than others, Says Mr. Mather. "There is no doubt that manufacturing is coming back. The question is—will it be American or foreign-owned?"

41.
POSITIVE MONITORING

Vico E. Henriques

Automated measurement systems clearly offer employees the opportunity
to gain greater control over their own working conditions in an atmosphere of impartiality previously unavailable.

Does computer monitoring of work demean employees by impersonally
measuring their performance? Or does it actually inject a new sense of fairness,
flexibility and competitiveness into the workplace?

Before addressing these questions, some background is necessary. As more
and more employees work at computer terminals, electronic measurement of
their productivity is growing too fast for anyone to have a picture of exactly
how many employees are involved. However, a study done last year for the
U.S. government reported that several million employees were being
monitored to some extent. Most of this work force is engaged in clerical tasks
such as data entry, word processing, claims processing and customer service.

Computers designed to enhance clerical work collect data on systems users
as part of their normal functioning. In the last five years, the presence of more
sophisticated software coupled with the increasing computerization of clerical
tasks has significantly increased the opportunities for monitoring. Managers
can now have access to employee productivity data with a choice of detail and
frequency levels. The resulting data can be used to set productivity goals,
identify problems, improve accounting or to price products and services.

EMPLOYEE REWARDS

These management opportunities can be matched by an equally attractive
set of possibilities for employees. Automated measurement can, for example,
allow an organization to more easily identify its high-achieving employees and
reward them appropriately. The rewards are often incentive pay for work
accomplished above a certain level. In other cases, rewards such as promotion
and public recognition are used.

Automated measurement can also contribute to fairer, more flexible working conditions. For example, the computer has no biases. It treats everyone

equally regardless of gender, race, religion, physical impairment, previous job experience or other factors that can be the basis for a discrimination suit against management. The computer gives the employee and manager the employee's performance record in an essentially irrefutable form.

When, then, do these systems sometimes meet with resistance from those who can benefit from them?

To an extent, the blame lies with management. When systems are improperly designed, poorly managed or inadequately explained to employees and managers, they backfire. The results are lower productivity, poorer work quality and greater absenteeism and turnover.

You should note that like any technologically based technique, automated measurement has some potential drawbacks. At this point, though, management has had enough experience with computer monitoring to anticipate and avoid many trouble spots. The improved productivity and high levels of satisfaction in the work force possible with measurement are not pipe dreams. These goals, however, cannot be reached without a clear understanding of how successful monitoring systems are structured. The following are some of the points that must be considered.

- Employees should be told when and why their work is being measured. Any change in the system and the reason for the change should be explained.
- Managers must create reasonable work standards that account for different types of tasks as well as short-term variations in employee performance.
- The frequency of measurement should be no more than what is needed to make the required productivity evaluations.
- Successful systems give employees complete access to their own records. This reduces the chance for error and assures employees that management is using the system in a reasonable and forthright way.

Only by applying these ground rules for establishing successful automated measurement systems can management expect monitored employees to increase productivity. Ignoring these rules can only lead to more problems than the most rigorously applied monitoring system could possibly correct.

Automated measurement systems clearly offer employees the opportunity to gain greater control over their own working conditions in an atmosphere of impartiality previously unavailable. Monitoring is an exciting new managerial tool because these positive results for employees are not achieved at the organization's expense. On the contrary, computer monitoring can increase productivity noticeably while making the work environment more flexible and opening up new opportunities for employees.

Vico E. Henriques is president of the Computer and Business Equipment Manufacturers Association, Washington, D.C.

42.
MEASURING TECHNOLOGY: A CASE STUDY OF OFFICE AUTOMATION

Ik-Whan Kwon
John W. Hamilton

Managers often do not see how they can take advantage of information technology to improve their operations. To overcome this attitude requires education and performance objectives for information-based technology solutions. The challenge is to find applications of technology to gain productivity.

There has been considerable focus on productivity in the business community in recent years. Many organizations have invested significant amounts of capital to improve plant and operational productivity. The levels of productivity have increased and unit costs have decreased. The example of Chrysler and its recovery from near bankruptcy can be attributed to two key items: the leadership of Iaccoca and major gains in productivity. While all productivity gains are not brought about by technology, it would be almost impossible to attain the gains without robotics, computer-augmented functions such as computer-aided design (CAD), or even simple billing and payroll systems, and other technology driven activities.

The productivity gains that have been attained in the factory have not been achieved in the office. Studies indicate that the potential productively gains in managerial/professional/clerical performance could be as high as a 30 percent improvement. A productivity gain of 15 percent would highly impact profit.[1] One of the difficulties in the office environment is the measurement of productivity gains. For example, a plant inventory manager can meet the objective to reduce inventory levels by the use of an automated system, which provides the cost savings needed to justify the original investment. However, it is often hard to measure the productivity gains of office systems and translate these gains into "real" returns on investments. This article measures the productivity gains from the office automation of a large service company.

In general, there are six major functions in any office activities:

1. Document creation—the creation and revision of letters, memos, and reports
2. Mail—the sending and receiving of letters, memos, and reports
3. Information filing/retrieval—the filing and retrieval of letters, memos, and reports
4. Scheduling—the scheduling of meetings, equipment, and facilities
5. Analysis—time spent in analyzing business, technical, and managerial problems/opportunities
6. Reading—time spent in reading letters, memos, and any business professional material.

We assumed that employee productivity gains would be attained by a decrease in the amount of time that would be spent on document creation, mail, information filing/retrieval, and scheduling, but that an increase in time spent on analysis and reading would lead to productivity gains.[2]

STUDY TECHNIQUE

A team was established that consisted of both departmental user personnel and information systems staff members. Also, human-resources specialists and special consultants were included to provide conflict resolution when required. Improvement factors and value-gain goals were determined and identified as project targets.

The general requirements phase focused on a needs assessment to determine what type of office "tools," such as work processing and electronic mail, would be provided to each category of employee.[3] The analysis of data requirements and information flows aided in the revision of policies, procedures, and the need for additional procedures. This analysis also provided information regarding the need for participants to access data and information that was of a sensitive nature. To insure that appropriate computer resources were available, volume projections for transaction rates, data-entry requirements, document-creation demands, and similar requirements were made to forecast the required level of technology to attain the performance goals for the project. The final step was the selection of the most effective *technological solutions* for the office system.

EDUCATION AND TRAINING

The education and training phase provided technical training for the departmental users. This was a key step in the implementation process and was of immense value in reducing resistance to the project, in setting realistic expectations regarding the system objectives, and in providing well-trained and motivated users and systems staff. Effective training can shorten the implementation time and reduce overall project costs.

The application phase included a survey to determine what functions or activities would be implemented at a group level, such as a subdepartment, and what activities would cross departmental and sub-departmental bounds. The group applications with the greatest potential for payoff were given priority over individual applications. The individual applications were supported by a "consulting staff" for office applications. The project did not provide any traditional information-systems type of application development. No programming was done during this project. The applications were supported by the software tools that were provided within the office system.

The last phases of the project included the installation of computer equipment, the implementation of office support functions, application support of specific office activities, and finally the project analysis.

The group study consisted of over 100 employees, and was comprised of managerial, professional, technical, and clerical personnel. Studies were conducted in two time periods. Office automation was not available to the study group during the first period and provided the basis for a control-group measurement. The second study was carried out after the implementation of an office system.[4] Using the same department in two different time periods minimized social, demographic, and environmental factors that would influence the study results.

MEASUREMENTS

The measurement unit was the number of hours expended in eight different activities as an indicator of change between two time periods.[5] The activities were: document creation, mail handling, information search/filing, scheduling, analysis, reading/research, meetings, and telephone activity. These activities were categorized into three groups based on the possible impact that would be attributed to office automation technology; a reduction in time spent on performing the activity, an increase in time available for the activity as a result of office automation, and a neutral effect.

We assumed that the office automation would decrease the time spent on document creation, mail handling, information search/file, and scheduling. The total hours available to office activities would be increased due to hours saved. For example, employees would have more time for reading, research, or analysis. We speculated that activities such as meetings and telephone usage were not affected by the office automation.

RESULTS

Based on the two studies, it was possible to allocate the total time spent by each employee into the eight activities or functional areas (Table 1). In

Table 1
Time Value Allocations

Functional Areas	Controlled Group		Experimental Group		Time Value Changes
(1)	Proportion (2)	Hours (3)	Proportion (4)	Hours (5)	(6)
Group I					
Documentation	0.233	60,580	0.250	65,000	+4,420
Mail Handling	0.104	27,040	0.085	22,100	−4,940
Information	0.085	22,100	0.072	18,720	−3,380
Scheduling	0.041	10,660	0.031	8,060	−2,600
Group II					
Analysis	0.085	22,100	0.110	28,600	+5,207
Reading/Research	0.039	10,140	0.050	13,000	+2,860
Group III					
Meeting	0.170	44,200	0.175	45,500	+1,300
Telephone	0.100	26,000	0.100	26,000	0
Total Gains	0.857[a]		0.873[a]		13,267

[a]Due to other activities, the total does not add up to 1.00.

general, the time values for Group 1 were reduced because of office automation. One exception was an increase in document creation time, which may have been due to an increase in technology available for this type of activity. A substantial gain (more than 60 percent) was attained for Group II activities. Group III activities indicated essentially no change as a result of the office automation.

A total of 13,000 hours were gains, confirming the original assumption.

CONCLUSIONS

This study assumed that there would be positive time-value savings from the use of office automation. There have been disputes over productivity attributed to the use of technology in support of knowledge-workers. This study demonstrated that time-value could be gained/saved by using technology.

Challenges arise from two basic areas: the measurement unit for knowledge-based activities and the approach used in managing office automation technology. Porter's value-chain approach allows an organization to be structured in such a way that measurable functions at a macro-level are possible.[6] An example would be numbers of orders processed. The introduction of office technology and the derived benefits per unit of work can clearly be measured. Managers often do not see how they can take advantage of information technology to improve their operations. To overcome this attitude requires education and performance objectives for information-based technology solutions. These objectives could take the form of goals similar to sales goals. The challenge is to find applications of technology to gain productivity.

REFERENCES

1. American Productivity Center, Computer Conference on Information Workers, "A Final Report for the White House Conference on Productivity," Houston: American Productivity Center, 1983, pp. 14-15.
2. Tomquist, B. and Hermansson, S., "Automation and the Quality of Work Life at the Swedish Telephone Company," *Highlights of the International Conference on Office Work and New Technology*, Cleveland: Working Women Education Fund, 1983, pp. 82-83.
3. Beers, B., "Information-Resources Planning: Strategy for Success," *Todays Office*, November, 1984, pp. 20-26.
4. Meyer, N. D., "Power and Credibility in Office Automation," *Datamation*, August 1, 1985, pp. 97-100.
5. Conway, D. L., "Common Staffing Systems, in *White Collar Productivity*, New York: McGraw-Hill, 1983.

6.   Porter, M. E. *Competitive Advantage—Creating and Sustaining Superior Performance*, New York: The Free Press, 1985, p. 36.

Ik-Whan Kwon is professor and chairman of the Department of Management Sciences, Saint Louis University. John W. Hamilton is director of information systems technology at United Van Lines, Inc.

43.
OVERCOMING BARRIERS TO PRODUCTIVITY

Wayne L. Wright

> When enlightened managers provide a positive environment in which the organization's productivity needs and the individual's personal needs are both being met, Americans actively participate in creative teamwork that surpasses the best efforts of the conformist Japanese.

Few managerial topics have generated more analysis, debate or mistakes in recent years than the so-called Japanese style of management.

"So-called," because there is a strong body of evidence indicating much of what falls under this heading was adapted from Western culture.

The Japanese studied and analyzed different philosophies and techniques, sorted out what made sense in terms of their culture, and then adapted these to fit their needs.

Several of the better, more successful companies in the United States have embraced these concepts for years; the primary difference is that the Japanese practice what they preach more often and with more consistency than do Americans.

Almost all of the "Japanese" practices work well in the United States, but not by using little bits here and there. A holistic approach tailored to each individual organization is necessary.

For example, attempts to incorporate quality circles onto an organization burdened with negative employee attitudes and severe distrust of management consistently fail.

The Japanese characteristics of interdependence, strong familial feelings, respect for the "face" (and space) of others, and maintenance of harmony are natural results of millions of people learning to survive together on a small island with few natural resources.

These traits, plus an ethnically homogeneous population with enormous behavioral sameness, characterize Japanese lives.

Conversely, Americans come from diverse backgrounds; tolerate behavioral differences; and worship freedom, individuality and the entrepreneurial spirit in a vast young country rich in natural resources.

The subsequent values and behavioral differences are inevitable.

The Japanese strength comes primarily from their homogeneity and willingness to subjugate individuality to the team process.

They readily identify themselves as part of a team (family, company) rather than as individuals; Japanese workers do what's good for the company even though they might be unhappy in their jobs.

Behavioral controls originate not only within the individual but from peer pressure as well.

Japanese management has simply *designed systems around* these predominant employee values.

American strength comes from diversity and enlightened self-interest.

A willingness to be open, candid, honest, and even different is a powerful force in properly channeled toward common goals.

This does not mean Americans are adverse to teamwork—most are not.

But to put forth maximum effort Americans must first be convinced that what's best for the team is also best for themselves.

When enlightened managers provide a positive environment in which the organization's productivity needs and the individual's personal needs are both being met, Americans actively participate in creative teamwork that surpasses the best efforts of the conformist Japanese.

Americans, however, cannot and will not strive toward organizational excellence until managers eliminate the barriers that frustrate their efforts.

BARRIERS TO PRODUCTIVITY TAKE MANY SHAPES

Barriers are conspicuously evident in poor and mediocre organizations and noticeably absent in many of the more successful groups. Specifically, they focus on several key aspects of the organization.

Lack of Direction. Failure to use a systematic, strategic approach to managing human resources can create a personnel nightmare.

If management wants everyone pulling in the same direction, that direction must be identified with as much detail as possible.

This requires carefully designed and fully comprehended objectives and strategies—what we are trying to do, how we are going to do it, and how we know when we are succeeding.

Lacking that, there can be no clear understanding of, or commitment to, the company's objectives.

The result will be much like alternate wheels in a gear box, with about half the people heading in the wrong direction—a sure-fire recipe for chaos.

Every organization has a psychological environment. Most, unfortunately, are cultures that have evolved haphazardly.

The most effective American organizations have designed their cultures ahead of time and work to the plan.

If you want excellence, you first design it, and then build it in; that is what the Japanese do so well.

Most Japanese and many successful American organizations spend most of their time analyzing *what* they are trying to accomplish rather than making quick decisions on *how* to accomplish specifics when the overall direction is unclear. (If the American railroads had understood sooner that they were not in the railroad business but the transportation industry, they would probably still be with us in strength.)

Monthly, quarterly and yearly decision-making mentality and repeated changes in direction are the results of such management failure.

Managers in successful organizations set the course, analyze and approve supporting strategies, and then stay out of the detailed "how to" decisions.

Top management in Japan *leads;* American tends to push employees.

Poor organizational structure. Poor organization is a major barrier that creates negativism, divisiveness and blocks positive communication, involvement, and teamwork.

Vertically, most structures have too many levels, including management.

Coupled with a mentality that requires rigid adherence to a fixed organizational structure, the result is an organization that's top heavy, inflexible, costly, and inefficient.

Japanese organizations and the resultant hiring, training, and assignments, on the other hand, are structured for the maximum amount of flexibility and versatility.

This is based on the belief that breadth of knowledge is at least as important as depth, and maybe more so.

Individual jobs, including management jobs, are broadly defined.

Specialists are few and far between, and employees think of themselves as part of a company rather than part of a profession.

Trust in the individual leads to individual accountability, instead of unnecessary staff watchdogs.

Horizontally, most American organizations suffer from too many inflexible, specific job descriptions and job classifications.

These contribute to inefficiency as well as to employee dissatisfaction. This is but one of the undesirable by-products of logical, digital, inflexible job-evaluation systems.

Detailed written job descriptions and narrowly defined job classifications ultimately serve only one purpose—to tell people what they *cannot* do.

Some of the most distressing words management can ever hear are, "But, it's not my job."

On the other hand, broad-based descriptions and classifications not only allow for greater efficiency and cost savings to the company, but also encourage versatility and job satisfaction for employees—a real win/win environment the Japanese know how to achieve.

PAY SYSTEMS ARE MISUNDERSTOOD AND PERCEIVED TO BE INEQUITABLE

Pay and Pay Systems. Far too many organizations continue to cling to systems and levels of pay that are not understood by employees, or are understood and perceived to be unfair.

External equity is rarely a problem insofar as fairness is perceived.

Internal equity more often than not, however, is a problem, and one that is completely controllable by management.

Problem systems are characterized by multiplicity of pay levels or job classification structures or both and attempt to use complicated merit pay concepts.

In addition, these problem systems are frequently job evaluation systems (alleged to be simple and objective) that elicit zero credibility.

To almost any American observation, Japanese pay systems would be considered totally unworkable. The equal pay for equal work concept is nonexistent, having been replaced with a pay based on need.

Two individuals working side by side may be paid rates that vary 50 percent or more if one is older, has more company service, and has a large family.

This system works, because both individuals in this example agree that the difference is appropriate.

Any system supported by employees will work, which is what American management needs to learn.

Pay policies represent extreme examples of values bias.

Compensation "experts" design systems that feel good to them, and therefore, by definition, are not understood or accepted by most others.

There seems to be an unwritten rule that says we cannot have pay systems that are simple, easy to understand, and easy to administer. Instead, we have bell-shaped curves, forced distributions, matrices, and maximums, mid points, and incentives that don't exist.

These barriers persist through failure to follow three simple steps. First, analyze what is to be accomplished by the pay system. Next, honestly evaluate whether these goals are appropriate and acceptable and, finally, design a simple system to attain these goals.

Managerial Selection and Training. The most significant differences between typical American and Japanese managers are manifest in their at-work behavioral expectations.

Americans are trained that success in climbing the corporate ladder goes to those who are the most competitive, aggressive, and rational (two and two *always* equals four).

Those individuals who have the right combination of these characteristics hit the "fast track" and attain increasing authority, power, and status.

The Japanese, including Japanese operations in the United States, don't even consider hiring or promoting individual superstars.

They opt for those capable of being helpful, supportive, and emotional leaders in a team environment (two and two equals five is OK if it works).

New graduates hired into most Japanese organizations can expect to be observed for as many as 10 years before any attempt is made to designate those with managerial abilities.

During that time, they are judged on their ability to cooperate—not on how competitive they can be.

Most approaches to selection, training, and promotion of managers are woefully lacking in the analysis of people skills.

Would you hire or tolerate a secretary who could not type, or a truck driver who could not drive? Of course not. Then why do so many American managers continue to survive, receive big bonus increases, and even get promoted when they cannot effectively deal with people?

In general, performance-review systems judge managerial people skills negligibly, if at all.

This does not go unnoticed by the manager—you get what you pay for.

Organizations spend millions of dollars each year on managerial training programs to teach them how to deal effectively with people.

Then they are placed in situations in which their role models in upper management contradict many of their newly learned skills.

Which has more impact on their behavior in interacting effectively with those they manage? Will they believe what they see or what they hear?

If *all* training programs reinforce what they teach, then managers will be appropriately trained and more sensitive to the needs of their people.

We/They Symbols. Glaring status symbols always have a negative effect on the work force.

The "haves" love them, but attainment of status often becomes more important than effectively pursuing the goals of the organization.

The "have-nots" hate status symbols because they feel less important.

Being singled out as different, better, or special is not only not expected in the Japanese culture, it is unwanted.

To be treated differently is an embarrassment and causes the recipient to "lose face."

Recognition and rewards are oriented to the team, not to the individual.

In situations in which there are differences, they are typically subtle.

For example, the manager of a large department would not have an ornate separate office, but his desk may be facing a different direction.

Everyone recognizes rank has its privileges, and that's OK.

The further one advances in an organization, the more individual freedom, the more pay, the more responsibility one receives.

Unnecessary we/they divisions, however, are those that serve no purpose except to physically or psychologically separate one group of employees from another.

This occurs because outmoded assumptions imply that people cannot be important unless they look important and are treated differently and better than others.

In simplest terms, we/they symbols are designed merely to feed the egos and self-importance of certain members of the organization.

The assumption is that they would be less effective, particularly in management positions, without these status symbols. The truth is, they are often less effective *because* of them.

FOR MANY EMPLOYEES, JOB SECURITY IS A TACIT CONCERN

No Job Security. Although not as prevalent as Americans sometimes assume, lifetime employment is a key factor in many Japanese organizations.

Everyone assumes employment for the long haul and acts accordingly.

Voluntary terminations and layoffs are virtually unknown.

With this commitment and knowing that business cycles also exist in Japan, management uses many contract and temporary employees to absorb unpredictable swings in manpower needs to protect the permanent positions.

Lifetime employment or absolute job security for all employees in most American organizations is not realistic and isn't even desirable.

For qualified employees, however, organizations need to manage their affairs to maximize long-term employment.

Job security is a key issue for many employees and although this concern is mostly unspoken, it exists and should be a primary concern of management.

Unions and government agencies often assume management has no concern, and consequently we have seen the evolution of external protection and limitations.

Turnover is expensive and its short-term costs are obvious. Longer-term costs with regard to loss of continuity are real but less measurable.

In addition, turnover not only includes indiscriminate terminations (a primary cause of employee dissatisfaction), but also includes continuous cycles of layoff, recall, layoff, ad infinitum.

When employees feel, even with good performance and commitment on their part, management is not trying to avoid layoffs, significant barriers are created that keep employees from really turning on and giving total commitment.

Management commitment, manifested in long-term planning and program design, can eliminate much of this instability, even in a fluctuating market. The Japanese understand this.

Lack of Systematic Employee Involvement. Employee involvement—participative management—is probably the most important opportunity for management today. Employee involvement does not mean soft or permissive management nor does it mean decision making by popular vote.

It simply means using the knowledge and experience of *all* employees when there is a reasonable expectation that those involved have the ability and desire for positive contribution.

Intelligently handled, a regular system of employee involvement can reap huge rewards for an organization. This is one of the areas where the Japanese outdo most Western organizations.

"Japanese-style management" is based on the premise that the total exceeds the sum of the individual parts.

Although a system of participative management can enhance a positive employee-relations environment, it also can significantly affect productivity, quality, and profitability.

Most Japanese managers have an amazing amount of patience when faced with decisions that have broad-based impact within their organizations.

They continue discussion and analysis, seemingly forever, if there is significant, though minority, opposition to a plan.

Most Americans find this disconcerting, preferring, at least, to get several opinions and then quickly fashion and issue a decision.

Under any system, implementers undermine decision makers when they disagree with or don't understand a decision.

The Japanese eliminate this possibility by getting support and understanding before the decision is made.

Ensuring all levels of the work force are appropriately involved in the decision-making process yields positive results in many areas.

It stimulates cooperation and understanding between work groups; improves communications; and allows a systematic, broad-based analysis of what is working well, not so well, and why.

The ability to achieve understanding and support of management decisions before the fact reduces time spent in retracing steps and revising decisions.

Possibly the greatest attribute of the Japanese style of management is that it develops genuine leaders rather than insensitive dictators.

Ill-Conceived Hiring/Training. Selection, hiring, and training practices based on incorrect assumptions lead to misfits, mismatches, turnover, and dissatisfaction.

Too often, organizations hire employees who are incompatible with corporate culture or the work group to which they are assigned.

Typically, the amount of time, money, and effort invested in the selection process varies directly with the level of the position to be filled.

For example, entry-level people are often hired by the human resource department.

The immediate supervisor may meet the new hires for the first time when he or she reports for work.

Following a new-employee orientation, the employee is placed in a training program (usually on the job) and told a probationary period must be served.

This probationary period theoretically serves to determine if the employee can do the job, wants to do the job, will come to work regularly and on time, has the proper attitude toward work, and is compatible with the corporate culture.

If an employee fails on any of these criteria, we terminate the employee, write off the expense, trot in a new group, repeat the process, and hope for the best.

Because of the permanence of employment, the necessity for teamwork and the unyielding dedication to quality, the Japanese are very meticulous in hiring decisions and training programs.

To ensure the applicant is compatible, the selection process often includes interviews with the applicant's family.

To establish quality in the work force and overcome hiring barriers, carefully detail the organization and positions, and then take the time necessary in interviewing and offer employment only to those who are compatible with your organization and with the work group to which they will be assigned.

Actively involve managers and supervisors in screening and hiring decisions.

It may also be necessary to implement a pre-employment training program to assess employee ability before the hiring decision.

Search out all of these primary barriers to organizational effectiveness and whittle them down to size.

Get rid of out-of-date, irrelevant assumptions and design an environment that enhances and encourages excellence for the organization.

It may not be "Japanese," it may not be "textbook," it may not have ever been done before—but it *will* be an effective and rewarding undertaking.

Wayne L. Wright was vice president of human resources at the Nissan Motor Corp., Smyrna, Tennessee, before becoming a corporate trainer and management consultant.

44.
MEASURING PRODUCTIVITY IN THE AUTOMATED OFFICE

Leilani E. Allen

> One simple thing managers can do is almost guaranteed to improve the productivity of their group—give them the big picture. Study after study has confirmed that employees who understand the larger implications of their work, how their job ties in with other functions, and the dependency and interrelationships of the tasks, work more productively.

The assumption is made that we can eliminate people but still get the job done, or that we can keep the same people but do substantially more. How is this magic to be accomplished? Largely through information systems (I/S). I/S, and especially office automation, has become the torchbearer in the quest for productivity. Yet, as many who have undertaken the mission know, the object remains elusive.

By and large, we have done a poor job in analyzing the effect of information systems on productivity. We have demonstrated that grouping tasks, automating routine tasks, improving standardization, creating user-oriented interfaces and the like allow the work to flow through more smoothly and with fewer errors. However, we still have great difficulty in actually measuring productivity improvements. The problem is two-fold: selecting the appropriate measures of productivity, and conducting scientifically valid studies that show productivity improvements.

QUANTITATIVE MEASURES

Many people equate measurement with quantification. Consequently, we have relied almost exclusively on quantitative measures such as number of items produced (claims, checks, line of code, etc.). These measures are easy to count, the results appear clear and unequivocal, and they do demonstrate that a change has taken place. The problem is that item counts may well be measuring the wrong thing—throughput, as opposed to productivity. Moreover, they are often prone to the classic "apples versus oranges" fallacy.

Take, for example, the difficult and complex job of programming. Capers Jones published an excellent study that demolished such classic measures of programmer productivity as lines of code or defects.[1] He showed that comparing development efforts using third generation languages like Cobol with fourth generation languages would inevitably yield a lower score for the more advanced languages, since the latter required fewer lines of code. Does this make the Cobol programmer more productive?

To avoid such apple and orange comparisons, we have to use a different basis for evaluation. The purist might argue that every task is unique. Perhaps, but there are certainly broad categories that can be established between which comparisons are valid. One classification scheme would be to rate tasks on degree of difficulty, using such generic measures as:

• Degree of technical skill or experience required
• Number of required interfaces (human or logical)
• Degree of controversy associated with the product or technique
• Degree of creativity required.

These criteria can be used to rate how long any number of activities will take. The productivity analysis would then count "number of type A tasks, type B, etc." Thus, an insurance claim that involved multiple physicians, experimental procedures or much follow-up would be given a higher rating than a claim for a routine physical, because of the greater number of interfaces and degree of experience required by the claims processor. In a programming environment, the Cobol-based effort would score relatively low on novelty and creativity; the fourth generation language (4GL) project, especially if it were the first of its kind, would be at the other end of the scale. Thus, more weight would be given to the completion of each 4GL module. Even if the two projects took the same amount of elapsed time, the 4GL programmers would be considered more productive because they had a more difficult chore to begin with.

Note that this is a relative, not absolute scale, which means we avoid the onerous task of establishing "ideal" or "average" completion times. Employees quite rightfully resent and resist such efforts. Productivity analyses have often floundered because of this resistance. The relative scale makes comparative analysis both more equitable and more realistic.

QUALITATIVE MEASURES

However, many tasks, especially managerial tasks, do not lend themselves to quantification, even at this level. Can we judge a manager's productivity on how many memos she produced each day? Or how many employee evaluations he completed? Or how many bright ideas were generated in a given month? How can we tell? The purist would argue that we can break down any job into its constituent parts, but would handling more tasks necessarily make for better performance?

Hence the need to measure quality, not just quantity. That sounds good, but how do we carry it out in practice? We certainly cannot do it by simply looking at errors or defects. Let's face it. For most higher-order human activities, quality is a subjective judgment. Sometimes a productivity improvement can only be measured by the fact that the person *feels* more productive. This is a perfectly legitimate measure. Properly supported with case-in-point examples, subjective evaluation is one way of demonstrating improvement. That manager who just bought a personal computer should be asked to show, for example, that doing the annual budget on a spreadsheet as opposed to manually saved a few days of time. Or by using financial models to do "what if" analysis, the evaluation of two competing R&D projects was quicker or more comprehensive. These results should be verified with colleagues and supervisors.

The key point to remember is that the individuals doing the evaluation should not only be the ones who have a vested interest in the outcome. We don't let accountants audit themselves; we bring in outsiders who have as much to gain in finding negatives as positives. The same is true in the implementation of information systems. Another team, from a different user area or a different group within I/S, should audit the results.

Over the long term, the only genuine way to demonstrate quality is to focus on the end results of productivity improvements, which is the corporate bottom line. Did the fact that we could do a budget in half a day using a spreadsheet instead of four days manually lower operating costs? Did the use of a financial model for "what if" analysis on product pricing result in increased revenue by beating out the competitions? Did the enhancements to the order entry system reduce customer lead times, and has the sales force used this fact for competitive advantage? Did putting the customer-service group on-line increase repeat business?

BEFORE-AND-AFTER COMPARISONS

The first principle to observe in conducting productivity analysis is to always conduct before-and-after comparisons. This sounds like a truism, yet I am amazed at how many companies implement systems to improve productivity without ever measuring what productivity is to begin with, or what factors influence productivity the most. If we don't know what something is now, how can we show that it is changed?

We also have to be very careful about documenting our assumptions. For instance, we might examine historical records and assume that a claims processor can handle at best 50 claims per day. This might be because it is simply beyond the physical and mental capacities of an individual to do more, no matter how we change the system. Or the clerk might well be able to do more but is constrained by operational or procedural rules that have nothing to do with the automated system. Removal of these constraints might well bring about productivity increases, but the automation effort itself had nothing to do with it.

Conversely, the expected productivity improvements might never be realized simply because the operational constraints are still there. Other key assumptions include:

- Volume and mix of work
- Processing time requirements
- Number and type of interfaces with other activities
- Work schedules
- System dependencies

A before-and-after analysis must take great care to validate assumptions. Otherwise, the conclusions might well be erroneous. Just because something "has always been done this way" does not mean it will (or should) continue.

Consider the case of a customer-service department. The clerks were responsible for handling customer calls about lost shipments, refunds, status of the order, etc. The supervisor complained that the on-line system had poor response time and was causing the clerks to be unproductive. Customers were on hold for many minutes and the sales department was in an uproar over the poor service.

Upon closer examination, the systems analyst discovered that the clerks had no problem accessing the on-line customer database and were experiencing response times of 3-8 seconds. However, after each call they were required to complete a lengthy incident report, which consumed 5-10 minutes. This was because user management was dissatisfied with the timeliness and detail in the existing computer reports and wanted to see the full story in each case. As long as the requirement for a manual report was in force, no amount of system tuning could improve the clerk's productivity.

TIME FRAMES FOR EVALUATION

Another factor we have to consider in before-and-after analyses is the time frame for evaluation. Most people who confront a new system or technology will experience a *decline* in productivity while they are learning the system and adjusting their work habits. This is an immediate effect and of short duration.

From there the productivity curve usually rises rapidly and dramatically—10-fold improvements are not unheard of. Clearly, any measurements taken at this interval, which typically lasts from 3-12 months after system implementation, will tell a rosy story. And, if the system was designed to meet a short-term need, the story is accurate.

Over the long term, productivity will plateau and eventually start to decline again. Here a system enhancement can be brought into play, and the productivity analysis can begin again. The point is that the timing of before-and-after evaluations is not whimsical, nor should it be done to be convenient with the analyst's schedule. The timing is a direct result of the objective of the project in the first place.

Time frames can be tricky. Many operations have peak periods of the year when processing loads are high. For a retail establishment, the peak period is typically Thanksgiving (the start of the Christmas buying season) through mid-January (the end of the Christmas return season). Productivity measurements taken during this period are likely to show improvement, simply because the work force has been geared up to handle the extra load. At the same time, many less-than-essential activities, which would normally lower productivity, may have been put on hold. The result may be a measure of productivity improvement that applies during peak season but not the rest of the year.

HAWTHORNE EFFECT

Another factor to be aware of when studying any work process is the so-called Hawthorne effect, first discovered during the early part of this century as a result of studies conducted at Western Electric's Hawthorne works near Chicago. Here, researchers found that the presence of an observer changed the behavior under examination. The special attention made workers work more productively, which obviously affected the results. Human beings simply work differently when under observation, and a productivity analyst will have to take care to correct for this problem. Ideally, both direct and indirect measures should be taken. For example, data gathered by observation of the employees' work should be supplemented with survey evidence or automated transaction or job counts. Another strategy is to tell the workers that one thing is being studied, when in fact something else is the true subject of the analysis. Thus, they might be told that the ergonomics of their workstation was the focus of the research when in fact it was their interaction with a given software system. As long as this deceit is not detrimental to the workers, it can be part of an analyst's set of techniques.

MULTIPLE VARIABLES

This brings us to a major factor that can affect our analysis—the existence of multiple variables that can influence productivity. In scientific laboratories we can conduct very controlled experiments that carefully isolate each factor and measure its impact. With human beings, that is not possible. Multiple variables can often skew the results of our study.

For example, take the series of studies conducted by IBM and others over the last five years to demonstrate the effect of sub-second response time on programmers productivity.[2] In most cases, response time was reduced and productivity increased.

However, in most of these studies, other factors were also at work. In one case, each programmer was given his/her own terminal, where previously they had to share terminals. Since the measure of productivity is time on the system is it any wonder that an improvement was realized? One may argue that productivity would have improved regardless of what response time was. In another case, a wide array of productivity-improvement tools were made available to the programmers. Was it their presence, or the reduced response time, that resulted in an increase in the number of transactions per hour? This does not disprove the response time-productivity equations, but it does show how careful we have to be in evaluating changes.

CONTROL GROUPS

In the absence of a scientific laboratory, we can still use some scientific research principles. One of these is to use a control group. If, for instance, we have 100 clerks to begin using a new system, why not keep 10 percent on the manual system for a few weeks to show the impact of the change? Granted, this requires a representative sample and a little extra administrative effort, but it should demonstrate the effect of the new system. If we are buying an application generator or other aid for the programming staff, give it to one group only and compare their performance with another group doing similar tasks. Did the package have a measurable impact on productivity? If a design team has questions about the ergonomics of a particular screen design, have half the users in a pilot group use one design and half use another.

ONE EASY STEP FORWARD

The techniques outlined above will certainly require work and discipline. Most things worth having do. But all managers can do one simple thing that can be almost guaranteed to improve the productivity of their group—give them the big picture. Study after study has confirmed that employees who understand the larger implications of their work, how their job ties in with other functions, the dependency and interrelationship of tasks, work more productively. They make better decisions on scheduling; they understand the need to stay informed and to inform others of changes; and they can adjust the work flow. All of these can help eliminate those annoying fits and starts that prevent us from completing projects on time within budget.

REFERENCES

1. Capers, Jones. *Programming Productivity*, New York: McGraw-Hill, 1985.
2. Arvind J. Thadhani, "Interactive User Productivity," *IBM Systems Journal*, Vol. 20, no. 4 (1981) and "Factors Affecting Programmers' Productivity During Application Development," *IBM Systems Journal*, Vol. 23, no. 1 (1984). See also G. N. Lambert, "A Comparative Study of System Response Time," in this same issue. Harold Lundy, "Justifying Subsecond Response Time," *Computerworld In-Depth*, (11/21/83); Dick Smith, "A Business Case for Subsecond Response Time," *Computerworld In-Depth*, (4/18/83); and Robert T. Hedrick, "Improving Productivity at Northern Trust," *Datamation*, (5/15/86).

Leilani E. Allen is president of Knowledge Consortium, an Oakland, CA-based research and consulting firm specializing in strategic information systems planning.

45.

MANAGING "TECHIES": AUTOMATION WON'T WORK WITHOUT PEOPLE

Keith Denton

Increased dependence upon highly trained technological specialists presents real challenges and risks to the manager because computer technology means more dependence on people, not less.

The growth of computer specialization and technology does not mean the individual becomes less important. On the contrary, your personnel and management of them will become more—much more—important. A manager expecting computer technology to improve productivity is frequently disappointed with the results. It may not produce the expected increase in efficiency or accuracy. The primary problem is not the computer system, but the people that implement it. Success of the system may require redefined roles, changing duties, new responsibilities and acceptance of these changes.

Increased dependence upon highly trained specialists, technicians and professionals with scarce analytical abilities can present real challenges and risks to the manager. The risk becomes real because computer technology means greater dependence on people, not less. This can be an uncomfortable thought when you think about the lack of commitment and concern many employees have for their organizations. Recent studies show that only about 22 percent of employees say they perform to their full capacities. Furthermore, only 44 percent of employees say they put a great deal of effort into their jobs.

Managers must try to obtain greater centralization and control. Advanced technology is only a tool: it still will require the human hand to be useful. Superior computer tools will only achieve maximum results when they are managed by supportive and properly trained personnel.

This training begins at the managerial level. One of the basic skills needed is to have a working knowledge of the computer. Its power and influence continue to grow to the point where it is almost impossible to imagine managers being able to function without being computer literates. Its ability to gather

353

data, analyze its impact and locate optimum solutions through tedious evaluation of alternatives make it extremely valuable.

The ability of computers to develop optimum solutions is based on the use of sophisticated and complex mathematical models that develop near optimum choices. Therefore, the second skill managers will need is a familiarity and understanding of mathematical and quantitative tools.

The manager also needs to become humanistic—using technology through, not in spite of, the human worker. For each level of management there are a variety of areas in which this skill will be needed.

Upper management faces the challenge of hiring and promoting more technically oriented people who both understand and use the new technology. The problem is that the vast majority of these computer engineers, technologists and office technicians are usually very knowledgeable and interested in technical matters but show little interest in the behavioral and psychological aspects of their jobs.

These technical people will have to assume leadership roles and develop people-management skills. One way to do this is to set up a series of special sessions on solving specific people issues that they will face in their jobs. By defining specific problems to be solved, there is a natural appeal to the strong analytical nature of most technically oriented people. The task might include such subjects as how to reduce absenteeism, grievances and the number of work slowdowns. The important aspect of setting up these training sessions is to clearly define the problems, then concentrate on providing instructions on how to use specific motivational and communication tools. The important thing to remember when developing managerial training programs for technically oriented personnel is to have them develop the habit of using their great analytical skills in the unfamiliar area of motivation and communication.

It is also useful to show them how to improve their writing skills. Technical people can communicate easily between themselves but often do not do as good a job when dealing with nontechnical managers. Since many of these people must explain concepts to those outside their discipline, it is important for them to be able to write clear, concrete and concise memos and reports free of jargon and technical shorthand that occurs between specialists.

While upper management must concentrate on generating interest and training in the art side of management to its technical people, middle managers face a different problem. Often these managers have technicians and experts working directly for them. They also frequently have to seek the advice of these people about highly complex and technical tasks. It is at this level where the marketing or accounting employee must be willing to broaden their skills in order to become a generalist manager—one who has a basic understanding of what each technical person's job involves. This requires learning the basic language of specialists and technical people within the manager's scope of influence.

Professional development for the middle manager must focus on developing a basic understanding of technical jobs and what they consist of. Managers cannot afford to lose control through lack of understanding. In many cases a basic orientation and training program similar to that given to new employees may be necessary if middle managers are to understand the scope of the modern technological organization. It can be of great value for the middle manager to spend several weeks working with the computer, design department, operations or other technical areas within the company.

For the first-line managers and others who must directly manage technical employees, there are several human resource challenges. For example, advanced technology does not necessarily make employees happier. In fact it has its own problems. High technology often produces high boredom, since many decisions—which were once made by people—are now made by machines.

Whether it is office personnel with word processors or blue-collar workers and robots, there are problems to be solved. There are the normal fears and apprehension when technology is introduced. Frequently, there are the complaints of stress due to the demands of the technology.

People need human contact and social interaction. In highly automated and technically oriented situations, there can be a feeling that the environment is alien and cold. It is necessary to recognize that these feelings can exist and do present a barrier to productive work. Managers in these situations can plan to make the high-tech work environment as human as possible by at least including such things as warm colors, open space. It may also require enriching techniques like job rotation so that human contact is still possible.

In addition to the special concerns of the differing levels of managerial personnel, there may be a more fundamental change occurring due to technological changes. It may soon be necessary to change our attitudes and perceptions about what types of people you want in your office. The type of personnel needed by management in the technological future may be different than those normally chosen. They will be thinkers who like and understand the power of technology. Often they are reflective, choosing to consider options instead of reacting with immediate action, since they have less need to act on limited information. Technology can increase the data available to make accurate decisions, but it requires investigative skills. These reflective and investigative people are sure to be highly educated, with great self-confidence about their specialized ability. They will expect to be involved in a major way with decisions that affect their areas.

In addition, an attitude that shows lack of commitment and concern for the company can be a problem. It has been a problem long before computer bar codes and technology. With great dependence on a few key people, it will be even more critical to make sure these people are committed and properly trained. From office personnel to electronic experts, their opinions and productivity will be critical to the organization. The key to future success in a technological world is not the technology but those who implement, operate and apply the technology.

Training technical specialists to deal with people problems and middle managers on the technical aspects of jobs is necessary if an organization is to prosper. In addition, first-line managers must be made aware of both the negative as well as positive impact technology can have on employees.

Keith Denton is associate professor of management at Southwest Missouri State University in Springfield, MO.

BIBLIOGRAPHY

Arnett, Harold E. and Schmeichel, Neill R., *Increasing Productivity in the U.S.* (Montvale, NJ: National Association Accountants., date not set).

Bailey, David, ed., *Productivity Measurement: An International Review of Concepts, Techniques, Programs and Current Issues* (Hampshire, England: Gower Publishing Company, 1981).

Bain, David L., *The Productivity Prescription: The Manager's Guide to Improving Productivity & Profits* (New York: McGraw-Hill, 1986).

Barra, Ralph, *Putting Quality Circles to Work: A Practical Strategy for Boosting Productivity & Profits* (New York: McGraw-Hill, 1983).

Batstone, Eric and Gourlay, Stephen, *Unions, Unemployment and Innovation* (New York: Basil Blackwell, 1986).

Blecher, John G., Jr., *Managing for Productivity* (Houston, TX: Gulf Publishing Company, 1987).

————, *The Productivity Management Process* (Oxford, OH: The Planning Forum, 1983).

Benge, Eugene and Hickey, John, *Morale & Motivation: How to Measure Morale & Increase Productivity* (New York: Franklin Watts, 1984).

Bergen, S. A., *Productivity & the R&D Production Interface* (Hampshire, England: Gower Publishing Company, 1983).

Bilson, Tora K., *New Technology in the Office: Planning for People* (Scarsdale, NY: Work in America Institute Inc., 1985).

Balke, Robert R. and Mouton, J., *Productivity: The Human Side* (New York: AMACOM, 1982).

Blau, Gary, *Human Resource Accounting* (Scarsdale, NY: Work in America Institute Inc., 1978).

Bodkin, Ronald G., *Wage-Price-Productivity Nexus* (Philadelphia, PA: University of Pennsylvania Press, 1966).

Bowey, Angela M. and Thrope, Richard, *Payment Systems & Productivity* (New York: St. Martin, 1985).

357

Buehler, Vernon M. & Shetty, Y., *Productivity Improvement: Case Studies of Proven Practice* (New York: AMACOM, 1981).

Burnham, Donald C., *Productivity Improvement* (New York: Columbia University Press, 1973).

Carkhuff, Robert R., *Interpersonal Skills & Human Productivity* (Amherst, MA: Human Research Development Press, 1983).

————, *Sources of Human Productivity* (Amherst, MA: Human Research Devevelopment Press, 1983).

Chinloy, Peter, *Labor Productivity* (Cambridge, MA: Abt Books, 1981).

Chorfas, Dimitris N., *Office Automation: The Productivity Challenge* (Englewood Cliffs, NJ: Prentice-Hall, 1982).

Clark, Kim B., *The Uneasy Alliance: Managing the Productivity-Technology Dilemma* (Cambridge, MA: Harvard University Press, 1985).

Connolly, Paul, M., *Promotional Practices & Policies* (Scarsdale, NY: Work in America Institute, Inc., 1985).

Cummings, Thomas, G. and Molloy, Edmund S., *Improving Productivity & the Quality of Work Life* (New York: Praeger, 1977).

Dessler, Gray, *Human Behavior: Improving Productivity at Work* (Reston, VA: Reston, 1980).

————, *Improving Productivity at Work: Motivating Today's Employees* (Reston, VA: Reston, 1983).

Dogramci, Ali, *Measurement Issues & Behavior of Productivity Variables* (Norwell, MA: Kluwer Academic Publishers, 1986).

Doyle, Robert J., *Gainsharing & Productivity: A Guide to Planning, Implementation & Development* (New York: AMACOM, 1983).

Edwards, Kenneth R., *The Perspective of Organized Labor on Improving America's Productivity* (Columbus, OH: National Center for Research in Vocational Education, 1983).

Eilon, Samuel, *Applied Productivity Analysis for Industry* (Elmsford, NY: Pergamon, 1976)

Fein, Mitchell, *Rational Approaches to Raising Productivity* (Norcross, GA: Institute of Industrial Engineers, 1974).

Fernandez, John P., *Child Care & Corporate Productivity: Resolving Family-Work Conflicts* (Lexington, MA: Lexington Books, 1985).

Flamholtz, Eric G. and Das, T. K., *Human Research Management & Productivity: State of the Art and Future Prospects* (Los Angeles, CA: University of California Institute of Industrial Relations, 1986).

―――, *Human Resource Productivity in the 1980s* (Los Angeles, CA: University of California Institute of Industrial Relations, 1982).

Freund, James and Wieand, Kenneth, *Discussion of Some Factors Affecting Labor Productivity* (St. Louis, MO: Institute for Urban & Regional Studies, Washington University, 1967).

Fuchs, Victor R., *Production & Productivity in the Service Industries* (Cambridge, MA: National Bureau Economic Research Inc., 1969).

Gedye, G. R., *Works Management & Productivity* (Devon, England: David & Charles, 1979).

Gibson, Price, *Quality Circles: An Approach to Productivity Improvement* (Scarsdale, NY: Work In America Institute, Inc., 1982).

―――, *Quality Circles: One Approach to Productivity Improvement* (Elmsford, NY: Pergamon, 1982).

Goldberg, Joel A., *A Manager's Guide to Productivity Improvement* (New York: Praeger, 1986).

―――, *The National Directory of Centers for Productivity and Quality of Working Life* (New York: National Center Public Productivity, John Jay College, 1982).

Greenwood, Frank and Greenwood, Mary, *High Productivity Organization: Managing in the Eighties* (Reston, VA: Reston, 1985).

Gregerman, Ira B., *Productivity Improvement: A Guide for Small Business* (New York: Van Nostrand Reinhold, 1984).

Guest, Robert H., *Work Teams & Team Building* (Elmsford, NY: Pergamon, 1986).

―――, *Innovative Work Practices* (Elmsford, NY: Pergamon, 1982).

————, *Work Practices* (Scarsdale, NY: Work in America Institute, Inc., 1982).

Guggenheim, Gus N., *Protocol for Productivity* (Gresham, OR: Guggenheim Research Association, 1982).

A Guide to Worker Productivity Experiments in the United States (Nutley, NJ: Moffat Publishing Company Inc., 1981).

Guzzo, Richard A., *Program for Productivity & Quality of Work Life* (Scarsdale, NY: Work in America Institute, Inc., 1984).

————, *A Guide to Worker Productivity Experiments in the U.S.* (Elmsford, NY: Pergamon, 1983).

Hanks, Kurt, *Up Your Productivity* (Los Altos, CA: William Kaufmann Inc., 1986).

Hayes, John P. and Sandman, William E., *How to Win Productivity in Manufacturing: How to Reduce Queues & Increase Profits* (New York: AMACOM, 1982).

Heaton, Herbert, *Productivity in Service Organization: Organizing for People* (New York: McGraw-Hill, 1977).

Henderson, Richard L., *Compensation Management: Rewarding Performance* (Reston, VA: Reston, 1985).

Hinrich, John R., *Controlling Absenteeism and Turnover* (Scarsdale, NY: Work in America Institute, Inc., 1980).

Holzer, Marc and Halachmi, Arie, *Strategic Issues in Public Sector Productivity: The Best of Public Productivity Review* (San Francisco, CA: Jossey Bass, 1986).

Huddleston, Kenneth F., *Productivity Is the Problem* (Columbus, OH: National Center for Research in Vocational Education, 1982).

Ingle, Sud, *Quality Circles Master Guide: Increasing Productivity with People Power* (Englewood Cliffs, NJ: Prentice-Hall, 1982).

Katzell, Raymond A., *A Guide to Worker Productivity Experiments in the United States: 1971-75* (Scarsdale, NY: Work in America Institute, Inc. 1977).

Kearsley. G. P., *Cost, Benefits, & Productivity in Training Systems* (Reading, MA: Addison-Wesley, 1982).

Kendrick, John W., *International Comparisons of Productivity & Causes of the Slowdown* (Cambridge, MA: Ballinger Publishing Co., 1984).

————, *Improving Company Productivity: Handbook with Case Studies* (Baltimore, MD: Johns Hopkins University Press, 1986).

————, *Interindustry Differences in Productivity Growth* (Mercer, PA: American Enterprise Publications, 1983).

————, *New Developments in Productivity Measurement & Analysis* (Chicago: University of Chicago Press, 1980).

King, J. R., *Improving Productivity (New York: American Society of Civil Engineers, 1983)*.

Krinsky, Leonard W., Stress & Productivity (New York: Human Science Press, 1984).

Lawlor, Alan, *Productivity Improvement Manual* (Westport, CT: Greenwood Press Inc., 1985).

Lawrence and Aft, *Productivity Measurement & Improvement* (Reston, VA: Reston, 1983).

Lebov, Myrna, *Human Resource Productivity* (New York: Executive Enterprise Publications Inc., 1985).

Lee, Mary D. and Hackman, J. Richard, *Redesigning Work: A Strategy for Change* (Scarsdale, NY: Work in America Institute Inc., 1979).

Levine, Michael, *Inside Productivity* (New York: Executive Enterprise Publications Inc., 1986).

Levitan, Sar A. and Werneke, Diane, *Productivity: Problems, Prospects, & Policies* (Baltimore, MD: John Hopkins University Press, 1984).

Luke, Hugh D., *Automation for Productivity* (Melbourne, FL: Robert E. Krieger Publishing Company Inc., 1972).

Lustgarten, Steven, *Productivity & Prices: The Consequence of Industrial Concentration* (Mercer, PA: American Enterprise Publications, 1983).

Machemehl, A. E., *Improving Performance Evaluation Procedures* (New York: AMACOM, 1983).

Mansfield, Edwin, *Technology Transfer, Productivity & Economic Policy* (New York: W. W. Norton, 1983).

Massrik, Fred, *Participative Management* (New York: Pergamon, 1983).

Maverick, Lewis, *Productivity: A Critique of Current Usage* (Carbondale, IL: Southern Illinois University Press, 1955).

Meltzer, Loren, *Worker Alienation* (Scarsdale, NY: Work in America Institute, Inc., 1978).

Moses, Joseph L. and Byham, William C., *Applying the Assessment Center Method* (Elmsford, NY: Pergamon, 1978)

Moss Kanter, Rosabeth, *The Change Masters: Innovation for Productivity in the American Corporation* (New York: Simon & Schuster, 1983).

Mundell, Marvin E., *Improving Productivity & Effectiveness* (Englewood Cliffs, NJ: Prentice-Hall, 1983).

Murphy, John W. and Pardeck, John T., *Technology & Human Productivity: Challenges for the Future* (Westport, CT: Greenwood, 1986).

Prais, S. J., *Productivity & Industrial Structure* (New York: Cambridge University Press, 1982).

Productivity Through Work Innovation (Elmsford, NY: Pergamon, 1982).

Regan, John F., *Even More Productivity: Expanding Effectiveness & Efficiency in Plant* (Windsor, CT: Swansea Publishing Co., 1987).

Ross, Joe, *Productivity, People & Profits* (Reston, VA: Reston, 1981).

Rubin, Irwin M., *Task-Oriented Team Development* (New York: McGraw-Hill, 1978).

Schermerhorn, J. R., *Productivity Guide: Resource Manual* (New York: Wiley, 1985).

Schuster, Frederick E., *The Schuster Report: The Connection Between People & Profits* (New York: Wiley, 1986).

Schutz, Will, *The Truth Option* (Berkley, CA: Ten Speed Press, 1984).

Sears, Woodrow H., Jr., *Back in Working Order: How American Institutions Can Win the Productivity Battle* (Glenview, IL: Scott Foresman, 1984).

Shade, Bernard N. and Mohindra, Raj, *Winning the Productivity Race* (Lexington, MA: Lexington Books, 1985).

Shetty, Y. K. and Buehler, Vernon M., *Productivity & Quality Through People: Practices of Well-Managed Companies* (Westport, CT: Greenwood Press Inc., 1985).

Silver, M. S., *Productivity Indices: Methods & Applications* (Brookfield, VT: Gower Publishing Company, 1984).

Spencer, Lyle, *Calculating Human Resource Costs Benefits: Cutting Cost & Improving Productivity* (New York: Wiley, 1986).

Stankard, Martin F., *Productivity by Choice: The 20-to-1 Principle* (New York: Wiley, 1986).

Sumanth, D. J., *Productivity Engineering & Management Productivity Measurement, Evaluation, Planning & Improvements in Manufacturing* (New York: McGraw-Hill, 1984).

Townsend, Robert, *Further Up the Organization: How to Stop Management from Stifling People & Strangling Productivity* (New York: Knopf, 1984).

Ullman, John E., *The Improvement of Productivity: Myths and Realities* (New York: Praeger, 1980).

Werther, William B., Jr., *Productivity Through People* (St. Paul, MN: West Publishing Company, 1986).

Wright, Oliver W., *MRP II: Unlocking America's Productivity Potential* (New York: Van Nostrand Reinhold, 1985).

INDEX